Of Poetry and Politics:
New Essays on Milton and His World

MEDIEVAL & RENAISSANCE

TEXTS & STUDIES

VOLUME 126

Of Poetry and Politics:
New Essays on Milton and His World
edited by
P. G. Stanwood

Medieval & Renaissance texts & studies
Binghamton, New York
1995

Library of Congress Cataloging-in-Publication Data

Of poetry and politics: new essays on Milton and his world / edited by P. G.
Stanwood
     p. cm. — (Medieval & Renaissance texts & studies; 126)
    Includes index.
    ISBN 0-86698-131-4
    1. Milton, John, 1608–1674—Criticism and interpretation. 2. Politics
and literature—Great Britain—History—18th century. 3. Political poetry,
English—History and criticism. 4. Prophecies in literature. 5. Sex roles in
literature. I. Stanwood, P. G. II. Series: Medieval & Renaissance texts &
studies; v. 126.
PR3588.O3 1994
821′.4—dc20   94–20124
CIP

This book is made to last.
It is set in Bembo, smythe-sewn
and printed on acid-free paper
to library specifications

Printed in the United States of America

CONTENTS

Milton's autograph of a scenario for the sacrifice of Isaac, Sarah's second tragedy, in the Trinity manuscript. By courtesy of the Master and Fellows of Trinity College, Cambridge, from the facsimile published by the Scolar Press. [Transcribed on page 139, note 19].

ABBREVIATIONS

This list includes literary and critical works most frequently cited.

AV   "Authorized" or King James version of the Bible (1611)

Apology   *An Apology against a Pamphlet Called "A Modest Confutation of the Animadversions upon the Remonstrant's Defense against Smectymnuus"*

Barker   Arthur Barker, *Milton and the Puritan Dilemma* (Toronto: Univ. of Toronto Press, 1942)

Bennett   Joan S. Bennett, *Reviving Liberty: Radical Christian Humanism in Milton's Great Poems* (Cambridge: Harvard Univ. Press, 1989)

Binns   J. W. Binns, *Intellectual Culture in Elizabethan and Jacobean England: The Latin Writings of the Age* (Leeds: Francis Cairns, 1990)

CE   *The Works of John Milton,* ed. Frank Allen Patterson, et al., 18 vols. + 2 vols. index (New York: Columbia Univ. Press, 1931–40)

CG   *The Reason of Church Government Urged Against Prelaty*

CPW   *The Complete Prose Works of John Milton,* ed. Don M. Wolfe et al., 8 vols. (New Haven: Yale Univ. Press, 1931–40)

Danielson   *The Cambridge Companion to Milton,* ed. Dennis Danielson (Cambridge: Cambridge Univ. Press, 1989)

Darbishire   *The Early Lives of Milton,* ed. Helen Darbishire (London: Constable, 1932)

ELH   *English Literary History*

Fish   Stanley Fish, *Surprised By Sin: The Reader in "Paradise Lost"* (Berkeley: Univ. of California Press, 1967)

Fletcher   Harris F. Fletcher, *The Intellectual Development of John Milton,* 2 vols. (Urbana: Univ. of Illinois Press, 1956–61)

Fowler   *The Complete Poems of John Milton,* ed. John Carey and Alastair Fowler (London: Longman, 1968)

French   *The Life Records of John Milton,* ed. J. Milton French, 5 vols. (New Brunswick, NJ: Rutgers Univ. Press, 1949–58; New York: Gordian, 1966)

Hill   Christopher Hill, *Milton and the English Revolution* (New York: Viking Press, 1977)

Hughes   *John Milton: Complete Poetry and Major Prose,* ed. Merritt Y. Hughes (New York: Odyssey Press, 1957)

Hunter   *A Milton Encyclopedia,* ed. William B. Hunter, 9 vols. (Lewisburg, PA: Bucknell Univ. Press, 1978–87)

JEGP   *Journal of English and Germanic Philology*

Loewenstein   *Politics, Poetics, and Hermeneutics in Milton's Prose,* ed. David Loewenstein and James Grantham Turner (Cambridge: Cambridge Univ. Press, 1990)

MP   *Modern Philology*

MQ   *Milton Quarterly*

MS   *Milton Studies*

McColley   Diane McColley, *Milton's Eve* (Urbana: Univ. of Illinois
              Press, 1983)

Mendle   Michael Mendle, *Dangerous Positions: Mixed Government,
              the Estates of the Realm, and the Making of the "Answer to the
              xix propositions"* (University: Univ. of Alabama Press,
              1985)

Nelson   *Records of the Early English Drama: Cambridge,* ed. Alan
              H. Nelson, 2 vols. (Toronto: Univ. of Toronto Press,
              1989)

Nyquist   *Re-Membering Milton: Essays in the Texts and the Tradi-
              tion,* ed. Mary Nyquist and Margaret W. Ferguson
              (New York and London: Methuen, 1987)

Of Prelat   *Of Prelatical Episcopacy*

Parker   William Riley Parker, *Milton: A Biography,* 2 vols. (Ox-
              ford: Clarendon Press, 1968)

PL   *Paradise Lost*

PMLA   *Publications of the Modern Language Association*

PR   *Paradise Regained*

Ref   *Of Reformation Touching Church Discipline in England*

Ricks   Christopher Ricks, *Milton's Grand Style* (Oxford:
              Clarendon Press, 1963)

SA   *Samson Agonistes*

SP   *Studies in Philology*

Staveley   Keith Staveley, *The Politics of Milton's Prose Style* (New
              Haven: Yale Univ. Press, 1975)

ACKNOWLEDGMENTS

I am pleased to acknowledge the helpfulness of a number of persons who have made this volume possible, beginning with the advisory council of the Fourth International Milton Symposium. Most of these twenty-five eminent scholars read and responded to a substantial share of the large number of papers originally submitted to the Vancouver symposium. Almost all of this council met over a memorable luncheon during the symposium itself where the idea for this book was first discussed. I was urged to undertake the editing of it, but to keep in mind the generally expressed desire that the resulting book should be a coherent volume, and not a diverse set of conference proceedings. Subsequently, I asked a small group from the council to advise me in making the difficult judgment of which papers given at the symposium should be included in such a collection. I am therefore grateful to Roy Flannagan, Lee Johnson, John Roberts and John Shawcross for their advice—and especially to Professors Flannagan and Johnson, who read all of the papers given at the symposium; but I must absolve them from the responsibility of final decisions, for which I am accountable. Mario Di Cesare, director of Medieval & Renaissance Texts & Studies, graciously encouraged the volume from its inception, arranging for the review of the manuscript by four anonymous readers whose advice and often very detailed comments helped immeasurably in clarifying issues that resulted in timely revisions. To him, and to the MRTS Editorial Board, and to Lee Hoskins, Priscilla Finley, and the dedicated editorial and production team, my deep thanks. I should also like to thank my English Department colleagues at the University of British Columbia who gave me support in organizing the symposium on which this volume is founded, especially Herbert Rosengarten, Dennis Danielson, and Lee Johnson, and most notably Mark Vessey who helped at every stage in the planning of the symposium.

On behalf of all Miltonists and literary scholars, I wish to recall yet once more the great contribution to humane letters—and to Milton studies—of Northrop Frye, who joined the advisory council but whose illness and death occurred not long before the symposium in which he had wished to take part. Finally, I should like to remember gratefully Louise Forest, my own college teacher of forty years ago, who first introduced me to Milton—to a love both of his work and of the literature of the seventeenth century.

P. G. Stanwood

INTRODUCTION

MILTONISTS IN THIS LAST DECADE OF THE TWENTIETH CENTURY are as eager as they always have been to uncover the meaning, to explore the form, to know the age, and to realize the magnitude of one of the most remarkable and compelling of all English writers. Critical emphases shift, however, and the kind of historical and biographical study once so fashionable now seems inadequate and often naive. Thus, contemporary study of Milton has responded to most of the inventions and insights of critical theory, especially to the demands for "contextual-izing" the writing and for interpreting its broadly political strains. The essays brought together here consequently share the wish to discover Milton's use of the past, which was of course present to him. Although his present is not ours, we may still come to know it and to participate in it, even as Milton himself directs us to do.

Although the organizers of the Fourth International Milton Sympo-sium, held at the University of British Columbia, in August 1991, announced no special topic and welcomed papers on any subject related to Milton and his times, they soon discovered that certain areas of common interest quickly emerged. The more than two hundred papers that were submitted clearly grouped themselves around only a few themes, and those seventy papers selected for the program represented them well. From this number come the twenty-one essays of the present volume, all in revised and expanded form, together offering a unified study illustrative of the best and most typical work on Milton today. The essays by Louis Martz, Mary Ann Radzinowicz, and Balachandra Rajan were originally given as plenary addresses, and their chief con-cerns—of "prophecy and poetry," "gender," and "politics"—usefully form the organizing heads of this book and are reminiscent of the cohering principles underlying the conference itself. Not included here on account of space and their more specialized emphasis are Joseph Summers' talk on "The Making of *The Muse's Method*" and the panel discussion, chaired by Gordon Campbell, with Barbara Lewalski and John Shawcross, which featured William Hunter's challenge that the *Christian Doctrine* is not Milton's work. This volume thus aims to focus above all on issues of context—the unifying and common theme of the Symposium.[1]

The essays naturally group themselves around three aspects of this contextualization, forming three interrelated sections. The first of these begins with Louis Martz's call to listen for Milton's prophetic voice, the sound of which in fact reverberates throughout this book and inspires the words that we hear. Martz compares the Milton of *The Reason of Church Government* and of the *Second Defense* with the major prophetic writers of the Old Testament, notably Isaiah, particularly in terms of their self-introductions. The prophet first reveals himself in the middle of his work, as in the sixth chapter of Isaiah or in the fifteenth and following chapters of Jeremiah; and in a similar way, Milton identifies himself and his role at the half-way point both in *Church Government* and the *Second Defense*. Also, the voice of the poet-prophet occurs in the *third* book of *Paradise Lost,* not at the beginning of the epic. Through a remarkable set of analogues, Martz helps us to see how Milton may be understood as a writer of prophecy. Moreover, he encourages us to look more carefully at Milton's Latin prose so that we may recognize in it the clues that characterize the man who would warn and waken his country.

That we should heed the voice of the prophet requires in the first instance our comprehension of it. This first essay sets the tone whose cadences we may now follow. The salutary reminder that Milton's Latin

---

[1] Roy C. Flannagan describes the week-long Symposium and reprints abstracts of all the session papers in *MQ* 25 (1991): 151–72. William B. Hunter's argument for "The Provenance of the *Christian Doctrine*" appears in *Studies in English Literature* 32 (1992): 129–66, along with the responses by Barbara K. Lewalski and John T. Shawcross and Hunter's answer to them. Hunter offers further evidence for his position in "The Provenance of the *Christian Doctrine:* Addenda from the Bishop of Salisbury," *Studies in English Literature* 33 (1993): 191–207, and also 34 (1994): 153–203. See also Gordon Campbell, "The Authorship of *De Doctrina Christiana,*" *MQ* 26 (1992): 129–30. Joseph H. Summers' address appears as *"The Muse's Method:* Its Making and Early Reception" in a special issue of the *George Herbert Journal* 16 (1993), which collects his essays on Renaissance literature.

demands much closer attention than many scholars have given to it brings a welcome answer in John Hale's study of the Latin verse. How can we discover its tone and so not miss the meaning but become alert to the "intensity" that includes self-awareness? Hale's reflections on the ode *Ad Joannem Rousium* lead to the discussion of another Pindaric experiment; for Stella Revard writes of *Lycidas* by showing how Milton transforms the mythic techniques of his classical model. One poet raises himself on the shoulders of another, the second seeing with the first, not further but differently.

We may follow another fashioning of the poetic voice in Lee Johnson's attentive study of Milton's method of building patterns of perfection. He begins by asking how Milton can depict "innocent perfection" on its own terms, how he can create with ordinary language "the illusion of innocence." Johnson focuses on the morning hymn of Adam and Eve in *Paradise Lost,* 5.153–208, by describing the circles that surround the passage, with its "symmetrical patterns of symbolic order." Milton, therefore, would seem to be finding a voice that speaks powerfully of the once universal yet now ineluctable light of paradise. David Robertson, adding an important point in this conversation, next writes of "private thought and self-enclosure," a comment occasioned by J. B. Broadbent's wise but misleading assertion some thirty years ago that Milton's characters soliloquize only when they are fallen. Robertson shows how the soliloquies, especially of Adam and Eve, are used for the fashioning of a new self. We may profitably look at *Paradise Lost* as a whole through the perspective of book 12 and see its complete and prophetic design. The idea of depicting universal human or sacred history in one work of art, such as Milton allows Michael to do in his display of the future for Adam, is common in medieval and Renaissance painting and sculpture, and, as Douglas Chambers shows, in a number of important tapestries. The synoptic illustrations of these tapestries recall Milton's similarly typological interpretation of history in the last book of *Paradise Lost,* providing a paradigm of the whole poem for the reader; in book 12, indeed, Milton transforms providence within time, and unites the "moral, doctrinal and scriptural in one event."

The achievement of *Paradise Lost,* like the books of Isaiah 1 (chaps. 1–39) or Jeremiah, is the work of one person who sees into history and warns his contemporaries against the wickedness and tribulations that inhibit faith and corrupt morals; but with an instructed heart, they may discover redemption instead of desolation. The situation of the poet in awful circumstances may be clear enough, but that of the dramatist poses a different situation. If dramatists were, as T. H. Howard-Hill suggests, the authors of the television scripts of their day, then Milton's disclaimer, at the beginning of *Samson Agonistes,* of not intending his work for the stage, must be taken quite seriously, and at face value. Arguing from contemporary statements and documents, Howard-Hill reminds us that later critics elevated Shakespeare and his generation of dramatists so that they might claim the title of "poet" alongside Milton. But such an attitude ignores the "cultural hegemony" of Milton's poetry and the essentially "popular" and marginal work of Shakespeare. Milton himself took no significant interest in him or in the theater of his time, nor did he value any of its works. Yet *Samson Agonistes* is a kind of drama, even if it is not "contemporary," and we need to explore its significance. In his essay on "Directing the Audience in *Samson Agonistes,*" Michael Spiller shows how we as critical readers may inhabit the same "meta-poetic space" of Milton's personae, who depart calm and purged, ready to revisit the monument of Samson, to recall his story with delight and imitate his virtues. This is "the delight that accompanies wisdom," the end of the prophet's—and the poet's—knowledge.

The second section of this volume approaches Milton in another but complementary way. Working from the Trinity manuscript, Mary Ann Radzinowicz discovers four heroines in Milton's sketches of trage-dies he planned to write: Sarah, Lot's (unnamed) wife, Dinah, and Tamar. Milton's portrayals of these "tragic women" of Genesis are various and revisionary, and in interpreting them, Radzinowicz is able to apply some of the newer modes in Milton studies, especially gender criticism, new historicism, and biblical poetics. In her closely argued essay, Radzinowicz says much about Milton's "gender sensitivity" as well as his historical and hermeneutic interests. The important issues raised in this essay provide an appropriate prelude to the more particular, mainly gender oriented studies that follow. Dayton Haskin discusses sonnet 9, "Lady that in the prime of earliest youth," with its striking allusion to the book of Ruth and the cluster of associations proceeding from the imagery of providence and fruitfulness. Milton, he concludes, provides a description, perhaps personal, of an ideal of female virtue. Michael Wilding takes up the issues of sexuality, egalitarianism, and common ownership in *Paradise Lost* by forcefully blaming Satan for unequivocally perverting right action and all just boundaries, a point which leads him to the conclusion that the alleged issue of inequality (or equality) in Eve's temptation is no issue after all. Then, in a cogent discussion of Milton's supposed vow of celibacy, John Leonard sorts out

the common confusion between Revelation 14 and 19, between celibacy and pre-marital virginity, and concludes from a careful reading of the
poetry that the case for Milton's vow is unfounded. Finally, Donald
Friedman leads us to reflect on the mutuality that underlies sexual
difference and gender, and on the paradise that "preserves a visionary
memory of the universe of the 'two great sexes' as they existed in their
freedom from exclusive definition and the tyranny of appearances."

The third part of the book marks the convergence of word and
world, of Milton's *political* response to his circumstances. Balachandra
Rajan begins by reflecting on Milton's use of imagery, especially in
Paradise Lost, that evokes the Orient. Usually, the effect is pejorative, as
in the great description of Pandemonium, "which far / Outshone the
wealth of *Ormus* and of *Ind*"—or diminishing; for his unstated, and
perhaps unconscious intention here, and especially in *Paradise Regained,*
is to set religious faith over against the claims of empire. But in *Paradise
Lost,* according to Martin Evans, the ambiguity of Milton's implicit
appropriation of the east and his exploitation of India finds decided
shape. In "Milton's Imperial Epic," Evans recommends *Paradise Lost* as
a "colonial" drama in which the various characters take on roles appropriate to their natures: Satan is a type of the Renaissance explorer and
adventurer, Adam and Eve are victims of colonization, God's emissaries
are imperial agents. The many contradictions and ambivalences of
Milton's narrative obviously permit no easy allegory; but Evans aims
chiefly to alert us to the likely impact of the New World in seventeenth-century culture, and particularly to the greatest protestant poem
of the age.

Milton, of course, lived in an obviously revolutionary time, of civil
war, religious strife, tyranny, and rebellion. Few thoughtful persons
could avoid the pressure of taking sides, and so Milton quite predictably
aligned himself with those he believed might save his nation from the
"artificer of fraud." Milton sought to combat rebellion in terms that are
in fact charged with the energy of the antagonists; by forcing opposing
ideologies to confront each other, he achieves a resonance filled with
the voices of linguistic and political ambiguity. In this political context,
Gary Hamilton, in the essay that follows, addresses *Paradise Regained*—a
work descriptive of the inwardness of public struggle. But Jesus is not
otherworldly; he is a non-conformist, who insists on privateness. He
remains "a private person" who, at the end of his trial in the wilderness,
"Home to his Mother's house private returned." In his cogent argument, Hamilton writes of the relevance of the Conventicles Act (1664),

which, through its enforcement, led to the suppression of private places of worship. While Milton would have demurred at that action, he yet could approve of private worship inspired by the presence of the Holy Spirit. In an unexpected turn that anticipates the final essay of the book on the sacrament of the word, Hamilton reminds us that Jesus returns to a quiet place where he may minister, not, as the gospel accounts inform us, to a public forum.

The first three essays in this last section display Milton's poetry in a variety of political contexts; the last four concentrate primarily on his prose treatises. The essay that bridges these parts is an exercise in current historical bibliography which seeks to show the special social circumstances of a book and its author. Peter Lindenbaum studies Milton as a professional author who had a sense of proprietorship over *Paradise Lost* and his last publications. We see him as a practical man who understands commercial value and his own ability to profit from it. Milton is, accordingly, a writer with an economic sense, one who knows *politics* according to the marketplace. Such a feeling for the affairs of this world befits the democratic Milton, whose republican affections began early and remained with him for the rest of his life. Arguing from the well known passage in *Of Reformation* in which Milton idealizes the character of Parliament, Janel Mueller traces the development of Milton's republicanism, identifying it with his discourse on "estates." By the time of *Eikonoklastes,* Milton's attitudes, of course, are clearly fixed. But his condemnation of the *Eikon Basilike,* Achsah Guibbory urges, is based essentially on the grounds of what he sees to be false idolatry; for Milton aims to break with the past in order to display the ideal "puritan" revolutionary.

While Milton attacked tyranny of all kinds, no one has hitherto noticed the sort called "grammatical," which Wyman Herendeen describes in his vital essay on *Accedence Commenc't Grammar.* Through pertinent examples, Milton manages to free his own grammar book from the ideology implicit in contemporary rival grammars; and the language in which Milton instructs his students is preeminently one of social reform. Indeed, we should probably not be surprised to know that even a grammatical treatise, properly construed, grows out of a political and an historical context which gives to it shape and uniqueness. Finally, Ken Simpson's study of the anti-episcopal tracts not only clarifies the doctrinal setting of these works, but it points toward the "burden" of the poet-prophet who would reveal the word through the inspiration and government of the Spirit.

   This book ends where it began, for the need to describe Milton's
sacramental theology lies at the heart of Simpson's study which tries to
describe the significance that Milton gives to the scriptures and to the
words of those who desire to interpret them. The issues Simpson raises
and toward which most of the essays in this book tend are contextual—
we are asked over and again to confront Milton's own time and learning, and his own words, to hear the voice of the prophet, and to listen
for his silences. We should not overlook the solemnity and the quietness
of this call, even in the frequently contentious treatises. In *Of Reformation,* Milton rails against the episcopacy but in order principally to say
that "the very essence of Truth is plainnesse, and brightnes; the darknes
and crookednesse is our own."[2] Milton regularly insists on the obvious-
ness of truth, teaching that "the deep mistery of the Gospel, is the pure
simplicity of doctrine."[3] He abhors the grip of tradition, irrationality,
intemperance, pompous authority, ritual without substance. Yet Milton's
purpose is always to reform and improve the church and state, a point
set out with great power in the splendid preface to the second book of
Church Government, to which Louis Martz called our attention at the
beginning of this present collection, where Milton characteristically
urges "the honest liberty of free speech" so that "the call of wisdom and
virtu may be heard every where."[4] Here indeed is the prophet who
cries, "Here am I. Send me."

UNIVERSITY OF BRITISH COLUMBIA

---

[2] See *Of Reformation,* in *Complete Prose Works of John Milton,* ed. Don M. Wolfe et al.,
(New Haven: Yale Univ. Press, 1953–82), 1:566.

[3] See *Reason of Church Government,* in CPW 1:826.

[4] Ibid., 1:804,819.

Part I

THE PROPHETIC VOICE

Louis L. Martz

MILTON'S PROPHETIC VOICE: MOVING TOWARD PARADISE

ONE OF THE MOST IMPORTANT DEVELOPMENTS IN RECENT Miltonic studies—perhaps the most important—lies in the renewed interest in Milton's prose. This development is partly due to the "new historicism," with its concern for signs of political power, partly to the older British concern for revolutionary history, led by Christopher Hill, and partly to the interest in Milton as prophet aroused in the 1970s by scholars such as William Kerrigan and Joseph Wittreich. All these tendencies have now reached a culmination in two books published in 1990: the collection of essays on Milton's prose edited by David Loewenstein and James Turner, and Loewenstein's own book *Milton and the Drama of History*.[1]

At the same time revisionist historians in England have been altering our views of the context in which Milton's prophetic voice appeared. Nicholas Tyacke, for example, has given a fresh view of the conflict between Calvinism and the resurgent advocates of free will during the first forty years of the seventeenth century. Two recent books by Conrad Russell have freshly explored the complex causes of the English Civil

---

[1] See Christopher Hill, *Milton and the English Revolution* (New York: Viking Press, 1978); William Kerrigan, *The Prophetic Milton* (Charlottesville: Univ. Press of Virginia, 1974); Joseph Anthony Wittreich, Jr., " 'A Poet Amongst Poets': Milton and the Tradition of Prophecy," in *Milton and the Line of Vision,* ed. Wittreich (Madison: Univ. of Wisconsin Press, 1975); J. A. Wittreich, *Visionary Poetics: Milton's Tradition and His Legacy* (San Marino, Calif.: Huntington Library, 1979); David Loewenstein and James Grantham Turner, eds., *Politics, Poetics, and Hermeneutics in Milton's Prose* (Cambridge: Cambridge Univ. Press, 1990); David Loewenstein, *Milton and the Drama of History* (Cambridge: Cambridge Univ. Press, 1990).

War.[2] Russell's massive book of 1991 bears the significant title *The Fall of the British Monarchies, 1637–1642*—monarchies, for the book explores in detail the interrelated events of the three kingdoms, England, Scotland, and Ireland, those events that precipitated Milton's entry into the field of politics. Russell shows King Charles's profound responsibility for the outbreak of war, with the result that we can see more clearly the reasons for Milton's bitter attacks upon Charles as tyrant.

In the context of such recent studies I want to consider Milton's prophetic voice as it develops within the structure of his writings, both in prose and in poetry. I turn first to the emergence of that voice in the middle of *The Reason of Church Government*—that surprising and rather embarrassing revelation of Milton's poetical hopes and dreams, while he apologizes for seeming to delay the fulfillment of those hopes by diversion into the "cool element of prose," the work of "my left hand." As recent critics have said, this slighting of his prose is spoken only in relation to this one treatise, as he compares his present writing with his exalted view of what he hopes to accomplish in the greater realms of poetry and drama. Some twenty years ago, in a book prophetically entitled *The Politics of Milton's Prose Style*, Keith Staveley speculated that in Milton's next prose treatise, the *Apology*, "Milton began trying to write prose with his right hand, began trying to perceive it as a medium which might give full and free expression to his poetic ideals, and began developing a voice of sufficient range and flexibility to perform this task."[3] In 1974 the collection of essays on Milton's prose edited by Michael Lieb and John Shawcross had shown the rightness (or right-handedness) of that view; thus the title of their book, *Achievements of the Left Hand*, takes on a certain perhaps deliberate irony, for the essays in this collection, like those in the later collection, show Milton gradually devoting his best talents to the achievement of what Joseph Wittreich calls "The Crown of Eloquence."[4]

But the remark about his "left hand" does apply to *The Reason of*

[2] Nicholas Tyacke, *Anti-Calvinists: The Rise of English Arminianism, c. 1590–1640* (Oxford: Clarendon Press, 1987); Conrad Russell, *The Causes of the English Civil War* (Oxford: Clarendon Press, 1990) and *The Fall of the British Monarchies, 1637–1642* (Oxford: Clarendon Press, 1991).

[3] Keith W. Staveley, *The Politics of Milton's Prose Style* (New Haven: Yale Univ. Pres, 1975), 48.

[4] Michael Lieb and John T. Shawcross, eds., *Achievements of the Left Hand: Essays on the Prose of John Milton* (Amherst: Univ. of Massachusetts Press, 1974).

Church Government—a work that, in accord with its title, clings so closely to reasoning that it does not often rise to eloquence: the treatise lacks the full power of prophetic invective and the full power of prophetic vision that mark the great Latin defences of the English people. But the personal revelation in the middle rises far above the rest in eloquence. The question is: Why does this powerful passage occur in the middle? Indeed, why does it occur at all?

A look at the Old Testament prophets may help to explain this surprising example of self-identification, self-dramatization, self-fashioning. The biblical prophets tend to provide a careful staging for the emergence of their prophetic voices, sometimes at the beginning, sometimes in the middle, and sometimes throughout their books of prophecy. Ezekiel is the most dramatic at the outset, with his setting among the exiles by the river of Chebar and the great vision of the chariot of Deity which conveys to him and to us the authority and authenticity of his prophetic visions. The prophet must identify himself in two ways: as one among his suffering and sinful people, and as one whose voice rises above disaster to speak for God, in the basic Greek meaning of the word *prophet:* "one who speaks for another."

Amos waits until well past the middle to identify himself, for we should discount the historical data which the ancient Hebrew editors have added in the opening verses of the prophetic books. The voice of Amos begins with a powerful poetic denunciation, subtle and dramatic. He begins by predicting the total destruction of Israel's pagan enemies: Damascus, Gaza, Tyre, Ammon, Moab: "For three transgressions of Moab, and for four," says the voice of God, "I will not turn away the punishment thereof . . . But I will send a fire upon Moab, and it shall devour the palaces of Kirioth: and Moab shall die with tumult, with shouting, and with the sound of the trumpet. . . ." But suddenly that refrain turns against Judah and Israel:

> Thus saith the Lord; For three transgressions of Judah, and for four, I will not turn away the punishment thereof, because they have despised the law of the Lord, and have not kept his commandments . . . But I will send a fire upon Judah, and it shall devour the palaces of Jerusalem. Thus saith the Lord; For three transgressions of Israel, and for four, I will not turn away the punishment thereof; because they sold the righteous for silver, and the poor for a pair of shoes. . . . (Amos 2.4–6 AV)

The prophet, we see, makes no distinction between religious and social evil: apostasy is the root cause of social injustice. This prophet has his eye upon the present, not primarily upon the future. His predictions of future disaster are designed to inspire a reform of the present, and his predictions of possible redemption are designed to encourage a renewal of the present. It is only after six and a half chapters of such denunciation that we come upon Amos in a dramatic confrontation with his priestly opponent Amaziah, who cries:

> O thou seer, go, flee thee away into the land of Judah, and there eat bread, and prophesy there;
>
> But prophesy not again any more at Bethel: for it is the king's chapel, and it is the king's court.
>
> Then answered Amos, and said to Amaziah, I was no prophet, neither was I a prophet's son; but I was an herdman, and a gatherer of sycomore fruit:
>
> And the Lord took me as I followed the flock, and the Lord said unto me, Go, prophesy unto my people Israel.
>
> Now therefore hear thou the word of the Lord: Thou sayest, Prophesy not against Israel, and drop not thy word against the house of Isaac.
>
> Therefore thus saith the Lord; Thy wife shall be an harlot in the city, and thy sons and thy daughters shall fall by the sword, and thy land shall be divided by line; and thou shalt die in a polluted land.... (7.12–17)

Thus Amos, a layman, is speaking against the minions of the king's chapel and the king's court—against prelatical episcopacy.

Jeremiah is the prophet whom we know best in his personal life, for he dramatizes himself and his emotions from beginning to end of his book, while the most personal of his self-revelations come more than a third of the way into his work, in chapters 15 through 20, where Jeremiah laments his suffering and persecution in words that Milton cites near the beginning of his own self-revelation: "This is that which the sad Prophet *Jeremiah* laments, *Wo is me my mother, that thou hast born me a man of strife, and contention*" (Jer. 15.10). And then a little later:

> If he [the modern prophet] shall think to be silent, as *Jeremiah* did, because of the reproach and derision he met with daily, and *all his familiar friends watcht for his halting* to be reveng'd on him for speaking the truth, he would be forc't to confesse as he confest, *his word was in my heart as a burning fire shut up in my*

bones, I was weary with forbearing, and could not stay (Jer. 20.9; CPW 1:802–3).

But even more important is Milton's well-known allusion to Isaiah, as Milton describes the primary source of poetic power: "devout prayer to that eternall Spirit who can enrich with all utterance and knowledge, and sends out his Seraphim with the hallow'd fire of his Altar to touch and purify the lips of whom he pleases" (CPW 1:820–21). Isaiah's account of the coal-bearing seraph occurs in the sixth chapter of his book, half-way through the opening section of twelve chapters that constitutes a distinct and complete composition in itself. After the so-called "Book of Immanuel" (chapters 6–12), Isaiah veers off into a totally different mode of writing, with the chapters containing the "burden" of the various surrounding nations devoted to destruction—"burden" being a translation of the Hebrew word meaning "utterance" or "oracle," but generally taken, as here by Milton, to mean the grievous fate foreseen by the prophet for the idolatrous enemies of Israel (*OED,* "Burden" III.8).

Chapter six of Isaiah, with its biographical self-authentication, is preceded by five chapters almost wholly given over to denouncing the apostasy of Israel, with its accompanying evils of social injustice. Then suddenly, unexpectedly, chapter six presents the calling of the prophet, with his vision of the seraphim. At first the prophet is reluctant to undertake the charge—this is the stance of nearly all prophets from Moses on down to Amos, Jeremiah, and Isaiah, who now cries: "Woe is me! for I am undone; because I am a man of unclean lips, and I dwell in the midst of a people of unclean lips." But after the seraph bears to his lips the purifying coal, he hears "the voice of the Lord, saying, Whom shall I send, and who will go for us? Then said I, Here am I; send me" (Isa. 6.5,8). Milton adopts essentially the same traditional stance of reluctance and acceptance.

But why place the prophetic self-revelation in the middle of a treatise? We can see the effect in Isaiah and Amos and to some extent in Jeremiah. The first parts of these prophetic books present the picture of a world of utter corruption: apostasy, pursuit of riches, neglect of the poor, thievery in high office, vanity in female dress and ornament, fornication, drunkenness, murder. But who is making these violent denunciations? What right has this voice to denounce his own people? In the middle comes the identification and authorization of that voice. He is not one of the numerous confraternities of accepted and accommodating prophets. He is a dissenting voice chosen to convey the word of the

Lord. He has been reluctant to undertake the task: Amos has his flocks
and his sycamores to tend. But God insists and so the prophet agrees:
"Here am I; send me." I will do what I can, even with my left hand.

Now, having revealed his identity, the prophet Isaiah goes on in the
next five chapters to reveal that denunciation is not his only role. Now
he mingles comfort with continued denunciation, and gradually a promise of redemption emerges in the words that we can all now sing, thanks
to Handel: "For unto us a child is born, unto us a son is given: and the
government shall be upon his shoulder: and his name shall be called
Wonderful, Counsellor, The mighty God, The everlasting Father, The
Prince of Peace" (9.6). Here is a promise of reformation, if only the
nation, or at least a remnant of the nation, will return to truth and
righteousness. These messianic chapters then reach their climax in the
pastoral vision of chapter eleven: "The wolf also shall dwell with the
lamb, and the leopard shall lie down with the kid; and the calf and the
young lion and fatling together; and a little child shall lead them" (11.6).
After these five chapters of dominantly redemptive vision this self-con-
tained section concludes, in the brief chapter twelve, with a psalm of
praise. Note the construction: five chapters of denunciation; a middle
chapter of self-revelation; then five chapters of redemptive vision, with
a pendant of praise. The self-revelation of the prophet becomes the axis
upon which the voice changes from denunciation to consolation.

One can see how *The Reason of Church Government* follows this pattern, rather than a pattern of traditional oratory. The first half, the first
book, is devoted to destroying the arguments for prelacy, not with the
full virulence of the biblical prophets, nor with the "sanctified bitterness" of Milton's later prose—but still with a tart and acid tone designed
to corrode and disintegrate the arguments of the prelates. After the biographical excursus of book 2 the arguments gradually move into a more
positive area, reaching a climax in the impassioned argument for the role
of the layman in the fully reformed church. This is an argument for
which the biographical "digression" of the lay prophet has carefully prepared the way. The work then concludes with a brief oration addressed
to the "Lords and Commons" of England—a conclusion performed in
a high style that shows clearly how different this is from the reasoning
mode of the treatise proper.

If it seems strained to find here an analogy with the opening twelve
chapters of Isaiah, we should consider that these chapters constitute, for
Christian readers, one of the most important passages in the Old Testament—indeed a passage equalled in importance only by its counterpart,

the story of the Fall. Furthermore, these twelve chapters constitute the opening of the entire sequence of the books of biblical prophecy. Likewise, we might say, *The Reason of Church Government* opens Milton's career as prophet, for in his preceding treatises the sense of mission is not so clearly realized.

Still a problem remains: *why* does the biblical prophet and his successor, John Milton, feel that he must so graphically introduce himself, or the prophetic version of himself? An answer may be suggested by the Chinese prophet and sage, Confucius, conversing with his disciples, in the adaptation by Ezra Pound in canto 13. "We are unknown," says Confucius, "You will take up charioteering? / Then you will become known,"

> "Or perhaps I should take up charioteering, or archery? Or the practice of public speaking?"

Now the charioteering of Ezekiel is rather more symbolic than this, but the end is much the same: to become known, to be recognized. For the prophets are outsiders—"Church-outed by the Prelates," and so they must define and dramatize themselves in order to assert their authority. The prophet is a dissenting voice arising unexpectedly from the midst of history. He seeks an active engagement with that history; he seeks to change the movement of history from decline and corruption toward the ideal of faith, honesty, justice, and love in which man and woman were created in Paradise. Thus the personal excursus arises from the midst of *The Reason of Church Government* to define the public speaker as a voice worth listening to.

Twelve years later, in the *Second Defence,* Milton again declares his presence and authority at even greater length, and again, in the middle of the treatise. Here he has a much more obvious reason for his personal discourse: he has been attacked personally; he must defend his character. But why do this in the middle of the work? Why not do it at the outset, by way of leading into his bitter attack upon his opposition? Other ends are accomplished by thus placing his personal defense in the middle, after the vicious excoriation of Morus. In this placement the prophet can, like Jeremiah in his thirty-eighth chapter, be seen arising from the dungeon, the mire of controversy in which he has been imprisoned, carried upward by the armpits toward a more exalted vision: the eulogy of Bradshaw, the eulogy of Fairfax, the eulogy of Cromwell, and the brief praise of other revolutionary leaders, some of them, like Bradshaw and Fairfax, currently out of favor with Cromwell. Milton's self-defense indeed creates a quaternion of major revolutionary heroes: Milton, Bradshaw, Fairfax, Cromwell.

But the most significant portion of the *Second Defence* does not lie in these heroic eulogies, important as they are; it lies in the solemn prophetic warnings near the close, where Milton shows his grasp of the immediate political situation, sensing accurately the divisions and corruptions that are threatening the success of the true Reformation. His praise of leaders now out of favor stresses the need for unity. At the same time he warns that too much stress is being placed upon military victories, in England, Ireland, Scotland, and on the sea, while at home the urgent issues of a troubled society are being neglected, and self-seekers profit from the turmoil:

> Many men has war made great whom peace makes small. If, having done with war, you neglect the arts of peace, if warfare is your peace and liberty, war your only virtue, your supreme glory, you will find, believe me, that peace itself is your greatest enemy.... Unless you be victors here as well, that enemy and tyrant whom you have just now defeated in the field has either not been conquered at all or has been conquered in vain. For if the ability to devise the cleverest means of putting vast sums of money into the treasury, the power readily to equip land and sea forces, to deal shrewdly with ambassadors from abroad, and to contract judicious alliances and treaties has seemed to any of you greater, wiser, and more useful to the state than to administer incorrupt justice to the people, to help those cruelly harassed and oppressed, and to render to every man promptly his own deserts, too late will you discover how mistaken you have been, when those great affairs have suddenly betrayed you and what now seems to you small and trifling shall then have turned against you and become a source of ruin. (CPW 4:680–81)

Milton, in these closing pages, has his eye upon the present, and he seems to realize that the cause is in grave danger. Nevertheless, in his final sentence he asserts his presence as one "who could rightly counsel, encourage, and inspire, who could honor both the noble deeds and those who had done them, and make both deeds and doers illustrious with praises that will never die" (CPW 4:685–86). We need the Latin to appreciate Milton's essential point: "non defuisse qui monere recta, hortari, incitari, qui egregiè tum facta, tum qui fecissent, condecorare, &

victuris in omne aevum celebrare laudibus potuerit" (CE 8:254). Note
the last word: *potuerit*—one who was able. The prophet's confidence defines the voice of one who was able to reach out from the midst of
present trouble into a future that will in some way justify all his efforts.

The Latin is everywhere essential if we are to grasp the greatness of
this treatise and the craft and care that Milton has expended in speaking,
as he was well aware, to the entire humanistic audience of Europe. His
Latin style here stands at a far remove from the frequently extended sentences, the sometimes curiously involved syntax (or lack of syntax) in his
English prose—the style that Thomas Corns has fruitfully examined in
terms of "transformational-generative grammar," with its "left-branch-
ing," "self-embedding," and "right-branching" elements.[5]

Corns's analysis tends to reinforce an uneasiness that I have felt with
efforts to read Milton's complex English sentences in terms of classical
rhetoric. His English prose seems rather to have the quality and movement of spoken, extemporaneous English, with the sort of branching
and digression along a main point that we all make in spontaneous oral
composition. I have noticed this oral, branching, digressive quality in
Thomas More's polemical English prose, in contrast to his humanistic
Latin writing. Is there, perhaps, something in the nature of polemical
writing in English that differentiates it, essentially, from classical form?
Such polemic is addressed to a broad English audience, not attuned to
the niceties of Latin style; the aim is to hit quickly, hit hard, hit again,
hit to knock out. Thus the long sentences come to have their branching
and self-embedding qualities. Milton himself has suggested the point in
the biographical excursus of *Church Government,* where the straggling
sentence illustrates exactly what he is saying:

> Next if I were wise only to mine own ends, I would certainly
> take such a subject as of it self might catch applause, whereas
> this hath all the disadvantages on the contrary, and such a sub-
> ject as the publishing whereof might be delayd at pleasure, and
> time enough to pencill it over with all the curious touches of
> art, even to the perfection of a faultlesse picture, whenas in this
> argument the not deferring is of great moment to the good
> speeding, that if solidity have leisure to doe her office, art
> cannot have much. (CPW 1:807–8)

[5] Thomas N. Corns, *The Development of Milton's Prose Style* (Oxford: Clarendon Press,
1982).

Notice how in the middle the sentence seems to start anew—"and such a subject. . . ." Note too the colloquial shift in "and time enough to pencill it over. . . ."

In the *Second Defence* the style is not thus "multi-branching": it is terse, condensed, tightly unified by all the devices that Latin rhetoric could use, all the emphatic, linking assonance, all the emphatic suspensions and inversions that an inflected language can sustain. The Latin must be read aloud to savor its effect. But first, the difficult translation:

> As for myself, to whatever state things may return, I have performed, and certainly with a good will, I hope not in vain, the service which I thought would be of most use to the commonwealth. It is not before our own doors alone that I have borne my arms in defence of liberty; I have wielded them on a field so wide, that the justice and reason of these which are no vulgar deeds, shall be explained and vindicated alike to foreign nations and to our own countrymen; and by all good men shall no doubt be approved; and shall remain to the matchless renown of my fellow-citizens, and as the brightest example for after-ages. (CE 8:253)

> Ad me quod attinet, quocunque res redierit, quam ego operam meam maximè ex usu reipublicae futuram judicavi, haud gravatim certè, &, ut spero, haud frustra impendi; meáque arma pro libertate, non solùm ante fores extuli, sed etiam iis ita latè sum usus, ut factorum minimè vulgarium jus atque ratio, & apud nostros & apud exteros explicata atque defensa, bonis certè omnibus probata, & ad meorum civium summam laudem, & posterorum ad exemplum praeclarè constet.

The Latin shows at once how English syntax forces a reversal of Milton's emphatic placement of his main verbs: *impendi* (I have performed) in the third line, and *constet* (will endure, will stand forever) at the very end. Note too the subtle hesitation of the passage translated with difficulty as "I have performed, and certainly with a good will, I hope not in vain, the service. . . ." The Latin reads: "haud gravatim certè, &, ut spero, haud frustra impendi." "Not unwillingly certainly, and, as I hope, not in vain have I performed [this work]." The elegance of the parallel phrasing reinforces the hesitation, just as the later balance of "& apud nostros & apud exteros" stresses the breadth of Milton's audience. The assonance that runs throughout is evident—I hope—from an oral reading, as in the resonant *m* (and other) linked sounds of the final words: "& ad meorum civium summam laudem, & posterorum ad exemplum praeclarè constet." Such devices create a subtle oratorical harmony sought and understood by the humanistic ear.

The assonance of Milton's phrasing points to a quality that runs throughout the treatise, especially notable in the tribute to Bradshaw:

> At length, on a request from the parliament that he would preside on the trial of the king, he refused not the dangerous office; for to skill in the law, he added a liberal mind, a lofty spirit, with manners unimpeached, and beholden to no man. This office ... he executed and filled with such steadiness, such gravity, with such dignity and presence of mind, that he seemed destined and created by the deity himself for this particular act ... and he so far surpassed the glory of all tyrannicides, as it is more humane, more just, more full of majesty, to try a tyrant, than to put him to death without trial. He was otherwise neither gloomy nor severe, but mild and gentle.

Here Milton pulls out all the stops of humanistic rhetoric, taking melodious advantage of case and verbal endings:

> Tandem uti Regis judicio praesidere vellet, à Senatu rogatus, provinciam sanè periculosissimam non recusavit. Attulerat enim ad legum scientiam ingenium liberale, animum excelsum, mores integros ac nemini obnoxios; unde illud munus ... ita constanter, ita graviter, tanta animi cum praesentia ac dignitate gessit atque implevit, ut ad hoc ipsum opus ... ab ipso Numine designatus atque factus videretur; & Tyrannicidarum omnium gloriam tantum superaverit, quantò est humanius, quantò justius, ac majestate plenius, Tyrannum judicare, quàm injudicatum occidere. Alioqui nec tristis, nec severus, sed comis ac placidus.... (CE 8:156–59)

The -am and -um endings are strong at the beginning, followed by the balancing of *integros* and *obnoxios, constanter* and *graviter,* the sonal affiliation of *videretur* and *superaverit,* the linkage of *humanius, justius, plenius,* and the alternate parallels of *tristis, comis,* and *severus, placidus.* These highly crafted, resonant cadences play an essential part in Milton's defense of himself and of his nation. For his handling of Latin shows that the revolution was not the work of barbarians, but the work of men

educated to the finest level of Renaissance culture, men who have inherited the language, the wisdom, and the judgment of the ancients.

And more than this. It seems likely that Milton's saturation in
writing such Latin, along with his immersion in Latin correspondence
for the Council of State, may have something to do with the peculiar
style of *Paradise Lost*. Of course Milton read Latin from boyhood and
wrote Latin verses in his youth. But nothing in Milton's earlier experience with Latin could have matched the five years of concentration on
the writing of Latin prose that he experienced in the years 1650–1655,
just before he began the sustained composition of his long-delayed epic.
Yes, Milton in *Paradise Lost* wrote English like (what is for us) a dead
language. But for Milton that language was vigorously, immediately,
living in his mind. Was it, then, the vital, immediate presence of Latin
in his mind that made it possible for him to create those great suspended
cadences, those echoes of Latin rhetorical devices, in *Paradise Lost*? If this
is so, then Milton's prose is indeed inseparable from his highest poetical
achievement.

Beyond this possible stylistic affiliation a larger structural analogy
may appear when we compare *Paradise Lost, The Reason of Church Government,* the *Second Defence,* and the biblical prophets, especially Isaiah.
As I have argued in *Poet of Exile,* the first two books of *Paradise Lost* are
not essentially located in hell.[6] Through Milton's similes the action is
translated from hell into the landscapes and seascapes of the earth, while
his roll-call of the pagan deities that led to Israel's apostasy recalls the
biblical prophet's denunciation of the abominations of Damascus, Gaza,
Ammon, and Moab. The result is that the opening two books come to
represent a prophetic denunciation of the evils of the fallen world. In
these two books the high epic manner marks Milton's achievement of a
brief epic—Satan's epic—where the voice of the narrator is quite different in tone and manner from the voice that emerges at the outset of
book 3. In books 1 and 2 the voice is distant and austere, sometimes explanatory, but more often minatory, condemnatory, while recounting
the evils of Satan and humankind:

> In Courts and Palaces he also Reigns
> And in luxurious Cities, where the noise
> Of riot ascends above thir loftiest Tow'rs,

---

[6] Louis L. Martz, *Poet of Exile: A Study of Milton's Poetry* (New Haven: Yale Univ. Press,
1980; reissued as *Milton: Poet of Exile,* 1986), 188–92.

> And injury and outrage: And when Night
> Darkens the Streets, then wander forth the Sons
> Of *Belial*, flown with insolence and wine.[7]
>
> (1.497–502)

> O shame to men! Devil with Devil damn'd
> Firm concord holds, men only disagree
> Of Creatures rational, though under hope
> Of heavenly Grace; and God proclaiming peace,
> Yet live in hatred, enmity, and strife
> Among themselves, and levy cruel wars,
> Wasting the Earth, each other to destroy....
>
> (2.496–502)

Who is this speaker who so vividly and violently denounces the wickedness of humankind? By what right does he speak? The answer, or part of the answer, comes in the prologue to book 3: he is a blind bard and prophet, suffering from the loss of the sight of nature's beauty and of what is to him the human face divine; yet not the more he clings to love of poetry, love of humankind, and love of God, hoping that divine grace will grant him the illumination that he seeks. The tone here is intimate, affectionate, and though the minatory voice emerges again in his account of Limbo, the dominant manner of this voice throughout books 3 and 4 is not condemnatory. The personal prologue to book 3 thus becomes, as with Isaiah, the pivot upon which the poem moves from denunciation of evil toward a pastoral promise of redemption. The intimate tone recurs in the brief prologue to book 4, where the poet shows his pity for the fate that he foresees for "innocent frail man," whom he has earlier declared (speaking for God) "sufficient to have stood, though free to fall." Now he seems to throw his theology to the winds, and asks for the voice of an older prophet:

> O for that warning voice, which he who saw
> Th' *Apocalypse*, heard cry in Heav'n aloud,
> Then when the Dragon, put to second rout,
> Came furious down to be reveng'd on men,
> *Woe to the inhabitants on Earth!* that now,
> While time was, our first Parents had bin warn'd

---

[7] All quotations from Milton's poetry follow Hughes.

> The coming of thir secret foe, and scap'd
> Haply so scap'd his mortal snare....   (4.1–8)

This concern, pity, and affection for mankind dominates the voice of the bard in Paradise; even his condemnation of shame is tempered with pity and regret:

> Then was not guilty shame: dishonest shame
> Of Nature's works, honor dishonorable,
> Sin-bred, how have ye troubl'd all mankind
> With shows instead, mere shows of seeming pure,
> And banisht from man's life his happiest life,
> Simplicity and spotless innocence.   (4.313–18)

His hymn to wedded love (4.736–75) thus properly becomes the climax of this book, where Milton manages to embed his praise of the wedded state within the political context of his times, attacking first the set prayers of the once established, then disestablished, and now re-established church:

> This said unanimous, and other Rites
> Observing none, but adoration pure
> Which God likes best, into thir inmost bower
> Handed they went....   (4.736–39)

Now he moves on into his attack on Catholic celibacy:

> Nor turn'd I ween
> *Adam* from his fair Spouse, nor *Eve* the Rites
> Mysterious of connubial Love refus'd:
> Whatever Hypocrites austerely talk
> Of purity and place and innocence,
> Defaming as impure what God declares
> Pure, and commands to some, leaves free to all.
>   (4.742–47)

Then he praises "all the Charities / Of Father, Son, and Brother"—and thus embroils himself in current controversy, for I wish, too, that Milton had somehow managed to work in the charities of Mother, Daughter, and Sister. But he is, yes, here he is, *patriarchal.* After this comes his culminating attack on the *mores* renewed in the Restoration:

> Court Amours,
> Mixt Dance, or wanton Mask, or Midnight Ball,

Or Serenate, which the starv'd Lover sings
To his proud fair, best quitted with disdain. (4.767–70)

As with Isaiah, prophetic denunciation of the sins of society is not left
behind even in the Book of Immanuel; but these condemnations in
both prophets are folded within and softened by affection and concern:

Sleep on,
Blest pair: and O yet happiest if ye seek
No happier state, and know to know no more.
(4.773–75)

But, you may ask, how can Milton's vision of paradise in book 4 be
regarded as a book of redemption, akin to Isaiah's Book of Immanuel?
I think it is redemptive in its promise because it is spoken by the redeemed voice of one who appreciates the goodness of God's creation—
the voice of one who maintains within his mind a vision of essential,
original goodness that is not lost, so long as it can be maintained by
even a remnant of the human race. The structure of Milton's first four
books can thus be seen as modelled on traditional prophetic strategy:
denunciation at the outset, revelation of the prophetic identity in the
middle, followed by affectionate evidence and promise of redemption.
The 240 lines that follow after the hymn to wedded love support this
promise of redemption by showing the vigilance of the garden's angelic
guards and the power of God revealed in the scales of heaven.

Current critics are right, then, to argue that we should give up the
view that Milton's many years of work with prose constituted a regrettable
interruption in his plans to create great works of poetry and drama. The
prose works, we can now see, provided an essential training-ground for the
dual voice of the prophet denouncing evil and offering hope, a training
that may have provided both a model of style and a model of structure.

But perhaps no model was really needed for that structure. Perhaps
prophecy intuitively moves toward such a structure, where the prophet
first explores his position, then, having gained confidence in his mission,
the prophet manifests his authority in a personal revelation, and from
here moves on to the message of redemption. This is what the poet-
prophet H. D. has done in her wartime *Trilogy* of the 1940s, proclaiming herself a successor to the prophet of the book of Revelation at the
outset of the second of her three books of prophecy. Walt Whitman too
waits until near the middle of his "Song of Myself" to reveal who that
self is:

> Walt Whitman, an American, one of the roughs, a
>   Kosmos,
> Disorderly fleshly and sensual ... eating drinking and
>   breeding,
> No sentimentalist ... no stander above men and women
>   or apart from them ... no more modest than
>   immodest.
>   * * * * *
> Through me many long dumb voices,
> Voices of the interminable generations of slaves,
> Voices of prostitutes and of deformed persons,
> Voices of the diseased and despairing, and of thieves and
>   dwarfs. ...   (1855 version)

This personal revelation of his mission acts as a pivot upon which Whitman's poem turns from a surface view of American scenes and actors—"In me the caresser of life wherever moving"—toward passages of grim suffering and death: a military massacre, a bloody battle at sea, the hounded slave, "the mashed fireman with breastbone broken." "I am the man ... I suffered ... I was there," says the prophet, who now reveals himself as the comforter for all afflicted humankind:

> I seize the descending man ... I raise him with resistless
>   will
> O despairer, here is my neck,
> By God! you shall not go down! Hang your whole
>   weight upon me.

Not exactly the language and cadence of Milton, but the essential mission is much the same. "I am the man ... I suffered ... I was there." "Here am I. Send me."

YALE UNIVERSITY

John K. Hale

THE PRE-CRITICISM OF MILTON'S LATIN VERSE, ILLUSTRATED FROM THE ODE "AD JOANNEM ROUSIUM"

I

"PRE-CRITICISM" MEANS IN GENERAL WHAT ONE DOES BEFORE making a critique, but in particular the recovery of a poem's conditions of understanding. These conditions of understanding poetry vary from period to period and from language to language; and vary, for the modern reader, both in kind and in degree. Thus the pre-criticism of the Hebrew Bible is so rare and major an undertaking that for centuries it has been a distinct, named science—Old Testament "Introduction" (*eisagoge, introductio*). Contrariwise, the poems of Shakespeare or Milton are felt to be so much more directly accessible to English-speakers that there exists no distinct, named science of the conditions of understanding them. But what is the position with Milton's *Latin* poems?

These poems find many obstacles to appreciation. The obvious one is that their being in Latin deters many readers. But further, they face the dilemma that by closely emulating Roman poetry they can be faulted for either doing it incorrectly or too well, slavishly. Here, however, pre-criticism helps. For we can appropriate much of what Gordon Williams says concerning the conditions of understanding classical Roman poetry.

> So it is essential, before proper critical judgment can be made of Roman poetry, to grasp and apply certain criteria of understanding. The pleasure to be got from reading poetry must be

worked for, and a reader needs to be able to set a poem in its
original context by a process of historical reconstruction.[1]

The next step, however, is to ask how far this applies to Milton's neo-
Latin: this, though imitating the Roman poets in many respects, has the
constraints and ambitions of his own time.

Because the present essay cannot undertake all of this for all of the
poems, it illustrates from one poem how pre-criticism may be done. It
offers a variety of methods of approach, new in themselves, or in their
emphases, or in being applied to Milton. Thus I begin with three contexts of understanding which use new research: (i) the way Milton's own
world regarded the publishing of Latin poems; (ii) the way he himself
regarded such publishing; and (iii) the chronology and occasions of his
composing.

II

The first two contexts of understanding are clarified by J. W. Binns's
survey, *Intellectual Culture in Elizabethan and Jacobean England: The Latin
Writings of the Age.*[2] Binns explains how Latin verse composition was
viewed at schools and universities when Milton was there, writing most
of the Latin poems of his which survive. To put it briefly, Latin verse
had the social and political function of "celebrating and reinforcing
royal power." Just as royalty paid visits to Oxford and Cambridge to
"mobilize them in support of the national interests and religion of
England," so the universities flowed with Latin occasional verse when
royalty visited or married, was born or died. Latin verse was a sign of
power—cultural power, placed at the service of political power, in
hopes (often) of association with it. For prestige and preferment rode on
the resulting verse anthologies that issued from the two university
presses: prestige for the institutions, preferment for the versifiers. Binns
explores the process by which an editor was selected and invited, then
used his contacts to get contributors of verses; but also, crucially, how

---

[1] Williams, *The Nature of Roman Poetry* (London: Oxford Univ. Press, 1970), vii. His own
book and the larger one it is based on (*Tradition and Originality in Roman Poetry* [Oxford:
Clarendon Press, 1968]) are "in this sense a pre-critical analysis" (viii).

[2] Binns, *Intellectual Culture* (Leeds: Francis Cairns, 1990), chap. 2, esp. 37. While Binns's
titular coverage stops at 1625, he has read and draws on most Latin work mentioned in the
Short-Title Catalogue, hence to 1640, so that at all events he covers the period of Milton's
training, and most of his writing, in Latin verse.

he would secure eminent contributors of liminary verses—prefatory puffings—to increase the mana of the whole thing.[3]

Milton did *not* contribute. Although this path to prominence among the intelligentsia surely lay open to him, he did not take it. The silence must be noted, however hard to interpret. Seeking to explain it, one can discern signs in his early Latin subjects of the incipient radical.[4] But firmer inference comes from the pattern of his verse publishing to 1645. He published several English poems before 1640, all anonymously. His first Latin publication was in that year, still anonymously. If he sought reputation or position at all through poetry, it could be only among the select circle who knew the hidden identity of the author. All this changed in 1645, when he brought out the poems of twenty-one years, in four languages, under his own full name—an action which for England anyway is unprecedented and individual. True, university anthologies and friends' books gave him patterns of self-presentation,[5] but the effect as a whole is new.

This, then, is how I would connect the new departure with the norm of Latin verse publishing as Binns describes it. By 1645, Milton had declared where he stood politically and controversially, and he uses Latin verse as part of the big, new, personal gesture which is *Poems of Mr. John Milton, Both English and Latin.* Milton moves towards Latin publishing when it suits him, and not in the old way which Binns describes but in a new one.

The writing, as distinct from publishing, of his Latin poems is a third context which needs reconstructing if we are to ground criticism upon relevant pre-criticism. Though I have no new datings to propose, a new emphasis is needed, since the poems come from three widely-spaced epochs of his life—a pattern distinctive, not to say odd. Most of the 1645

---

[3] If Binns's account of the linking of verse with preferment through print seems mechanical, I would reply that it is formidable (like the cognate prosopographical history of Ronald Syme) because it relies on masses of hard evidence. Or if it seems to make its subjects look servile by writing to catch a bishop's eye, I would reply that every regime incorporates recruitment methods into the power structure itself, and that for Latin verse to have a place in this structure gives to it—if not the versifiers—both interest and dignity, and also heightens the importance of Milton's absence.

[4] "Elegia prima," concerning the joys of being "sent down" from Cambridge to London; "Elegia quarta," commiserating with Thomas Young as an exile from England, the "dura parens" (line 87).

[5] I have discussed this point in "Milton's Self-Presentation in *Poems . . . 1645,*" *MQ* 25 (1991):37–48.

Poemata were written in his school or university years.[6] All the rest, except the *Ode,* came from 1638–39, his time in Italy, where it was Latin verse, precisely, that opened doors for him into the academies.[7] The ode sits all by itself in 1647, a by-blow of the 1645 *Poems* and the Civil War.

It becomes natural to ask, why this alternating of spurts and spaces? In the first place, Milton composes Latin when he shares a Latin-verse-writing milieu, and not when he doesn't. But to go deeper, he compos-es to and about the friendships made through Latin. Not in the early poems on prescribed themes, of course, but in all the ones on self-chosen themes.[8] They celebrate given friendships in the first period; chosen ones on the Italian journey; both together in the *Epitaphium Damonis* which closes it off; and the *Ode to Rouse* is a late windfall, a *felix culpa.* These poems neither center on public matters nor bare the soul. They uphold an ideal of humanist *amicitia,* known through per-sonal experience, a congenial audience, and consequent fame. An audience is entailed, of the friends, and their friends, and those like them. In turn, audience implies purpose, namely to win its respect, and so a humanist fame—glory.

So a further "context of understanding" needs defining—the scope which Latin verse gave for occasional poems attesting diverse friendship. His best Latin poems are all occasional. They weave the choice of Latin, and of the particular Latin meter, into the occasion and friendship celebrated. Certainly Milton's English poems show a similar witty decorum. Nonetheless, Latin gives peculiar opportunities for such decorum. Each relationship is at once congenially romanized by the Latin medium, raised or idealized along with—as part of—the selecting of Roman models and genres. He greets a Roman friend who is sick, using Catullus's "limping" meter ("Scazontes"). He bids farewell to the dead friend to whom he had written elegiac verse-letters by using the higher meter, hexameters.

---

[6] Even *Ad patrem,* 1632: Milton graduated M.A. in that year.

[7] See *Reason of Church Government* (1642): "But much latelier in the privat Academies of *Italy* . . . perceiving that some trifles which I had in memory, compos'd at under twenty or thereabout . . . met with acceptance above what was lookt for . . ." (CPW 1:809). Between 1632 and 1638 "barbitoque devius/ Indulsit *patrio*" (that is, English verse only; see the text of the ode given below, lines 9–10). Latin verse writing had similarly attracted Joachim du Bellay when he went to Rome.

[8] Thus not in the series of Gunpowder Plot epigrams, but in the voluntary verse letters to Charles Diodati and Thomas Young.

Thus concerning my illustrative case of the ode to John Rouse we should ask why he wrote an ode, in Latin, to Rouse, on 23 January 1647; and why praise-poetry addressing, not one of its traditional subjects like a prince or a city or a victor, but a librarian. The answers are not obvious, since the ode has no one clear ancient model, and its meter is (unusually) purpose-built. But context puts the right questions, and creates the right expectations and criteria, because it lets us feel appropriate surprise.

To sum up so far: the "criteria of understanding" prompted by these contexts show what Milton attempts; only on that basis can we assess his achievement; and the attempts themselves must interest Milton scholarship.

III

Turning now to explication of the ode, I address some typical questions raised by its neo-Latin—bearing in mind that the typical highlights the untypical, and that both are to be examined by new methods for a changed emphasis.

The Ode *Ad Joannem Rousium*: Text and Translation

The text of the ode and the translation which follow are those of Gordon Campbell.[9]

Jan. 23 1646 [Old Style]

Ad *Joannem Rousium* Oxoniensis Academiae Bibliothecarium

De libro Poematum amisso, quem ille sibi denuo mitti postulabat, ut cum aliis nostris in Bibliotheca publica reponeret, Ode.

Strophe 1
Gemelle cultu simplici gaudens liber,
Fronde licet gemina,
Munditieque nitens non operosa,
Quam manus attulit
Juvenilis olim,
Sedula tamen haud nimii Poetae;
Dum vagus Ausonias nunc per umbras
Nunc Britannica per vireta lusit

---

[9] John Milton, *The Complete Poems*, ed. B. A. Wright, with introduction and notes by Gordon Campbell (London: Dent, 1980). I am grateful for permission to quote from this edition.

Insons populi, barbitoque devius
Indulsit patrio, mox itidem pectine Daunio   10
Longinquum intonuit melos
Vicinis, et humum vix tetigit pede;

Antistrophe
Quis te, parve liber, quis te fratribus
Subduxit reliquis dolo?
Cum tu missus ab urbe,
Docto jugiter obsecrante amico,
Illustre tendebas iter
Thamesis ad incunabula
Caerulei patris,
Fontes ubi limpidi   20
Aonidum, thyasusque sacer
Orbi notus per immensos
Temporum lapsus redeunte caelo,
Celeberque futurus in aevum;

Strophe 2
Modo quis deus aut editus deo
Pristinam gentis miseratus indolem
(Si satis noxas luimus priores
Mollique luxu degener otium)
Tollat nefandos civium tumultus,
Almaque revocet studia sanctus   30
Et relegatas sine sede Musas
Jam pene totis finibus Angligenum;
Immundas volucres
Unguibus imminentes
Figat Apollinea pharetra,
Phineamque abigat pestem procul amne Pegaseo?

Antistrophe
Quin tu, libelle, nuntii licet mala
Fide vel oscitantia
Semel erraveris agmine fratrum,
Seu quis te teneat specus,   40
Seu qua te latebra, forsan unde vili
Callo tereris institoris insulsi,
Laetare felix; en iterum tibi
Spes nova fulget posse profundam
Fugere Lethen, vehique Superam
In Jovis aulam remige penna;

Strophe 3
Nam te Roüsius sui
Optat peculi, numeroque justo
Sibi pollicitum queritur abesse,
Rogatque venias ille cujus inclyta   50
Sunt data virum monumenta curae:
Teque adytis etiam sacris
Voluit reponi quibus et ipse praesidet
Aeternorum operum custos fidelis,
Quaestorque gazae nobilioris
Quam cui praefuit Ion
Clarus Erechtheides,
Opulenta dei per templa parentis,
Fulvosque tripodas, donaque Delphica,
Ion Actaea genitus Creusa.   60

Antistrophe
Ergo tu visere lucos
Musarum ibis amoenos,
Diamque Phoebi rursus ibis in domum
Oxonia quam valle collit
Delo posthabita
Bifidoque Parnassi jugo:
Ibis honestus,
Postquam egregiam tu quoque sortem
Nactus abis, dextri prece sollicitatus amici.
Illic legeris inter alta nomina   70
Authorum, Graiae simul et Latinae
Antiqua gentis lumina et verum decus.

Epodos
Vos tandem haud vacui mei labores,
Quicquid hoc sterile fudit ingenium,
Jam sero placidam sperare jubeo
Perfunctam invidia requiem, sedesque beatas
Quas bonus Hermes
Et tutela dabit solers Roüsi,
Quo neque lingua procax vulgi penetrabit, atque longe
Turba legentum prava facesset;   80
At ultimi nepotes
Et cordatior aetas
Judicia rebus aequiora forsitan
Adhibebit integro sinu.
Tum livore sepulto
Si quid meremur sana posteritas sciet
Roüsio favente.

Ode tribus constat Strophis totidemque Antistrophis una demum epodo clausis, quas, tametsi omnes nec versuum numero nec certis ubique colis exacte respondeant, ita tamen secuimus, commode legendi potius quam ad antiquos concinendi modos rationem spectantes. Alioquin hoc genus rectius fortasse dici monostrophicum debuerat. Metre partim sunt κατὰ σχέσιν, *partim* ἀπολελυμένα· *Phaleucia quae sunt, spondaeum tertio loco bis admittunt, quod idem in secundo loco Catullus ad libitum fecit.*

Ad Joannem Rousium
Jan. 23, 1646
To John Rouse, Librarian of Oxford University

An ode on a lost volume of my Poems, which he asked to be sent to him a second time that he might place it in the public library with my other books.

Strophe 1 (lines 1–12)
Two-part book, cheerful in your single covers, but with a double leaf, shining with the unlaboured elegance once given you by a youthful hand—industrious, but hardly that of a poet—wandering, he sported now in the Ausonian shades, now in the green fields of England unconcerned with the public. Withdrawn, he gave himself up to his native lute, and then presently with Daunian quill sounded a foreign strain to his neighbours, and scarcely touched the ground with his foot;

Antistrophe (lines 13–24)
Little book, who deceitfully carried you away from your brothers, when sent from the city at the persistent requests of my learned friend you were proceeding upon your famous journey to the cradle of blue Father Thames, where the clear fountains of the Aonides are, and the sacred Bacchic dance known to the world as the Heavens turn through the flight of time, and will be famous for ever?

Strophe 2 (lines 25–36)
But what God or demi-god has compassion for the original native qualities of our race (if we have atoned sufficiently for our earlier faults, effeminate luxury and degenerate idleness) and will take away the abomination of civil war, and what divinity will recall nourishing studies and the banished muses now without a home in almost the entire land of England? Who, using Apollo's quiver will pierce the foul birds threatening us with their talons, and drive away the plague of Phineus far from the river of Pegasus?

Antistrophe (lines 37–46)
But, little book, although by the bad faith or negligence of my messenger you have at some time strayed from the company of your brothers,

though some cave or hiding place now possesses you, where perhaps you will be rubbed by the base callous hand of a stupid peddlar, rejoice in your good fortune. Behold, new hope shines that you may be able to run away from the depths of Lethe and be borne on soaring wings to the courts of Jove above.

Strophe 3 (lines 47–60)
For Rouse wishes you to be part of his property, complains that you are missing from the full number promised him and asks that you come to him, to whose care are entrusted the famous monuments of men. He wants you to be placed in the sacred inner chambers over which he presides, the faithful keeper of immortal works and the treasurer of riches more excellent than the golden tripods and Delphic offerings entrusted to Ion in the splendid temple of his divine father—Ion, the famous grandson of Erechtheus born of Actaean Creusa.

Antistrophe (lines 61–72)
Therefore you will go to view the delightful groves of the muses, and you will go again to the divine home of Phoebus where he dwells in the Vale of Oxford, preferring that to Delos and the cleft summit of Parnassus. You will go in honour, since you go away with a distin-guished fate, urged by the entreaty of a favouring friend. There you will be read among the great names of authors who were the ancient lights and true glory of the Greek and Latin peoples.

Epodos (lines 73–87)
You then, my labours, whatever this barren genius has brought forth, were not in vain. Now at last, I bid you hope for peaceful rest and, having endured envy, the blessed dwellings which good Hermes and the expert care of Rouse shall give you, where the impudent tongue of the vulgar shall not penetrate, and the faithless crowd of readers will remain far off. But our distant descendants and a wiser age will perhaps, with honest mind, bring fairer judgement to all things. Then, with malice buried, a sane posterity will know, thanks to Rouse, the worth of these poems.

The ode has three strophes, the same number of antistrophes, and ends with an epode. Although all parts do not correspond exactly in the number of lines, nor are the metrical sections fixed, I have divided it thus, however, to facilitate reading and not because of respect for an ancient method of versification.

In other respects this sort of poem should perhaps have been more correctly called monostrophic. The metres are in part related and in part free. The Phaleucian lines twice admit a spondee in the third foot; Catullus readily did thus in the second foot.

IV

The first typical question raised is the inherent dilemma of humanist Latin, and must be faced as soon as the sixth word. In place of "fronde ... gemina" (the "double leaf" of the lost copy of *Poems*), Thomas Warton[10] conjectured "fronte gemina" (the "double edge" of a Roman papyrus-roll). There being no reason to doubt that Milton's scribe wrote "fronde" in the MS, nor that he approved the scribing, Warton was claiming that it was incorrect (non-classical and un-Roman) Latin to use "fronde" of a book: the classical exemplars had not, and could not, so Milton should not. He was claiming that—as early as line 2—our poet had blundered.

However, since strophe 1 is describing the actual book, *Poems ... 1645*, "gemelle ... liber" in line 1 does not require the fiction that it was a scroll which got lost. Nor would double "edge" describe the book since that would lose the main point, namely its separate Latin and English paginations and "twin" title-pages. What is more, because "fronde" secures an updating pun on "fronte" which would not work in the opposite direction, Milton has achieved not a blunder but a witty gambit. In short, the Latin starts off by establishing the English subject as Roman, so that the reader can gain a heightened sense of that subject, which next, however, is recognised as not solely similar but different.[11]

The pleasure of attentive reading in fact comes from the variety of this playing upon similarity and difference. Take lines 10–11, "pectine *Daunio* / Longinquum intonuit melos" (my emphasis). The emphatic epithet "Daunio" can mean "Italian" or "from Apulia," for Horace uses it both ways in his odes. So Milton tells Rouse he wrote some of the poems when visiting Italy. But Horace had boasted of his humble birth in Apulia, in his famous ode about *his* poetic achievement ("Exegi monumentum aere perennius"). So "Daunio" sends a double and decisive Horatian signal, a witty one here to prepare for sonorous ones in strophe 2.

Allusion is not limited to Horace, of course. It is eclectic, and as intertextual as anyone could hope for.[12] Consider the poem's address

---

[10] *Poems upon Several Occasions*, ed. Thomas Warton, 2d ed. rev. (London, 1791).

[11] A kindred instance is "remige penna" (line 46). The well-known Vergilian "remigium alarum" ("oarage of wings") is brought into view, then varied.

[12] Neo-Latin well exemplifies the intertextuality prized and emphasized by recent schools of literary theory like structuralism, though I do not recall its being used as the paradigm case it is. There is no other way to read it with understanding.

to occasion: it addresses the lost book about the intended recipient, as a cunning way of addressing the recipient about the book. Precedents do exist in Ovid and Propertius; yet their situations, and their fancies, are distinct.[13] Milton, as Ezra Pound would have commanded him to, "makes it new."

He does so throughout, by a more striking eclecticism. We soon leave Roman exemplars for Greek ones: Oxford's river, the Thames, is linked with Mount Helicon, home of the Muses; and thus the scholars of Oxford can be viewed as a "thyasus sacer" or band of god-inspired dancers. The purist can object that Milton has switched gods, from the Muses to Bacchus. Too bad—soon he moves again, to Apollo (strophes 2 and 3)!

Rather than simply following and enjoying the eclecticism, however, I would stress progression. That is, we notice a sequence of predominant exemplars: from Ovid and Propertius to Horace; then from Romans to Greeks in the antistrophe; and so to Horace again, the Horace this time of the odes of expiation and prayer concerning civil war.[14] Horace is finally subsumed with Vergil and Euripides into climactic mention of the Harpies, "immundas volucres," now to be driven off with Apollo's help (33, 35).

"Eclectic" is after all too pallid a word for such coherent, imaginative progression. A better word might be "contaminatio," the charge brought against Terence that he "adulterated" his plays by their mingled Greek and Roman subject-matter. Terence's so-called adulteration is his glory. Roman poets, in all the genres they took over from the Greeks, set out to make use—different, personal, original use—of their Greek exemplars; for their subjects, figures, diction, allusion. They did it not simply to create Roman counterparts, but more boldly, to blend Greek with Roman into "a poetic world of the imagination that was neither Greek nor Roman but an invented amalgam of both."[15] As Romans

---

[13] Ovid *Amores* 1.12 and Propertius 3.23, discussed by Stella P. Revard, "*Ad Joannem Rousium:* Elegiac Wit and Pindaric Mode," in *Urbane Milton: The Latin Poetry,* ed. James A. Freeman and Anthony Low, *MS* 19 (1984): 205–26 (210 for the personification). See also Ovid *Tristia* 2.1.

[14] See esp. *Odes* 1.2.25ff. ("quem vocet divum populus ruentis / imperi rebus ... cui dabit partis scelus expiandi / Iuppiter?"). Cf. also 47–49 with Milton's strophe 2: "neve te nostris vitiis iniquum / ocior aura / tollat." Milton echoes both the questioning ("Quis deus?") and the intercession ("*Tollat* nefandos civium tumultus").

[15] Gordon Williams, *The Nature of Roman Poetry,* 61. A good recent instance of the tracing of the process in Milton's Latin is Gordon Campbell, "Imitation in *Epitaphius Damonis,*" *MQ* 19 (1984): 165–77.

stood to Greeks, so Romans stood to earlier Romans. But so also the
neo-Latin humanist stood to these Romano-Grecians.

Thus in the present ode the long first sentence flows through thirty-
six[16] lines of varying successive dominant allusion, like a river rising, to
raise the whole occasion to a noble finality: let some god or hero
remove civil war, atone all citizens, and restore to us the life of mind
(the Muses, 31). I discern aptness and echoism in the climbing of
thought and tone, since the sentence began quietly with a book lost in
the siege of Oxford, to rise to thought of all that is lost by civil wars.

V

One must next confront the metrics, most difficult of all the eclectic
features. The problem is, how to face the difficulty briefly. I shall sketch
the general neo-Latin dilemma for prosody, then summarize a recent general answer and apply it to Milton; then more fully state the acute form of
the dilemma for this ode, so as to affirm that we should start from Milton's
own remarks and designs—in other words, proceed "pre-critically" again.

Renaissance humanists modeled their scansion on that of the Roman exemplars, but could not do it with full accuracy; for since they
could not reconstruct all Roman pronunciation, they could not hear the
whole of the Romans' verse rhythms. Besides, they licensed for their
own composition a very wide range of usage, ignoring the changes in
pronunciation during the 150 years between (say) Lucretius and Martial.
Being thus misconceivedly eclectic, their scansion alienates the reader of
classical Latin.[17]

---

[16] The punctuation of the MS is unclear at lines 12 and 24, but the first printed text (that
of *Poems . . . 1673*) shows a semi-colon in both places. That entails a single period running
to line 36, unless we take the question mark after line 14 to close off the sense. As against
that, lines 15–24 which follow the question mark make far better sense taken with lines 1–12
("quis te . . . subduxit . . . cum tu missus ab urbe tendebas iter") than with line 17 onwards
("Cum tu missus etc. . . . Modo quis deus"). In short, lines 15–24 are a set of subordinate
clauses, and easier to subordinate backwards than forwards. However, the *1673* pointing
confirms that lines 1–24 as a whole move the thought onwards, too—because the loss of the
book is seen next in the context of other and greater losses, those of the civil war. This leaves
unsolved the puzzle of line 36, where the sense requires a second question mark, but neither
MS nor *1673* has one.

[17] Examples: (i) final -o of verb, normally long in Golden Latin, is frequently shortened
in humanist Latin; (ii) final open vowel, short by nature and left short when the following
word begins with the double consonant first of which is s- ("magna *scientia*," "inclyte
spiritus")—something which happens only rarely in Golden Latin—is done habitually in the
humanists. See Ford, next note.

Yet since *every* humanist did these things, can one call them sole-cisms? The situation resembles that of our own intelligentsia telling the barbarians never to split an infinitive. This position is argued, with the theory and practice of George Buchanan in mind, by Philip J. Ford:

> What is surprising is that scholars should continue to evaluate Neo-Latin according to classical rules rather than according to its own, verifiable standards. It is as if one were to judge a Palladian villa according to the criteria of a classical temple; for Palladio, no less than the Renaissance poet, based his works on classical precedent and theory.[18]

Thus Milton, when employing ancient meters, feels their pulse to the extent, and in the way, that Buchanan and other humanists did. Which means, in practice, most of the time: the percentage of divergent practice is systematic, and not large—just enough that one might find the result pleasantly distinctive. At any rate, when I measured a more subtle aspect of scansion, I found Milton's practice to strike the mean between his two main models, Vergil and Ovid.[19] Not rules, but only his ear, could have produced this result. It demonstrates, in fact, that prosody is not a matter of rules. Rather, it is an aspect of sound which intersects with all the others, and exists for the sake of memorable meaning.

Nevertheless, this general answer to the humanist metrics dilemma will not suffice for the *Ode to Rouse*, whose meters flout Roman practice—untypically, in fact consciously so. As elsewhere, therefore, one must ask what Milton attempted and why before assessing whether he achieved anything thereby.

Roman odes came in stanzas, which repeated their meter with considerable strictness (as Horace's Alcaics, or Sapphics). Milton's ode does not repeat meters with much strictness. He comments on one liberty he took, imitating Catullus in this respect but going beyond him.[20] He says too that in several respects his meter is "monostrophic"

---

[18] Ford, *George Buchanan, Prince of Poets* (Aberdeen: Aberdeen Univ. Press, 1982), esp. chap. 2.

[19] For the variation in relationship between quantitative and accentual pulse in the fourth foot of the hexameter throughout *Epitaphium Damonis,* see *MS* 16 (1982): 115–30.

[20] Milton's note, written in 1673, explains the more striking departures from Roman precedent: incomplete response in number of lines and metrical sections, meters partly related and partly free, thus a monostrophic feeling, departures from the already free-spirited scansion of Catullus in the phalaecians. See Campbell's edition, 546.

(through-composed, rather than recurrent). Once again he did have
some precedents: not in classical Latin, but in later Latin such as the
choruses of Seneca's plays, and above all in Greek, in the odes of Pindar.
Here is a major exemplar and influence, mentioned by E. M. W.
Tillyard and analyzed more fully by Stella Revard.[21] The influence
goes far beyond metrics, to the whole tone and stance of praise-poetry
at the highest level of ardor, and moreover, to some specific linkage of
praising with the role of poet, especially when value is assailed by war
but survives and transcends it:

> The great Emathian conqueror bid spare
> The house of Pindarus.   (Sonnet 8.10–11)

So prosody links with theme and tone and occasion, revealingly.

Yet Pindar still does not suffice to explain Milton's metrical attempt.
Sometimes he follows the meters of tragic lyric—which befits the
Euripidean allusions (strophes 2 and 3). Sometimes he goes beyond even
his Greek models as he more obviously exceeded his Latin ones. Even
E. K. Rand, rightly urging that Milton availed himself of "the glorious
formalism and glorious freedom of Greek" for his Latin, may have
understated.[22] The metrics are eclectic, and startling, for the sake of
tour de force.

VI

That, however, makes the reader ask, why? To resolve the metrical apo-
ria pre-critically only triggers further questions, such as, What was
Milton up to? Who was Rouse? Is it not unusual to address a praise-
poem to a librarian, even Bodley's? And what was he to Milton on 23
January 1647 that he merited an ode so audacious? The questions are
the appropriate ones, in the appropriate order. For this penultimate
exercise of pre-criticism, one must infer from internal evidence (the
thought of the ode itself), then from external evidence, then combine
the two.

---

[21] E. M. W. Tillyard, *Milton* (London: Chatto and Windus, 1930), 171–72; Revard, see
n. 13 above. In view of the vogue of Pindarics in the seventeenth century, the ode may be
influenced by contemporary neo-Latin imitations of Pindar as well; but for the licensed fervor
and rhapsodic swirl he surely goes back to the source.

[22] E. K. Rand, "Milton in Rustication," in *SP* 19 (1922): 115.

The thought moves thus: from description of the apostrophized *Poems 1645* (strophe 1), to its missed home in Oxford where the "learned friend" Rouse beseeches its sending ("docto amico," 16): oh, who is to end[23] the civil war and the befouling destruction which so thwarts the muses of England (strophe 2)? Wherever you are, little lost book (antistrophe 2), Rouse wants you to join his "treasure" (peculium, 48), and wants you to enter the "sacred shrine" ("adytis sacris," 52), which he guards. Rouse is the "faithful keeper" of eternal works (54), "treasurer" ("quaestor") of a "nobler treasure" ("gazae") than that which Ion guarded for Apollo at Delphi.[24] Thus you, my book, will see Oxford, like but greater than Delphi, through the prayers of my friend.[25] You will be read there in the Bodleian along with the Greek and Latin exemplars (70–72). And thus (Epode) my work will not have been in vain: free from ill-will, you will be kept safe in the "blessed dwelling" given you by Hermes and Rouse (75–77). A posterity saner than we are will read you, thanks to Rouse:

> Tum livore sepulto
> Si quid meremur sana posteritas sciet
> Rousio favente.   (85–87)

Milton fills the ode with role-words describing and praising Rouse. Rouse is a "friend" (twice), a "treasurer," "guardian," priest, and guarantor of justice and fame for the poet.

I take this quite literally. Milton was thrilled by Rouse's interest, and its persistence ("jugiter obsecrante," 16). The ode—no ordinary covering-letter!—responds with ardor. Rouse (aged 72) would not have been a close personal friend, but his office and his actions released Milton's ardent love of what he took them to stand for.

We can grasp that symbolic standing by recalling that in one of the prose works which Rouse had requested (*Areopagitica*) Milton said "a good book is the precious life-blood of a master-spirit, embalmed and

---

[23] "Tollat" is present subjunctive, not future indicative, as some translations give it; i.e., its force is yearning or hortative, just as when Horace uses it (see n. 14 above).

[24] Notice the diction of the phrase: the temple has as guardian a Roman-sounding "quaestor," who is at once compared to the Greek Ion, while the treasure is referred to by an oriental loan-word, "gazae" (Persian?). I suspect that the hybridizing of diction is to chime with the diversity of the Bodleian treasures.

[25] "Amici" may mean instead "your friend"; but if the absence of the possessive adjective means Rouse befriends author *and* book, that sense would be still more apt.

treasured up on purpose to a life beyond life." Milton "hopes" his book is good (75); and let it anyway face fair judgment by joining Rouse's (Bodley's) indubitable classics. So to put it in general terms, Rouse and the Bodleian and the ode celebrate right relations of parties to the humanist ideal of fame.

External evidence confirms and strengthens the point. As librarians go, Rouse was heroic, as Milton through Oxford connections[26] would know. Rouse refused to lend a library book to the king. He went and explained why not: the statutes of the pious founder, and his own oath of office, forbade it; the laws and religion forbade it. The king accepted the refusal, too. And this episode (of December 1645) enabled Rouse's successor, Barlow, to refuse a similar request in 1654 from Cromwell. The accounts speak of the "sacred" reasons of trust and law which compelled such heroic book-guardianship.[27]

Thus, in his own domain, Rouse stood for the prevailing of law and religion and conscience, even in time of civil war. His stand chimes with Milton's humanist idealism, whether Greek, Latin, or modern. All three worlds intersect in the ode. But not least the Latin one, for he draws on the Roman horror of civil war at the climax, and he addresses Rouse like the many Romans of the dying Republic who had to communicate across party lines in time of civil war with their sundered family or friends.[28]

Moreover, whereas Rouse's office stood for high and precious principles, his actions to Milton stood for something more personal—the encouragement, if not recognition, implicit in the request for a copy of the *Poems*. Milton was making sure the Bodleian received not only his prose pamphlets on public concerns but also his poems on (mainly) private occasions. I would link to Rouse's response, and to this prospect of being (despite upsets) *fully* represented in the library, the high spirits and youthful panache of the performance. These do require explanation: they are unlike the tone of any other poem by Milton, not solely those of the 1640s.

---

[26] He had had friends at that university (Diodati, Gil), and while living at Horton had matriculated there, probably so as to use the Bodleian. If he knew John Selden, as well as reading him in the period 1640–45, here would be a further link.

[27] W. D. Macray, *Annals of the Bodleian Library, Oxford* (London: Rivington, 1868), 44–82, esp. 45, 71–72 on the Charles I incident ("the will and statutes of the *pious* founder should be *religiously* observed"), and 75–82 on the Cromwell incident ("his Highness . . . commended the prudence of the Founder, who had made the place so *sacred*"), my emphases.

[28] Not forgetting that Milton's own brother was on the other side.

VII

Tone, indeed, is my final objective in these exercises of recovery. In understanding a poem the concept of tone—albeit indefinable—is irreducible. Tone includes how one reads aloud for meaning and expression. Tone includes the stance of speaking voice to subject, recipient, and occasion (all the elements which we have been treating and which comprise decorum). Yet it is perhaps easiest to define correct tone from mistakes of tone. That is, once the reader mistakes the tone of voice of a poem's utterance, for instance by reading hyperbole as burlesque or by missing the places where assertion turns ironical, that reader cannot recover the desired understanding. Tone may in fact outweigh (because it subsumes) other conditions of understanding.

In the ode we have seen that the tone is continually rising. It rises to moments of hyperbolical ardour, as at line 36 (the evil pestilence that is civil war) or line 60 (the treasures of the Bodleian as "temple"). We need to know, nonetheless, whether the tone is solely of ardent hyperbole, or to put that another way, how long the Pindaric rapture continues. Certain details alert us to something not only magniloquent but laughingly so, an intensity including self-awareness. Take Milton's climactic assurance that his poems will be safe from now on because Rouse and the god Hermes[29] will keep them safe. "Rouse and Hermes" (77–78) . . . an invincible team, no doubt, but a whimsical yoking. And what they vouchsafe is called "sedes beatas" (76), the name of Elysium, the destination of virtuous souls in the *Aeneid*.[30] Now,

---

[29] Hermes = Mercury was often linked with eloquence and poetry, and also with learning and prophecy. He was conductor of souls into the after-life, and (as Hermes Trismegistus) initiant into secret wisdom. Since he was also the patron of thieves (!) we need to select the relevant attributes here: eloquence—poetry—learning, but possibly also guiding souls to new life.

[30] *Aeneid* 6.639, cf. *Paradise Lost* 1.5 ("blissful seat"). My point is that the Vergilian sonority must accompany the borrowed phrase, but so does an awareness that its new application is a scaling-down. That is, the entire ode is whimsical in being an address to a *little* book: it assumes and renews the witty deprecation of the old "Go, little book" topos. However, the *joining* of Hermes with *sedes beatas* insinuates the idea of the afterlife of spirit in writings, which libraries as a sort of treasure-guarding temples enable. Thus the tone is light although—or is it because—the idea is credal.

A similar tonal range informs the third antistrophe through the repetition of "ibis" (63,64,67) and its modulation into "abis" (69). I find a playful insistence on the book's completing its journey *this* time (and it did, for it is still in Bodley), but more of an excited vision of its dwelling among the treasures of Apollo (63ff.). So with "abis" by the pun on *abis*

Bodley is a wonderful library (it even smells right), but surely not thus immune from all mutability? In such details the youthful hyperbole seems *prima facie* played off against an amused maturity. And the "prima facie" of pre-criticism clarifies an issue which criticism proper, or judgment, or evaluation, cannot then avoid confronting in due time. When hyperbole can be juxtaposed with detachment, or even inhabit the same phrases, the tone of the whole is made rarer and more compelling; for its combination of youth and maturity is not matched anywhere else in Milton's verse.

VIII

The ode is thus all of a piece, and so are the contexts and methods we have illustrated. All alike relate by decorum. Pre-critically, therefore, Milton's ode emerges as a harmonious, audacious experiment.

We still have to ask, does it achieve what it attempts? Here, pre-criticism hands on to judgment. The reader will, however, have noticed that a tone of delight at Milton's bravura playing has crept into some of these "pre-criticisms." Yet I do not retract; for where this happens, there is being revealed in the object a presumptive excellence.

To generalize, finally: pre-criticism should launch interpretation and evaluation. Even if the points of transition from one to another cannot be pinpointed, the transition itself is legitimate. Pre-criticism guides and forms attention rightly. That in turn makes an implicit admiration actual, yet only when attention finds enough to feed on.[31]

UNIVERSITY OF OTAGO

/ *ibis*, its going away from the author is entailed by its going to Rouse. He being the "friend" of worthy books (69), Milton hints here at the cooperating of god and human which becomes explicit in the *epodos* (Rouse and Hermes).

[31] I must record thanks to friends who helped me with the paper before it was read at Vancouver, especially Doug Little and Agathe Thornton, and the Otago Classics Department Seminar, to whom I read an early version.

Stella P. Revard

ALPHEUS, ARETHUSA, AND THE PINDARIC PURSUIT IN *LYCIDAS*

BY THE TIME MILTON CAME TO COMPOSE *LYCIDAS,* HE HAD been experimenting with different kinds of ode forms for well over ten years, and he would continue to think about the potentials of ode, especially Pindaric ode, for at least ten more, as his reference to the magnific odes of Pindar in *The Reason of Church Government* and his adaptation of Pindaric stanzas in the Rouse ode amply testify.[1] Milton's earliest ode, "On the Death of a Fair Infant," boasts some clear Pindaric signatures. He opens with the extravagant figure of the blasted flower; he uses an extended digression in the myth of Winter, and he develops several exemplary portraits, as, for example, that of Astraea. The tripartite organization and the digressive techniques of the Nativity Ode also suggest Pindaric influence. "L'Allegro" and "Il Penseroso" are experiments in the hymn-ode, and "L'Allegro," in particular, as I have argued elsewhere, is modelled partly on Pindar's *Olympia* 14.[2] *Lycidas* proceeds even further with Pindaric experiments. I am not the first to suggest Pindaric influence in Milton's monody. Both F. T. Prince and Clay Hunt thought that the verse techniques of *Lycidas* had affinities with the Pindaric ode and came to Milton indirectly through the medium of the Italian canzone.[3]

---

[1] See Hughes, 669. All quotations of Milton's verse and prose are from this edition.

[2] Revard, " 'L'Allegro' and 'Il Penseroso': Classical Tradition and Renaissance Mythography," *PMLA* 101 (1986): 338–50.

[3] See Clay Hunt, *"Lycidas" and the Italian Critics* (New Haven: Yale Univ. Press, 1979); F. T. Prince, *"Lycidas* and the Tradition of the Italian Eclogue," *English Miscellany* 2 (1951): 95–105; also *The Italian Element in Milton's Verse* (Oxford: Clarendon Press, 1954).

Milton termed his pastoral lament *Lycidas* a monody; critics since
James Holly Hanford in 1910 usually call it a pastoral elegy; and scholars, investigating the relevant traditions, compare the poem to everything from eclogue to idyll to ode. A monody, I hasten to say, as the
Renaissance critics Scaliger and Puttenham agree, is simply an ode for a
single rather than the choral voice.[4] It is perfectly logical then to inquire whether Milton's monody for a single voice owes anything to
Pindar's choral odes. An ode for a single voice, such as Milton's shepherd swain sings for his dead companion, is the proper complement to
the kind of occasional choral odes that Pindar wrote to celebrate heroes
of the ancient world, both living and dead.

There are two ways, I think, that Milton approaches Pindaric ode
in *Lycidas:* first and simplest, by using certain Pindaric devices such as
thematic figures and mythic digression in the structuring of his ode,
second, by writing a poem whose ostensible subject is different from its
real one. The ostensible subject or occasion of Milton's ode is to offer
the official lamentation for the dead Lycidas, who "must not float upon
his wat'ry bier / Unwept" (12–13). In this it follows Pindaric ode,
which is always offered to commemorate an official occasion and is
always addressed to a specific person on that occasion, usually an athlete
who has been victorious in one of the games, though occasionally to
another person to celebrate another event, as, for example the founding
of the city Aetna in *Pythia* 1. In his odes, Pindar not only commemo-
rates an occasion, but also probes the issues of life and death, success and
failure, joy and grief, good and evil. Each ode raises some problem
central to human life and considers through a series of passages, some
juxtaposed abruptly against one other, a universal question about human
beings and their relations with the gods. The probing usually takes the
form of a series of so-called digressions, often about a central myth or
myths. Pindar never proceeds directly; it is the very essence of his ode
that as he celebrates the ostensible occasion he has come to commemo-

---

[4] James Holly Hanford, "The Pastoral Elegy and Milton's *Lycidas*," *PMLA* (1910): 403–
47. Both Scaliger and Puttenham define monody as a funeral song. Scaliger puts it simply:
"Etiam monodia dictus cantus lugubris" (*Poetices, Libri Septem* [1581], 129). Puttenham goes
further to call it a funeral song for a single voice: "Such funerall songs were called *Epicedia* if
they were song by many, and *Monodia* if they were vttered by one alone" (*The Arte of English
Poesie* (1589), a facsimile reproduction [Kent, Ohio: Kent State Univ. Press, 1970], 63). Balachandra Rajan in "*Lycidas*" in the *Milton Encyclopedia* and Scott Elledge in *Milton's "Lycidas"*
(New York: Harper and Row, 1966) cite Scaliger's and Puttenham's definitions of monody.

rate, he raises other basic questions about human existence that are important to him. Many times these questions involve those very issues of good and evil, life and death that are so important in *Lycidas* as well.

The opening figure in *Lycidas*—the shattered garland—resembles strongly the bold opening figures of Pindaric ode, not only in its striking poetic vividness, but also in its allusive design. Milton begins his monody by shattering the would-be laurel crown that he would bestow or gather to himself—both actions are implicit in the statement—the laurel crown that was the victory reward both for the poet and for the athlete in the Pythian games in Apollo's honor. Death has shattered Lycidas's garland; untimely plucking shatters the garland the poet-swain would pluck as would-be poet. The paradox in the action is implicitly Pindaric. The poet's responsibility in epinician ode or in monody is to bestow the crown of praise—this the poet knows. Yet tragic circumstance can make him reflect on the appropriateness of bestowing that crown. Consider Pindar's reticence and anguish of heart (ἀχνύμενός θυμόν, 5–6) at the beginning of *Isthmia* 8 when he comes at a time of national mourning, just at the end of the wars with Persia; he must invoke the Muses, but he hesitates to do so.[5] Yet especially in times of sorrow, he knows, if human beings somehow are to go on, the poetic garland must be bestowed—indeed it is part of the process that gives comfort and ultimately relief to the sick at heart. We must not fall "orphaned" of garlands, he asserts. In the opening section of *Lycidas* Milton works his way from the figure of the shattered garland to the assertion of the appropriateness—indeed the necessity to lay poetic praise—Lycidas "must not float upon his wat'ry bier / Unwept" (12–13).

The Pindaric ode at its best is a very delicate poise of seemingly discordant parts. Take, for example, *Pythia* 12, an ode, composed of four strophes or stanzas, commemorating the victory of Midas, a Sicilian flute player in a Pythian contest. At first, it seems no more than a perfunctory compliment to the winner of a flute contest, which narrates the origin of flute playing in Pallas Athene's invention of the flute after hearing the wailing of the gorgon-sisters of Medusa, whom Perseus slew. Pindar opens with an invocation that praises Midas's native city and invokes its ruling goddess:

[5] Citations of Pindar's verse are from Pindar, *Carmina*, ed. C. M. Bowra (Oxford: Oxford Univ. Press, 1935). Also see Pindar, *The Olympian and Pythian Odes*, ed. Basil L. Gildersleeve (London: Macmillan, 1908).

ὦ ἄνα,
ἵλαος ἀθανάτων ἀνδρῶν τε σὺν εὐμενίᾳ
δέξαι στεφάνωμα τόδ' ἐκ Πυθῶνος εὐδόξῳ Μίδᾳ
αὐτόν τέ νιν ῾Ελλάδα νικάσαντα τέχνᾳ τὰν ποτε
Παλλὰς ἐφεῦρε θρασειᾶν Γοργόνων
οὔλιον θρῆνον διαπλέξαισ᾽ ᾿Αθάνα

(*Pythia* 12.3–8)

O Mistress,
Be gracious with the favor of men and gods,
Receive this crown from Pytho in behalf of glorious
          Midas
the one who has conquered in Hellas in the art that
          once
Pallas Athene invented, weaving it from the dreadful
          dirge of the bold Gorgons.

After this introduction, the ode appears to digress erratically from its subject, when, with the naming of Perseus as the slayer of Medusa, Pindar goes on gratuitously to recount the story of Perseus's birth, his killing of the gorgon, and his vengeance for his mother. What is Pindar's purpose both in introducing Perseus into the ode and in recounting his adventures in such detail? If he had merely been celebrating flute playing, there would appear to be none. But Pindar's true aim in the ode transcends his honoring the flute player Midas and even the beauty of flute playing. For as he considers the miraculous invention of lovely music from hideous wailing, he is also reflecting on how often for human beings beauty comes out of ugliness, victory out of defeat, and miracle from the commonplace. But these miracles can come about only when the gods aid human beings to transcend the limits of their mortal nature. Side by side in the ode are Athene, the all-powerful, all-wise virgin goddess; the gorgons, once beautiful women, transformed to snaky-haired monsters; the great hero Perseus; and the flute player Midas, for whom the ode was composed. What do they have in common; how has Pindar made their stories interlock in an ode that ostensibly is no more than a celebration of a flute victory? The clue lies in the figure of Athene and her relationship to the human beings in the poem—to the gorgons, to Perseus, and even to Midas the flute player. As a goddess, she has the power to transform both human beings and things—and transformation is one of the crucial issues in the poem. First of all, Athene transformed the gorgons from lovely maidens like herself to snaky-haired horrors, who turn all to stone. She petrified their beauty, and they in turn petrify all who look on them. But, curiously enough this transformation works two ways. Athene not only can transform lovely maidens to gorgons, but she can also transform the wailing lament that they raise for their sister into lovely polyphonic music. For the sound of the gorgons' wailing is the inspiration for the flute music that Athene creates. It is a wailing that Perseus hears, both after he kills Medusa and when he turns the king of Seriphos and his subjects to stone with the head of the Gorgon:

> τὸν παρθενίοις ὑπό τ᾽ ἀπλάτοις ὀφίων κεφαλαῖς
> ἄιε λειβόμενον δυσπενθέι σὺν καμάτῳ,
> Περσεὺς ὁπότε τρίτον ἄνυσσεν κασιγνητᾶν μέρος
> ᾽ενναλίᾳ Σερίφῳ λαοῖσί τε μοῖραν ἄγων.   (9–12)

the (sound) which Perseus heard coming from the horrible
maidenly heads of serpents with anguished suffering,
when he conquered the third of the sisters
and brought death to sea-girt Seriphos and its people.

Athene uses her divine power to guide the hero Perseus, transforming him also in turn. She leads him to the gorgons, assists him in killing Medusa, and inspires him to take Medusa's head to effect the liberation of his mother, Danae, by turning the king who has imprisoned her into stone along with his subjects. With the introduction of Danae Pindar works a still more intricate metaphoric transformation. As the gorgons are lovely maidens imprisoned in ugliness, Danae is a maiden imprisoned because of her loveliness, first confined to the brazen tower and then to her island prison. She is liberated from both by divine intervention and her sorrow is ultimately transformed to joy. When she is first captive, Zeus comes to her in the brazen tower and impregnates her with the hero Perseus who ultimately frees her from a second captivity. Zeus came to Danae, as Pindar reminds us, in a stream of gold. Here Pindar works his most daring metaphoric transformation. As he describes Perseus's conception from the spontaneously-flowing stream of gold, he links it with the flute music, itself golden and flowing, that also was conceived when through divine intervention its sorrowful wailing became beautiful music.

In the final strophe of the ode, Pindar binds up his moral, connecting now the figure of the flute player Midas with the hero Perseus, as he had earlier connected the antithetical figures of the gorgons, Danae, and Athene. Joy does not come to light, comments Pindar, without laboring or pain. The flute music was born of the pain of the gorgons, Perseus from the laboring pain of his mother, and Danae's liberation from captivity through the pain of the islanders and king turned to stone. Even the flute player Midas, if the legend that the Scholiasts hand down is true, won victory from apparent pain and defeat. As he was playing, his mouth piece broke and he was forced to play upon the reeds, but nonetheless was victorious.[6] Pindar's ode reaches beyond the celebration of a flute-player or even the celebration of the origin of flute-music to comment upon a universal truth—how the divine has the power to transform human experience, bringing joy or sorrow, success or failure.

I have dealt with *Pythia* 12 in detail in order to illustrate the complex way in which Pindar connects apparently digressive material within the body of his ode. The kind of metaphoric transformation that I have been illustrating in *Pythia* 12 is common throughout the corpus of Pindar's odes. As a poet, Milton works in *Lycidas* in a similar way, I believe, bringing together the figures of the dead poet Lycidas, Orpheus, Apollo, St. Peter, Alpheus and Arethusa, Michael, and Christ in order to work metaphoric transformations very like Pindar's. The example of Pindar, a poet Milton admired, is subtly present. Like Pindar's odes, *Lycidas* is an ode that transcends its occasion. As Pindar comes to praise a hero, Milton, or the uncouth swain who is his spokesman in the ode, comes to lift a song for the dead. His apparent purpose is to lament, but involved in that lament, as inextricably as in Pindar's celebration of victory, is an investigation into the way in which the divine within human life can bring a man sorrow or joy. Lycidas is dead; what can the living poet expect from a divine dispensation that seems savagely to cut off human expectation, just when it is about to be fulfilled? If the underlying image in *Pythia* 12 is the flowing stream: of melody, of lament, of generative power—now golden, now brazen and dissonant— the underlying image of *Lycidas* is water: the water that drowned Lycidas; the wat'ry tears—melodious and lamenting; the water that causes the sisters of the sacred well to revive their song; the fresh-water stream that bears the head of Orpheus in contrast to the Alpheus's amorous stream that pursues the fountain nymph Arethusa and mingles its waters with hers; the water of triumph on which Christ walked; the water of

---

[6] Gildersleeve, 365.

other streams in the kingdom of the blest. The water image has been studied by Brooks and Hardy and other critics, but no one has commented on how Milton's treatment of it as a linking image resembles Pindar's tactics with linking figures.[7] Water flows as persistently in Milton's ode as the stream of gold in Pindar's and its meaning changes as it is linked now with one, now with another figure. It destroys Lycidas and Orpheus; it is the medium of Alpheus's and Arethusa's transformation; it triumphs as Christ rises from the ocean like a resurrected sun; and it is the final benison for the saved Lycidas whose oozy locks are laved with nectar pure—heaven's transformed water.

Milton's use of both brief and extended mythic digression owes as much to Pindar as his treatment of the transformed image. The introduction of the first mythic figure occurs just at the point when Milton poses the question, why did the nymphs not save Lycidas? As though to reply, he poses two other interlinked questions—"Had ye been there—for what could that have done?" and next "What could the Muse herself" (57–58), leaving the rest of the question incomplete. At this point, he introduces Orpheus as the first of a series of figures to whom he will contrast Lycidas. He chooses, just as Pindar had for Perseus, only very select details of his story—his birth from the Muse mother, his enchantment of Nature and her lament at his death, his dismemberment by the "rout that make the hideous roar" (61), and his voyage down the Hebrus to the Lesbian shore as the "hoary visage," decapitated by the Bacchantes. The connection of Orpheus with Lycidas seems at first deceptively direct—both are young poets who suffered untimely deaths. But the resemblance masks two decided differences. Lycidas was neither so divinely favored as Orpheus, nor so tragically nor violently destroyed. And perhaps, though Milton is not ready to assert it, he was not abandoned by Heaven after all.

The example of Orpheus provokes a second poetic sigh and still more impassioned questioning. Why should anyone serve a muse, who begrudges thanks and abandons her children to a blind and fury-ridden fate? The question brings upon the scene the next important mythic figure in the ode, Orpheus's poetical father, Phoebus Apollo, the god of

---

[7] *Poems of Mr. John Milton* (New York, 1951), 169–86, reprinted in *Milton's "Lycidas": The Tradition and the Poem*, ed. C. A. Patrides (Columbia: Univ. of Missouri Press, 1983), 140–56. Also see Wayne Shumaker, "Flowerets and Sounding Seas: A Study in the Affective Structure of *Lycidas*," *PMLA* 66 (1951): 485–94, reprinted in *Milton's "Lycidas": The Tradition and the Poem*, 129–39.

poetry and the patron of poets, who, as Pindar tells us in *Pythia* 1, holds
the lyre in common right with the Muses. As with the appearance of
Athene in *Pythia* 12, Apollo's appearance here raises the level from the
human to the divine. Further, it bridges the gap between Orpheus and
Lycidas. Phoebus is presented in his roles of divine father to Orpheus
and patron god of poets, so metaphorically a father to Lycidas as well.
As such, he affirms that heaven does not abandon the poet nor deny
him just fame; one must consider Jove's ultimate purposes in all things.

Phoebus's speech—dramatic or epic in its style—is another instance
of Milton's adopting a Pindaric device. Pindar does not use the device
of dramatic speech except in very special instances when he wishes to
give vivid realization to a moment in a narrative or an odic sequence. In
Olympia 1, for example, Pindar is telling the story of how Tantalus's son
Pelops, having been restored to his father, wishes to seek fame and the
hand of Hippodamia in marriage by taking part in a very dangerous
chariot competition with her father. At the climactic moment, when
Pelops has come to the seashore alone to seek the aid of the god Posei-
don, Pindar breaks from the narrative and gives us Pelops's prayer to the
god. The prayer makes vivid for us the sincerity, the courage, and above
all the piety of this young man, a young man whose father Tantalus,
after all, had been guilty of the greatest impiety. It is a turning point in
the ode, for the young man is rewarded with victory—and Pindar makes
an interesting point for his patron Hieron, who has also just been
victorious in a chariot race, urging him implicitly to follow the example
of the humble and pious son, who attributes his success to the god's help
and not to his arrogant father, who sinned against the gods. Pindar uses
dramatic speech in other odes to bring the word of the god to human
beings. In *Olympia* 13 we hear the voice of the goddess Athene urge
Bellerophon on to heroic daring—as she tells him to bridle the winged
horse Pegasus. In *Pythia* 3 we hear the voice of Apollo as he determines
to save his son Asclepius from death, even as he has determined to
punish Asclepius's mother. In *Nemea* 10 we hear the voice of Zeus
speaking in reply to Polydeuces and granting his request that he honor
Castor and permit him to share his immortality. Moments of crisis
provoke Pindar not just to describe the action but to present it with
dramatic voice. Dramatic speech often in Pindar's odes marks a point of
encounter of the mortal with the god, a point when the god must
decide on a matter of crucial importance for that mortal.

Dramatic speech punctuates the narrative not once but several times
in the central "digressive" section of *Lycidas*. Apollo replies to the shep-

herd swain; St. Peter pronounces on the fate of the unworthy shepherds. Phoebus Apollo interrupts the swain's angry indictment of divine justice and reassures him that Jove's judgment is just, as Pindar's Apollo in *Pythia* 3 or Pindar's Zeus in *Nemea* 10 had offered reassurance of the faith and justice of the divine. In *Lycidas* the swain asserts that "*Fame* is the spur that the clear spirit doth raise," a fame prematurely dashed to disappointment (70); Phoebus replies, "*Fame* is no plant that grows on mortal soil" (78), correcting the swain's vision as he repeats the key word. With a simple rejoinder Phoebus changes the perspective from mortal to immortal.

The ode now proceeds with a diverse procession of mythic figures: first, Arethusa (Alpheus will join her later), then Triton and Hippotades, next Camus and St. Peter. These figures appear dramatically in the poem to disclaim responsibility for or to express sorrow at Lycidas's death and to present alternate perspectives on the question of human mortality. They are both thematically and dramatically differentiated. Triton and Hippotades, representing nature as sea and wind, and Camus, representing human society, speak only from the perspective of earth, and so are unable to account for Lycidas and his fate. Peter, however, representing both human and divine realms, can speak authoritatively. As with Orpheus and Apollo, Milton focuses selectively on Peter's roles as pilot of the Galilean Lake, holder of the keys of heaven, and shepherd of the church, for in these roles he is related both to the pastor Lycidas and other shepherds, able to offer earthly guidance and heavenly sanction. Peter is a Christian father to the shepherd Lycidas, for he is the head of the church, just as Apollo is poetic father both to Orpheus and Lycidas as the head of the poetic congregation. Like Phoebus, he raises the dialogue from the earthly to the divine, vindicating Heaven of the charge that it does not value the just and promising the punishment of the unjust. Once more Milton uses the device of dramatic speech to make his point vivid. Just as Athene in Pindar's ode had brought Danae and Perseus from their unfortunate beginnings to triumph and liberation, punishing those who had done them evil, Peter assures us that the just shepherd will be saved, the unjust punished with swift heavenly vengeance.

But in many ways it is the treatment of Arethusa and Alpheus that demonstrates Milton's most subtle use of Pindar's mythic techniques. Why are they invoked, Arethusa, immediately after the Phoebus, and Alpheus after the Peter passage in the poem? Arethusa had fled from Alpheus, who pursued her undersea and joined his waters with hers as she was transformed in Sicily into a fountain. In one aspect she is the tragically pursued nymph, who loses her life and her form in attempting to escape an unwanted lover. In another, she is the miraculously transformed being, who attains her true purpose in joining as fountain to river with that lover she first fled from. Both Arethusa and Alpheus experience a sea-change; both undergo a kind of death in order to attain as transformed gods immortality in another realm. Pindar in *Nemea 1* names Sicily as the " Ἄμπνευμα σεμνὸν Ἀλφεοῦ," the holy breathing place of Alpheus, the site where the river god attained his second breath as the immortal husband of Arethusa.[8] From the human perspective, Alpheus in vain pursuit of a fleeing nymph heard a dread voice that shrunk his streams; from the divine perspective that voice gave him renewed life in Sicily. Milton's mythic figures, like those of Pindar, hold the key to his ode's meaning.

Once he has identified Lycidas with Alpheus, Milton can work further transformations in the final sections of the poem. He announces the transition as he names both Alpheus ("Return Alpheus") and Arethusa, associating her now with the "Sicilian Muse," the restored Persephone, who brings the flowers of the spring and whom Pindar also invoked in *Nemea 1*. The flowers do honor to the dead Lycidas, who has been linked both to the tragically destroyed Orpheus and the resurrected Alpheus. In order to make the final transition to the Christian consolation and the vision of Lycidas, redeemed in Heaven, Milton undertakes one more mythic digression—the undersea passage that associates the dead Lycidas with two figures from antiquity—Alpheus, whose undersea journey Lycidas metaphorically also undertakes, and Arion, the poet, who was saved from drowning by the dolphins. Lycidas's dolphins, as J. Martin Evans has observed, recall the Arion story and also other mythic accounts of salvation.[9] Ultimately, however, it is not the dolphins or the power of the mythic figures from classical antiquity that saves Lycidas, even though Milton has metaphorically

---

[8] Alpheus and Arethusa appear also in Theocritus, in Moschus (where the story of the river god and the nymph are told), in *Aeneid* 3. See J. Martin Evans, *The Road from Horton: Looking Backwards in "Lycidas"* (Victoria, B.C.: Univ. of Victoria Press, 1983). Also see Edward W. Tayler, "*Lycidas* in Christian Time," in his *Milton's Poetry: Its Development in Time* (Pittsburgh: Duquesne Univ. Press, 1979), reprinted from *Huntington Library Quarterly* 41 (1978): 103–17, a condensed version of which appears in *Milton's "Lycidas": The Tradition and the Poem*, 303–18.

[9] See J. Martin Evans, " '*Lycidas*' and the Dolphins," *Notes & Queries* 25 (1978): 15–17.

linked them with him. The resurrected Alpheus and the rescued Arion point to the one who alone can effect Lycidas's resurrection. The angel of the guarded mount calls Lycidas homeward, and like the day-star risen, he mounts high "Through the dear might of him that walk'd the waves" (173). The vision of Lycidas, redeemed in Heaven, hearing the songs of the solemn troops and sweet societies, not sunk beneath the waves, is directly dependent, however, upon the mythic transformations that Milton has effected at the center of the ode.

Lycidas is a composite poem, made up of many strands from different traditions, part pastoral idyll, part lament for the dead, part commemorative ode in the Pindaric mode. In naming his poem a monody, Milton suggests the Greek model. By imitating its techniques of mythic transformation Milton can convey by implication, by allusion, by digressive design his most deeply held beliefs. The consoling affirmation of the final passage—"Henceforth thou art the Genius of the shore, / In thy large recompense, and shalt be good, / To all that wander in that perilous flood" (183–85) even has the ring of Pindar's *sententia*. In recognizing the source of these techniques, we can finally give due credit to what one great poet learned from another.

SOUTHERN ILLINOIS UNIVERSITY, EDWARDSVILLE

Lee M. Johnson

LANGUAGE AND THE ILLUSION OF INNOCENCE IN
PARADISE LOST

WE CANNOT ENTER THE GARDEN OF EDEN IN BOOK 4 OF *Paradise Lost* and look upon the "mysterious parts" of the innocent Adam and Eve or upon Eve's "wanton ringlets" in a spirit of complete simplicity and purity: not only do we observe with the fallen Satan as our companion, but our perceptions, including those of the poet himself, are subject to the complex connotations and associations which characterize our use of language.[1] To some, "words alone are certain good"[2] but not to the epic's narrator, who, as if acknowledging the hopelessness of painting a credible verbal picture of innocent life, continually calls attention to the "guilty shame" and "dishonest shame" that evoke innocence only by contrast and by a sense of absence (4.313). As the unhappy turns in the careers of Satan, Adam, and Eve demonstrate, linguistic self-subversion, irony, and ambiguity, including, at its lowest, downright bad puns, inhere in the expression of fallen natures. Such a language drifts ineluctably into waywardness and perverse complexity and is, by definition, inadequate to the task of depicting innocent perfection on its own terms. But a poet need not be limited to the depiction of innocence solely by its absence: the illusion of its presence is within the domain of artistic symbolism.

It would appear that, for the purpose of dramatizing the state of

---

[1] *John Milton: Complete Poems and Major Prose*, ed. Merritt Y. Hughes (New York: Odyssey Press, 1957), 285 (4.306,312). Subsequent citations of *Paradise Lost* are from this edition and are indicated in the text by book and line numbers.

[2] W. B. Yeats, "The Song of the Happy Shepherd," *The Collected Poems of W. B. Yeats* (New York: Macmillan, 1956), 7.

innocence, Milton's poetic style displays a remarkable bond between his language and the use of uncomplicated symbolic formal patterns. In exploring the nature of those patterns, we find that they are restricted to books 4, 5, and 8 of *Paradise Lost*: precisely those portions of the epic in which Adam and Eve are described or act in their unfallen condition. We shall not come upon anything similar to Milton's art of innocence elsewhere in *Paradise Lost* or throughout *Paradise Regained* and *Samson Agonistes*: all such passages and works chiefly concern fallen experience and conditions and thus have their own appropriate modes of presentation.[3]

The symbolic patterns associated with the style and language of innocence lend a sense of authenticity to the early speeches of the innocent Adam and Eve. Among those early speeches, the one which displays the most concentrated example of the patterns we shall now consider is Eve's love-lyric "Sweet is the breath of morn":

> Sweet is the breath of morn, her rising sweet,
> With charm of earliest Birds; pleasant the Sun
> When first on this delightful Land he spreads
> His orient Beams, on herb, tree, fruit, and flow'r,
> Glist'ring with dew; fragrant the fertile earth   645
> After soft showers; and sweet the coming on
> Of grateful Ev'ning mild, then silent Night
> With this her solemn Bird and this fair Moon,

---

[3] The difficulty of finding the right words and thoughts for paradise is admirably summarized by Ira Clark, "A Problem of Knowing Paradise in *Paradise Lost*," *MS* 27 (1991): 183–207. Finding words and thoughts for fallen conditions leads A. Bartlett Giamatti to go so far as to posit a "Satanic style" of ambiguities and dissonance; see *The Earthly Paradise and the Renaissance Epic* (Princeton: Princeton Univ. Press, 1966), 303ff. Without pausing to qualify such views, we must respect the impulse that leads to them. Perhaps Peter Berek's guidelines for a distinction between innocent and fallen language are as fair as anyone's:

> Milton, I suggest, has used a certain kind of 'poetical' manipulation of facts by means of language as a powerful metaphor for corruption, and, conversely, uses patterns of words that give the effect of imitating rather than manipulating reality as a way of presenting figures of innocence and perfection. (" 'Plain' and 'Ornate' Styles and the Structure of *Paradise Lost*," *PMLA* 85 [March, 1970]: 246).

Moving from questions of diction to the larger arena of forms, we might wish to consider the function of unrhymed sonnets and the divine proportion as ways of expressing and redeeming fallen language: see Lee Johnson, "Milton's Blank Verse Sonnets," *MS* 5 (1973): 129–53; for the divine proportion, see Lee Johnson, "Milton's Epic Style: The Invocations in *Paradise Lost*," *The Cambridge Companion to Milton*, ed. Dennis Danielson (Cambridge: Cambridge Univ. Press, 1989), 65–78.

And these the Gems of Heav'n, her starry train:
But neither breath of Morn when she ascends   650
With charm of earliest Birds, nor rising Sun
On this delightful land, nor herb, fruit, flow'r,
Glist'ring with dew, nor fragrance after showers,
Nor grateful Ev'ning mild, nor silent Night
With this her solemn Bird, nor walk by Moon,   655
Or glittering Star-light without thee is sweet.

(4.641–56)

The principal effect of the passage is one of enclosure and depends on the careful placement of key words. The lyric's opening line, "Sweet is the breath of morn, her rising sweet," illustrates the effect in miniature by using the same word in its first and tenth syllables. The effect continues throughout the series of clauses that completes the initial part of the passage: "pleasant the Sun," "fragrant the fertile earth," and, finally, "sweet the coming on / Of grateful Ev'ning mild." What is being enclosed, of course, is the scale of creation from "morn" to "Ev'ning mild," settings for the sun and moon whose importance and interdependence are emphasized by their use as end-words in their respective lines.

The same phrases and images reappear in the second part of the lyric: the sun and moon again serve as end-words for their lines, but Eve's sense of the harmonious interrelationships among things would not be "sweet" without Adam as her companion. Eve's lyric on the mutual support and pairing of all things ends as it begins: the word "sweet" encloses the cycles and images of day and night in a circle, which, as a symbol of fullness and perfection, is appropriate to Eve's innocent state of being. The sixteen lines of Eve's lyric, which has been described mistakenly as a sonnet, are actually much more interesting and strictly unified in their use of key words to establish patterns of enclosure and circularity of evident symbolic value.[4]

By touching on the fullness of the scale of creation, such patterns of enclosure are notable, not for their exclusion or limitation of possibilities, but for their participation in a graceful range of complexity. In the

---

[4] For a discussion and notes on Eve's love-lyric as a Petrarchan-style sonnet, see Barbara K. Lewalski, *"Paradise Lost" and the Rhetoric of Literary Forms* (Princeton: Princeton Univ. Press, 1985), 188, 344 n. 42; also, Barbara K. Lewalski, "The Genres of *Paradise Lost*," *The Cambridge Companion to Milton*, ed. Dennis Danielson (Cambridge: Cambridge Univ. Press, 1989), 88.

verse paragraphs which immediately precede and follow Eve's love-lyric, Adam anticipates and echoes the imagery and form of Eve's speech. The phrase "Night bids us rest" concludes Adam's speech before Eve's lyric begins, and the words "night" and "rest" appear in the opening lines of Adam's verse paragraph as well, thereby encircling his thoughts on the mutually supportive cycles of their days and nights (4.610–33). As in Eve's lyric, so here the cyclical imagery and diction are at one with the formal design of the speech. After her lyric has ended and in response to her question about the role of starlight during their sleep, Adam considers the physical and spiritual natures of light and sound in relation to earth and earth's inhabitants. The speech is thirty lines long (4.659–88) and divides neatly into two fifteen-line halves (659–73; 674–88). In the first half, Adam notes the relationship of the stars to the sun: both sources of light, in a downward movement, irradiate the "earth," the word which appears prominently near the beginning (661) and end (672) of this portion of his speech. In the second half, he calls attention to the relationship of "Millions of spiritual Creatures," including perhaps angels, to their creator as the music of their praise rises from earth to "heaven," the word which surrounds this portion of the speech (676, 688). Thus, "Earth" and "Heaven" delimit their respective halves of the verse paragraph and, serving as end-words at the beginning (661) and conclusion (688) of the entire speech, circumscribe the mirror-effect of downward and upward motions of first physical and then spiritual forms of energy that ultimately "lift our thoughts to Heaven." Eve's love-lyric and the two surrounding speeches by Adam indicate that, to Milton, the presentation of the state of innocence is no mere study in reductive simplicity. Instead, the interaction of linguistic and formal symbols in these passages is sufficiently complex to create a coherent sense of an innocent reality that is complete in itself and that gives the impression of not needing to be encumbered with help from an additional and fallen level of discourse.

Opposed to the circles of perfection that befit the innocence of Adam and Eve is the surrounding presence of Satan, whose speeches and activities initiate and conclude book 4. Enclosing the perfection of Eden and its inhabitants is not enough, however: he needs to break through, as his attempt at the ear of Eve demonstrates. The measure of his success is suggested at the beginning of book 5 when Eve recounts her troubled dream, which begins with images similar to those of her love-lyric in book 4. The morning sun and evening moon with their attendant birds have been replaced by "the night-warbling Bird, that now awake /

Tunes sweetest his love-labor'd song" and by a moon that shines "with more pleasing light" (5.40–42). In her dream, Eve says, "I rose as at thy call, but found thee not" (5.48). The theme of loving interdependence among all things has been replaced by Satan's theme of self-sufficiency.

Adam's explanation of the dream as a product of wayward faculties seems to satisfy Eve, but their restoration to untroubled innocence is completed by their morning-hymn which ensues shortly thereafter (5.153–208). Standing as the summation of Milton's art of innocence, the hymn, given its importance and complexity, is best seen whole with line-numbers and divisions noted in the margin:

> These are thy glorious works, Parent of good,
> Almighty, thine this universal Frame,
> Thus wondrous fair; thyself how wondrous then!   155
> Unspeakable, who sit'st above these Heavens
> To us invisible or dimly seen
> In these thy lowest works, yet these declare
> Thy goodness beyond thought, and Power Divine: $\underline{7}\uparrow$
> Speak yee who best can tell, ye Sons of Light, $20\downarrow$ 160
> Angels, for yee behold him, and with songs
> And choral symphonies, Day without Night,
> Circle his Throne rejoicing, yee in Heav'n;
> On Earth join all ye Creatures to extol
> Him first, him last, him midst, and without end.   165
> Fairest of Stars, last in the train of Night,
> If better thou belong not to the dawn,
> Sure pledge of day, that crown'st the smiling Morn
> With thy bright Circlet, praise him in thy Sphere
> While day arises, that sweet hour of Prime.   170
> Thou Sun, of this great World both Eye and Soul,
> Acknowledge him thy Greater, sound his praise
> In thy eternal course, both when thou climb'st,
> And when high Noon hast gain'd, and when thou fall'st.
> Moon, that now meet'st the orient Sun, now fli'st   175
> With the fixt Stars, fixt in thir Orb that flies,
> And yee five other wand'ring Fires that move
> In mystic Dance not without Song, resound
> His praise, who out of Darkness call'd up Light. $\underline{20}\uparrow$
> Air, and ye Elements the eldest birth $5\downarrow$ 180

Of Nature's Womb, that in quaternion run
Perpetual Circle, multiform, and mix
And nourish all things, let your ceaseless change
Vary to our great Maker still new praise.   5↑
Ye Mists and Exhalations that now rise   20↓   185
From Hill or steaming Lake, dusky or grey,
Till the Sun paint your fleecy skirts with Gold,
In honor to the World's great Author rise,
Whether to deck with Clouds th' uncolor'd sky,
Or wet the thirsty Earth with falling showers,   190
Rising or falling still advance his praise.
His praise ye Winds, that from four Quarters blow,
Breathe soft or loud; and wave your tops, ye Pines,
With every Plant, in sign of Worship wave.
Fountains and yee, that warble, as ye flow,   195
Melodious murmurs, warbling tune his praise.
Join voices all ye living Souls; ye Birds,
That singing up to Heaven Gate ascend,
Bear on your wings and in your notes his praise;
Yee that in Waters glide, and yee that walk   200
The Earth, and stately tread, or lowly creep;
Witness if I be silent, Morn or Even,
To Hill, or Valley, Fountain, or fresh shade
Made vocal by my Song, and taught his praise.   20↑
Hail universal Lord, be bounteous still   4↓   205
To give us only good; and if the night
Have gather'd aught of evil or conceal'd,
Disperse it, as now light dispels the dark.   (5.153–208)

Here patterns of enclosure and circles which symbolize innocent perfection receive their most highly developed expression in the entire epic. Direct addresses to the creator frame the hymn which in its body consists of direct addresses to different aspects of the creation. After the opening seven lines of praise to God and before the final four lines on the need for God's protective bounty, the hymn displays forty-five lines on the celestial and terrestrial elements of creation (160–204). These forty-five lines are symmetrically balanced: the first twenty address the celestial universe, then comes a middle section of five lines on the physical elements of the creation, and finally twenty more lines on the praise that comes from the earth. At the exact midpoint of these forty-five lines is the phrase "Perpetual Circle," which describes how the elements intermix to form all things. Images and metaphors of circles dominate the hymn as well. The "Sons of Light" addressed at the beginning of the first twenty-line section "Circle" God's throne, the "Fairest of Stars" provides a "bright Circlet" to crown the morning, the fixed stars are whirled about in the moving "Orb," and the entire passage is encircled by the word "Light" which serves as the end-word for lines one and twenty. The counterbalancing twenty-line section on the terrestrial scale of creation uses the word "praise" to end its major clauses, a praise that, according to other important words at the ends of lines, must "rise" and "ascend" as the passage touches on various aspects of earthly life associated with the springing forth of the morning light.

The symmetrical patterns of symbolic order just described would appear to counter the epic narrator's claim which immediately precedes the morning-hymn: namely, that such utterances from the innocent Adam and Eve are "Unmeditated" and spontaneous, occurring "in Prose or numerous Verse" (5.149,150). The "various style" (146) to which the narrator calls attention leads Joseph Summers to note the variety of strophic and syntactical lengths in the morning-hymn and to suggest that such variety is intrinsic to Milton's idea of perfection.[5] Now, it is demonstrably the case that the internal structure of the hymn is irregular and, by avoiding predictable lengths in its sections, fosters a sense of freedom; at the same time, it is equally demonstrable that the hymn fulfills strict patterns of symbolic order through its images, the placement of key words, and its overall design. Milton's articulation of the artistic principle in question also characterizes, of course, the "Mystical dance" of the angels and planets, whose motions are "regular / Then most, when most irregular they seem" (5.620–24). The striking conjunction of freedom and strict form in the morning-hymn, then, is no coincidence, as if we had simply caught Adam and Eve on a good day, but is one of Milton's most telling demonstrations of what characterizes the state of innocence: spontaneous perfection.

At the conclusion of Adam and Eve's morning-hymn, the epic's

---

[5] Joseph H. Summers, *The Muse's Method: An Introduction to "Paradise Lost"* (London: Chatto and Windus, 1962), 77–78. For another way of dividing the morning-hymn, see John Hollander, *The Figure of Echo: A Mode of Allusion in Milton and After* (Berkeley: Univ. of California Press, 1981), 39.

narrator observes, "So pray'd they innocent, and to thir thoughts / Firm peace recover'd soon and wonted calm" (5.209–10). Looking back, we have no difficulty in seeing how the morning-hymn accomplishes such a firm support to the theme of innocence. Its patterns of circular imagery and symmetry recall Eve's love-lyric in book 4 but on a larger scale and in a much more elaborate way, thereby reasserting the perfection of being assigned to Adam and Eve at the outset. The morning-hymn also recalls the scale of creation which here receives one of the most detailed and extensive treatments to be found in the epic. By this means, the theme of interdependence among all things is unequivocally restated and removes any traces of self-sufficiency as suggested by Satan to Eve in her dream. Looking ahead, we can anticipate Raphael's visit to Eden: in particular, his presentation of the scale of creation as a great tree of life (5.469–505). After listening to Raphael's speech, Adam provides a key to the symbolism with which we have been dealing: he is pleased with how the angel has

> the scale of Nature set
> From centre to circumference, whereon
> In contemplation of created things
> By steps we may ascend to God.   (5.509–12)

Of course, the orderliness of the spheres and circles of existence is a measure of the primal condition of perfection.

"So pray'd they innocent," but to read innocently is another matter. Even in the morning-hymn, the magnificent purity and control of style and expression cannot eliminate opportunities for verbal dissonance. When Adam and Eve call upon the "Fairest of Stars" to praise God with the planet's "bright Circlet" and "Sphere," it is difficult not to think of Venus as Lucifer, the morning star. Were Adam and Eve to know of Satan as the false Lucifer, as they will after the departure from Eden brings a tragic depth to their experience, they could not pray so confidently and avoid wrestling with language. For the reader, the problem is similar to that raised by Eve's "wanton ringlets" in book 4. The morning-hymn's "Mists and Exhalations" that nourish "the thirsty Earth with falling showers" and usher in the terrestrial praise of the creator present a related problem, given that in book 9 Satan enters Eden "involv'd in rising Mist" and moves about like "a black mist low creeping" (9.75,180). In the overall context of the poem, Milton's imagery seems designed to complicate and compromise depictions of innocence, leading to further considerations of what has been lost along with the simplicity of language.[6]

Within passages designed to express innocence, however, the function of circular patterns of enclosure is to temper linguistic complexity by supplying images of pure form that resist misinterpretation and by exemplifying those images through the symmetrical positioning of key words or other elements of poetic structure. The resulting language is purified, as it were, by the formal ritual of symbolic patterns, which are evident once more in our final example of dramatized innocence: Adam's account of his initial consciousness as a living being (8.249–91). The remarkable internal structure of the opening forty-three lines of Adam's long verse paragraph reveals a deft use of enclosure. The opening eight lines (249–56) and concluding nine lines (283–91) frame the central portion of twenty-six lines, which present Adam's first sensations and thoughts and which divide exactly in half. The key word in the framing lines around the central portion is "sleep," displayed prominently as the end-word of lines 253 and 287. Adam's account of his life's beginnings, which are thus literally and symbolically rounded with the word "sleep," then ensues (257–82), with each thirteen-line section being virtually the mirror-image of the other. In the first thirteen-line section, Adam's enchantment with the heavens prompts him to stand erect and then peruse the pastoral images around him before attending to his own physical abilities. What he has done is to go symbolically from the ethereal source of his being to an intuition of a scale of creation around him that ascends from "Hill, Dale, and shady Woods" to "Creatures that liv'd and mov'd" and, finally, to himself. In the second thirteen-line section, he is able to speak and name all that he

[6] The expressive ambiguities and dissonances of Milton's style have long elicited first-rate comments; in addition to the items by Clark, Berek, and Giamatti cited in n. 3, Ricks, Swaim, and Leonard have provided astute and provocative observations on the complexity of Milton's words. When Christopher Ricks says, "with the Fall of Man, language falls too," he shows how corruptions infect words such as "wanton," "error," and numerous others: see *Milton's Grand Style* (Oxford: Clarendon Press, 1963), 109–11. In *Before and After the Fall: Contrasting Modes in "Paradise Lost"* (Amherst: Univ. of Massachusetts Press, 1986), Kathleen Swaim discusses the morning-hymn and its troublesome "Fairest of Stars" as well as adding to our sense of puns and ambiguities in Milton's diction (70, 185–86). Most thoroughly and admirably, John Leonard's *Naming in Paradise: Milton and the Language of Adam and Eve* (Oxford: Clarendon Press, 1990) corroborates and extends Ricks's work: Leonard's final chapter, "Prelapsarian Language and the Poet," is especially relevant throughout to our consideration of subtleties in the morning-hymn and in Edenic language generally (233–92).

perceives, repeat almost verbatim the images he has noted, and he concludes by inferring the existence of "some great Maker" to account for the existence and design of the world. The entire twenty-six lines thus end almost where they began. A sense of heavenly origins encircles Adam's creation, but the end has the additional creative glory of a self-reflexive and ordered language that enables him to express an exact sense of being happier than he knows. His first perceptions, first words, and first encircling sense of perfection all harmonize precisely to give the illusion of primordial innocence.

In the fallen world, however, great poets have repeatedly lamented the indeterminacy of language and have accordingly explored the greater precision which may be forged through symbolic form. Now, Milton is not unusual in employing symbolic form to control the waywardness of language when it relies on verbal meanings alone. Other instances pervade the history of poetry, and a few words should be added to distinguish between the tempering effect of symbolic form on language for general purposes in contrast to the depiction of innocence as a particular problem. Since we have been concerned with circles and spheres especially, let us use these figures to illustrate a few distinctions. Sometimes circles and spheres appear as basically uncomplicated descriptive images without having to perform larger tasks associated with symbolic form: such is their function, for example, in depicting elements of creation in book 7 of *Paradise Lost*. More often, though, their symbolic possibilities prove irresistible. To Ben Jonson, Donne, Herbert, Marvell, Dryden, and others in Milton's century, to name a few, circles and spheres have symbolic value that focuses the themes of major poems. To T. S. Eliot in our century, the *Four Quartets* employ circles and patterns of enclosure to break away from the linear tyranny of time and the instability of words, which in "Burnt Norton" are said to

> strain,
> Crack and sometimes break, under the burden,
> Under the tension, slip, slide, perish,
> Decay with imprecision, will not stay in place,
> Will not stay still.[7]

---

[7] T. S. Eliot, "Burnt Norton," *Four Quartets* (London: Faber and Faber, 1959), 19 (5.149–53). The subsequent citation of "Burnt Norton" is indicated in the text by section and line numbers.

As a result, the *Four Quartets* attempt to set their images on a higher plane of symbolism in which beginnings and ends circle towards one another because

> Only by the form, the pattern,
> Can words or music reach
> The stillness, as a Chinese jar still
> Moves perpetually in its stillness.
>   ("Burnt Norton," 5.140–43)

Thus, the word "stillness" is carefully positioned to enclose the simile of the Chinese jar in a demonstration of theme through the clarity of a formal pattern. To Eliot, circles are important for containing still, central points in a turning world of words. As such, the formal pattern uses language to evoke a sense of something beyond language, a transcendent order or symbol of permanence. There is necessarily a gap between temporal and symbolic realities as form supplements language. That gap or sense of dislocation is inherent in the nature of fallen language, which perforce relates to a fallen world, and is therefore characteristic of most symbolic discourse. By contrast, innocent perfection requires that there be no sense of dislocation.

The presentation of innocence presupposes acts of perception in which reality and appearance are indistinguishable in the union of language and symbolic form. In this respect, perhaps no poet since Milton has pondered the relationship of language to pure form so carefully as has Wordsworth, who, in his treatment of the theme of innocence, is even capable of expressing the process of perception by which innocence may be attained. An example of his ability to create a sense of innocence is in "Home at Grasmere" as the poet describes the sensation of living in that place:

> 'Tis, but I cannot name it, 'tis the sense
> Of majesty, and beauty, and repose,
> A blended holiness of earth and sky,
> Something that makes this individual Spot,
> This small Abiding-place of many Men,
> A termination, and a last retreat,
> A Centre, come from whereso'er you will,
> A Whole without dependence or defect,

Made for itself; and happy in itself,
Perfect Contentment, Unity entire.[8]

The sensation Wordsworth cannot name is, of course, innocent perfection, which he is attempting to apply to his home ground. Language can only approximate that sensation, and so the passage, as it progresses, carefully refines its terms, using circles and patterns of enclosure to control the description, which becomes increasingly abstract and aligned with the purity of geometrical form, until it concludes in the line "Perfect Contentment, Unity entire" in which words of two syllables enclose those of three.[9] Here, as in the examples from *Paradise Lost*, all elements of language are coordinated to serve the symbolism of pure form and even express the process by which that coordination or union of perceptions is achieved. Wordsworth's memories of a more perfect state of being are, of course, at the heart of his endeavor to give them a life in the present throughout his major poetry, just as they are the source of the symbolic forms he employs in that endeavor. In *Paradise Lost*, Milton attempts a fiction which may seem even more daring: a sense that his innocent Eden is no mere memory but a perception of perfection on which memories will be based. For both Milton and Wordsworth, the results show, at the very least, how an illusion of perfection may be suggested beyond the capabilities of verbal meaning alone. At the most, a poignant sense of something ranging from the archetypal to the Platonic may be awakened as the particularities of language fade into insignificance.

UNIVERSITY OF BRITISH COLUMBIA

[8] *Wordsworth's Poetical Works*, ed. Ernest de Selincourt and Helen Darbishire, 5 vols. (Oxford: Clarendon Press, 1949), 5:318.

[9] In this passage from "Home at Grasmere," the symbolism of geometrical form goes beyond the local qualities of diction to the design of the entire verse paragraph in which our passage serves as the conclusion. Echoing Milton's Edenic language, Wordsworth places his careful evocation of Grasmere in the overall pattern of a divine proportion, a geometrical way of interrelating smaller and larger sections of a verse paragraph into a symbol of interaction between temporal and timeless realities. The circles of innocent perfection which occupy us here thus reside in an overall context of geometrical symbolism which is suited to the fallen world and which, as indicated in n. 1, is also a key ingredient in Milton's art. Wordsworth's example, which blends a local pattern of innocence (the circle) with a larger design of experience (the divine proportion), is a superb triumph of his rational imagination that introduces rich complexities which deserve a separate discussion: see Lee Johnson, *Wordsworth's Metaphysical Verse: Geometry, Nature, and Form* (Toronto: Univ. of Toronto Press, 1982), 194–97.

David Robertson

SOLILOQUY AND SELF
IN MILTON'S MAJOR POEMS

J. B. BROADBENT'S ASSERTION THAT "THE CHARACTERS OF
Paradise Lost do not soliloquize until they have fallen"[1] has been so
readily accepted that it seems to have become a critical commonplace.[2]
Yet Broadbent's claim challenges us in at least two ways. Firstly, it
invites us to test the truth of the statement—are the characters in fact
fallen before they break into soliloquy? This is particularly challenging
where Eve and Adam are concerned, for both soliloquize *before* actually
biting into the fruit. Broadbent therefore forces us into a consideration
of what precisely constitutes the Fall in *Paradise Lost*.

Secondly, Broadbent's comment challenges us to consider what the
role of soliloquy is in the poem, and even in Milton's other major
works. Are we to see the soliloquy as a form of speech peculiarly
appropriate to, or even only available to fallen beings, as Broadbent's
comment would suggest? Or is it no more than a dramatic device taken
over into the epic from the presentation of character on stage?

If Broadbent is right, Adam and Eve must have fallen before they
actually eat of the fruit. A fair amount of ink has been spilled over the
question of when and how exactly the Fall takes place in *Paradise Lost*,

---

[1] J. B. Broadbent, *Some Graver Subject: An Essay on "Paradise Lost"* (London: Chatto and Windus, 1960), 80.

[2] For example, Catherine Belsey claims that "it is not until after the Fall that Adam 'expresses himself' in soliloquy" (*John Milton: Language, Gender, Power* [Oxford: Blackwell, 1988], 89).

but it is not my intention to review the debate here.[3] In point of fact
the text is quite specific that the characters are sinless until an overt act
of rebellion is performed. Eve, on being shown the tree which has
wrought the "miracle" of giving the snake reason and speech, is specifically said by the narrator to be "yet sinless" (9.660).[4] And nature sighs
and groans only *after* the fruit has been tasted, not during the dialogues
or soliloquies leading up to the act. A simple analogy will clarify the
point I wish to make. Under a just and impartial legal system the intention to commit an offense is not enough to convict a person. One can
always reverse an intention and choose not to commit the act. And
although Gordon Teskey aptly points out that "in *Paradise Lost,* only a
choice can be perverse, never an event in itself,"[5] choices are reversible,
but an act is irreversible, and is therefore punishable, even if the perpe-
trator subsequently feels remorse.

In *Christian Doctrine,* Milton recognizes this distinction. "Each type
of sin," he says, "has two subdivisions.... These subdivisions are evil
desire, or the will to do evil, and the evil deed itself." Milton compli-
cates matters for us postlapsarian beings by regarding evil desire as part
of original sin, but Adam and Eve before their fall "could not have been
subject to original sin.... Their sin was what is called 'actual' sin." And
actual sin "is the evil action or crime itself."[6] Adam and Eve, therefore,
could have drawn back from their intention to fall right up to the
moment of eating the fruit and thus remained sinless.

In a subtly argued article, John S. Tanner notes that "*Paradise Lost*
represents Edenic evil as emerging both in a sudden, discontinuous
instant of free choice and within a long, continuous psychological drama

---

[3] A number of critics have regarded the parting scene (9.205–385) as the true beginning
of the Fall. See for example, Fredson Bowers, "Adam, Eve and the Fall in *Paradise Lost,*"
PMLA 84 (1969): 264–73; Eric Smith, *Some Versions of the Fall* (Pittsburgh: Univ. of
Pittsburgh Press, 1973), 28; and A. G. George, *Milton and the Nature of Man* (London: Asia
Publishing House, 1974), 143. On the other hand, Stella Revard, "Eve and the Doctrine of
Responsibility in *Paradise Lost,*" *PMLA* 88 (1973): 69–78, and Mary Nyquist, "Reading the
Fall: Discourse in *Paradise Lost,*" *English Literary Renaissance* 14 (1984): 199–229, argue very
eloquently against this view.

[4] Milton's poetry is quoted from *The Poems of John Milton,* ed. John Carey and Alastair
Fowler (London: Longman, 1968).

[5] Gordon Teskey, "From Allegory to Dialectic: Imagining Error in Spenser and Milton,"
PMLA 101 (1986): 10. He, too, reads Eve as being totally sinless "until she enters into direct
contradiction with truth" (13–14).

[6] *Christian Doctrine* 1.11, quoted from CPW, 6:388; 390; 391.

of seduction." However, even within the drama of seduction the text of *Paradise Lost* argues specifically that it is possible to think evil, and therefore sinful, thoughts and yet remain sinless, for Adam tells Eve after her disturbing dream in book 4 that

> Evil into the mind of god or man
> May come and go, so unapproved, and leave
> No spot or blame behind: (5.117–19)

As Tanner says, the instant of free choice within the poem forms a scheme which "is ethical; in it sin bisects an innocent 'before' from a guilty 'after.'... Ethically, the Fall collapses into an act, a rupture located in a specific instant: 'she pluck'd, she eat: / Earth felt the wound' ... Before this Eve is 'yet sinless.'"[7]

Broadbent is therefore wrong: Adam and Eve are still unfallen when they speak their first soliloquies in book 9. Nevertheless, Broadbent's insight is valuable in that it challenges us in the second way mentioned above, namely to consider whether soliloquy is a form of speech particularly appropriate to fallen beings.

Before examining the way Milton uses soliloquies, perhaps it is necessary briefly to explore the nature and use of soliloquy as it had developed up to the seventeenth century. In the theater the soliloquy is an obvious stage device with a history reaching all the way back to Greek drama. It has been used for a number of purposes: to report action that has already occurred or that was occurring off-stage; to disclose and deliberate on plans for future actions. But its most delicate use by the time Milton was writing was to present a character's innermost thoughts and feelings to the audience. It "can appear to be a true thinking aloud."[8] The soliloquy is also used by Shakespeare, among others, "to engage the spectator directly, to throw him a face-to-face challenge to agree or disagree...."[9] For example, in *Othello,* Iago's claim that the "advice is free I give and honest" (2.3.345) cannot be accepted as the truth, nor can it be seen as simple thinking aloud, in the sense of the character revealing his innermost and secret thoughts without dissembling in any way. The audience are perfectly aware that

---

[7] John S. Tanner, " 'Say First What Cause': Ricoeur and the Etiology of Evil in *Paradise Lost,*" *PMLA* 103 (1988): 50.

[8] Elizabeth Burns, *Theatricality: A Study of Convention in the Theatre and in Social Life* (London: Longman, 1972), 54.

[9] J. L. Styan, *Drama, Stage and Audience* (London: Cambridge Univ. Press, 1975), 153.

even here he is lying—this time not just to the other characters, but more importantly, to himself and to them, the audience.

In this way, then, the soliloquy can indeed reveal a character's true mental processes and deepest motives, not always by a straightforward presentation of them, but by the tension between the words spoken and the knowledge that the audience or reader possesses. In the epic the uses of the soliloquy are no different. Here too the reader is both directly engaged by the soliloquy, and challenged to examine the words for their truth or falsehood. However, the reader must suspend disbelief in the unnaturalness of this mode of address. This is something that Jun Harada ignores in his otherwise excellent article, "Self and Language in the Fall." He claims that the characters themselves choose this artificial, dramatic device as a form of behavior, and builds a theory around this. In brief his theory is that "the mechanism of soliloquy ... functions to make the reader realize the internal relationship between the form of talking to one's self and the speaker's state of self-enclosure."[10] Harada is here placing far too much weight on soliloquy as realistic behavior, for his point would have been just as valid had he based it on the relationship between private thought and self-enclosure.

If the soliloquy, then, is an artificial form of behavior which it is unwise to take literally, we can still consider the uses to which Milton puts the soliloquy in his major poems. There are nine soliloquies in *Paradise Lost:* the fallen Satan delivers five during the course of the poem, and Adam and Eve each speak one before and one after their falls.[11] In this sense Broadbent's claim is correct: *most* soliloquies in the poem are indeed spoken by fallen beings. Perhaps this is significant, for if we look at what the soliloquies are concerned with, we can see a pattern emerging. John M. Steadman points out that Satan's soliloquies "advance the action by portraying an *internal* act that precedes the external, physical act."[12] This is an important insight, but he fails to

[10] Jun Harada, "Self and Language in the Fall," *MS* 5 (1973): 213.

[11] Satan's soliloquies are at 4.32–113; 4.358–92; 4.505–35; 9.99–178; 9.473–93. Eve's are at 9.745–79 and 9.795–833. Adam's are at 9.896–916 and 10.720–862. I have not included Adam's first reported speech here (8.273–82), firstly because it is a recreation by Adam of his actual speech, and secondly because most of it is in fact a series of appeals and questions to inanimate objects which Adam addresses as if they were animate, not knowing any better, having just been created himself.

[12] John M. Steadman, "Milton's Rhetoric: Satan and the 'Unjust Discourse,'" *MS* 1 (1969): 81.

define exactly what the internal act is. He is content to see Satan's soliloquies as "fairly straightforward expressions of his actual feelings and purposes" (80). A closer examination of Satan's soliloquies will clarify the nature of the internal act.

Satan's first soliloquy begins with an address to the sun, which brings him to a remembrance of how he fell. This leads him to a consideration of the reasons for his fall: pride, ambition, and ingratitude. He understands that God "deserved no such return," and that he himself is really to blame for his own condition: "Hadst thou the same free will and power to stand? / Thou hadst" (4.66–67). The use of the second person pronoun here is complex. In one way it reminds readers that the text is also applicable to themselves: they too have free will and power to stand even in the postlapsarian world. But at least just as importantly it exposes Satan's divided view of his self. It exposes the gap that has opened up between what he once was and what he is now. The momentary exposure of the gap also allows the possibility of a move towards reducing or closing the gap, but this Satan rejects, and instead chooses to reinforce and widen it: "Be then his love accurst." This positioning of the self as object, as second person, is unnecessary for an unfallen being, who has a perfectly unified, unchanging self.

Satan understands "that a grateful mind / By owing owes not." This moment of clear-eyed understanding of the nature of his sin and the true reasons for it,[13] so different from the rhetoric of his public speeches in books 1 and 2, leads him to despair, which he expresses as:

> Which way I fly is hell; my self am hell;
> And in the lowest deep a lower deep
> Still threatening to devour me opens wide,
> To which the hell I suffer seems a heaven.　(4.75–78)

In considering whether repentance might still be possible, Satan compares his public image and private state:

> is there no place
> Left for repentance, none for pardon left?
> None left but by submission; and that word
> Disdain forbids me, and my dread of shame

---

[13] Tanner very usefully draws attention to the fact that motives such as pride and envy "mask etiological tautologies. . . . Such 'causes' simply throw explanation back upon free self-determination. Beyond this we cannot go" (49).

> Among the spirits beneath . . .
> . . . .
>   Ay me, they little know
> . . . .
> Under what torments inwardly I groan;
> While they adore me on the throne of hell,
> With diadem and sceptre high advanced
> The lower still I fall, only supreme
> In misery; such joy ambition finds. (4.79–83,86,88–92)

Satan here articulates his discovery of the gap which has opened up between his public and private selves. His recognition of this gap forces him into a revision of his private self to bring it closer to his public role. This process culminates in this soliloquy in the exclamation, "all good to me is lost; / Evil be thou my good" (4.109–10). What the reader is shown actually happening throughout this soliloquy, therefore, is Satan creating, through a dialectical process of self-examination, a totally evil self, one that has never quite so consciously existed before.[14]

His next soliloquy follows a very similar pattern. He sees Adam and Eve for the first time, is struck by their beauty and resemblance to God, and realizes that he "could love [them], so lively shines / In them divine resemblance." Being moved almost to love reawakens his better, compassionate self, which he then proceeds deliberately to repress. This same movement of sympathy, almost empathy, and then repression of his feelings is repeated twice more before he finally succeeds in overcoming his better self:

> And should I at your harmless innocence
> Melt, as I do, yet public reason just,
> Honour and empire with revenge enlarged,
> By conquering this new world, compels me now
> To do what else though damned I should abhor.
>   (4.388–92)

---

[14] Teskey has also noted this aspect of Satan's characterization. Satan, he says, "is revealed to himself and to us through repeated efforts of antithetical self-definition . . . Satan can only imagine what it is he has become by defining himself as the opposite of an other—God in particular, goodness in general—that represents what he is attempting to exorcise from himself" (20, n. 5). My reading clearly differs from this, in that I identify the dynamics of Satan's self-definition not in exorcising anything, but in bringing his private self more into line with the public role he has chosen to play.

Again we see the tension between the private and public selves forging a new evil self. The narrator drives home the point, emphasizing the political dimension as he does so: "So spake the fiend, and with necessity, / The tyrant's plea, excused his devilish deeds."[15]

The third Satanic soliloquy in book 4 seems to be a more traditional direct address to the audience, in that it serves to allow the reader to hear Satan's mind working on the problem of how to bring about the Fall of Man. We literally hear the hatching of the plot. However, this does not add anything to Satan's self-definition.

The two soliloquies in book 9, however, both present a situation similar to the first two, in book 4. Both reveal to the reader a process of deliberate repression of all finer feelings in order to create the Satanic self he feels his public role demands. As he searches through the garden for the snake, Satan is once again struck by the beauty of paradise. He is clearly delighted by the "Terrestrial heaven" he is passing through. But once again he deliberately represses and denies his pleasure and emotion: "With what delight could I have walked thee round, / If I could joy in aught" (9.114–15). His public role is once again appealed to, but this time the selfish nature of his tyranny is clearly revealed:

> To me shall be the glory sole among
> The infernal powers, in one day to have marred
> What he almighty styled, six nights and days
> Continued making . . .   (9.135–38)

The price he has to pay, however, is high. As he contemplates what it will feel like to enter the serpent, the horror is obvious:

> O foul descent! That I who erst contended
> With gods to sit the highest, am now constrained
> Into a beast, and mixed with bestial slime,
> This essence to incarnate and imbrute,
> That to the highth of deity aspired;
> But what will not ambition and revenge
> Descend to? Who aspires must down as low

---

[15] In *Tenure of Kings and Magistrates* (1649), Milton had defined a tyrant not in the usual terms of arbitrariness or cruelty, but in terms of selfishness: "A Tyrant whether by wrong or right comming to the Crown, is he who regarding neither Law nor the common good, reigns onely for himself and his faction" (CPW 3:212).

> As high he soared, obnoxious first or last
> To basest things.   (9.163–70)

He here discovers one of the lower deeps within himself which threatens to devour him. A moment later, as he enters the serpent through the
mouth, he is indeed symbolically devoured.

But perhaps the clearest example of Satan's self-definition comes in
his final soliloquy. The narrator compares the effect the sight of Eve has
on him to the effect a beautiful fresh country girl has on a city dweller,
and the narrator specifically notes that Eve's beauty suddenly makes him
forget his evil intention:

> Such pleasure took the serpent to behold
> This flowery plat, the sweet recess of Eve
> Thus early, thus alone; her heavenly form
> . . . .
>   . . . overawed
> His malice.   (9.455–57, 460–61)

Now when Satan recovers from his distraction, he has to remind himself
of who and what he is:

> Thoughts, whither have ye led me, with what sweet
> Compulsion thus transported to forget
> What hither brought us, hate, not love, nor hope
> Of Paradise for hell, hope here to taste
> Of pleasure, but all pleasure to destroy,
> Save what is in destroying, other joy
> To me is lost.   (9.473–79)

Having just felt such overwhelming pleasure that he stands "abstracted
. . . / From his own evil" and struck "stupidly good," he immediately
denies in these lines the capacity for any such emotion, and in so doing
again continues the work of creating his devilish self, the self that is
necessary for him to carry through his cruel plan. So, in each of the
three soliloquies examined, the internal act has been an act of self-
creation which represses his better, gentler self, thus reducing the gap
between his evil public role and his private self.

These soliloquies trace the process of creation of a self that had its
origin in sin, and, as Tanner remarks, sin "irrupts in an instant of radical
self-determination" (49). However, the sinful self is not immediately
fully formed, but must be gradually defined and learned. The process

delineated in *Paradise Lost* is one in which Satan defines his self as one approaching closer and closer to his evil public role. It is a self defined only in terms of himself and in relation to the evil other of his fellow fallen angels.[16]

Adam's and Eve's soliloquies are equally concerned with the creation of new selves. It is a critical commonplace to say that Eve convinces herself to fall in the soliloquy she delivers after the serpent finishes his temptation. She does this by using good scientific, deductive reasoning which depends upon the "objective" evidence of her senses (the serpent has eaten, has gained new powers, and is still alive, therefore . . .), and in so doing begins to create a new, independent self which will be unbound by the old prohibitions: "What fear I then," she says, "what hinders?" She is not yet fallen, though she is falling. The questions she asks remind the reader that the answers are available to her: she could, and should, have reminded herself that what she should fear, what hinders her, is God's one clear prohibition. She could have answered her questions, drawn back, and remained sinless. But of course she does not.

After her fall she rapidly continues this process of forging a new self, the start of which is signalled to the reader by the question: "But to Adam in what sort / Shall I appear?" Her new, duplicitous self is, like Satan, able to represent one emotion as its opposite. And, like Satan again, she is concerned to fashion a self which is consistent with this public persona (how she will appear to Adam) she now discovers she has. Her realization that God could replace her, and that Adam would be married to another woman, awakes in her the first sting of jealousy. However, she quickly decides to make sure that Adam shares her fate: "So dear I love him, that with him all deaths / I could endure, without him live no life" (9. 832–33). Alastair Fowler appositely observes that in these lines "in effect she is planning to kill Adam to ease her own mind."[17] In easing her mind, however, she reveals that it is herself, a new sinful self which she is creating, that she loves.

---

[16] In fact, being cut off from God and from their past in Heaven, all the fallen angels are forced to create their own sense of self in relation to themselves and to each other. Their language displays their lack of familiar anchorage points for their selves. Satan's first words in the poem are "If thou beest he," revealing that he cannot recognize his closest associate, Beelzebub. Moloch seems unsure whether the fallen angels' "substance be indeed divine." And Mammon advises the angels to "seek / Our own good from ourselves, and from our own / Live to ourselves" (1.84, 2.99, 252–54).

[17] Carey and Fowler, 905.

The precise status of the speech that I identify as Adam's first soliloquy (9.896–916) is slightly problematic. It is either not spoken aloud for Eve to hear, but is rather an internal monologue which the reader is privy to (for the narrator tells us that "First to himself he inward silence broke"), or alternatively it is a true soliloquy which is not addressed to Eve, even though she may be able to hear it (for the narrator inserts between this speech and the next the comment "So having said ... / ... his words to Eve he turned" [9.917–20]). Either way, it is clear that the speech is not part of the dialogue between Adam and Eve, and must therefore be regarded as a soliloquy of some kind.

In this soliloquy, too, a process of forging a new self is at work. It is noticeable that Adam is more concerned with the effect of Eve's fall on himself than with Eve's fate. He rapidly moves from "How can I live without thee" to a self which can even perceive Paradise as composed of "wild woods" (9.908–10). Like Eve, he too contemplates the possibility of God creating another Eve, but, like Eve again, rejects it on selfish grounds: "yet loss of thee / Would never from my heart" (9.912–13). Adam's process of falling here is a falling into self-love, which accords well with St. Thomas Aquinas's statement that "inordinate self-love is the cause of all sin."[18]

Adam's second soliloquy (10.720–862) is concerned with the construction of a fallen self. It too is filled with self-love. He never gives a thought to Eve, to how she might be coping with her altered state. His thoughts revolve around his own problems: "What can I increase / Or multiply, but curses on my head?" (10.731–32). And like Satan and Eve, he too finds that he has taken on a new public role or persona which is some distance from his old self, when he imagines the attitude of later generations towards him (10.733–37 and 819–22). This gap is revealed vividly when he suddenly changes from subject to object position as he ponders God's justice for the first time:

> Inexplicable
> Thy justice seems; yet to say truth, too late,
> I thus contest; then should have been refused
> Those terms whatever, when they were proposed:
> Thou didst accept them; wilt thou enjoy the good,
> Then cavil the conditions? And though God

---

[18] St. Thomas Aquinas, *Summa Theologicæ*, trans. John Fearon (London: Blackfriars, 1968), vol. 25, 1a2æ, q. 77, art. 4, p. 173.

> Made thee without thy leave, what if thy son
> Prove disobedient, and reproved, retort,
> Wherefore didst thou beget me?   (10.754–62)

This positioning of the self as object, as second person, has only been available to Satan before, as noted above.

In other ways, too, the pattern of his thinking resembles Satan's first soliloquy, forming a dialectic of evasions, in which he blames God for his situation, followed by moments of insight when the truth of his condition "Comes thundering back" on his "defenceless head" (10.814–15). The difference is that this time the process leads to a positive conclusion in that Adam is forced to admit that

> all my evasions vain
> And reasonings, though through mazes, lead me still
> But to my own conviction: ...   (10.829–31)

And so Adam has reached the first stage of repentance, recognition of sin.[19] In so doing he has taken the first step towards forging the kind of postlapsarian self which is required of a Christian, even though the soliloquy ends on a note reinforcing the parallel with Satan:

> O conscience! into what abyss of fears
> And horrors hast thou driven me; out of which
> I find no way, from deep to deeper plunged!
>   (10.842–44)

His self-enclosure, which is despair, prevents him from moving further along the road to true repentance, and he will have to wait for Eve to show him the way forward.

Nevertheless, the fallen self that Adam begins to fashion in this soliloquy is radically different from Satan's. He rejects all movements leading him further into sin, and sets about creating a fallen self that will allow a return to God. He accepts his punishment and the consequences it implies for his radically changed self: "I submit, his doom is fair, / That dust I am, and shall to dust return" (10.769–70). Similarly, he comes to accept that his new self is one which justly includes the "sense of endless woes" for he can convince himself that "On me, me only, as the source and spring / Of all corruption, all the blame lights due"

---

[19] See *Christian Doctrine* 1.19, CPW 6:468.

(10.832–33). Although he himself realizes that he has gone too far in
these lines, and has fallen into self-love and self-pity, this allows him to
understand how divided and self-contradictory his self is (again in the
second person):

> Thus what thou desirest
> And what thou fear'st, alike destroys all hope
> Of refuge . . .   (10.837–39)

But despite this, his creation of a fallen yet submissive, humble self will
save him from being "from deep to deeper plunged" along with Satan.

The opening soliloquy of *Samson Agonistes* reveals that Samson's
predicament and condition closely resemble Adam's in his second
soliloquy. Both give way to despair, and both are afflicted by a sense of
Heaven's desertion. Like the angels at the opening of *Paradise Lost,* and
like Adam and Eve after their falls, Samson too is faced with a gap
between "what once [he] was, and what [is] now" (22) that challenges
his familiar sense of himself, and that forces him to reassess his identity.
His opening soliloquy is concerned with precisely this distance:

> Why was my breeding ordered and prescribed
> As of a person separate to God,
> Designed for great exploits; if I must die
> Betrayed, captived, and both my eyes put out,
> Made of my enemies the scorn and gaze;
> To grind in brazen fetters under task
> With this heaven-gifted strength?   (*SA* 30–36)

His complaint leads to the bitterly ironic "Ask for this great deliverer
now, and find him / Eyeless in Gaza at the mill with slaves" (40–41).
But this descent into self-pity brings him up short at the realization that
his thoughts are blasphemous: "Yet stay, let me not rashly call in doubt
/ Divine prediction" (43–44). Just as Adam's self-pity forces him to
realize his own divided self, so Samson's leads him to a closer understanding of his divided self: "Whom have I to complain of but myself?"
(46). He does not quite achieve the object position that Adam does, but
he does come close to such a view of himself.

At the beginning of the poem Samson is, as Mary Ann Radzinowicz elegantly argues,

> a divided self, one aspect of whom proposes inflexible codes of
> behaviour on the other. Both selves are present as subjects: "if

I must die" are the words of a self-solicitous subject; "I must
not quarrel" is the comment of a self-denying subject. . . . In
experiencing the torments of his divided self, he tries to protect
his vulnerable core by playing off his private self against a
public self and by assuming an external role in public life, the
role of a laboring fallen hero.[20]

At the beginning of the poem, there is no doubt that the self-solicitous
self is predominant. Yet the self-denying self is aware that he must look
within himself for the reason for his plight:

> what if all foretold
> Had been fulfilled but through mine own default,
> Whom have I to complain of but myself?
>
> (SA 44–46)

The aspect of himself that he now identifies as the cause of his condition
is, however, the wrong one: "O impotence of mind, in body strong!"
(52); "strength is my bane, / And proves the source of all my miseries"
(63–64).

The impassioned complaint about loss of sight which follows this
has obvious spiritual connotations which the text itself makes clear:

> O first-created beam, and thou great word,
> Let there be light, and light was over all;
> Why am I thus bereaved thy prime decree?
>
> (SA 83–85)

Although the theological dimension of the complaint which these lines
lead the reader towards is obvious, there is another aspect, which links
backwards to Samson's previous words. He asks:

> if it be true
> That light is in the soul,
> She all in every part; why was the sight
> To such a tender ball as the eye confined?
>
> (SA 91–94)

This also can be read as referring to God illuminating the soul. But it
also raises the idea of internal light, of understanding, of literally *insight*.

---

[20] Mary Ann Radzinowicz, *Toward "Samson Agonistes": The Growth of Milton's Mind*
(Princeton: Princeton Univ. Press, 1978), 18.

It is precisely this that Samson lacks at the beginning of the poem, as is proved by his wrong identification of the source of all his miseries.

Despite his regular attempts to begin the formation of a humble self ("But peace, I must not quarrel with the will / Of highest dispensation" [*SA* 60–61]), his lack of insight prevents him, at this stage of the poem, creating a self truly capable of humility and repentance. His self-pity instead perversely reinforces his pride, and he positions himself, rather like Satan, down as low as he aspires; he has, he says, "Inferior to the vilest now become / Of man or worm" (73–74). He is exposed "still as a fool," "dead more than half." Only pride, not true humility, can support such a vision of the self. And so the proud, self-pitying self that he affirms in the final half of his soliloquy is unable to make the advances that Adam is capable of. Those changes in his self that will bring him the possibility of a new relationship with God are precisely the ones that he will have to make as the poem progresses, and which form the dramatic process of the poem.

In *Paradise Regained* there are three soliloquies, one by Mary and two by the Son. Mary is, by definition, a fallen being, and so, to extend Broadbent's claim, we might expect her to soliloquize. Mary's brief appearances in *Paradise Regained* are so low-key that most critics seem to do little more than note her presence in the poem.[21] But even a Protestant poet can allow the second Eve an important role. In fact, Mary's own soliloquy in book 2 is important, for it shares the same basic structure as Adam's soliloquy after the Fall. It begins with a moment of human doubt and even bitterness at her fate: "O what avails me now that honour high / To have conceived of God" (*PR* 2.66–67). She then goes on to complain about the difficulties and dangers of her life since the birth of Jesus. Her expectations are all of trouble, "as old Simeon plain foretold" (87). And her complaint reaches its height in the bitterly ironic comment, "this is my favoured lot, / My exaltation to afflictions high" (91–92). This concentration on her own feelings and disappointments is remarkable in the second Eve. It comes very close to a selfish questioning of God's wisdom. But it does not quite go so far. She has

---

[21] For example, Radzinowicz mentions her name just twice, on consecutive lines on p. 333, in a book of over 400 pages. And in *Poet of Exile: A Study of Milton's Poetry* (New Haven: Yale Univ. Press, 1980), Louis L. Martz does no more than briefly describe the process of her thoughts (255).

learned to be patient and to trust her difficult son, and to wait humbly
for God to clear her understanding:

> when twelve years he scarce had seen,
> I lost him, but so found, as well I saw
> He could not lose himself; but went about
> His Father's business; what he meant I mused,
> Since understand.   (*PR* 2.96–100)

She is fully human, and her resigned "But I to wait with patience am
inured" (102) could be echoed by many a mother throughout history.
But it is exactly this humble acceptance of God's will, her deliberate
creation, or perhaps confirmation of a self that can say "Afflicted I may
be, it seems, and blest; / I will not argue that, nor will repine" (93–94)
which redeems her and saves her from her own selfish complaint: the
narrator reinforces this conclusion with his parting glance at her as she
"with thoughts / Meekly composed awaited the fulfilling" (107–8). She
is, then, the structural equivalent of Eve in *Paradise Lost,* tempted by
selfish concern to question God's ways, but finally able to overcome her
self and trust in God's providence.

The hero of *Paradise Regained* is very different from the characters
of *Paradise Lost* or *Samson Agonistes,* for Jesus is the perfect human being.
Yet he is nevertheless nothing more than an ordinary man, as is made
clear at the beginning of the poem by God the Father, for Satan

> now shall know I can produce a man
> Of female seed, far abler to resist
> All his solicitations.   (*PR* 1.150–52)

And even Satan, having completed his tests to discover whether the Son
of God is merely human, finds that Jesus is "firm / To the utmost of
mere man both wise and good, / Not more" (*PR* 4.534–36).

Although Jesus appears completely sure of his identity as the Son of
God and has no doubts about his faith, he is as yet unsure about how he
is to fulfill his Father's will. At the beginning of the poem, his first
words, which strongly and disturbingly echo the opening of Samson's
soliloquy, indicate that he is confused about the contrast between what
he knows to be his destiny and his life circumstances:

> O what a multitude of thoughts at once
> Awakened in me swarm, while I consider
> What from within I feel myself, and hear

> What from without comes often to my ears,
> Ill sorting with my present state compared.
> (PR 1.196–200)

The intensive soul-searching described in this speech, and indeed in Samson's, recalls the Puritan emphasis on searching one's life and soul for evidence of God's grace. It also brings up the problem, familiar to members of radical sects in the seventeenth century, of how one can be sure that the signs of grace one finds are not just selfish imagination. Jesus is able to solve this problem by a study of the scriptures:

> I again revolved
> The Law and prophets, searching what was writ
> Concerning the Messiah, to our scribes
> Known partly, and soon found of whom they spake
> I am.   (PR 1.259–63)

Jesus is doing exactly as he should, using the Bible in precisely the same way as Milton does in *Christian Doctrine* to ensure that his theology is founded firmly: "The rule and canon of faith ... is scripture alone ... In controversies there is no arbitrator except scripture, or rather, each man is his own arbitrator, so long as he follows scripture and the Spirit of God."[22]

The doubt expressed in the opening lines of the soliloquy clearly focuses the reader's attention on the gap between what Jesus feels himself to be and the public role that he is now expected to take on. In an attempt to reduce this gap he reviews his life, commenting on the way his self-definition has changed. When he was a child he thought himself "born to promote all truth, / All righteous things" (*PR* 1.205–6), but also "to do / What might be public good" (1.203–4). But he understood the means by which he was to achieve these ends wrongly: he imagined "victorious deeds," "heroic acts" which would "subdue and quell o'er all the earth / Brute violence and proud tyrannic power" (1.218–19). And despite the fact that even at that stage of development he understood that it is "more humane, more heavenly first / By winning words

---

[22] CPW 6:585. It is also worth quoting another passage here, which emphasizes Milton's literal view of the nature of scripture as being illumination by the Holy Spirit: "We have, particularly under the gospel, a double scripture. There is the external scripture of the written word and the internal scripture of the Holy Spirit which he, according to God's promise, has engraved upon the hearts of believers" (587).

to conquer willing hearts, / And make persuasion do the work of fear"
(1.221–23), he is still prepared to have to use force on the "stubborn."

His mother's revelation of his authentic identity as the Son of God
forces him into the examination of scriptures for confirmation of what
she says. With confirmation of his identity he gains deeper insight into
the kind of self that he must become: a self which must accept "many a
hard assay even to the death, / Ere I the promised kingdom can attain"
(1.264–65). The baptism he regards not as further confirmation of
identity, but rather as a sign that the time is "Now full, that I no more
should live obscure" (1.287).

The memories Jesus calls to mind in this first soliloquy thus serve to
show that he is convinced of his identity and his mission, but does not
know "How best the mighty work he might begin / Of saviour to
mankind" (PR 1.186–87).[23] Nevertheless, he is confident that God will
reveal his will:

> And now by some strong motion I am led
> Into this wilderness, to what intent
> I learn not yet, perhaps I need not know;
> For what concerns my knowledge God reveals.
>
> (PR 1.290–93)

So saying, he displays precisely the attitude that Eve should have taken
on being led to the Tree of Knowledge. His review of how his self-
definition has changed and developed has brought him to the point
where he is ready to be tested.

Jesus's second soliloquy is very short (PR 2.245–59), but it is just as
important as the first. It comes directly after the first temptation, the temptation of the stones, has failed. At the end of that temptation Satan has un-
settled Jesus's mind with a "sly preface to return" which has left Jesus "vacant" (2.115–16). This, we are told by the narrator, causes Jesus to review
his sense of self and his mission again, just as he did in the first soliloquy:

> tracing the desert wild,
> Sole but with holiest meditations fed,

---

[23] Martz sees the process of discovery in the Son in rather different terms. He claims that
Jesus has to discover "what it means to be pronounced the Son of God" (252). Martz argues
that the poem thus presents every reader with a process of self-discovery, so that they, too,
can appreciate what is involved in being a son of God. Such a view is not at odds with my
reading, but it does have a different emphasis.

> Into himself descended, and at once
> All his great work to come before him set;
> How to begin, how to accomplish best
> His end of being on earth, and mission high.
>
>   (2.109–14)

If Jesus's self-identity is based upon nothing but himself, he will indeed be left vacant, and so he must once again descend into himself to confirm that he is truly the Son of God.

Traces of these unspoken meditations are to be found in the second soliloquy. Jesus's problems have been complicated during the time of the devils' council by the onset of hunger.[24] The opening line of his solilo-quy, "Where will this end" (*PR* 2.245), suggests not only that he is concerned about his hunger, but also that his descent into himself during the unspoken meditations has not been completed, and that this second soliloquy is perhaps the conclusion of those extended meditations. The line also echoes the questionings of God's wisdom that are found in

---

[24] The poem is ambiguous about whether Jesus is hungry during the first temptation. William B. Hunter claims that "the worst confusion of the whole poem is generally acknowl-edged to be the time when Jesus first becomes hungry and when the first night falls" ("The Double Set of Temptations in *Paradise Regained*," *MS* 14 [1980]: 184). I do not wish to address the problem of when the first night falls. However, the difficulty over hunger can, I think, be explained by a glance at the biblical text Milton was following. Hunter himself recognizes that the poem is at least partially based on Luke 4.1–13. But he ignores the fact that the Bible text is explicit that Jesus was in the wilderness "*Being forty days tempted of the devil*. And in those days he did eat nothing: and when they were ended, he afterward hungered*" (my emphasis). Luke then proceeds to tell the story of the three temptations, but leaves it open whether these temptations occurred during the forty days of fasting or after Jesus became hungry. Luke also leaves open exactly how long Jesus was in the wilderness. Hunter is therefore wrong when he rejects Barbara Lewalski's statement that "Christ does not actually experience hunger until Book II" (*Milton's Brief Epic* [Providence: Brown Univ. Press, 1966], 202) on the grounds that "this ignores the biblical account that Jesus was hungry before the first temptation" (184). In fact, if Hunter had argued that Milton was following Matthew 4.2–3, he would have had a case, for Matthew is arguably much clearer about the sequence of events, placing the three temptations after Jesus had become aware of his hunger. What makes an appeal to Matthew problematic is that Milton follows Luke's order for the temptations, not Matthew's.

I suggest that Milton is interpreting the text of Luke in such a way that he places the temptation to turn stones into bread during the forty days of fasting, when, according to Mark, Jesus was either constantly or regularly tempted by the devil, but was not hungry. Milton's next temptation, to eat of the banquet, then takes place after Jesus has felt the first pangs of hunger, as is made explicit in the poem.

Adam's and Mary's soliloquies.[25] However, the perfect man immediately suppresses this by confirming his humble reliance upon God's providence. The moves of his self-fashioning here are obvious: his denial of independent virtue ("that fast / To virtue I impute not" [2.247–48]); his affirmation that hunger is not something important to him ("I content me," "Nor mind it, fed with better thoughts" [2.256,258]); and his affirmation of trust in God's providence. He thus creates and confirms the kind of self that would have saved Adam and Eve, and will render him proof against the temptations of Satan. Yet it is clearly a self which is wholly human, and therefore available for even fallen beings to emulate.

This analysis of the soliloquies in Milton's major poems has shown that although Broadbent's claim is far too strong, there does seem to be a germ of truth in it. The soliloquy proves to be an appropriate technique for the portrayal of a character forging a new self because it is a technique perfectly suited to revealing a character's state of self-enclosure, though not quite in the way that Harada proposes. It seems that all the characters who soliloquize perceive a gap between their former and present selves and the public role they now find they have to perform. The soliloquies trace the processs by which the characters attempt to bring their self-definition more into line with their altered circumstances. These acts of self-creation are the internal acts (to extend Steadman's insight) which make possible an external, physical act. In all these poems Milton uses soliloquy to present a dynamic sense of self which invariably involves a potential questioning of God's wisdom and providence, and therefore at least a possible movement away from God, before the characters (excepting Satan) discover how to construct a self which contains the capacity for movement in the opposite direction. In this way, Milton's soliloquies always expose at least the potential for dangerous self-enclosure in the character who soliloquizes, even in Jesus himself.

UNIVERSITY OF TAMPERE, FINLAND

[25] This feature of Milton's text provides yet another piece of evidence for reading Milton's Jesus as, from a strictly orthodox Christian point of view, an Arian interpretation of Christ. In one of the more recent considerations of this old problem, Thomas Langford argues that "Milton's depiction of a human Christ is not an Arian aberration from orthodoxy, but a reflection of the Bible he knew well, and which he regarded above the creeds" ("The Nature of the Christ in *Paradise Regained,*" *MQ* 16 [1982]: 63). This certainly emphasizes Milton's views on the primacy of scripture over received Church doctrine, but it does no more than show where Milton's reading of the Bible differs from orthodoxy rather than defend him from the Arian heresy.

Douglas Chambers

"IMPROV'D BY TRACT OF TIME": ART'S SYNOPTICON IN *PARADISE LOST* BOOK 12

THE FINAL BOOKS OF *PARADISE LOST* FOREGROUND A NARRA-
tological issue that has been evident throughout the poem and that is part
of the epic tradition: the difference between event and its narration.
Milton's method here is not simply his own but one that he shares with
(and inherits from) many works of visual art in the Renaissance, chiefly, as
I shall demonstrate, in the widely popular art of tapestry.[1]

As in much of the "synoptic" art of this period, time is as much a
meaning as a frame. Milton's poetic Adam who first sees and then hears
forward into our time is an Adam who listens in his time to a voice that
is outside of time. All of these times are also within the poem's time, the
time that we as readers inhabit in the process of reading.

It is in the identification of Adam's experience with the reader's in the
very process of reading that Milton's literary art is revolutionary. The
"visions" of the last two books are not simply parallel to our experience (as
Vergil's are to Augustan Rome); those visions are of the selves that we
discover. Our experience becomes like Adam's as his becomes like ours;
we turn from spectacle with its dangers of "idle show" towards the word,
from being spectators toward being understanders. In so doing, we touch
the poem into its real life, a life akin to that which the intelligent spectator
must give to Michelangelo's God in the Sistine Chapel. The hand of God
does not quite touch the hand of Adam; we make the connection by
understanding the meaning.

---

[1] Cf. Diane McColley's recent book, *A Gust for Paradise: Milton's Eden and the Visual Arts*
(Urbana: Univ. of Illinois Press, 1993).

The bases of this narratology are the artistic and historic conventions of typology that Milton shares with early modern works in the visual arts; these are a commonplace of Judaeo-Christian history. The kind of reading that they presuppose could also be found endlessly repeated in medieval drama, painting and sculpture.[2] The habit of depicting all sacred history in one work of art, however, has many complex narrative manifestations. The Ghiberti doors on the Baptistry in Florence are one example and Andrea Pisano's panels for the Duomo are another.

Similar "synoptica" would have been seen by Milton in the mosaics of St. Mark's in Venice or around the main door of San Petronio in Bologna where the door, as in Florence, becomes the entrance into true narrative meaning. Indeed, when Milton was staying in Florence the whole of the chancel (*tribuna*) of San Lorenzo, the Medici church which was next to the Paradiso Gaddi in which he was entertained, contained a cycle of frescoes by Pontormo depicting the sacred history of the world from the Creation to the Last Judgment. The creation of Eve and the Last Judgment are part of one narrative sequence.

Such works as Holbein's *Allegory of the Old and New Testament,* the title-page of the German New Testament, or an anonymous English-Netherlandish painting of the first quarter of the seventeenth century [fig. 1] indicate that this synchronicity was also a feature of protestant art. Johann Heinrich Glaser's engraving of Adam and Eve [fig. 2] takes the process one step further, however, hiding anamorphically under its ostensible subject (the Fall) its true significance, visible only in the true perspective of the instructed eye: the Redemption.

Even in Milton's England, the story of the sixteenth-century glass in the chapel of Hatfield House was a typological one, tracing the universal *historia salvationis* on a more modest scale than the more familiar early sixteenth-century windows at King's College, Cambridge, which Milton must have known.[3] At York, during the Civil War, Marvell's patron, General Fairfax, gave instruction to his troops not to destroy the medieval

---

[2] Barbara Lewalski, "Typological Symbolism and 'The Progress of the Soul' in 17th Century Literature," in *Literary Uses of Typology,* ed. Earl Miner (Princeton: Princeton Univ. Press, 1977), 104.

[3] For example, there are carvings in the Chapter House in Salisbury, on the screen at Exeter, and there is a series of wall paintings in Easby Parish Church near Richmond, Yorks. Cf. the series of four paintings of the Creation, the Brazen Serpent, the Last Judgment and the Glory of Paradise by the sixteenth-century Venetian, Andrea Vincentino, in the Basilica of the Frari in Venice.

Fig. 1. Anonymous seventeenth-century English-Netherlandish painting. *Allegory of the Old and New Law.* Courtesy of the Victoria and Albert Museum, London.

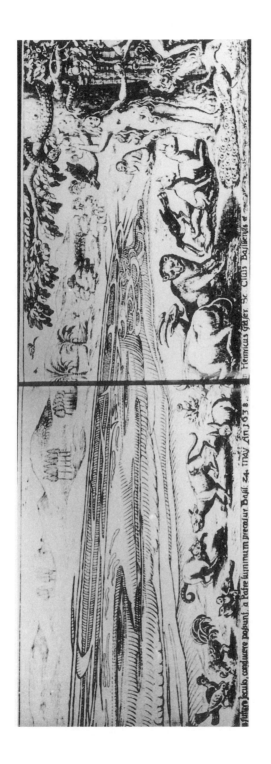

Fig. 2. Johann Heinrich Glaser. Anamorphic engraving. *Christ with the Crown of Thorns flanked by the Fall and the Expulsion*. 1638.

stained glass in the Minster, of which the jewel is John Thornton's great east window which traces again the story of redemption from the Creation of Adam through the Fall, and the Expulsion to the Apocalypse.

The Arena Chapel in Padua, painted by Giotto, however, is a more complex example of this sort of narrative cycle. It is also one that both Sir Henry Wotton and the Arundel circle, with whom Milton was acquainted, would have recommended to him. So dense is its subject that the viewer has to walk around the chapel three times in order to follow its narrative. In the process, what emerges is that the order in which events happened is not necessarily the order in which they are told or the order in which the viewer experiences them. Here the spectator moves beyond the world of typology into a narrative multivalency that implies his "erected wit" present in the "text."

This disjunction between what James Elkins has called "the order of occurrence," "the order of telling," and "the order of reading" reflects a common disjunction in Renaissance narratives, a disjunction that is instructive in the reading of *Paradise Lost*.

> It would be anachronistic to say that subversions are built into the structure of the pictorial narrative itself—but it is certainly true that the idea of complexity was already well developed in written narratives, so that visual artists were alert to the subversions that became fashionable in the time of Ariosto, Sannazaro, Boiardo, and Michelangelo. What the Renaissance did not give up was the essential referent, the story-line itself and its order(s) of occurrence.[4]

All of this directs us again to reading, to the necessity of our finding in diverse actions the one continuing thread of providential design. What Milton asks of his reader is only an extension of what contemporary engravers expected of theirs. In the title-page of Du Bartas's *Diuine Weekes* [fig. 3], the engraver (Renold Elstrack) presents us with the author's sense of a providential history in which the illustration takes us from the creation of Eve to the Fall, and then to Abraham and Isaac, Judith and Holofernes, Isaiah, and finally to Joseph and Potiphar's wife.

---

[4] Elkins, "On the Impossibility of Stories: the Anti-narrative and Non-narrative Impulse in Modern Painting," *Word & Image* 7 (1991): 355. I am indebted to Elkins for his account of the Arena Chapel and of the three orders of narrative.

Fig. 3. Renold Elstrack. Engraved title-page for Guillaume de Salluste Du
Bartas, *Diuine Weekes and Workes*. London, 1608.

"The relation of language to painting is an infinite relation," Michel Foucault has observed in writing about Velasquez's painting *Las Meninas:*

> It is not that words are imperfect, or that, when confronted by the visible, they prove superbly inadequate. Neither can be reduced to the other's term: it is in vain that we say what we see; what we see never resides in what we say.[5]

Ernest Gilman offers a response to Foucault by insisting on the primacy of our *experience* of the work over the so-called "terms" of the work itself.

> The experience of a witness to a literary text, and to a painting are comparable in a way the objects themselves are not. Both "reading" and "seeing" include a processional and an integrative, or reflective, phase which together generate reading.[6]

And he goes on to identify this simultaneous pattern of significance with the *dianoia* that Northrop Frye finds in Aristotle. Certainly at least some of these questions of art are as old as Aristotle's *topoi.*

This problem of right reading also presents itself more forcefully in relation to the most popular of the decorative arts in the late sixteenth and early seventeenth centuries, the art of tapestry. "In reading a narrative tapestry," Jill Levenson has observed,

> the observer had to discern a sequence of events and its implications from an immense composition of figures and details. He had to discover the chronology of episodes, the relationships among characters, the causal links between incidents, and the themes which informed the action. A storied tapestry which attracted and held its viewers' attention offered not only pleasure but also edification.[7]

That these tapestries strongly influenced late sixteenth and early seventeenth-century readings of classical mythology is no less in doubt than that

---

[5] Foucault, *The Order of Things* [*Le Mot et Les Choses*] (London: Tavistock Press, 1979), 9.

[6] Gilman, *The Curious Perspective* (New Haven: Yale Univ. Press, 1978), 10. Cf. G. K. Chesterton's defense of the symbolist paintings of George Frederic Watts, that they were not simply illustrative of an idea already extant in words, but responded to the same central myth from which the verbal description also arose.

[7] Levenson, "Shakespeare's *Troilus and Cressida* and the Monumental Tradition in Tapestries and Literature," *Renaissance Drama* 7 (1976): 46–47.

they also shaped expectations of a narrative that was both sequential and immediate, in other words, synoptic. The thousands of tapestry hangings in the collection of Charles I included not only the common secular histories of Meleager, Aeneas, Hercules, Hector, Hippolitus, Alexander, and Hannibal and Scipio, but sacred history as well.

Among the tapestries reserved for Cromwell's use from the sale of the King's goods we may be somewhat surprised to find *Twelve Peeces of y' History of. Pleasance. and Cupid*[8] and five of Vulcan and Venus,[9] the latter for his bedchamber. Less surprising, aside from the sets of classical and historical tapestries that included a set of twelve of the siege of Troy and four of the history of Charlemagne,[10] were the sets of tapestries of biblical events. Among those recorded as set aside "in His Highness [Cromwell's] Service" were a set of ten of the story of Abraham (*Inv.* 158:3), four of Joshua (*Inv.* 158:4), nine of Tobias (*Inv.* 158:5), eight of Hezekiah (*Inv.* 75:5), nine of Esther and Ahasuerus (*Inv.* 162:50), six of Samson (*Inv.* 342:213), and nine of St. Paul (*Inv.* 158:6).

The lesson of synoptic history is also the burden of the great sets of Brussels tapestries of the fifteenth and sixteenth centuries. Whether mythological or from sacred or secular history, these tapestries inhabit an aesthetic world where history is not the 'old mouse-eaten records' that Sidney abused, but the manifestation of transforming Providence within time. They bring into focus in one work both the sequential world of time and the eternal world of truth. Like Spenser's "short time's endless monument," they teach us to read truth in terms of value, not statistics, quality not quantity. Paradise, as Michael explains at the end of his instruction in books 11 and 12, is not a place in space and time. Eve's mistake has been to think of it in those terms. Paradise is an understanding of the spirit where, as Raphael has explained to Adam, men might

[8] Oliver Millar, ed., *Inventories and Valuations of the King's Goods,* Walpole Society, vol. 43 (London, 1972), 161:38, referred to in the text as *Inv.*

[9] Ernest Law, *The History of Hampton Court* (London, 1888), 2, 280. These tapestries were probably part of one of the three sets on this subject that were the first products of the Mortlake tapestry works (1622–25). They were based on cartoons from Henry VIII's set of Brussels tapestries, cartoons done by Giacomo della Riviera who also worked for the Barberini workshops in Rome. See George Wingfield Digby, "Masterpieces from Mortlake," *Discovering Antiques* 7 (London: B. P. C. Publishing, 1977): 157–58.

[10] Similar to these, and akin to the traditional "Triumphs of Petrarch" tapestries, was a set of tapestries for which both Rubens and Pietro da Cortona did the cartoons of the "Story of Constantine." A set of these was in the Palazzo Barberini when Milton was there in 1638.

at last turn all to spirit,
Improv'd by tract of time, and wing'd ascend
Ethereal, as wee, or may at choice
Here or in Heavenly Paradises dwell.   (5.497–500)

Michael's rebuke in books 11 and 12 is as much to the sentimental narrative reader as to Adam. And like Michael, but in a fallen world of confusing time, these tapestries instruct about a truth that outlasts time. Only in the world of art is this possible, and in graphic art it is especially obvious. "Graphic art had to summarize the account in one way or another; it could not indulge what J. Huizinga calls the 'quantitative method' of the large mediaeval romances."[11] No more could Milton's epic. His turning away from a romance subject (foregrounded at the beginning of book 9) is also an abjuration of romance form. The "notes" that are "turned to tragic" demand the sort of dramatic concision that is evident in the organisation of the Brussels tapestries.

If the collecting of paintings was confined to a relatively small circle in early seventeenth-century England, the same was not true of tapestries, with their obviously practical function in unheated stone houses. In 1650, the year before the onset of his blindness, Milton acquired from the king's goods "such hangings as shall bee sufficient for the furnishing of his Lodgings."[12]

Accounts of ordinary country-house collections of tapestries are harder to come by than the royal inventories. At Holyrood House, for example, we know that Mary Queen of Scots had a set of eight pieces of the Judgment of Paris, eight of the "*Saling of Aeneas,*" and eight of the labors of Hercules.[13] She herself was later the house-prisoner of Bess of Hardwick, the countess of Shrewsbury, who at Hardwick Hall had surrounded the High Great Chamber with a set of tapestries of the story of Ulysses.

At Kenilworth, Sir Philip Sidney's uncle, Robert Dudley, earl of Leicester, had in 1583 "six peeces of the history of Hercules," "seven pieces of Jesabell," "eight pieces of Judith and Holofernes," "five pieces of the story of David," "six pieces of the Story of Abraham," "five pieces of the story of Sampson," "nyne faire peeces of the story of Hippolitus," "eight pieces of the story of Alexander the Great," "six pieces of the story

[11] Levenson, 48.

[12] J. Milton French, *The Life Records of Milton* (New Brunswick, N.J.: Rutgers Univ. Press, 1950), 2:314.

[13] W. G. Thomson, *A History of Tapestry* (Menston, Yorks.: E. P. Publishing, 1973), 109.

of Namaan," "eight pieces of the story of Jacob," and "four pieces of Saul," along with a number of other biblical and historical hangings.[14]

Both sacred and secular tapestries taught similar lessons: not only that providence ruled in history but that the true significance of this history was to be found not in mere chronology but in observing the workings of eternity in time. The *Story of Abraham* that Leicester possessed was a tapestry set that was very popular and featured more than once in the Royal collection. It included *The Sacrifice of Isaac,* the last both a potent typology of the Crucifixion and the subject of a very popular multi-block engraving by Titian that also treated the subject synchronically.

This tapestry set was Brussels work, created by William Pannemaker about 1530; similar sets of the stories of Genesis were also very common. "A tapistrie of the *historie of the Creatioun* in worsett contening nyne peces," recorded among the movables in Holyrood House in Mary Queen of Scots' reign,[15] may well have been part of another Brussels set of the Creation (1525–1550) possibly by van Aelst, for which Raphael did the cartoons. Parts of this set still survive elsewhere, including *The Creation of the Animals, The Creation of Adam, Adam taken into the Garden, Adam Naming the Animals, Eve Presented to Adam, The Fall, The Judgment of Adam and Eve, The Expulsion, Adam Tilling, Abel's Offering, Cain and Abel,* and *Cain's Flight.*[16] A similar set exists of *The Story of Noah* and of *The Building of the Tower of Babel.* Raphael's famous cartoons for the New Testament were bought by Charles I as designs for the tapestry factory at Mortlake and preserved for state use by Cromwell.

To look at any of these sets of sacred histories without reading their significance is to reduce them to mere decoration. Their proper effect is that the viewer, like Adam, be "gently instructed" (12. 556). The Old (and New) Testament history they present is one that takes us to book 12 of *Paradise Lost,* and the meaning is the providential one that Adam begins to make happen by his accepting exclamation: "O goodness infinite, goodness immense! / That all this good of evil shall produce, / And evil turn to good" (12.469–71). Out of an understanding of sacred history comes Adam's (and the reader's) recognition of God's providence, "Merciful over all his works, with good / Still overcoming evil" (12.565–66). This "sum

---

[14] *Royal Commission on Historical Manuscripts. Lord De L'Isle and Dudley* (London, 1925), 1:278–79.

[15] Thomson, 109.

[16] These sets are in the Academia in Florence and Wawel Castle in Cracow.

of wisdom," as Michael calls it, is history's instruction to the faithful reader; out of the chaotic atomism of the postlapsarian world faith finds coherence.

Among the sets of tapestries in the Caroline collection was one of *The Seven Deadly Sins,* a set purchased by Cardinal Wolsey from Richard Gresham for the Legate's Chamber at Hampton Court. These anonymous Brussels tapestries formed only one of a number of similar sets.[17] In them are depicted "the religious history of the Redemption as it appears in the various cycles of Miracle Plays, and the moral allegory of the Conflict of Virtues and Vices—between themselves and in aiding or attacking Mankind."[18] D. T. B. Wood wrote also that it was "perfectly criminal, from an historical point of view, to treat one of these eight pieces as if it stood alone."[19]

In the 1659 inventory of Hampton Court, these tapestries were recorded as among Cromwell's goods "In Paradice Roome." What is most interesting about them to a reader of Milton is their demanding narrative scheme. Like Mantegna's famous series of paintings, *The Triumph of Caesar* (also reserved by Cromwell for the Throne Room at Hampton Court), these tapestries depended upon an almost kinetic narrative that moved through a series of distinct panels. But their scheme was even more dependent upon the reader's understanding eye than the complex set based on Petrarch's *Trionfi* that Cromwell also reserved to his use (here *The Triumph of Death over Chastity, The Triumph of Fame over Death,* and *The Trimph of Time over Fame*).

In *The Seven Deadly Sins* series we proceed from a tapestry of *The Creation and Fall* to one of *The Last Judgment* through eight panels in which historical, tropological, and anagogical are all present in one narrative. The consistent characters in each are "Homo" and Christ, and the story, like Milton's, proceeds from loss of Eden by man in the first panel to restoration by "one greater man" in the eighth. Wood has labeled these tapestries consecutively: *Creation, Deadly Sins* (2), *Allegorical Scenes from the New Testament, Combat of Virtues and Vice, Christ Inspiring Faith, Triumph of Christianity,* and *Last Judgment.*

The author of these tapestries, which were made in Brussels about 1520, is unknown, but the moral complexity of the scheme is that of the

---

[17] D. T. B. Wood, "Tapestries of the Seven Deadly Sins," *Burlington Magazine* 15 (1912): 215.

[18] Wood, 210.

[19] Ibid.

great *Author*. What the artist achieves is what Milton presents us with in
Paradise Lost—a union of moral, doctrinal and scriptural in one narrative
event. There is no escaping the focus of these events in the Homo who is
at their center, the Homo who is a mirror of the spectator. The groups of
figures are disposed into an upper and a lower series, the lower dealing
largely with the Fall and the upper with Redemption. But the two series
of narratives, even within one tapestry, cannot be dissociated; the story of
the lower must be read in terms of the upper.

The Homo who is Adam in the first tapestry, moreover, becomes us,
all mankind, in the second; this is our story. In the seventh of this series,
the *Triumph of Christianity* [fig. 4], Christ ascending to join the other
persons of the Trinity is flanked by other depictions in which he appears
with the apostles Peter and James and (with Chastity and Humility)
receiving his mother. And the Trinity, flanked by Mercy and Justice,
receives a kneeling man who faces Abraham and is presented by the grace
of God while an avenging angel drives down Envy, Despair, Avarice, and
the Tempter. Adam's story, Abraham's story, and Christ's story become part
of one story, the more so in that we identify ourselves with the "Homo"
who is its center. Man of the "first disobedience" and the "greater Man"
become, in Donne's phrase, companions of the Holy Ghost in the kingdom of heaven, where, in the eighth panel, Man, Nature, and Abraham sit
on the right of the throne.

This also is the position of the reader in *Paradise Lost,* a participant,
like Adam, in the narrative of which he is a part. The doctrine of the
"everlasting gospel"—that the gospel continues to be written in the hearts
and minds of its readers and is not a closed document—is one commonly
associated with Blake and the legacy of interregnum Muggletonians. But
such a reading of the New Testament is, as I have suggested, not confined
to radical protestantism. Moreover, its deprivileging of a single mode of
reading revitalizes Augustine's theory of allegory by reclaiming allegory
from mere *allegoria* in the narrow sense of received church (or even state)
doctrine. It places the reader firmly in an exegetical exercise—an act of
true "translation."

Milton's claim (in *Areopagitica*) that truth "may have more shapes than
one" is a celebration of the dialectical nature of truth. This also is the truth
that emerges in the long dialectical passages of *Paradise Lost,* not least in the
concluding books. There the opening two books are answered—not only
Satan's facile fatalism but his hierophantic reading of the text of the war in
heaven and his monarchic rhetorical stance, posing as a democrat. The

Fig. 4. Sixteenth-century Brussels tapestry. *Triumph of Christianity.* Courtesy of the Metropolitan Museum of Art, New York.

"wolves [who] shall succeed for teachers" and those who "spiritual Laws by carnal power shall force on every conscience" are Satan's heirs, yet they are ultimately powerless to pervert "written Records pure" that are "by the Spirit understood."

In place of heroic rant and syllogistic logic-chopping ("Fixt Fate, Free will, Foreknowledge," etc.) we find an angel guest (Michael) whose beauty "prime in Manhood where Youth ended" manifests his true heroism. If no longer "sociably mild" as Raphael was, nor "familiar" (in the original sense of *famulus*, "household"), Michael is nonetheless both mild and benign in his conversation. And he introduces Adam to our postlapsarian world where signs are not simply discovered but discover themselves to the adverting mind.

If Michael's answers are prompted by Adam's "whys," they are also explicatory of a series of narrative events (Cain and Abel, the Children of Israel, Noah, the Captivity, etc.) that is strikingly similar to the subjects of the great Brussels tapestries. Inside a historical narrative other historical narratives are being explicated, an explication in which process and change are of the essence and proper doubt is the instrument of faith.

Michael also introduces us to what we think of as modern epistemological and hence narratological problems. Is the "speculation" of 12. 589 a "comprehending vision" (the original sense), a mirror of things as they are and will be? Or is it, in a postlapsarian world, merely "a conjectural consideration"? How, at the simplest level, is Adam's attempt to read the future a reflection on our inability to read the past except in the distorting language of the present?

Of the visions of the modern artist, Paul Klee has written: "not only do they, to some extent, add more spirit to the seen, but they also make secret visions visible." "This being so," he writes elsewhere, "the artist must be forgiven if he regards the present state of outward appearances in his own particular world as accidentally fixed in time and space."[20] Klee's strong sense of the generative in creation, a principle that he calls the "primeval power [that] nurtures all evolution,"[21] is what Milton calls God, but Milton's stress on the generative power that "dove-like sat'st brooding on the vast abyss / And mad'st it pregnant" (1. 21–22) is no less than Klee's. What is more, this is a generative power that both the artist

[20] Paul Klee, *On Modern Art,* trans. Paul Findlay (London: Faber and Faber, 1966), 51, 47, 53 respectively.
[21] Klee, 49.

and the intelligent reader may share. Milton's plea that what is dark in him be illumined is answered in the working of the poem not only within his mind but among his readers.

The poet's flight is not only above the Aonian mount and the Stygian pool but the whole history of mankind, a history that is sequential but immediate to the spirit's understanding. Books 11 and 12 make plain not only to Adam but to the flagging reader that "only through time is time redeemed," and that to understand that is to be saved from time. "The deeper he looks," Klee says of the artist,

> the more readily he can extend his view from the present to the past, the more deeply he is impressed by the one essential image of creation itself, as Genesis, rather than by the image of nature, the finished product. Then he permits himself the thought that the process of creation can today be hardly complete and he sees the act of world creation stretching from the past to the future. Genesis eternal![22]

Adam's present is our past, his future our present. Real time, the time of Eden, is the time kept by the understanding soul in a garden in which Eden is continually renewed.

UNIVERSITY OF TORONTO

---

[22] Ibid.

T. H. Howard-Hill

MILTON AND
"THE ROUNDED THEATRE'S POMP"

I

IN A STRIKING MANIFESTATION OF CULTURAL PRODUCTION, scholars in the early part of this century collaborated to construct a myth of Milton's affiliation with contemporary drama and its *locus,* the theater. By the end of the nineteenth century, drama had become established as the dominant literary form of the early seventeenth century rather than a marginal kind of public entertainment. Milton's involvement with drama as a genre, witnessed by his *Arcades, Comus, Samson Agonistes,* and the original design of *Paradise Lost* as a tragedy, was undeniable. However, it became important to claim as well Milton's experience of the drama of his own time besides the knowledge of classical drama he gained from his education and subsequent reading. Neither Milton's attendance at public theaters nor his participation in school performances was closely investigated. Nevertheless, bold claims were made. Milton's "early enthusiasm for the English stage is well known," asserted James Holly Hanford in 1917, words echoed by Denis Saurat: Milton's *Elegia Prima* revealed "his love for the stage." Indeed, Harris Fletcher noted, "The disreputable theatres of the time" were as familiar to him as "the pomp and circumstance that frequently transformed the St. Paul's and West Cheap area."[1] On the other hand, even though "It is not difficult

---

[1] "The Dramatic Element in *Paradise Lost,*" *Studies in Philology* 14 (1917): 178–95, repr. in *John Milton, Poet and Humanist: Essays by James Holly Hanford* (Cleveland: Press of Western Reserve Univ., 1966), 224; Saurat, *Milton, Man and Thinker* (New York: Dial Press, 1925), 7; Fletcher, *The Intellectual Development of John Milton, Volume I: The Institution to 1625: From*

to find indications that Milton *was* hostile to the theater as it existed in his day" (Wagenknecht), "as one whose longstanding attitude toward drama was strongly positive though not uncritical, he must have opposed the move" to close the theaters in 1642.[2] However, Milton's comment on Tertullian in his commonplace book shows that he could distinguish the literary form, drama, from the site or mode of its initial publication, the theater; the distinction is frequently obscured in modern criticism.[3] The point is not insignificant, for if it appears that Milton's theatrical experience was negligible or nonexistent, it is reasonable to inquire through what other means Milton acquired that comprehensive knowledge of Elizabethan and Jacobean drama that, apparently, he possessed. Hence, Alwin Thaler in 1966: "That there are numerous points of contact between Shakespeare and Milton has, of course been common knowledge. . . ."[4] So common, indeed, that it is not surprising to read in Barbara Lewalski's *"Paradise Lost" and the Rhetoric of Literary Forms* that "Satan's use of a characteristic formal element from Elizabethan tragedy, the soliloquy," associates him "successively, and on a descending scale of moral worthiness, with various kinds of Elizabethan tragic heroes, villain-heroes, and tragic antagonists."[5] Yet, there is a disquieting lack of objective evidence that Milton either sought or acquired extensive acquaintance of contemporary English drama.

Modern readers who see Shakespeare pretty much as Cassius described Caesar, looming over the literature of his time like a Colossus, experience an almost instinctive revulsion to the notion that Shakespeare was merely one of a number of contemporary poets with whose works Milton may have been familiar, or to the idea that Milton was not quick to recognize the distinctive contribution of Elizabethan drama to English cultural history, employing and mentioning contemporary plays in his works. How could the studious Milton have failed to perceive what is

---

the Beginnings through Grammar School (Urbana: Univ. of Illinois Press, 1956), 431.

[2] Edward Wagenknecht, *The Personality of Milton* (Norman: Univ. of Oklahoma Press, 1970), 32; Roger B. Rollin, "Paradise Lost: 'Tragical-Comical-Historical-Pastoral,'" *MS* 5 (1973): 4–5.

[3] Ruth Mohl, ed., "Milton's *Commonplace Book,*" in CPW 1:489–91.

[4] *Shakespeare and Our World* (Knoxville: Univ. of Tennessee Press, 1966), 140.

[5] See Lewalski (Princeton: Princeton Univ. Press, 1985), 63. The presence of these features in Milton is explained, like many of the links between Shakespeare's plays and *Paradise Lost,* in that the dramatist and the poet depended (although indirectly at least in the first case) on the same sources and models.

so clear to us now? Or have neglected to acknowledge in his works a substantial indebtedness to the great works of the early English drama? At the least it is beneficial to examine the evidence that may exist for Milton's attitude to the contemporary theater and the plays written for it in order to answer such questions. Ultimately, it is more important to remove accretions of scholarly piety that encrust Milton's distinctive contribution to literary history. If the present assessment is correct, one should rather read Milton generally with attention to the profound influence classical literature had on him than as an author who readily adopted innovations from contemporary literature: in short, for instance, it is rather to Seneca that we should look for the models of Satan's soliloquies, as Marlowe, Kyd, and their successors did, than to the tragedies of the contemporary stage.

II

To show in some detail why it was important for later Miltonists to ally Milton with the contemporary theater would be worthwhile. However, the factual bases of their position need to be established before their cultural biases can be interpreted.[6] I propose here, therefore, only to examine the evidence that exists of Milton's familiarity with the English stage before undertaking a brief survey of his knowledge and use of the vernacular contemporary drama. The first task is the easier because of two circumstances that delimit Milton's opportunities for theater-going. On Friday, 2 September 1642, Parliament closed the public theaters, a prohibition so influential as to extend even to the Lord Mayor's show customarily presented at the end of October.[7] Further, if Milton had retained any disposition to view public spectacles after the restoration of the monarchy in 1660 reopened the theaters, it must have been diminished by his blindness in 1654. If Milton was a theater-goer, it must have been in the first years of his life. Turning then to the beginning of Milton's life, his father's ambitions for the precocious child and the circumstances of his upbringing make it intrinsically unlikely that the young Milton attended theaters before he set out on his grammar school education at St. Paul's School, "almost certainly late in 1620 or early in

---

[6] The last part of this paper contains some preliminary speculations on this topic.

[7] G. E. Bentley, *The Jacobean and Caroline Stage,* 7 vols. (Oxford: Clarendon Press, 1941–68), 2 (1941): 690; 7 (1968): 127.

1621, when he was twelve years old."[8] Milton's experience of contemporary theater would have been obtained within the subsequent twenty-one years to 1642 when he was in his thirty-fourth year.

Attendance at Paul's imposed arduous discipline on the young pupils. They worked from seven o'clock in the morning to five in the afternoon, with a two-hour break for lunch that afforded little enough time for their return to their homes for lunch, none for a surreptitious visit to a public theater. Their holidays were Sundays (when public performances of plays were prohibited), saints' days, and (possibly) a summer vacation, amounting to 153 days of the year.[9] It is sometimes claimed that the young Milton was exposed to public theater within the very precincts of Paul's, but, besides its establishment within the early Choir School of the Cathedral rather than in Colet's later foundation, the Children of Paul's company had ceased playing between 1606 and 1610, well before Milton attended Paul's School.[10] In common with grammar schools in London and elsewhere, the school participated in theatrical exercises designed to aid students in the acquisition of the "true laten speech" mentioned in Colet's statutes.[11] In his *De ratione studii* (1511), Erasmus had commended the Latin comedians: "Amongst Roman writers, in prose and verse, Terence, for pure, terse Latinity has no rival, and his plays are never dull. I see no objection to adding carefully chosen comedies of Plautus—the less obscene ones."[12] But there are indications that by Milton's time "school drama at Paul's was

[8] W. R. Parker, *Milton, a Biography: I. The Life.* (Oxford: Clarendon Press, 1968), 13. Ann Jennalie Cook (*The Privileged Playgoers of Shakespeare's London, 1576–1642* [Princeton: Princeton Univ. Press, 1981]) mentions that the twelve-year-old Milton went to the Fortune theater in 1611 (131). The claim was repeated—with the date corrected to 1621—by Andrew Gurr (*Playgoing in Shakespeare's London* [Cambridge: Cambridge Univ. Press, 1987], 199) who points out privately that because the Fortune was square, the language of Milton's letter to Diodati cannot apply to it. See also n. 36.

[9] D. L. Clark, *John Milton at St. Paul's School* (New York: Columbia Univ. Press, 1948), 44, 49. The red-letter days were later reduced by thirty and a Thursday afternoon half-holiday instituted. Fletcher suggests that "the school apparently held throughout the year, 'both wynter and sumer,' and there seem to have been no vacations in any sense, ancient or modern" (*Intellectual Development*, 1:162). However, it is hard to believe that as many as 153 holidays did not provide a continuous respite from studies in the customary holiday period.

[10] E. K. Chambers, *The Elizabethan Stage* (Oxford: Clarendon Press, 1923), 2:22–23.

[11] Clark, 101.

[12] Quoted in Clark, 104.

following the drama of the professional boy actors into eclipse."[13] McDonnell records performances by "the scholars of Pawles" at the Company of Mercers' hall in 1618 and 1619 but the next reference to a school performance is under the year 1626–27.[14] Milton could not have been involved in any of these three productions. Nevertheless, given the established vitality of performances of the Latin comedians intended to foster the acquisition of colloquial Latin as well as poise and polish in public rhetorical situations, it would be unwise to conclude that Milton had not had some experience of drama while at school. However, there is no evidence that he saw a play in a public theater before he left London for Cambridge; I think the likelihood is very small.

For Milton's later boyhood we can more confidently claim regular experience of the shows and quasi-dramatic entertainments London offered in profusion. Prominent amongst these and certainly the most regular were the shows given to celebrate the inauguration of the Lord Mayor of London on (usually) 29 October of each year, the day after he took office. Customarily, the Lord Mayor went in state from Guildhall down to the Thames and thence by barges to Westminster to be sworn in by the Lord Chief Justice. His return by water accompanied by the barges of the great livery companies was itself a magnificent spectacle but from time to time allegorical entertainments were also presented on the river. On the way to Guildhall the mayoral procession passed the yard of St. Paul's Cathedral where some of the main shows were mounted and later stopped at such locations as the conduit in Cheapside, not far from Milton's home in Bread Street, to watch other shows. Following dinner at Guildhall where there was often another entertainment, the whole party went to worship at St. Paul's, after which the Lord Mayor was escorted home with appropriate ceremonies. The formal shows were accompanied by the informal entertainments of the citizens but it is undoubtedly the allegorical devices contrived by such pageant-makers as Anthony Munday, Thomas Middleton, and John Webster that would have most interested the young Milton.

In 1619 while not yet eleven years old Milton may have witnessed part of Middleton's pageant for Sir William Cockayne, a Skinner.[15] *The*

---

[13] T. H. Vail Motter, *The School Drama in England* (1929; repr. Port Washington, N.Y.: Kennikat Press, 1968), 153.

[14] Michael F. J. McDonnell, *A History of St. Paul's School* (London, 1909), 159.

[15] For the most part the ensuing details were drawn from David M. Bergeron, *English Civic Pageantry, 1558–1642* (Columbia, S.C.: Univ. of South Carolina Press, 1971).

Triumphs of Love and Antiquity began on the river with a welcoming speech from Love, then the first land device presented a wilderness with fur-bearing beasts (an allusion to Cockayne's company), the device at the Little Conduit in Cheap showed a "Sanctuary of Fame," and as the procession moved towards Guildhall, Antiquity addressed the mayor from the "Parliament of Honour." Finally in the evening, the devices having accompanied the mayor to his house, Love concluded the pageant with a speech from the "triumphant Chariot of Love." The following year the little-known John Squire celebrated the installation of Sir Francis Jones, a Haberdasher, with *Tes Irenes Trophaea or The Triumphs of Peace*. This was his only composition in this form. It is interesting mainly for adoption of a dual and contrasting structure that employed mythological characters for the entertainment on the Thames and allegorical figures in the land devices, for purposes of moral instruction. The second river device presented the tableau of Mount Parnassus with Apollo and the Muses, each shown with a distinctive identifying property: Clio carried books, Terpsichore played on a lute, and Urania wore a robe sprinkled with stars. We need not give details of Middleton's 1621 show, *The Sun in Aries* or his *The Triumphs of Honour and Virtue* in 1622, or his show for land in 1623, *The Triumphs of Integrity,* when Munday devised *The Triumphs of the Golden Fleece* for the river entertainment. However, beyond being the last mayoral show Milton may have seen before Cambridge, John Webster's 1624 *Monuments of Honour* is significant. The water devices employed the sea figures of Oceanus, Thetis, Thamesis, and Medway, with a terrestrial globe circled about with the seated figures of seven famous English seamen (e.g., Drake and Hawkins). However, a unique innovation was the introduction of five famous scholars and poets in the "Temple of Honour," the first device on land, shown in St. Paul's churchyard. The figures were Chaucer, Gower, Lydgate, More, and Sidney. Bergeron was "struck by Webster's selection, especially the absence of Shakespeare" (208), but none of the poets had been an active contemporary of Webster's as Shakespeare had. Besides, a writer for the popular theater did not belong in such a company.

In the allegorical tableaux of the Lord Mayor's shows, the young Milton could have seen the physical representations, the living pictures, of mythological and allegorical characters already familiar to him from his reading. In them the icons and emblematic images of art and architecture were given life by the power of words and incarnated in the shapes of a theatrical tradition that extended from the first establishment of Christianity in England. These were the images that Milton took with him to Cambridge, long before he experienced the *sacre rappresentazioni* of Catholic Italy.[16] Bergeron characterizes Middleton's achievement in the pageant form in words that identify the mayoral shows as a contributory influence on the so-called morality elements of *Paradise Lost*.

> It is not far-fetched to view his whole pageant output as a vast morality play, thematically considered at least. Man comes up against the forces of Evil and Error, but he is led to the triumphant mount by Truth, and the path to salvation is enhanced by his encounters with Honour, Love, Fame, and Integrity— all confirming that the "salvation" will be manifest in good works as man creates harmony out of the wilderness or sails the rough seas of life. (200)

The dramatic foundations of Milton's morality-like allegories should not be sought in the crude "motions" presenting Adam and Eve, or in the Chester, "Coventry," or York Corpus Christi plays that Milton had had no opportunity either to see or read.[17] The allegorical pageants offered an influence all the more potent on account of their theatrical immediacy. Yet, so far as I can discover, scholars have given no attention to this subject.

Nor were the Lord Mayor's shows the only spectacles Milton had opportunity to view. On Sunday, 26 March 1620, the king made his first procession to St. Paul's. At Paul's Cross, Chamberlain relates, the

---

[16] See John G. Demaray, *Milton's Theatrical Epic: The Invention and Design of Paradise Lost* (Cambridge: Harvard Univ. Press, 1980), 26–28.

[17] Interestingly, I cannot find references to Milton's possible knowledge of such early morality plays employing personified abstractions as *Everyman*, save for Skelton's *Magnificence:* the only edition before the nineteenth century was printed in 1530 and survives in three variously-imperfect copies. There is a strong presumption that Milton saw neither copy nor performance, despite R. L. Ramsay's claim (see n. 47). However, Allan H. Gilbert ("Milton and the Mysteries," *Studies in Philology* 17 [1920]: 147–69), while admitting Milton "could never have seen them performed, or, so far as we know, have read them," is compelled to conclude "it seems probable, however, that he had some means of indirect access to them, or to other plays like them" (167)—or anything else. On the other hand, Hanford suggests that "he may well have watched as a child the puppet shows of Adam and Eve to which he alludes in *Areopagitica*" (*A Milton Handbook*, 5th ed. [New York: Appleton-Century-Crofts, 1970], 210), citing "A meer artificial *Adam,* such an Adam as he is in the motions" (CPW 2:527). It is startling to find Gilbert's tottering edifice and *Paradise Lost* both reduced to a children's show.

bishop of London (John King) preached on a text the king had given him, but "the better halfe" of the two hours "he spent in a patheticall speach for the repairing of Powles."[18] Then James banqueted in the bishop's house, received a purse of gold from the Lord Mayor and aldermen at Temple Bar, and rode through the streets where "The citizens stoode by companies with their banners and stremers" to Paul's where he was received by the prebends and clergy. On the other hand, the young Milton may have missed the opening of Parliament on 30 January 1620 to which the king and Prince Charles rode in great state: there was "the greatest concourse and thronge of people that hath ben seene, so that there was some hurt don by the breaking of two scaffolds and otherwise," Chamberlain reported (2:338). And on 19 February 1623/24, "The King went to the parlement on Thursday, with greater shew and pompe then I have seen," wrote Chamberlain again (2:546). But both events were outside Milton's neighborhood and for the second, at least, he should have been in school. However, he could scarcely have missed the extraordinary celebrations that accompanied Prince Charles's safe return from the Spanish marriage negotiations in Madrid, on Monday, 6 October 1623. Chamberlain reported:

> I have not heard of more demonstrations of public joy then were here and every where from the highest to the lowest, such spreading of tables in the streets with all manner of provisions, setting out whole hoggesheads of wine and butts of sacke, but specially such numbers of bonfires both here and all along as he [the Prince] went, . . . as is almost incredible: . . . at Blackheath there was fowreteen load of woode in one fire, and the people were so mad with excesse of joy that yf they met with any cart loaden with woode they wold take out the horses and set cart and all on fire . . . there beeing solemne service in Powles the singing of a new antheme was specially observed, the 114th psalme, when Israell came out of Egipt and the house of Jacob from among the barbarous people. (2:515–16)

In this manner the English people celebrated the deliverance of their Anglican prince from the serpentine entanglements of Spanish Catholi-

---

[18] *The Letters of John Chamberlain*, ed. Norman Egbert McClure. 2 vols. (Philadelphia: American Philosophical Society, 1939), 2:299.

cism. Likewise, the anniversary was celebrated with the ringing of bells and burning of bonfires (Chamberlain, 2:581). Shortly afterwards, on Sunday, 7 November 1624, by public command there was "great triumph and rejoycing for the goode forwardnes" of the match between Prince Charles and Henrietta Maria of France: "the organs in Paules playde two howres on their lowdest pipes, and so began to the bells, the bells to the bonfires, the bonfires to a great peale of ordinance at the Towre." The future author of *Eikonoklastes* was doubtless too young (fifteen) to share Chamberlain's prayer: "God graunt yt may prove worth all this noise" (2:558).

Thus if the seventeen-year-old Milton who went up to Cambridge early in 1625 had only a bookish knowledge of formal drama and that classical in origin, he had nevertheless experienced a variety of expressive spectacles: popular festivals, state processions, and civic pageants. And, never to be forgotten, he had participated in the seasonal drama of the Anglican calendar, the saints' days commemorating the founders and martyrs of the early church, the dolorous event of Good Friday, the joyous celebrations of the Resurrection and of the Nativity. Even a "normal, God-fearing, Jesuit-hating, Bible-reading Christian," as Parker (1:10) characterizes Milton at this stage of his life, could not have been unaffected by the dramatic qualities of the rituals in which he participated week after week. In these respects Milton was no different from his fellows. The point is that although lack of evidence and probability does not allow us to attribute extensive theatrical experience to the young Milton (particularly of adult drama in public theaters), he carried to Cambridge a larger freight of dramatic experience than is generally recognized.

III

Probably the definitive account of Milton's contact with the theater during his Cambridge years (1625–1632) is Harris Fletcher's chapter on "Milton and the Academic Drama."[19] He remarks that "No phase of Milton's life at Cambridge has been more misunderstood and even misrepresented than his general attitude toward the academic drama of his day, particularly his attendance at various performances and even participation in them" (360). Despite Fletcher's efforts (or, perhaps,

---

[19] *The Intellectual Development of John Milton* (Urbana: Univ. of Illinois Press, 1961), 2:360–66.

because of them) his comment remains true today. Fletcher grounded his argument on the certainty of "one or two facts about Milton and the various forms of dramatic performances at Cambridge in his day" (360). His first fact (claiming that student attendance at university plays was mandatory, and citing a Queens' College statute threatening the expulsion of students who refused to participate in or attend performances) was that Milton "saw a lot of such performances" (360).[20] However, the fact is that no university statute exists that requires students to attend university plays. Nonetheless, there are several orders from the vice-chancellor and heads of colleges that regulate the seating and behavior of students who attended the public performances of university plays presented for the entertainment of visiting dignitaries.[21] For instance, the order of 1622/23 commands "That all graduats, & students of this Vniversitie both at the publique Comodyes, & disputacions observe, & keepe ye auncient orders of ye Vniuersitie, & take their places accordinge to their degree, & Seniorityes ...," but attendance at the public plays was not mandated. At college exercises, however, it may have been otherwise.

The Queens' ordinance that Fletcher mentioned applied only to Queens' students and Queens' plays. The 1546/47 ordinance provided that if

> any youth (who is) a student of this college ... inferior to a master of arts (and is) not even a fellow should refuse to take part (in a comedy or tragedy), or be absent when the comedy or tragedy is being put on publicly, or in some other way behave obstinately or perversely ... [he] shall be expelled....[22]

However, fellow commoners and scholars who were not bachelors of theology were merely fined five shillings, unless they had a legitimate excuse. But even if Christ's College also possessed such an ordinance, it

[20] Fletcher cites James Bass Mullinger, *The University of Cambridge* (Cambridge: Cambridge Univ. Press, 1884), 2:74 as his authority. What Mullinger wrote was that performances of plays at Cambridge "were at this time a practice recognized by the authorities and encouraged by statutory enactments,—penalties even being sometimes imposed on those who refused to bear their part" (pp. 72–73), footnoting the Queens' College statute.

[21] See *Cambridge,* ed. Alan H. Nelson, *Records of Early English Drama,* 2 vols. (Toronto: Univ. of Toronto Press, 1989): 1:501–3 (1612–13); 1:537 (6 March 1614/15); 1:585–86 (1622/23).

[22] Nelson, 2:1117; 1:147.

was not relevant to Milton's period of residence. So far as extant records reveal, even though there were periodic payments to the town waits, trumpeters and other musicians from 1603 to 1632, Christ's put on no plays of its own.[23] It may or may not indicate the attitude of Christ's to performances of plays that whereas Clare, Emmanuel, King's, and St. Catharine's colleges contributed their "College Rate for ye Comedyes before ye King" on the visit of Charles in 1632, a Christ's College contribution is not recorded.[24] In fact, "Christ's College, a puritan stronghold, performed no plays after 1567–8" (Nelson, 2:713).[25] Indeed, the records show that the long tradition of academic drama at Cambridge—where it had always been more vigorous than at Oxford—was drawing to a close. After 1622–23 only Trinity and Queens' are recorded as having performed plays (Nelson, 2:714). The gradual prevalence of puritanism in a university notably Protestant at the beginning of the seventeenth century did not provide a sympathetic nursery for actors even of the classical drama. There was a persistent animus against the theater during Milton's time at university which led inevitably, it may be thought, to the eventual suppression of most forms of theatrical performance or organized festivities.

Nevertheless, Milton did have opportunities to see the plays, all comedies and mostly Latin, presented by Trinity and Queens' between 1625 and 1632.[26] Thomas Randolph's *Aristippus,* perhaps performed in November 1626, was published in 1630 with the sub-title, "the Joviall Philosopher: Demonstrativelie Prooving, that Quartes, Pintes, and Pottles, are sometimes necessary Authours in a Scholers Library," just the kind of composition, one might suggest, that would appeal to a serious-minded young scholar intended for the ministry. An untitled comedy written by one Edmunds was put on by Queens' in 1627–28, and Trinity presented Randolph's monologue, *The Conceited Pedlar,* perhaps on 1 November 1627. Thomas Vincent's Latin *Paria* was performed at Trinity for King Charles on 3 March 1628 and printed in

---

[23] See Nelson 1:599 (1625/26); 1:602 (1626/27); 1:605 (1627/28); 1:615 (1628/29); 1:623 (1629/30); 1:626 (1630/31); 1:629 (1631/32); 1:647 (1632/33).

[24] Nelson 1:630–33.

[25] But students of Christ's had cooperated in performances of George Ruggles's *Ignoramus* before the King in March and May 1615 (Nelson, 2:902–3).

[26] The following details are summarized from Nelson's "Chronological List of College Performances" (2:963–76) and "Cambridge Play Bibliography" (2:886–962). Fletcher's account of these plays in *The Intellectual Development* (2:363) is stuffed with errors.

1648. William Worlech wrote a comedy for Trinity in 1627–28 and Edmund Stubb's Latin *Fraus Honesta* of 1616 was presented again for the French ambassador in 1629, and printed in 1632. (But, "We know nothing of [Milton's] whereabouts during the spring, summer, and autumn of 1629" [Parker, 1:59].) Peter Hausted's Latin *Senile Odium* was performed probably in 1630 and published in 1633 but Thomas Pestell's Latin play, *Versipellis,* written for performance before the king in 1632 was not given or subsequently printed. Another Hausted comedy, *The Rival Friends* (printed 1632), and Randolph's *The Jealous Lovers* (printed 1632) were performed before the king and queen consecutively in March 1632. John Pory noted that Hausted's play, "being 7 howers long was very tedious to the Spectatours" (Nelson, 1:640). Later, he reported, "Dr. Buttes Master of Benet Colledge and Vicechancelour of Cambridge ... on Easter daye in the morning hanged himselfe with a three cornerd kercher" (Nelson, 1:643), being mortified by the reception of the comedy he had championed. Performances of university plays even before the highest dignitaries of the land were strenuous occasions. Before the earl of Holland and the French ambassador were honored, the university admonished the students

> That noe tobacco be taken in ye hall, nor any where else publikely ... nor before ye Comoedy begin, nor all the tyme thereof, any rude and immodest exclamations be made, nor anye humminge, hakeinge, whistlinge, hisseinge, or laughinge be vsed, nor any stampinge, or knockinge, nor any other such vncivill, or vnschollerlike, and boyish demeanor vppon any occasion ... (Nelson, 1:620–21)

Milton states in his *Apology* that he "was a spectator; they thought themselves gallant men, and I thought them fools...."[27] Even though

---

[27] CPW 1:888; Nelson, 2:859. Hugh G. Dick (ed., *Albumazar: a Comedy,* 1615, by Thomas Tomkis, University of California Publications in English, 13 [Berkeley: Univ. of California Press, 1944]) convincingly identified Tomkis's play as the source of Milton's reference to "Trinculo's, Buffons, and Bawds" in the *Apology* passage (pp. 54–55). Yet, persuaded by modern assertions of Milton's experience of the theater, he was obliged to postulate an unknown performance at Cambridge for Milton to view, one which left no trace at all in university records. However, three editions of *Albumazar* were in print before 1642, Q3 being published in 1634, the year of *Comus* (see n. 46). Alan H. Nelson, "Women in the Audience of Cambridge Plays," *Shakespeare Survey* 41 (1990): 333–36, provides another gloss on Milton's well-known passage.

these words were possibly composed more exactly to serve the purposes of argument than biography, we can take no impression from them that Milton attended performances of plays either enthusiastically or frequently. Still, whether or not Milton braved the often riotous performances of such plays, he was able at least to read most of them during his studies for the M.A. at Cambridge and during his subsequent studies at Hammersmith and Horton.

To other kinds of representational entertainment Milton had little access while at Cambridge. Writing to the university on 23 July 1603, James had commanded both the town and university authorities to

> restraine, inhibite and forbid ... all manner of vnprofitable or Idle games, plaies or exercises ... within 5 miles compasse ... Espetially, Bull-bayting, Beare-bayting, common Plaies, Publique shewes, Enterludes, Comodies & tragedies in the English Tongue, games at loggetes & nyneholes & all other sportes and games Whereby throngs, concourse or multitudes are drawne together, or whereby the younger sorte are or maie bee drawne or provoked to vain expence, losse of tyme, or corrupcion of Manners.[28]

(However, the king had continued, "it is not our pleasure and meaning hereby to abridge the studentes of their accustomed exercises in any kinde whatsoeuer within their seuerall Colledges.") The Letters Patent granted to the university in March 1604 were more amply specific in forbidding "any plays or scenes of actors; feats of rope-walkers, acrobats, or athletes; baitings of bears or of bulls; tricks and frivolities of jesters or those who carry about puppets; or in short other contentious contests or time-wasting spectacles...."[29] Such entertainments the university authorities should forbid and not even tolerate "by tacit consent," so that "it might be known how unworthy of the sophistication and seriousness of academics we consider these trifles, or rather, these corrupting influences upon their morals." This language may be thought to foreshadow Milton's well-known condemnation in the *Apology* of students intended for the church involving themselves in demeaning spectacles, but James's and Milton's attitudes were commonplace. For instance, the St. John's College statutes of 1529/30 had enjoined members of the college to

---

[28] From Nelson, 1:395–96, with some repunctuation.
[29] From Nelson, 2:1171; the Latin original is at 1:399.

"conduct themselves as becomes clerics … nor shall they watch forbidden shows or games/plays prohibited by ecclesiastical or common law.…" (Nelson, 2:1106).

The university statutes were enforced. In September 1611 Edward Worth was fined and admonished to leave Cambridge for showing puppet plays, and in March 1616/17 a company of actors led by Thomas Dounton and Edward Jubey were also expelled (Nelson, 1:553). In July 1619 the vice-chancellor caused a stir by closing down the games and sports ("horseraces, bull bayting, beare bayting, Loggattes, ninehoales, ryflinge, dicing") at Gogmagog Hills (Nelson, 1:571), which was "notorious as a place of resort," as Simonds D'Ewes wrote in his diary (Nelson, 1:572). In 1624 John Ellis was imprisoned for persisting in "shewinge an Elephant in Sturbridg fayer & taking mony of schollers & divers others for seeing him" (Nelson, 1:594). And as late as February 1629/30, when Lord Holland, the chancellor of the university, wrote to offer the university an opportunity to entertain the touring company of the Queen of Bohemia's players, the vice-chancellor and heads of colleges were prompt to refer to their charter to avoid licensing the actors, "comming now in time of lent a season fitter for humiliation, when also our Bachelors and Sophisters sitt daylie in the schooles for disputations.…" (Nelson, 1:626). Cambridge was not on the habitual route of touring companies and it is fairly certain that if Milton visited a public theatre during 1625–1632, it was not at Cambridge.

The notion that Milton was a frequent theater-goer in his early years is difficult to entertain seriously. Fletcher was determined to make him one. A generalized reference to speeches from Euripides' *Orestes* and *Hercules Furens* is bent to support a theory of college performances of Greek drama for which there is not an iota of circumstantial evidence. Even though Fletcher concedes that "so far as we know Milton himself never took part in the production or performance of any play while at Christ's" (361), he persists in maintaining the equally-unsubstantiated possibility of "his participation in the performance of plays by Aristophanes, Terence, Plautus, Aeschylus, Sophocles, and Euripides.…"[30]

---

[30] In *Prolusion I,* written in 1628, Milton imagined
these little speakers here, whom a short time ago he might have heard spouting in the buskined *Orestes* of Euripides, or more bombastically in the *Hercules* raging toward his death; at length their very slender supply of some little words being exhausted, parade in measured step with haughtiness laid aside, or crawl slowly off like certain little animals with their horns drawn in ("The Prolusions" trans.

However, the last recorded Cambridge performance of a play written by any of these authors occurred in 1609/10, Terence's *Andria* at Trinity, fifteen years or so before Milton reached Cambridge. Performances of Greek and Latin dramatists' works apparently were not so frequent as Fletcher appears to imply.[31] Fletcher concludes the discussion of his first point thus: "The performances that Milton so sneered at in the *Apology* may have been either college or university performances; but he certainly saw them" (361). There is no reason to believe that this is correct.

Fletcher holds this view so strongly that he raises "the suggestion that at one time or another Milton may have so successfully played the part of a female character in a college play that delightedly his colleagues dubbed him *Domina*" (365). The circumstances of drama at Cambridge I have mentioned above make the suggestion so implausible as hardly to be worth discussion. The young man educating himself for the ministry, who later regretted even his performance in the Vacation Exercise of

by Bromley Smith, *Works* [New York: Columbia Univ. Press, 1936], 12:120–23.)
This seems to describe recitation rather than dramatic performance.

[31] Nelson's "Chronological List of College Performances" (2:963–76) contains the following: a play by Terence at King's Hall, 1516/17; by Plautus at Queens', 1522/23; Plautus's *Miles Gloriosus* at Trinity Hall (?) in 1522/23 (?); a play by Terence at St. John's, 1534/35; Aristophanes' *Plutus* at St. John's in 1535/36 (?), a Greek dialogue in 1537/38, followed by a play by Plautus, and a Greek comedy in 1538/39 and again in 1539/40; Terence's *Adelphoe* at Queens' in 1547/48 followed by Terence's *Eunuchus* and Plautus's *Persa* in 1547/48; Aristophanes' *Peace* at Trinity in 1547/48(?); Plautus's *Poenulus* at Trinity in 1551/52; Euripides' *Hippolytus* at King's in 1552/53; Plautus's *Stichus* at Queens' in 1553/54 followed by Terence's *Eunuchus* and Plautus's *Poenulus* in 1554/55; Plautus's *Rudens* at Trinity in 1556/57; Seneca's *Oedipus*, Plautus's *Mostellaria*, and Euripides' *Hecuba* at Trinity in 1559/60, followed by Plautus's *Amphitruo*, Seneca's *Trojan Women* and *Medea* in 1560/61; Terence's *Adelphoe* and Plautus's *Curculio* at Jesus in 1562/63; Plautus's *Pseudolus* and Terence's *Adelphoe* and *Phormio* at Trinity in the same year; Terence's *Eunuchus* at Jesus in 1563/64; a play by Sophocles intended for performance in University College in 1563/64; Plautus's *Trinummus* and *Bacchides* in the same year; Plautus's *Stichus* at Trinity in 1564/65 followed by his *Asinaria* and *Menaechmi* in the next year; Plautus's *Bacchides* at Jesus in 1579/80; Plautus's *Persa* at St. John's in 1583/84; Plautus's *Mostellaria* (?) at Trinity in 1585/86; his *Miles Gloriosus* (?) at Queens' in 1591/92, culminating with *Andria* in 1609/10. In many instances only the producer rather than the title or author of the play is noted in the records, a fact which severely qualifies the following remarks; but some observations may be made. Aeschylus is not, *pace* Fletcher, included in this list where, in fact, Greek drama is sparse. Further, performances of Terence and Plautus become relatively infrequent after the 1560s. Neo-classical Latin plays appear quite early with Thomas Watson's *Absalom* at St. John's in 1539/40, as does English drama (Stevenson at Christ's in 1553/54), and they eventually usurp the position of the classical drama.

1628 (see Parker 1:44, 49) was surely of the temper evinced by Samuel Fairclough in 1615 who, on being nominated to the role of Surda, an old woman, in Ruggle's *Ignoramus*, objected that it was "unlawful for a man to wear Womens Apparel, even in a Comedy." His objection was based on Deuteronomy 22:5 (AV): "The woman shall not wear that which pertaineth to a man, neither shall a man put on a woman's garment: for all that do so are abhomination unto the Lord thy God." His biographer characterizes Fairclough's actions in terms which, *ceteris paribus*, are appropriate to Milton:

> Thus did this youth choose to lose the smiles of the Court, and to bear the frowns of the Vice-Chancellour, rather than to hazard the loss of the light of Gods countenance, or to endure the least lash of his own Conscience. He well understood the meaning of that saying, Populus me sibilat, At mihi plaudo; for indeed he was always a Theatre to himself, and although he could not Histrionem agere, act the Comedian, or ὑποϰϱίτεῖν play the hypocrite, either with God or men, or himself, yet he acted always as one that was resolved to die and go off the Stage of the world with a "well done, good and faithful Servant" spoken to him by the King of Kings, and the great Spectator and observer of all men.[32]

More than a touch of this attitude can be detected in Milton's later defense of his association with academic drama, the well-known passage in his *Apology against a Pamphlet* (1642):

> if it be unlawfull to sit and behold a mercenary Comedian personating that which is least unseemely for a hireling to doe, how much more blamefull is it to indure the sight of as vile things acted by persons either enter'd, or presently to enter into the ministery, and how much more foule and ignominious for them to be the actors.[33]

---

[32] Samuel Clarke, "Life and Death of Mr. Samuel Fairclough," *The Lives of Sundry Eminent Persons* (London: T. Simmons, 1683), 156–67 *bis*, quoted from Nelson 1:543–44, with speech marks added. Nelson (1:544) gives another instance of one Thomas Morgan who also objected to taking a woman's part in *Ignoramus*, was prevailed upon to act his part, and suffered an appropriate fate: he "afterwards removed unto Oxford, & suffer'd to play what part he would, and so relapsed to Popery" (Thomas Ball, *The Life of the Renowned Doctor Preston*, ed. E. W. Harcourt [Oxford: Parker, 1885], 32).

[33] CPW 1:888; Nelson, 2:859.

Milton's attitude to the participation of religious men in public plays was not so different from the view William Prynne had published a few years earlier in his *Histrio-mastix* (1633): "So the graver, better, and more studious sort (especially Divines, who by sundry Councels are prohibited from acting or beholding any publike or private Stage-playes, and therefore dare not to approach them) condemne them, censure them, come not at them. . . ."[34] However, the strongest refutation of the possibility that Milton had acted in a play at Cambridge is his very condemnation of the involvement in the theater of men intended for the ministry. Had he performed in a play he could well have confessed the fact in his *Apology* and, as a repentant offender, excused it as a youthful folly. Too many of his college friends survived in 1642 to reveal his culpability had he suppressed the fact of an early misdemeanor in the *Apology*. However, nothing in Milton's character or writings suggests that he was ever involved in theatrical performances.

IV

Fletcher's second "fact" about Milton's involvement in "the various forms of dramatic performances at Cambridge" (360) seems to be the well-known evidence of his participation in "various college exercises, private and public" and in "the public schools": "No matter how much he may have sneered at college theatricals in the *Apology*, . . . his own public performances were at least histrionic, and direct us to the suspicion that he himself participated in others of a more directly dramatic nature" (366). One wonders at Fletcher's determination to oppose the charge of Milton's hostility to drama—which patently lacks foundation—by involving him in theatrical performances. It is as if a man cannot love music if he does not play a musical instrument. This determination led him to the undocumented claim that "Milton referred several times during his university career to professional stage performances" (361), a statement that redirects attention to Milton's experience of the public theater. Since, as we have seen, he had no opportunity to witness performances by commercial theater companies in Cambridge, we

---

[34] Sig. 3R2^r, quoted from Nelson, 2:856. One should notice that both Prynne and Milton censure comedies specifically, a licentious form in the best of times. Earlier, in 1618, William Harrison the Catholic archpriest had forbidden priests to watch plays on the popular stage (I. J. Semper, "The Jacobean Theater through the Eyes of Catholic Clerics," *Shakespeare Quarterly* 3 [1952]: 45–51).

should examine when he could have attended theaters in London.

Sometime in March 1626, it seems, Milton fell out with his tutor and returned home to London (Parker, 1:29). While there he wrote a Latin verse-letter to his friend Charles Diodati, the *Elegia Prima* describing the pleasures of his unexpected vacation. Because Fletcher understands the seventeen-year-old Milton to refer to "professional stage performances" in part of the *Elegia Prima,* it is worthwhile quoting the passage in W. W. Skeat's translation.[35] Milton compared himself to Ovid, an earlier exile, who solaced his time with reading:

> Here may I dedicate whene'er I chuse,
>> Free hours to the quiet Muse:
> Each book I live by, all my mind inspires;
>> Me overply'd, then draws
> The rounded theatre's pomp, and all my applause
>> The rattling stage requires:
> Now gray Rogue—spendthrift Heir—now Suitor sighs—
>> Now (in Civilian guise)
> Soldier—now Counsel, flown with ten-year case,
>> In court devoid of grace
> Thunders his Norman jargon of the laws:
>> Now sly Slave's aidance, lent
> To amorous Son, puts hard Sire off the scent,
>> Or Maids, new fires that prove,
> Of love naught knowing, yet—unknowing—love.
>> Next, phrenzied Tragedy sways
> Her gory wand: wild-hair'd, with rolling eyes,
>> I watch her agonize;
> For somehow, though my gaze begetteth grief,
>> Yet gazing gives relief;
> Some bitter sweetness oft my tear allays:
>> As when, in piteous wise
> Yon ill-starr'd youth, his love-dream shatter'd, dies
>> Ere tasted Hymen's bliss;
> Or when from forth night's shades (the Styx recrost)
>> Some dread, avenging ghost
> Sounds with death-torch the depth of sin's abyss

---

[35] *Milton: Complete Poetry & Selected Prose, with English Metrical Translations of the Latin, Greek and Italian Poems,* ed. E. H. Visiak (London: Nonesuch Library, 1938; repr. 1952), 756.

> In guilty hearts that lies;
> Or Troy's illustrious Line, or Pelops', weep,
> Or Kreon's House that met
> Of her incestuous sires the monstrous debt.   (26–47)[36]

It is difficult to read this youthful effusion as evidence that Milton was familiar with "the disreputable theatres of the time" as Fletcher claimed. Not a phrase here suggests actual experience of the public stage. Rather, Milton describes the "garrulous stage" (to use J. Milton French's expression) in terms of the classical drama with which he had become increasingly familiar during his schooldays. Hence, we find the *senex,* the *adulescens,* the *miles gloriosus,* the *advocatus,* the *servus,* and the *virgo* from classical comedy, with the stories of Greek tragedy, perhaps transmitted through Seneca, who was more familiar to a young Latinist. But the merchants and housewives of English domestic drama, the gentlemen and ladies, the princes of the romantic comedies together with the clowns and jesters and the pert romantic heroines in boy's dress of the English stage do not figure in Milton's account any more than the kings and nobles who earlier held the stage in the history plays. There is not a detail that can be associated more closely with the plays that were being presented on the stage during 1625–26 than with the drama available to Milton's recollection from reading. When we consider how assiduously at this time and afterwards Milton strove to master the decorum of different kinds of writing, we cannot easily read these lines biographically. The reference to Ovid gives a possible clue to what Milton was doing here: Ovid had devoted books 3–5 of his *Tristia* to bemoaning the deprivations of his exile. Milton was made of sterner stuff: he was doing very well indeed, thank you, with reading and the pleasures of the town. It is, as Parker said, "a pale and politic foreshadowing of *L'Allegro* and *Il Penseroso.*" In fact, in the latter poem he

---

[36] The Latin text and a closer prose translation are available in *The Life Records of John Milton,* ed. J. Milton French (New Brunswick, N.J.: Rutgers Univ. Press, 1949), 1:756. Richard Hosley ("Elizabethan Theatres and Audiences," *Research Opportunities in Renaissance Drama* 10 [1967]: 9–14) interprets "sinuosi pompa theatri" as "the splendor of the curved theatre" and concludes that Milton must have visited "one of the large, round, open-air playhouses" (14) in London. He does not consider that Milton need not have attended performances to know that theaters were "curved"—a surprising characterization in any event—or that Milton had the Greek amphitheaters in mind.

describes tragedy in much the same classicized terms.[37]

After he returned to Cambridge, Milton's opportunities to view the productions of the public stage were limited to the summers and other periods in which the obscurities of his biographical records allow us to place him in London. The theaters were closed from 17 April to 12 November in 1630, for some time between 18 February 1630/31 and 10 June 1631, and for nearly seventeen months from 10 May 1636 to 2 October 1637, all on account of plague.[38] Nevertheless, there remained time during his sojourn in his father's house in Hammersmith for visits to the commercial theaters of the south bank, and even while he was living at Horton (1635–1638) he could have combined the theater with visits to the London booksellers (Parker, 1:147). That he did so is entirely inconsistent with the "decorum of character" we can associate with a man who, in the first years of his post-Cambridge period at least, still considered the ministry his vocation. Nevertheless, however few and intermittent the opportunities Milton had to visit the public theaters of London were, they did exist: no case can be made that he never saw a performance in the commercial theater. However, there is no incontestable evidence that he did, and the intrinsic likelihood he visited theaters frequently or habitually is very small. That probability is considerably diminished by consideration of the place that contemporary drama occupied in his writings.

V

James Holly Hanford claimed in 1917 that there was "no evidence that Milton ever outgrew his early love of Elizabethan drama."[39] To the best of our knowledge, as I have recounted, Milton's "love of Elizabethan drama" must have been formed mainly if not exclusively from perusal of ephemeral play quartos or the more dignified collections of plays by the best English dramatists of the time, e.g., the Jonson folios of 1616 and 1640, the Shakespeare folios of 1623 and 1632, or even the works of Beaumont and Fletcher published in 1647. It is disturbing but not surprising that Milton's reconstructed library contains only two such

[37] Parker, 1:30–31. *Il Penseroso,* lines 97–102 *(The Poetical Works of John Milton,* ed. Helen Darbishire, 2 vols. [Oxford: Clarendon Press, 1953], 2:144).

[38] See G. E. Bentley, "The closing of the theatres because of plague," in *The Jacobean and Caroline Stage,* 7 vols. (Oxford: Clarendon Press, 1941–68), 2:632–72.

[39] "The Dramatic Element in *Paradise Lost,*" 225, cited in n. 1.

titles.[40] One is William Cartwright's *Comedies, Tragicomedies, with Other Poems* (1651) which the compiler included because, Milton having praised one of Cartwright's poems, it "seems reasonable that Milton would have read more than one" (Boswell, 51). The other is the 1632 folio of Shakespeare's *Comedies, Histories and Tragedies* to which Milton had contributed his verse, "On Shakespeare." In fact, the only work of a contemporary English playwright that Milton verifiably read is Shakespeare's *Richard III* which he quoted in *Eikonoklastes*.[41] All the other citations of English dramatists in *Milton's Library* are marked as merely "possible or likely" or "doubtful." Of the other twenty dramatic titles listed (excluding *R3* and the "likely" Cartwright and F2), only two works are noted as "possible or likely": Jonson's *Pleasure Reconciled to Virtue* and *Poetaster*.[42]

The "fact" of Milton's use of *Pleasure Reconciled to Virtue* for the composition of his *Mask presented at Ludlow Castle (Comus)* is often repeated since Percy Simpson first asserted that Milton "had clearly studied *Pleasure Reconciled*" and then went on to set out the substantial *differences* between the two entertainments.[43] Independently, Enid Welsford commented that "*Comus* is reminiscent of *Pleasure Reconciled to Virtue*" and claimed that it "owes at least as much to *Pleasure Reconciled to Virtue* as it does to Peele's crude romantic play *The Old Wives Tale*": that is, we must conclude, nothing.[44] Both Simpson and Welsford ignored a substantial impediment to the notion that Jonson's masque influenced Milton. Before it was printed in the 1641 volume of Jonson's

---

[40] Jackson C. Boswell, *Milton's Library; a Catalogue of the Remains of John Milton's Library and an Annotated Reconstruction of Milton's Library and Ancilliary Readings* (New York: Garland, 1975). Of the collections of drama recorded by W. W. Greg (*A Bibliography of the English Drama to the Restoration* [London: Bibliographical Society, 1939–59], vol. 3), only seven collected editions were published after Milton's death in 1674. This does not mean that all the earlier-published collections were available in bookshops or private libraries.

[41] CPW 3:36.

[42] Marlowe's *Hero and Leander* and Shakespeare's *Venus and Adonis*, non-dramatic poems, are not considered.

[43] *Ben Jonson*, ed. C. H. Herford and Percy Simpson (Oxford: Clarendon Press, 1925), 2: 307–9. Cf. Ethel Seaton, "*Comus* and Shakespeare," *Essays and Studies* 31 (1945): 79: "Milton probably planned a masque with Peele's *Old Wives Tale,* Jonson's *Pleasure Reconciled to Virtue* consciously in mind." R. C. Fox noted that "Comus" occurs in *Poetaster*, III.iv.115 (*Notes & Queries* 9 [1962]: 52–53), but see n. 46 below.

[44] *The Court Masque; A Study in the Relationship between Poetry & the Revels* (Cambridge: Cambridge Univ. Press, 1927), 307, 314.

works, apart from the original manuscript, *Pleasure* apparently existed in a single scribal transcript "made for presentation to a courtier, either a performer or a patron."[45] (It is presently in the Duke of Devonshire's library at Chatsworth.) If other transcripts of Jonson's masque were made, they too were most likely in libraries inaccessible to Milton. The probability that Milton ever saw a copy of *Pleasure* is so small that it deserves no consideration.[46] If he did not read *Pleasure* in 1634, *Comus* could not have been influenced by Jonson's masque.

The list of contemporary plays in *Milton's Library* marked "doubtful" does not warrant close scrutiny. Three citations of Corpus Christi plays are owed to Gilbert's early article, and Ramsay's notion that Milton had access to Skelton's moral play, *Magnificence,* depended on a broad structural similarity to *Paradise Lost* that he constructed himself.[47] Further, the resemblances between Milton's *Mask* and Peele's "very scarce" *Old Wives Tale* first noted in the *Biographia Dramatica* were the common devices of romance found in such works as Ariosto's *Orlando Furioso*—which the *Biographia* mentioned—that Milton certainly had read.[48]

Such evidence from Milton's "library" does not encourage us to conclude that he was significantly indebted to the vernacular drama of his time in his own writings. The commonplace book which Milton kept from Horton days until after his blindness cites some writings in English (most prominently, Holinshed's *Chronicle*) and two dead English poets, Chaucer and Gower.[49] However, plays and playwrights are not mentioned, not even (as Parker noted) "any of the Greek tragedians."[50] Also, when Milton contemplated suitable subjects for dramas, as shown by the Trinity manuscript "probably made within a

---

[45] C. H. Herford and Percy and Evelyn Simpson, *Ben Jonson* (Oxford: Clarendon Press, 1941), 7:475.

[46] Parker, 2:791–92, n. 37, sums up the scholarship on the question, noting in particular the more immediate influence of John Fletcher's *The Faithful Shepherdess* and Erycius Puteanus's neo-Latin romance, *Comus,* both republished in 1634.

[47] For Gilbert, see n. 17. R. L. Ramsey, "Morality Themes in Milton's Poetry," *Studies in Philology* 15 (1918): 149–50.

[48] *Biographia Dramatica or A Companion to the Playhouse,* ed. David Erskine Baker, Isaac Reed, and Stephen Jones (London: Longman, 1812), 3:97; Boswell, *Milton's Library,* 11.

[49] Ruth Mohl, "Milton's *Commonplace Book*," CPW 1:510–13. George Buchanan is mentioned for his *Rerum Scoticarum Historia,* Sidney for his *Arcadia,* and Spenser for his *A View of the Present State of Ireland*.

[50] Parker, 2:801–2. He dates the Commonplace Book from late 1634 or 1635 to some time after Milton's blindness in 1654.

year or so after his return from the Continent" (Parker, 1:190) in 1639, where thirty-eight subjects for a British tragedy were listed, Milton's sources were the histories of Geoffrey of Monmouth, Holinshed, Speed, Stow, and others: no contemporary English play or playwright was mentioned.[51] Finally, setting aside the quotation from *Richard III* in *Eikonoklastes,* in all his voluminous prose works Milton never cites an English play or mentions an English dramatic writer.[52]

Indeed, were the subject to be thoroughly explored, it would not be surprising to learn that Milton, like most of his scholarly contemporaries, was not very interested in any form of contemporary English literature.[53] Harris Fletcher suggests Alexander Gill's influence on the young poet at St. Paul's school, reflected by an assortment of English poets cited in his *Logonomia Anglica* (1619; 1621).[54] Remarkably, however, only Jonson and Wither of the sixteen authors were alive when Milton was at St. Paul's. The dramatists Gill mentioned (Campion, Daniel, and Jonson) were included for their poetry: modern playwrights were not held up as models for schoolboy poets. Fletcher's further comment that Shakespeare was "the most striking omission" from Gill's work (1:404) gives occasion to consider the question of Milton's

---

[51] "Milton's Outlines for Tragedies," in *The Uncollected Writings of John Milton,* ed. Thomas Ollive Mabbott and J. Milton French, CE 18:228–45. A good illustration of Milton's attitude to Shakespeare in relation to his own poetic projects (pointed out by Roy C. Flannagan) is that in planning a tragedy based on Holinshed's account of Macbeth, Milton made no indication that he knew of Shakespeare's tragedy on the same subject.

[52] So far as can be detected from *A Concordance to the English Prose of John Milton,* gen. ed. Laurence Stone (Binghamton, N.Y.: Medieval & Renaissance Texts & Studies, 1985).

[53] In ninety-four inventories probated at Cambridge between 1560 and 1620, as recorded by E. S. Leedham-Green *(Books in Cambridge Inventories; Book-Lists from Vice-Chancellor's Court Probate Inventories in the Tudor and Stuart Periods* [Cambridge: Cambridge Univ. Press, 1986], nos. 110–93) only thirty-one copies of titles out of 11,021 are recognizable as British "literature" (0.28%), a category which here includes More's *Utopia.* Of these, nine are Latin works. There are *no* plays: Marlowe, Shakespeare, Jonson, and their colleagues do not appear even though Terence, Plautus, and Seneca are well represented. There is no *Mirror for Magistrates* apart from a copy of Blennerhasset's second part, no Spenser or Sidney (other than a single *Apology*), and only single copies of such popular works as Tottel's Miscellany and Lyly's *Euphues, the Anatomy of Wit.* Chaucer's *Works* (three copies), *Piers Plowman* (five), and *Utopia* (four, more likely Latin editions) are the exceptional English works. Only three collections (Denys, 4; Perne, 6; Lorkin, 5) contain half of the English literature.

[54] *Intellectual Development,* 1:186–87. Fletcher's conclusion that "by 1625, Milton had read and analysed a great deal of English literature and learned to love it" (187) is about as acceptable as the conclusions about Milton's knowledge and love of contemporary drama discussed earlier in this essay.

estimation and knowledge of Shakespeare's works.

A. C. Labriola and, more recently, John T. Shawcross have so effectively deconstructed the rickety edifice put together mainly during the first half of this century that I can be brief.[55] Milton mentioned Shakespeare's name only twice in his poetry. The first occasion was the derivative and formal tribute "On Shakespeare" added anonymously to the encomiastic verses of the 1623 Shakespeare folio in the second folio published by the Jaggards' successor Thomas Cotes in 1632.[56] It makes no specific reference to any of Shakespeare's plays although Milton had apparently read Jonson's poem on Shakespeare published in the first folio of 1623. I agree that it is most likely that Milton or his father acquired a copy of the volume in which Milton's first published work appeared.[57] Around 1631 perhaps, Milton employed similarly commonplace language in describing Shakespeare as "fancies childe" in contrast to the learned Jonson in *L'Allegro*. Ethel Seaton suggested some connections between Milton's *Mask* and Shakespeare's works, not all of which are implausible.[58] It is reasonable to believe that Milton had read Shakespeare at least after the publication of the first folio and definitely after F2 in 1632.[59] He had certainly read *Richard III* before 1649 when *Eikonoklastes* was published. Shakespeare is cited there as "the Closet companion" of Charles's solitudes during his captivity. Contextually, that is a pejorative reference: Charles should have occupied his leisure with more sober reading than popular stage-plays, but what could be expected from a monarch whose very piety was dissembled? Earlier in the pamphlet Milton wrote contemptuously of "quaint Emblems and devices begg'd from the old Pageantry of some Twelf-nights entertainment at *Whitehall*" (CPW 3:343). Even if Milton prized the theater of his time—a most unlikely conclusion—he patently recognized its value

---

[55] "William Shakespeare," *A Milton Encyclopedia*, 7:188–91. John T. Shawcross's "Shakespeare, Milton and Literary Debt," *John Milton and Influence: Presence in Literature, History and Culture* (Pittsburgh: Duquesne Univ. Press, 1991), 5–38, was published during the revision of this essay.

[56] Characterizing the "Epitaph" as "an excellent original encomium that brings together many commonplaces," Shawcross cannot determine the extent of Milton's reading or appreciation of Shakespeare's works from the poem (14).

[57] So Parker, 2:769, but a somewhat later date is possible.

[58] "*Comus* and Shakespeare," 68–80, cited in n. 43.

[59] Perhaps as early as 1641 or 1642: See Ralph A. Haugh, ed., *The Reason of Church-government*, CPW 1:833, n. 18, who records Milton's use of "Key-cold," a term found in *R3*, I.ii.5.

as a weapon in controversy. Milton's references to contemporary theater in "Il Penseroso" and in the prefaces to *Samson Agonistes* and *Paradise Lost* are brief and essentially derogatory, particularly by comparison with classical tragedy. There is small reason to exempt Shakespeare from the tendency of such comments or to give the contemporary theater and its products high standing amongst the influences on Milton's writings.[60]

In this event, how can we explain the persistent attempts to associate the greatest epic poet of the seventeenth century with its greatest dramatic poet? At the first they were "unhistorical" in the diachronic sense in that the modern scholars mainly ignored the contemporary reputation of drama in general as the least of the available modes of literary expression. In the public theaters—and even in the universities, as we have seen—drama was licentious and unruly, at the same time symptomatic of and provocative of social tendencies that all serious-minded citizens deplored.[61] In popular regard the theater of the young Milton's time had much in common with widespread modern perceptions of television. It may be significant for the advancement of their views that the modern Milton scholars wrote too early to perceive that comparison themselves. Towards the end of the nineteenth century Shakespeare had spearheaded a significant re-estimation of the standing of early drama which, detached from the demeaning physical circumstances of its origin and translated into the libraries of gentlemen and the increasingly respectable theaters of the universities, Broadway, and the West End, became to an extent the "classical" literature of the modern age.

By the turn of the century it was possible to place Shakespeare (and by association, Elizabethan drama) and Milton within a contrasting set of polarities. Shakespeare could be seen as writing within a native tradition of vernacular literature with a natural genius whereas Milton's art was learned, owing more to the examples and precepts of classical writers than to the concerns of his historical milieu. Shakespeare could be

---

[60] Shawcross could not "conclude that Milton's poetic voice was greatly affected by Shakespeare's" (38) but there is little reason to doubt that Milton recognized Shakespeare's achievement as a *poet*.

[61] The best recent comprehensive account of early attitudes to drama and the theatre is Jonas Barish, *The Antitheatrical Prejudice* (Berkeley: Univ. of California Press, 1981), esp. 4, "Puritans and Proteans" (80–131). Sir Thomas Bodley was not unusual in including play-books amongst the "baggage books" not to be preserved in his public library of Oxford: its early librarian even disposed of the Company of Stationers' deposit copy of the Shakespeare first folio.

regarded pre-eminently as a playwright whose work was enjoyably accessible to everyone. Milton, however, was a poet whose work appealed most to a smaller, cultivated elite. And too, whereas Shakespeare's plays were no more "religious" than entertainment could support, in much of Milton's poetry religious reference weighed almost to the point of didacticism. In effect, I suggest, the modern scholars who collaborated in the fiction of Milton's involvement with the vernacular drama of his young manhood felt it necessary to rehabilitate his status by re-authorizing his canon by association with the ascendant early drama. They reversed the direction of the process by which the playwrights Jonson, Middleton, Marston, Webster, and their fellows sought to validate their popular writings by claiming the title of "poet." Such are the whirligigs of time, however, that by about three hundred years after the poet Milton began to write at Cambridge, it became necessary to appropriate the formerly-marginal Elizabethan drama to Milton in order to re-establish his centrality within a renovated cultural hegemony. There is no substantial evidence that Milton either experienced the theater of his time or valued its products, but perhaps we should indeed fictionalize his history so that it embodies our values rather than his: "Milton, Our Contemporary."

UNIVERSITY OF SOUTH CAROLINA

Michael R. G. Spiller

DIRECTING THE AUDIENCE IN
SAMSON AGONISTES

I START FROM THE POSITION THAT *SAMSON AGONISTES,* WHICH
narratively is one of the simplest of Milton's poems, seems also one of
the most mysterious. Not only do we not know at all when it was
written—something for which Milton cannot be blamed (unless, as one
is tempted to think, the old man mischievously kept it hidden from the
eyes of Edward Phillips)—but we do not know in what mode it is to be
read: political, allegorical, tragical-historical; nor even in what cultural
tradition it sits: Greek, Judaic, or Christian. The result, as Anthony Low
has said, is that "there is no . . . agreement about the central question of
the play's spirit or meaning."[1] And, one might add, there is not even
agreement over whether it is a play; Milton calls it a tragedy, but also a
dramatic poem, which leaves its precise generic status unclear.[2]

   This is most un-Miltonic, for as I tell students when they feel
intimidated by Milton's verse, Milton is usually extremely concerned to
tell his readers why he is writing what they are reading. His strongest
metanarrative voice is that of the preface or prologue, as in *Lycidas,* and
the argument summaries of the books of *Paradise Lost;* slightly weaker,
because further into the poesis itself, is the narrator's voice, as in the

---

[1] Anthony Low, *The Blaze of Noon: A Reading of "Samson Agonistes"* (New York:
Columbia Univ. Press, 1974), 3. After summarizing some completely opposed views of the
Chorus and Samson and Manoa, Low adds, "There is no closer agreement about the central
question of the play's meaning." All quotations and line numbers are from the Hughes
edition.

[2] See William Riley Parker, *Milton's Debt to Greek Tragedy in "Samson Agonistes"* (Baltimore: Johns Hopkins Univ. Press, 1937), 4–10.

verse of *Paradise Lost;* and weakest of all, being embedded in the fictional world which that poesis creates, is the privileged voice of a character, such as the Attendant Spirit in *Comus.* Now *Samson* has both a preface and an argument, but these tell us nothing about the purpose or the effect of the poem (or tragedy) as he saw it.

The preface deals not with the specific poem, but with the genre to which it belongs: and in considering that, Milton is preoccupied with establishing its dignity, and referring its imputed seriousness to its medicinal powers. His following of "the Antients and *Italians*" is more a matter of decorum than of moral intent, and the splendid peroration of the second last sentence is somewhat oddly followed by a kind of "P.S.," asking us to note the circumscription of time within the space of about 24 hours." It is perhaps unfair to call this preface *pedantic,* preoccupied with details of form to the exclusion of statements of purpose; certainly it reveals nothing of Milton's intentions.

The argument is hardly more helpful; though it reveals, perhaps, Milton's sense of the relative importance of the incidents of the drama— would any modern reader, preparing a summary, reduce Dalila's incursion to "in the meanwhile is visited by *other persons*"?—it suffers, in point of revealing purpose, from having to adopt the narrative voice of a summarizer, a person who, like a friend whispering a synopsis in a theater before the curtain rises, always seems in a hurry to be finished, or like the arguer before each canto of Spenser's *Faerie Queene,* is animated by a hearty ethical simplicity. Milton's arguer seems actually inattentive to what even the characters within the drama make of the situation: to say of the catastrophe that Samson had done it "by accident to himself" is to ignore what Manoa says at 1590–91, and to pass over also the words of the Messenger just before, "Inevitable cause / At once both to destroy and be destroy'd." Whoever the narrator of the argument is, he seems a prologue "not in confidence / Of author's pen or actor's voice."

The limitations of the arguer do not matter in *The Faerie Queene,* because the fuller metanarrative voice of the main text takes over; but here, Milton has chosen to write a drama, and drama is distinctive among literary forms for not containing a narrator's voice. Even the polyglossia of the novel privileges a narrator's voice above those of the characters, but in a drama no voice is formally privileged, nor has Samson any Attendant Spirit to introduce him. Further, Milton elected to use for this source text the prose narrative of Judges 16, which itself has a purely annalistic voice; and for his dramatic models, the plays of Sophocles and Aeschylus, which do not direct their readers how to read them.[3] So *Samson Agonistes,* from various causes, is *reticent:* it is in this respect like Old Testament and Greek narratives, and unlike, say, the *Divine Comedy* or *Paradise Lost.* The prefatory voice is finicky and unhelpful, the arguer is naive or overhasty, and no character's voice is formally privileged.

But in trying to get behind this text's reticence as to its own purposes, we may note that unless a dramatist is deliberately undermining his own discourse, as Beckett and Pinter do, it is very hard for him to avoid the privileging of finality. All plays must stop, and most of them also end, so that the voice that is speaking when a play ends does tend to acquire a certain authority. There are various ways of signalling this authority to an audience. The Greek dramatists inclined to make the last speech of their chorus comprehensive and normative, however partial or confused the chorus might have been before;[4] and Shakespeare also likes to pull forward a character, like Horatio in *Hamlet* or Albany in *King Lear,* to deliver a verdict or evaluation. Sometimes, as with Prospero at the end of *The Tempest,* Shakespeare will take the character into the metamimetic space that exists between the world of the play and the world of the audience, and a character thus rank-shifted is privileged above his fellows.

Relevant to the end of *Samson Agonistes* is one of the signs of this kind of privileged finality, a metapoetic one: the speaker recognizes the existence, either of the audience or of the play that he or she has been in. Puck, for example, refers to himself and his fellows as "shadows" and asks for applause; the Attendant Spirit in *Comus* also speaks out of the stage world to an audience of attending mortals. To have a speaker recognize, by appropriate apostrophe or metaphor, that the world he or she has been "in" is a theater or a text, is to privilege that speaker by metapoetic transfer to a higher level of reality, and give his or her final words a kind of summative power.

To consider what kind of finality *Samson Agonistes* has, we must turn to its last speeches, where there is, admittedly, no recognition of the audience such as there is in *Comus,* but there is much that stops just short of it, so much, indeed, that it cannot be casual. In reading the

[3] Irene Samuel, "*Samson Agonistes* as Tragedy," in *Calm of Mind: Tercentenary Essays on "Paradise Regained" and "Samson Agonistes" in Honor of John S. Diekhoff,* ed. Joseph Anthony Wittreich, Jr. (Cleveland: Press of Case Western Reserve Univ., 1971), 253.

[4] See the note to lines 1745–48 in the Hughes edition.

speeches of Manoa (1708–44) and of the Chorus (1745–58), we find
continuous equivocation between the theatrical event and the biblical
event—for example, when Manoa exhorts, "Come, come, no time for
lamentation now" (1708), the words have the immediate sense that the
group should not stand around elegizing while they have the opportunity to reclaim Samson's body; but since the second Semichorus has not
actually been lamenting at all, Manoa's words seem to apply also to the
audience, with the sense that at this point in the text, the audience
should not lament, but take a different attitude. And since, by Milton's
insistence, the play is for reading, not acting, there is no actor's interpretation to overpower the ambiguity of the words in the reader's mind.
Tracing these equivocations we find a strong metapoetic presence, by
which the act of constructing the text is involved as one considers that
act of destructing Samson himself.

At the center of this is the beautiful passage in which Manoa describes
what he will create (and I use the word deliberately) for the dead Samson:

> I with what speed the while
> (*Gaza* is not in plight to say us nay)
> Will send for all my kindred, all my friends
> To fetch him hence and solemnly attend
> With silent obsequy and funeral train
> Home to his Father's house: there will I build him
> A Monument, and plant it round with shade
> Of Laurel ever green, and branching Palm,
> With all his trophies hung, and Acts enroll'd
> In copious Legend, or sweet Lyric Song.   (1728–37)

The informing principle of the poem may be Hebraic, as Harold
Fisch claims,[5] but here Milton has allowed Manoa to slide into a very
classical form of commemoration, proposing a permanent tomb with
laurel and palm, trophies and scrolls with long inscriptions. This late
Roman idea of the heroic monument is a very common presence in the
visual and literary arts of the Renaissance and seventeenth century, and
its commonness in literature is because among the *topoi* of praise it offers
a metaphor for poetic creation itself, from Horace's "Exegi monumentum aere perennius" through to Shakespeare's "Not marble, nor the

---

[5] Harold Fisch, *Jerusalem and Albion: The Hebraic Factor in Seventeenth-Century Literature*
(London: Routledge and Kegan Paul, 1964), 142.

gilded monuments / Of Princes, shall outlive this powerful rhyme." I might add that because the laurel tree is not an emblematic Old Testament plant, as the palm is, we are more likely to read it as a classical emblem of victory and of poetry.

The mention of Shakespeare's use of the *topos* of poetry as a monument leads me to Milton's own retroping of it in his lines on Shakespeare contributed to the second folio of 1632, a passage with strong similarities to Manoa's lines just quoted:

> Thou in our wonder and astonishment
> Hast built thyself a live long Monument.
> For whilst to th'shame of slow-endeavoring art,
> Thy easy numbers flow, and that each heart
> Hath from the leaves of thy unvalu'd Book
> Those Delphic lines with deep impression took,
> Then thou our fancy of itself bereaving,
> Dost make us Marble with too much conceiving.
>
> ("On Shakespeare," 7–14)

Though Manoa's lines are much less mannered, and less mannerist, than the young Milton's, the two passages share the idea of the text as monument, ever living, easy and flowing, and profoundly attractive to an audience. The textual features of the monument Manoa proposes, shaded with the laurel of poetic fame, prompt the thought that we, the readers, are now visiting Samson's monument in the text before us, where under the laurel of Milton's poetry Samson's deeds are hung, and his acts enrolled or inscribed in copious legend (the narrative parts of *Samson Agonistes*) and sweet lyric song (the choric songs). The prediction that youths and virgins will visit the tomb can then be taken as a prophecy that *Samson Agonistes* will continue to be read by the youth of the nation, those who should be fashioned and inspired by "grave, moral and most profitable poems." And if, in defiance of Milton's preface, we imagine *Samson* being *acted*, it is not difficult to see Manoa's intention to

> send for all my kindred, all my friends
> To fetch him hence and solemnly attend
> With silent obsequy and funeral train
> Home to his Father's house ...   (1730–33)

as a gesture which includes the audience, who have been and are solemnly attending and silently following the death of Samson and the close of *Samson Agonistes*.

In the final speech of the play, commentators have long noticed
that the Chorus of friends "from Eshtaol and Zora's fruitful vale" appear
to have a sophisticated awareness of how tragedy operates, derived from
Aristotle and Minturno:[6]

> His servants he with new acquist
> Of true experience from this great event
> With peace and consolation hath dismist,
> And calm of mind, all passion spent.   (1755–58)

This is so much a literary reflection of the theory of catharsis that it
moves the Chorus very definitely into metapoetic space: the "great
event" is thus simultaneously the narrated, and witnessed, death of Samson in the poem, and also the experience of reading it. (Again, it is to
the point to say that Samson is offered as a text for reading, not for
watching, and the reader who reads these words would have a memory
of the other two voices that have said this in the text: the voice of the
preface, and the voice of Aristotle in the epigraph on the title page.)
Greek tragic practice does suggest that the Chorus, though capable of assuming a very specific identity within the narrative—as men of Thebes,
or Trachinian maidens—also mediated between protagonist or deuterag-
onist and the live audience, notably so at the end, where the "we" of
the Chorus extends to include all those who have experienced the
events, both those who in the narrative witness them and those who in
the theater (or the armchair) witness them.

If we accept the Chorus in *Samson* as at the end more concerned
with our experience as audience than with theirs as men of Dan, the
next step may not seem so contentious. Since Manoa has already introduced the *topos* of the poem as monument, and the readers as worship-
pers or celebrants (Horace again is the source of the idea that a text is a
sacred object that will attract devotees down the ages),[7] we are now
reading all that is said on two levels, the narrative and the metapoetic. I
have already pointed to the double sense of the word "event"; let us

---

[6] See the discussion of theory of tragedy as it applies to *Samson* by John Steadman,
" 'Passions well Imitated': Rhetoric and Poetics in the Preface to *Samson Agonistes*," in *Calm
of Mind*, 175–207.

[7] His remark in the last ode of book 3 (30.8–9) that he will be an object of perpetual
praise for his verse achievements, "dum Capitolium / scandet cum tacita virgine pontifex,"
contrives to link his fame with the central holy ritual of Rome by suggestion, not direct
statement.

now look at the first lines of the Chorus's speech:

> All is best, though we oft doubt
> What th'unsearchable dispose
> Of highest wisdom brings about,
> And ever best found in the close.   (1745–48)

Milton's elliptical syntax leaves some room for argument here, but he seems to be saying that all works out for the best, and that this truth is best found at the end of on experience. But the Chorus's summative attitude warns us that the text, as well as the sequence of events, is now closing, and that things have therefore been disposed on two levels. Of experiences, God is the disposer; but of texts, the author; and as if to reinforce the point, Milton inserts a kind of prosodic pun,

> Oft he seems to hide his face,
> But unexpectedly returns ...   (1749–50)

where the neat introduction of a new rhyme draws attention to the point that as God turns round again, so the text turns to bring in a new set of rhymes. Next we have the affirmation that highest wisdom

> ... to his faithful Champion hath in place
> Bore witness gloriously ...   (1751–52)

"Place," like "close" and "event," is a word at once narrative and meta-poetic: the house of Dagon is the place where God has borne witness to Samson, but the text is the place where Milton has borne witness to *his* "Samson Agonistes"—Samson the Champion. And it is Milton who, by finishing his text, dismisses his obedient readers with "new acquist / Of true experience from this great event."

Milton would have been dismayed, or affronted, to hear himself compared to God; but in the *topos* of the poem as monument or building, the poet is the architect of his creation just as God is the architect of his. The conventional parallel between the book of the human writer and the book of Nature simply extends the idea that the poet is the God of his textual creation and of his imaginative world. And certainly in book 7 of *Paradise Lost*, Milton comes very near an identification of himself with Divine Wisdom. He refers to the Wisdom tradition that he knew of in the Old Testament and in neo-Platonic thought, in which Wisdom is a feminine attribute, metaphorized as a companion of the Deity: and in paraphrasing Proverbs 8.30, Milton adds a touch of his own:

Thou [that is, Urania] with Eternal Wisdom didst
    converse,
Wisdom thy Sister, and with her didst play,
In presence of th'Almighty Father, pleas'd
With thy Celestial Song.   (*PL*, 7.9–12)

The book of Proverbs says nothing about poetry in heaven; it is Milton's
delightful idea to make God pleased with poetry, and to make Wisdom
keep company in God's sight with the power of imaginative verse. The
poet whose verse offers truth is very near to heaven, possessing, as Milton
said of tragedy in his preface, both verisimilitude and decorum.

There might seem to be little delight or playfulness at the end of
Samson (though the line on which Samson dies, "I mean to show you
of my strength, yet greater, / As with amaze shall strike all who behold"
[1644–45], has the same kind of heavyweight humor as Satan and Belial
use after the cannonade in heaven); and yet, if we remember that
Manoa and the Chorus are both involved in a description not just of the
narrative events of which they have both been witnesses, but of the
poetic text of which we are the witnesses, we see that we are being
guided by Milton to a reading of the text that involves a kind of playfulness and delight consequent upon the perception of truth. For the
youths and virgins who will come to the monument of Samson, and
who in the metapoesis of the passage represent us, the audience, young
in relation to the antique heroism of the patriarchs of Judaea—these will
play, according to their sex: the youths with dreams of valor and adven-
ture, and the virgins with flowers laid on the tomb (itself a metaphor for
writing poetry). In relating the fate of Samson, the virgins will lament
only his poor marriage choice and the slavery of blindness it brought,
nothing else; what they have to say about Samson will be joyful and inspiring, whence the flowers.

Here, then, in a text that is at the end maneuvering its personae
forward into metapoetic space, is the delight that should be a paradigm
of our own reaction as readers of the text. We depart at once, calm and
purged; but after that, if we revisit the monument of Samson, we will
recall his story with delight, and imitate his virtues in action, thus turning word into deed and imagination into virtuous action, as humanist
poetic theory traditionally prescribes. God has so disposed Samson's life;
and His wisdom, using celestial song through Milton, has so disposed
Samson's story that this will be the result. Indeed, there is even a sense
of social urgency in the exhortation to Israel (standard term for a regen-

erated Britain) to "find courage to lay hold on this occasion."

The text turns out to be less reticent than we had thought. Milton respected the Greek tragic form by refraining from authorial intrusion, but he did not on that account refrain also from indicating to his readers how they should respond. If it seems paradoxical that violence and destruction should issue in calm and the strewing of flowers, we may remember that this is also the sequence of events in *Comus* and *Lycidas*. It is the metapoesis of the last fifty lines that assures us that Manoa, and after him the Chorus, speak (if I may use a Miltonic pun) in an authorized fashion, and guide us to the delight that accompanies wisdom. Perhaps *Samson Agonistes* **was** written by Milton in old age, a man of "unaffected cheerfulness and civility": for we can say of Samson, both text and hero, what William Riley Parker very movingly says of Milton in his last days: "Death, when it came to this man, would be the end of a song."[8]

UNIVERSITY OF ABERDEEN

[8] William Riley Parker, *Milton: A Biography*, 2 vols. (Oxford: Clarendon Press, 1968), 1:639. The phrase "unaffected cheerfulness and civility" is Deborah Milton's, quoted by Parker on the previous page.

Part II

GENDER AND
PERSONAL IDENTITIES

Mary Ann Radzinowicz

MILTON ON THE
TRAGIC WOMEN OF GENESIS

WHEN MARGARET THATCHER CEASED TO LEAD THE TORY
party, the Shakespeare scholar Muriel Bradbrook wrote,

> I felt *2 Kings 9* was the text. "And Jehu said Who is on *my*
> side? . . . Throw *her* down. . . . And they threw her down."
> Mrs. Thatcher went to the Lord Mayor's Banquet disguised as
> Elizabeth I, with a kind of ruff.

Professor Bradbrook sees Thatcher's fall as a toppling of Jezebel, reading
in the Old Testament political not religious typology. She glosses scripture through the Seneca-like nemesis of *The Mirror for Magistrates*; she
understands the fate of contemporary women through gender-politics
and assumes that the historical books of the Bible did so too. With an
irony fearless of anachronism, she scans the Bible as a coherent political
text applicable to all times.

I want to take a leaf out of Professor Bradbrook's model and to
glance at Milton through some of the newer modes in Milton studies—
gender criticism, new historicism, and biblical poetics—by examining his
multiple interpretations of parts of a sacred text to which he ascribed
unicity. To do so, I turn to Milton's readings of the stories Genesis tells
of four women, a good place from which to look at current nomina-
tions of him as a proto-feminist.[1] Milton proposed a literary use of four

---

[1] See, for example, James Grantham Turner, *One Flesh* (Oxford: Clarendon Press, 1987),
266–87; Joseph Anthony Wittreich, Jr., *Feminist Milton* (Ithaca: Cornell Univ. Press, 1987),
2–53; but see also John Guillory, "From the Superfluous to the Supernumerary: Reading

women in Genesis as heroines in tragedies he planned to write. In the event, however, he surrendered them almost wholly to specific seventeenth-century causes: sexual, political, and religious. Milton's proposed and actual uses of the stories divulge the non-literary circumstances that affected his reading of the Bible. By revealing modes of Miltonic allusion not yet observed, I hope to complicate our understanding of his biblical poetics, to contextualize it politically, and at the same time to interrogate his idea of woman.

My argument is that Milton interprets women in Genesis on at least three distinctive levels variously combined. First, he is interested in sexual difference and in the distinctiveness of woman's biological, social, political, and religious experience. All four of the women figure in Genesis as responding with unusual independence to the authority of God and men, responding uniquely as women; Milton does not elide but rather emphasizes the distinctiveness of their experiences from those of men. He reads otherness not only, for example, in Sarah's laughter as a sign distinct from Abraham's (Gen. 18.12 and Gen. 17.15–17), but in the actions of Lot's wife, Dinah, and Tamar as impossible to Lot, Jacob's sons, or Judah (Gen. 19.26 and 18.18–21; Gen. 34.2 and 34.25–31; Gen. 39.24 and 39.25–26). His biblical scenarios embody and integrate a woman's as well as a man's point of view. His readings organize sexual difference and show its power in women to create a gendered sense of self.

Second, Milton as an historian interests himself in the ethical, political, and social *relativism* of the gender concerns the four stories incorpo-

---

Gender into *Paradise Lost*," in *Soliciting Interpretation*, ed. Elizabeth D. Harvey and Katharine Eisaman Maus (Chicago: Univ. of Chicago Press, 1990), 70.

Parallel to the reinterpretations of Milton based upon feminist insights are reinterpretations in feminist studies of Genesis of the very women about whom he thought to write tragedies. These are, of course, anachronistic measures of Milton's protofeminism, but they make very interesting reading to Miltonists, nonetheless. For a good recent selection, see Adela Yarbero Collins, "The Historical-Critical and Feminist Readings of Genesis 1.26–28," in *Hebrew Bible or Old Testament?*, ed. Roger Brooks and John J. Collins (Notre Dame: Univ. of Notre Dame Press, 1990), 197–200; Tamar Frankiel, *The Voice of Sarah* (San Francisco: Harper, 1990), 1–37; Alice L. Laffey, *Wives, Harlots and Concubines* (London: SPCK, 1990), 21–41; Elaine Pagels, *Adam, Eve and the Serpent* (New York: Random House, 1988), xvii–xxviii; Letty Russell, ed., *Feminist Interpretation of the Bible* (Philadelphia: Westminster Press, 1985), 73–86; Savina Teubal, *Hagar the Egyptian* (New York: Harper and Row, 1990), 87–110; Phyllis Trible, *Texts of Terror* (Philadelphia: Fortress Press, 1984), 9–36; and John van Seters, *Abraham in History and Tradition* (New Haven: Yale Univ. Press, 1975), 167–91.

rate. He notes historical changes in marriage customs, ceremonial law, fullness of revelation, and the like, and from these historical changes he argues human responsibility for human institutions instead of priestly or godly regulation of the whole fabric of life. So he points out that Abraham and Sarah were married before the incest bar extended to half sisters (Gen. 20.12; CPW 6:756)[2] and he justifies under Levirate law Tamar's recruiting the seed of her father-in-law Judah to secure an heir[3] (Gen. 38.12–26; CPW 8:555), even though she resorts to the disguise of a harlot. He does not read women of the Old Testament through the invariant lens of the New, from the anachronistic standpoint of Christian typology, where female types are comically limited to two: the helpless mother and the good prostitute. (The epistle to the Hebrews specifies only those two in Sarah and Rachav, and Milton planned tragedies on each, but also on numerous other types.) Instead Milton is careful to root his four women in their own historical circumstances while giving their stories psychological contemporaneity.

Finally and contrariwise, without claiming their exemplarity for his own society, Milton uses the stories polemically to comment on social and political power in his own times. He uses them sometimes to legitimate male dominance in a theocratic state, and sometimes to expose the self-interest, inequity, fraudulence, or ambivalence of both masculinist and prophetic claims. Sometimes critical opinion differs on which he is doing,[4] as it has differed in the case of Dalila in *Samson Agonistes*.[5]

The indifference of the New Testament to the actual variety of

---

[2] I have used *A Scripture Index to John Milton's "De Doctrina Christiana"* by Michael Bauman (Binghamton, N.Y.: Medieval & Renaissance Texts & Studies, 1989) to identify Milton's allusions to Genesis in the theological tractate, referring both to the Columbia and Yale editions of the work. I have used the vols. 19 and 20, index volumes to *The Works of John Milton*, ed. Frank Allen Patterson (New York: Columbia Univ. Press, 1940), to identify allusions to Genesis throughout his works. All quotations from Milton will be either to that edition, identified CE in the text or to *The Complete Prose Works of John Milton*, ed. Don M. Wolfe (New Haven: Yale Univ. Press, 1982), identified in the text as CPW. All quotations from the Bible will be to the King James Version (AV) save where noted.

[3] I have borrowed the summary from James C. Nohrnberg, "The Keeping of Nahor," in *The Book and the Text*, ed. Regina Schwartz (Oxford: Blackwell, 1990), 162.

[4] See, for example, Stanley Fish, "Wanting a Supplement," in *Politics, Poetics, and Hermeneutics in Milton's Prose*, ed. David Loewenstein and James Grantham Turner (Cambridge: Cambridge Univ. Press), 63–64, and Susanne Woods, "Elective Poetics and Milton's Prose," idem., 203.

[5] See Joseph Anthony Wittreich, Jr., *Interpreting Samson Agonistes* (Princeton: Princeton Univ. Press, 1986), x–xxii and 3–52.

tragic women in Genesis authorized Milton's freedom in the literary
treatments he planned. What were those plans and what became of
them? In the Trinity manuscript, Milton entered eight subjects for tragedy from Genesis.[6] He named them tragedies, though most would have
ended happily for the good and unhappily only for the evil; supplying
them with Greek epithetic titles, he shaped them according to classical
parallels. Some episodes he only listed as titles. For some he supplied
dramatis personae; for some, a note on plot or structure. The Genesis
tragedies were: the expulsion from paradise, Adam in banishment, the
flood, Abram in Egypt, the sacrifice of Isaac, the destruction of Sodom,
Dinah vindicated, and Tamar pregnant. Each story, in the Bible and in
Milton's scenario, calls attention to a central female character. The four
stories Milton earmarked for a literary treatment he never gave them revolve around women who lived after the flood: Sarah, Lot's wife,
Dinah, and Tamar. They are the heroines I shall trace, using the tragic
sketches in the Trinity manuscript as the base for assessing the political,
gender, and religious determinants of biblical allusion in Milton. His
other plot proposals—the expulsion from Paradise, Adam in banishment,
and the flood—made it into *Paradise Lost.* So did Abraham, but not by
way of the Trinity manuscript plots featuring Sarah. Choosing those four
plots, Milton's choice falls on women threatened, punished, or vindicated as women: wives, mothers, a sister, and a daughter-in-law. The women
fear the sexual depravity of the alien society in which they sojourn; but the
patriarchs, assumed to protect them, prove not less dangerous; God's
indifference or hostility to their special interests is a final menace.

All four are influential in founding Israel.[7] All assist the devious
twists of destiny, setting aside primogeniture to make patriarchs of
younger favored sons.[8] All four may seem mere adjuncts to the history
of patriarchy, serving Abraham, Lot, Joseph, Judah. But all four are in-

---

[6] These are conveniently listed in biblical order with duplicates reconciled in *The
Uncollected Writings of John Milton,* ed. Thomas Mabbott and J. Milton French, CE 18, 220–
235. A printed text of the Trinity Manuscript is also given in "Notes on Milton's *Paradise Lost*
and Other Biblical Scenarios" by James Holly Hanford, ed. John M. Steadman, CPW 8:554–
560. *John Milton: Poems, Reproduced in Facsimile from the Manuscript in Trinity College, Cambridge, With a Transcript* (Menston, Yorks.: Scolar Press, 1972) affords a legible photocopy,
together with a transcript made by W. A. Wright in 1899, when he printed his facsimile.

[7] See Joel Rosenberg, *King and Kin* (Bloomington: Indiana Univ. Press, 1986), 70–73;
and Robert Alter, *The Art of Biblical Narrative* (New York: Basic Books, 1981), 6.

[8] See Cheryl J. Exum, " 'Mother in Israel,' " in *The Feminist Interpretation of the Bible,* 74, 79.

volved in the swerves of power away from those patriarchs. Patriarchs are polygamous and enjoy concubinage, but ensure their lineage by strict endogamous matings. The four women are all problematic child-bearers, whose lack of heirs threatens stability. Sarah and Tamar bear children only under difficult circumstances, one postmenopausal,[9] the other a widow. Both achieve motherhood only as exceptions to the incest bar, one with her half-brother, one with her father-in-law. Lot's wife's motherhood is restricted to two daughters who replace her in Lot's bed. If Dinah, the cause of the slaughter of the whole male population of Shechem, has any issue, tradition holds that it comes from marriage to her brother Simeon and lacks a history.

Milton brings all but one of the four women together once, when in *The Likeliest Means to Remove Hirelings Out of the Church* he argues that while pre-Mosaic moral practices express a developing ethical sensibility in Israel, they are not binding on subsequent generations: "To what end servd els those altars and sacrifices [Sarah] . . . circumcision [Dinah] and the raising up of seed to the elder brother [Tamar]?" (CPW 7:284). The uniting and argument hint at how Milton's scenarios interrogate any allegorically consistent interpretation of Genesis. The Bible inconsistently explains Israel's stable foundation.[10] On the one hand, the nation's landholding is explained as absolute, the result of ancestral purchase, treaty, inheritance, and divine covenant. Land is permanently acquired by legal purchases such as Abraham makes to secure Sarah a burial plot (Gen. 23.4–18), gifts such as Pharaoh or Abimelech give him (Gen. 12.16 and Gen. 20.14–16), his inheritance from his father Terah (Gen. 12.5), and God's covenant with him freely renewed (Gen. 12.2–3; 13.15–17; 15.18; 17.4–8). On the other hand, Israel's landholding is explained as contingent on righteousness, as in the flood (Gen. 6.9–9.17) or the destruction of Sodom (Gen. 19.1–35),[11] when the land itself is defaced for unrighteousness. The stories of the four women invoke and perplex orders of stability: Israel as God's gift or God's reward, an

---

[9] As feminist and comparativist, Savina J. Teubal in *Hagar the Egyptian* suggests that Sarah is a priestess sworn to chastity, whose barrenness owes nothing to excessive age and is set aside by YHWH in a narrative designed to explicate the relationship of Arabs and Jews by way of Hagar and Sarah.

[10] I am indebted to Joel Rosenberg, *King and Kin*, 88–89, for the subsequent description.

[11] On the intertextual relationship of the flood to the destruction of the cities of the plain, see Harold Fisch, *Poetry with a Purpose* (Bloomington: Indiana Univ. Press, 1988), 70–74. The two stories thematize Israel's moral responsibility.

absolute heritage or a merited payment for family or tribal morality.

Finally, the mythic strength of patriarchy is qualified by the central roles the four play in the political foundation of Israel; they do not install matriarchy in place of patriarchy, but they do act heroically. In three of Milton's four cases, Genesis is so sympathetic to the women that Harold Bloom conjectures that the J text was written by one.[12] In all four Genesis occludes patriarchal individuality by changing the names of the patriarchs, electing the sons of special wives above those of other wives or slaves, or by submerging the patriarchs into tribal entities. Personal names in Genesis are identified with national or place names so that the stories of mythic heroes become the vehicles of national history.[13] Tamar fails to bear children with the privately named Er and Onan, but succeeds with her father-in-law Judah, whose name may be taken to mean Southern Kingdom, the geopolitical equivalent of, say, South Carolina or South America (Gen. 38.1–30). The metamorphosis of Lot's wife into a pillar of salt (Gen. 19.23) results in his daughters' bearing Moab and Ammon, fathers of nations that carry their names (Gen. 19.36–38). Ammonites and Moabites are cousins of Israel. But Israel—as Jacob, Abraham's grandson, becomes when he is re-named (Gen. 32.29)[14]—is legitimate while Ammon and Moab are illegitimate; the names within the family history label those two nations' inferiority to Israel. Biblical stories convey both private and political meaning. To conclude with my introduction, then, Milton's four women are decisive in the geopolitical allegory of Genesis and rich in human implications. Milton understands them in both modes across the pattern of his prose and poetic allusions. His readings co-opt the historicity for polemic and expand the human sympathy due them as women. He planned literary treatments they could sustain, he made polemical uses they invite; they were attractive to him because of that double possibility.[15]

[12] See Harold Bloom, *The Book of J* (New York: Grove Weidenfeld, 1990), 10, 311.

[13] See Edward L. Greenstein, "Genealogy as a Code in Genesis," in *Approaches to Teaching the Hebrew Bible as Literature,* ed. Barry N. Olshen and Yael S. Feldman (New York: Modern Language Association of America, 1989), 104.

[14] See Nahum M. Sarna, ed., *The JPS Torah Commentary: Genesis* (Philadelphia, New York, Jerusalem: The Jewish Publication Society, 1989), 304–5.

[15] Milton's *inclusion* of the four women I shall treat is easier to explain than his exclusion of several others from literary plans. The stories of Hagar and Ishmael, of Isaac and Rebecca, or of Jacob and his two cousin-wives Rachel and Leah, themselves sisters, are not on the face of it less interesting than those of Sarah, Dinah, and Tamar. Nor is Lot's wife obviously more interesting than his daughters, who induced an alcoholic blackout in their father in order to

Milton listed two tragedies involving Sarah. The first he cryptically entitled "Abram in Aegypt" (Gen. 12.11–20) but he did not work up its theme (the sister-wife theme, varied at Gen. 20 and echoed at Gen. 26.1, 6–11). He planned a second tragedy, entitled it "Abram from Morea or Isack redeemd" (based on Gen. 22), and fully sketched that plot. In Genesis, Sarah's story and Abraham's election are inextricably bound: Abraham is not elect without Sarah, even though through Hagar and Keturah he produces many tribes (Gen. 25.1–18). Genesis says that Sarah is both exceptionally beautiful and barren. Had Milton worked out the scenario for "Abram in Aegypt," it could have begun when Abram told Sarai: "This is thy kindness which thou shalt show unto me; at every place whither we shall come, say of me, He is my brother" (Gen. 20.13). On the point of entering Egypt, Abram explains that Egyptians desiring Sarai could ignore a brother but would have to kill a husband to enjoy her. She is abducted, but he is well treated on her account. Her captor Pharaoh learns the truth of her weddedness when he and his house become impotent. When Abram prays for him and they recover, Pharaoh instructs his men to see them safely off with gifts.

A good number of years later, Abram, again on alien soil but now called Abraham since he has been circumcised and promised Isaac, tells Abimelech, the local ruler, that Sarah is his sister. She is now named Sarah, having overheard the annunciation of Isaac, and must now be nearly ninety, other motives perhaps than her exceptional beauty inspiring her abduction.[16] This time, no physical congress occurs between Sarah and Abimelech; during the night, God visits Abimelech in a dream and predicts his death for interfering with a married woman. Abimelech assures God of "the innocency of my hands" (Gen. 20.5); God advises him to restore Sarah and have Abraham intercede for him. When Abimelech asks Abraham for an explanation of the deception, he is given two: First, he always calls Sarah his sister when in a country where God is not feared. Second, she *is* his sister, "the daughter of my father, but not . . . of my mother" (Gen. 20.12). In its combined Genesis

---

perpetuate the race upon him, after what they took to have been apocalyptic destruction of all male stock.

John M. Steadman suggests that while Milton was not deterred from considering the same subjects a number of dramatists had already treated (CPW 8.547), he may have omitted such themes as Jephthah's daughter, Esther, and Judith because of "their popularity with earlier epic or dramatic poets." I cannot offer a better explanation.

[16] See Sarna, *The JPS Torah Commentary: Genesis*, 141.

versions, the story is uncannily similar to that of the two abductions of the beautiful Helen of Troy by Theseus and then when she is married to Menelaus, by Paris.[17]

In his nonliterary treatments Milton answers several questions about Abraham and Sarah. Ought Abraham to pass Sarah off as his sister even if she is? Milton says no for two reasons: (1) to ask Sarah to say she is his sister shows distrust of God (CPW 6:568); (2) "though [the deception] was intended only to save his life, [it] was, as he might have learned from his previous experience in Egypt, likely to lead men who did not know the truth into sin and unlawful desire" (CPW 6:760–61). His plea of self-defense, far from mitigating Abraham's guilt, only exposes his lack of faith. Abraham hasn't understood Sarah's importance to the covenant; the promise of progeny seems to him all about male sexuality in its linkage to circumcision; he even suggests that God create nations from his son Ishmael (Gen. 17.18).[18] Milton also answers the question: ought Abraham to have accepted gifts from Pharaoh or Abimelech? He says yes, it showed high-mindedness or Abraham's "own dignity rightly understood" (CPW 6:735), whereas to accept a field from Ephron in which to bury Sarah would be low-minded, a burial plot deserving a market price, even the extortionate one he pays. And finally, he answers the question, do Pharaoh's or Abimelech's *people* need Abraham's prayers? Milton says yes. Even before the declaration of Mosaic law, God made adultery a capital offense. Tribes or nations become guilty for crimes committed by their heads. Pharaoh and Abimelech were guilty of adultery or its intent, so their people were justly plagued with impotence (CPW 6:386).

Milton's nonliterary allusions reveal all three levels of his interest in Sarah as the elect sister-wife. First, he shows his interest in the gendered identities of men and women. Sarah overhears in the annunciation of Isaac an emphasis on female not male sexuality; circumcision is not mentioned in her hearing and she thinks ruefully of her menopause and Abraham's inability to give her pleasure. So she laughs at what she hears. Rebuked by the angel, she denies laughing. Milton says her denial was dishonest and she should have apologized. He does not say that her laughter was a scandal or a threat; he distinguishes between Abraham's dangerously misleading deception of Abimelech and Sarah's earthier

---

[17] I have been anticipated on this point by Sarna, *The JPS Torah Commentary: Genesis,* 94.

[18] See Leslie Brisman, *The Voice of Jacob* (Indianapolis: Indiana Univ. Press, 1990), 36.

social lie concealing only a private joke (CPW 6:760). Second, Milton
reveals his historical interest in changes in sexual mores, noting that half-
sister marriage is permitted in the patriarchal period but that even then
adultery is a capital crime (CPW 6:757). Third, Milton the polemicist
finds in the love of Abraham and Sarah the institution of an ideal marriage of "mutual love, delight, help and society of husband and wife,
though with the husband having greater authority" (CPW 6:355).
Sarah's docile complicity in her own abduction is used, that is, to endorse male dominance and not to challenge it.

In the Trinity manuscript, Milton sketched a full scenario for the
sacrifice of Isaac, Sarah's second tragedy. In Genesis the story is called a
test of Abraham: the father is told to sacrifice his beloved son, takes him
to a mountain and ties him to a pyre, at which God interdicts the
human sacrifice, a ram is substituted, and the father and son return
home.[19] Milton's scenario takes every opportunity to emphasize the
equivocal in this story. He creates a scene in which Abraham's puzzled
friends explain his strange secret mission as the collapse of his reason
from misplaced zeal or superstition. In Sarah, he draws a well-developed
character, strong to insist that love of one's son is as sacred as obedience
to one's God. He introduces an ally monarch in Melchizedek, not a
priest. He limits his cast of characters to the human in order to question
what exactly is being tested in Abraham. Is it Abraham's obedience in
acceding to God's demand for human sacrifice, or is it his understanding

[19] The scenario reads:

Abram from Morea, or Isack redeemd. the oiconomie may be thus the fift or sixt
day after Abrahams departure, Eleazer Abrams steward first alone and then with
the chorus discours of Abrahams strange voiage thire mistresse sorrow and
perplexity accompanied with frighfull dreams, and tell the manner of his rising by
night taking his servants and his son with him next may come forth Sarah her
self, after the Chorus or Ismael or Agar next some shepheard or companie of
merchants passing through the mount in the time that Abram was in the mid
work relate to Sarah what they saw hence lamentations, fears, wonders, the
matter in the mean while divulgd Aner or Eshcol, or mamre Abrams confederats
come to the hous of Abram to be more certaine, or to bring news, in the mean
while discoursing as the world would of such an action divers ways, bewayling
the fate of so noble a man faln from his reputation, either through divin justice,
or superstition, or coveting to doe some notable act through zeal. at length a
servant sent from Abram relates the truth, and last he himselfe comes in with a
great Train of Melchizedec whose shepheards beeing secret eye witnesses of all
passages had related to thir master, and he conducted his freind Abraham home with
joy. (CPW 8:557–58) [This passage is reproduced as the frontispiece, page viii].

of God's true nature? Has God covenanted with Abraham because Abraham is righteous and obedient or because God is righteous and desires to raise human morality to a new height?[20] Finally, Milton draws a Sarah, like Mary in *Paradise Regained,* kept in the dark, who suffers whatever Abraham's test be, obedience or faith, becoming the vehicle of every human emotion involved in the scene. Milton forgoes Isaac's touching question, "where is the lamb," and all the apparatus of piety; he substitutes Sarah's nightmares during the horror of her week-long fear. He reverses the emphasis of Genesis deliberately, that text silent about Sarah's and rich about Isaac's responses.

Milton again reveals his threefold interest in gender: plainly he is alert to the distinctive experience of a woman, whose sense of womanliness provides her core identity. Milton reads Abraham as having no doubt that God means him to kill Isaac. In *Christian Doctrine* he acquits him of falsehood for telling his servants that he would return with Isaac:

> He himself was quite sure that his son would be sacrificed and left behind. Had he not been sure of this, what sort of trial of

---

[20] This equivocality in the sacrifice of Isaac is similar to an equivocality in the verse in Abram's first dialogue with God in which Abram is promised progeny and trusts God, Gen. 15.6, "And he believed in the Lord; and he counted it to him for righteousness." Milton knew that the preponderant rabbinic midrash read the verse: "And because Abraham put his trust in the Lord, the Lord reckoned it to Abraham's merit," but that a minority of rabbis including Rambon and Abravanel rendered it: "Abram trusted God and attributed the covenant to God's righteousness." The verse applies to the equivocality of the test of Abraham; it is a test of his power either to obey or to learn. In the outcome, too, Isaac is spared either because Abraham righteously performs a work of obedience or in order that he sees that God righteously desires human purity of faith, not human sacrifice. In *Christian Doctrine* (CPW 6:487) Milton cites the verse to show that mankind is saved "not through the works of law but through faith," taking the majority position. Milton then applies verse 15.6 to the sacrifice of Isaac (CPW 6:490). Abraham's faith or trusting obedience in offering his son as a sacrifice is "counted to him for righteousness" and rewarded by the return of Isaac and by the better understanding of God's pure mercy. I suggest that Milton gave the alternative position to Sarah and Abraham's friends in his scenario, however.

Brisman, *The Voice of Jacob,* 55–60, offers the most interesting modern version of the Abravanel and Rambon readings and their bearing on the sacrifice of Isaac. (On 37, he notes the textual incongruity between the famous statement of pure "faith" of verse 6, followed by a demand for a sign in verse 8.) But see also Sarna, *The JPS Torah Commentary: Genesis,* 113, 359, for a Hebracist reading and van Seters, *Abraham in History and Tradition,* 227–248, for an important archaeological historicist interpretation. For an analysis of the political twist Milton gave to the testing of Abraham, see my essay " 'In those days there were no kings in Israel': Milton's Politics and Biblical Narrative," *The Year's Work in English Studies* 21 (1991): 242–52.

faith would there have been? But he was an intelligent man and he realized that it was not his servants' concern to know what was going on, and that it was convenient that they should not know for the time being. (CPW 6:763)

Sarah does not agree with Abraham, but with the companions Milton invented: superstition and blind zeal have unhinged him. Since Sarah doesn't hear God's second command—"Lay not thine hand upon the lad, neither do thou anything unto him" (Gen. 22.12)—revealing his will to forfend the human sacrifice, she may even consider that God is woman's arbitrary enemy. Second, Milton's scenario substitutes historical literalism for sentiments of piety. He elaborates Abraham's patriarchal household in a way similar to the face-value interest he took in the historicity of adultery and incest in the wife-sister story. In nonliterary polemic, too, he secularizes Melchizedek to argue against tithes and for independent congregationalism and an unpaid clergy. His Melchizedek is an ally given a share of military spoils and not a priest subsisting on tithes.[21] Finally, Milton refuses to endorse Abraham's faith as exemplary, writing: "not examples but express commands oblige our obedience to God or man," a sharply literal rebuff to typologists. Milton is silent about Sarah's typological significance; the epistle to the Hebrews, enrolling her amongst the heroes and heroines of faith, has regard simply to her conceiving Isaac: "Through faith also Sarah herself received strength to conceive seed, and was delivered of a child when she was past age, because she judged him faithful who had promised." Save in connection with marriage, all Milton's readings of Sarah are revisionary.

What does Milton make of Lot's wife? In Genesis, when God tells Abram that owing to the depravity of the Sodomites he will utterly destroy the cities of the plain, Abram bargains: might not the presence of

---

[21] In *Considerations Touching The Likeliest Means to Remove Hirelings Out of the Church,* CPW 7:258, Milton writes of Melchizedek's support for Abram in battle (Gen. 14):

> Melchisedec, besides his priestly benediction, brought him bread and wine sufficient to refresh *Abram* and his whole armie; incited to do so, first, by the secret providence of God, intending him for a type of Christ and his priesthood; next by his due thankfulnes and honor to *Abram,* who had freed his borders of *Salem* from a potent enemie: *Abram* on the other side honors him with the tenth of all, that is to say, (for he took not sure his whole estate with him to that warr) of the spoiles.

This Melchisedec Milton transfers from Gen. 14 to the end of his tragic scenario, with the effect of surrounding Abraham with historical human beings and activity, an emphasis that urges a humanistic reading.

fifty, forty-five, thirty, twenty, or even ten innocent men save the cities? He extracts from God the promise that for ten the city would be saved.[22] Ten could not be found. Milton wrote a very full scenario for that tragedy, entitling it "Cupids funeral pile. Sodom Burning." In one nonliterary use of the material, he instanced God's pact with Abraham as proof of God's justice, noting in *The Doctrine and Discipline of Divorce:*

> [H]e hath taught us to love and to extoll his Lawes, not onely as they are his, but as they are just and good to every wise understanding. Therefore *Abraham* ... seem'd to doubt of divine justice, if it should swerve from that irradiation wherwith it had enlight'ned the mind of man, and bound it selfe to observe its own rule. *Wilt thou destroy the righteous with the wicked? that be far from thee; shall not the Judge of the earth doe right?* Therby declaring that God hath created a righteousness in right it selfe, against which he cannot doe. (CPW 2:297–98)

God's contract to obey his own laws of justice is the theme Milton shapes from the story of Lot; but for Lot's wife's story, his emphasis falls on human freedom to choose. That Milton's personal Bible shows signs of great wear and tear at chapter 18 of Genesis may indicate his sense of an ambiguity in its meaning.

Milton's literary plan reveals just as strong an interest in historical and political mores as in religious and sexual ones. In Genesis, God's bargain with Abraham is immediately followed by a scene in which the Sodomites show their depravity. Two angels arrive in the city and accept Lot's hospitality. While they feast with him, the Sodomites demand them for homosexual rape. Lot offers instead his two daughters, virgin though betrothed. The Sodomites warn him that he is an alien living in their city on sufferance, not their moral mentor, and threaten to break down the door. The angels blind them with a blaze of light,[23] and, as

---

[22] Harold Bloom, "From J to K: the Uncanniness of the Yahwist," in *The Bible and the Narrative Tradition,* ed. Frank McConnell (New York: Oxford Univ. Press, 1986), 205–6, and again in *The Book of J,* 28, finds the bargaining so grimly comic that he suspected the redactors of cutting out from the Akedah a similar argument on Abraham's part for his son's life.

[23] Milton cuts the scene in Genesis in which the Sodomites are struck momentarily blind and grope in vain for Lot's door. He does argue in self-defensive polemic, however, after he himself had become blind, that blindness is not God's punishment for wrongdoing but afflicts both the righteous and unrighteous, citing Isaac and Jacob as righteous blind:

the Sodomites grope around for the door, instruct Lot to take his household and leave the city to its destruction. Lot argues and makes conditions, until the angels catch his wife and daughters by the hands and
rush them off, saying, "Escape for thy life; look not behind thee, neither
stay thou in the plain; escape to the mountain, lest thou be consumed"
(Gen. 19.17). When Lot's wife looks back she is turned into a pillar of
salt. The cataclysm follows.

Milton's scenario substitutes a wholly unscriptural scene for the
threatened sodomizing of the angels and Lot's offer to yield the virginity
of his daughters in place of his guests. First Milton devises an anthropo-
logical ritual: the "Gallantry" of Sodom process with song and dance to
the Temple of Venus, Urania, or Peor; learning of the noble guests,
they send two "of thire choysest youth with the preist to invite them to
thire citty solemnities it beeing an honour that thire citty had decreed to
fair *personages*" (CPW 8:558). The angels tell the priest they are from
"Salem" and a violent religious quarrel erupts. Here Milton splices briefly back to Genesis: the Sodomites denounce Lot for "praesumption, sin-
gularity [&] breach of citty customs." Milton then continues to impro-
vise history: the Sodomites fight Lot's shepherds. The angels intervene
to save him and warn Lot to take his "friends and sons in Law" out of
the city. When Lot meets one of them, "heer is disputed of incredulity
of divine judgments & such like matters." A chorus of angels "relat[es]
the events of Lots journy, & of his wife," and then Milton brings on
"ye king & nobles" to whom as thunder, lightening and fires com-
mence, the chief of the angelic Chorus explains the difference between
love and lust. The tragedy ends "with some short warning to all other
nations to take heed."

Biblical poesis is essentially multiplotted, not creating a figure in the
carpet but a scrolled panorama.[24] The destruction of the Cities of the
Plain is the thematic nexus of a larger story. Milton's nonliterary reading of
the story as thematizing divine justice renders the moral of Biblical narrative: the history of the developing ethical sensibility of Israel. His literary
scenario cuts into the larger web, however, as dramatically for Lot's story
as for Abraham's. He excludes the daughters but retains the only unnamed

[T]he patriarch Isaac himself, than whom no mortal was ever more dear to God,
lived blind no small number of years; and for some time, perhaps Jacob also his
son, of God no less beloved. (CPW 4:586)

[24] See Meir Sternberg, *The Poetics of Biblical Narrative* (Bloomington: Indiana Univ. Press,
1985), 81–84, and Robert Alter, "Sodom as Nexus," in *The Book and the Text*, 149–51.

patriarch's wife in scripture. As Sarah recalls Helen of Troy, and as Isaac resembles Iphigenia, Lot's wife more imprecisely evokes an abandoned Eury-
dice. Milton knows that the angelic words "don't look back" are a warning to her, not a command, and signify "don't let the grass grow under
your feet." He knows her metamorphosis into a pillar of salt etiologically
accounts for some geographical oddity in the rock-salt near the Dead Sea.
The Geneva Bible so read it and softened her accidental destruction with
the comment, it "touch[ed] the bodie only [and made] a notable monument of Gods vengeance to all them that passed that way."[25] In nonliterary use Milton considers her transformation the natural result of a human
flaw, not a divine punishment lumping her with the Sodomites. In *Christian Doctrine,* he proves that God does not absolutely decree anything left
in the power of human beings but gives them freedom of action, noting
that when Lot delayed his departure from Sodom to ask for the little city
of Zoar to be saved for him as a refuge, it was saved (Gen. 19.20–22;
CPW 6:155). Lot had a lucky freedom of will. Milton ascribes Lot's wife's
ruin to her "[s]eeking for knowledge of things which are hidden from
mankind" (CPW 6:649). She stood looking back to see the fireworks
and destruction caught up with her; she had an unlucky freedom of will.
Both Milton and Genesis sanction the destruction of Sodom: Milton's
only other references to it, literary or otherwise, disapprove its drunkenness and homosexuality (e.g., CPW 6:756; *PL* 1:503).

Once more, Milton's persistent interests are reflected both in the
scenario and in his nonliterary allusions. To Milton, Lot's wife clearly
experiences freedom and necessity very differently from Lot: Lot's procrastination illustrates his dutiful preciseness; his wife's procrastination, a
lethal curiosity. The details of the fertility worship of the Sodomites reveal Milton's historian's interest in pagan religions. He makes no polemical use of the Lot story, unless the inclusion of chastity and temperance
among one's duties to one's neighbors is polemical rather than prophylactic.

Milton's next postdiluvian heroine is Dinah, for whose tragedy he
supplies only a *dramatis personae.* That *dramatis personae* is telling, however. In the Bible (Gen. 34), Dinah's story is the most pitiful of the four.

[25] See *The Geneva Bible: a facsimile of the 1560 edition,* with an introduction by Lloyd E.
Berry (New York, 1969). John T. Shawcross, "Milton's Bibles," in *The Milton Encyclopedia,*
2.163, confirms that the 1560 edition is generally thought to have been in Milton's possession.

Sympathy is invoked for a defenseless Israelite virgin,[26] who speaks no word in her own defense and whose classical analogue is the pitiful Philomela. Dinah needs defense against the passion of her princely rapist Shechem, who keeps her prisoner while he negotiates to secure her as a wife; she is only freed when Levi and Simeon put the Shechemites to the sword (Gen. 34.26). She needs it against the indifference of her father Jacob, who coolly awaits her brothers' reactions to the rape; she is the daughter of Leah, the unloved wife, and not of Rachel, and the Shechemite alliance is worth having. She needs it against the self-right-eousness of her grieving and violent brothers Simeon and Levi, who avenge her by murdering Shechem and the entire male population, men who could put up no fight, for they were confined to their separate houses, weakened by having just been circumcised to meet Simeon and Levi's objection, "We cannot give our sister ... to one that is uncircumcised" (Gen. 34.24). Sympathy is invoked for Dinah, solely innocent. As for her brothers Simeon and Levi, Jacob on his death-bed denounces them, "Cursed be their anger, for it was fierce; and their wrath, for it was cruel" (Gen. 49.7) and prophesies the election will skip over them to light on Judah. Levi goes on to father a landless prelacy; Simeon, to disappear. Tradition has it that Dinah marries him, but she too vanishes from scripture. Though to be disinherited, Simeon and Levi speak the most powerful words of the story,[27] an unanswered question: "And they said, should he deal with our sister as with a harlot?" Having read in Shechem's offer of a rich dowry for Dinah a condescension like a prostitute's payoff, they murder the males, enslave the females and loot the city (Gen. 34.31). But looting is forbidden to the Israelites. Jacob abandons the city Shechem, buries the loot, and dedicates a new altar to

---

[26] More sympathy accrues to her in the J version of her story than in the E, according to Leslie Brisman, *The Voice of Jacob*, 96–98, and Richard Elliott Friedman, *Who Wrote the Bible?* (New York: Summit Books, 1987), 62–65. But her affective force is generally conceded, a force greater than that of her brothers or her father. Sternberg's support of the ethics and theology of Simeon and Levi, in *The Poetics of Biblical Narrative*, 444–81, is challenged by Elaine Fuchs, and Gilas Ramas-Rauch in *Mappings of the Biblical Terrain*, ed. Vincent L. Tollers and John Maier (Lewisburg, Pa.: Bucknell Univ. Press, 1990), 136–37, 160–64. The Geneva Bible criticizes Dinah's parents for permitting her to wander freely in the countryside, condemns Simeon and Levi for using the religious rite of circumcision as a military cover and deception plan, and imposes judgment against the people Shechem for the wickedness of its princes.

[27] Robert Alter, *The Art of Biblical Poetry* (New York: Basic Books, 1985), 47, is of that opinion.

God at Bethel. There Deborah, Rebekah's nurse, dies.

Milton's *dramatis personae* includes Deborah. The inclusion suggests that a literary treatment would not, as with the destruction of Sodom, have cut a dramatic segment from a web of meaning. By the inclusion of Deborah,[28] he extends the plot as far as her only association with Dinah, the verse announcing her death. Hanford has suggested:

> The messenger would doubtless have narrated the massacre and Rebekah's old nurse Deborah have prophesied the outcome— but where, when, and to whom. Milton is confronted with the difficulty of carving out a dramatic unit from the continuity of Hebrew history. (CPW 8:590)

But Deborah does not prophetically look ahead; she looks back. Her presence binds together a long sequence within the continuity of scriptural history. Her death cuts the last link with Jacob's generation as a prelude to the story of Joseph.[29] Hence Milton's *dramatis personae* hints at a historical thematization, not simply a dramatic shaping of Dinah's rape. Deborah's death closes off the Jacob cycle; Dinah's violation results in the inheritance swerving away from his elder sons. The outcome of the story renders a complex and ironic historical moral; human beings are free to make history, to make themselves into the makers of history. History then makes plain its verdict on history-makers. Milton's nonliterary reading of the episode renders that historical verdict. He faults the Shechemites for undertaking to be circumcised for political or economic motives and not religious conviction (CPW 6:668); he denies that Levi's tithes in any way constitute God's wish for his modern church (CPW 7:287–88). What was moral in Levi's time in relieving his necessity would be childishly ceremonial in Milton's England. God has left men free to determine his will by the analysis of the history of his people; he does not rule them by fiat.

---

[28] The Trinity manuscript gives the title "Dinah," followed by the note of a later poetical treatment, "vide Euseb. praeparat Evang.1.9.c.22," and then a list of characters headed "the Persons": "Dina, Debora rebeccas nurse, Jacob, Simeon, Levi, Hamor, Sichem, Counselers 2., Nuncius, Chorus" (CE 18:259; CPW 8:555).

[29] Partly to save him from Isaac's anger, Rebekah sent Jacob to seek marriage among her kinship; Esau had taken wives among the Hittites, a source of bitterness to his parents. Her family piety in urging endogamy on Jacob has seemed to Sarna, *The JPR Torah Commentary: Genesis,* 195, to compensate for her compliance in tricking Isaac into blessing the younger son. Dismissing Jacob, Rebekah promised to send for Jacob to return when it was safe; rabbinic tradition named the ancient nurse Deborah her messenger.

The last of the tragic women is Tamar, a widow cheated of her Levirate due (Gen. 38). She secures the heir to her husband's share in Judah's estate, the son she is owed by a brother-in-law, when she tricks her father-in-law Judah into taking her for a prostitute, risking execution as a common harlot under the double standard of patriarchal sexual behavior.[30] By Levirate law, on the death of her husband Er, Tamar is owed an heir to the fortune of the family into which she has married, to be fathered by her next eldest brother-in-law; but when the first such brother-in-law, Onan, is struck dead for spilling his seed on the ground in order not to divide his inheritance through compliance with the law, Judah withholds his last remaining son from Tamar. She tricks Judah into lying with her himself and, visibly pregnant, is condemned to death. But she has evidence of Judah's role and he acknowledges the proof together with her entitlement to an heir, and leaves her in peace. In the event, Tamar bears Judah twin sons, the only of his sons to survive.[31]

For the projected literary treatment of Tamar's story, Milton provides a title, a revised title and a conclusion. His first title is "Thamar Veiled," *veiled* referring to her disguise by the road Judah travels: "And she put her widowes garments off her, and covered her with a vaile" (Gen. 38.14). His second title cancels "veiled" and substitutes "Tamar pregnant": "Behold, she is with child by whoredom: and Judah said, Bring her forth and let her be burnt" (Gen. 38.24). Milton phrases its moral: "Juda is found to have bin the author of that crime which he condemn'd in Tamar, Tamar excus'd in what she attempted" (CPW 8:555). Clearly, Judah is tricked by a mettlesome heroine, whose audacity and wit are fully equal to the power of a male leader of his people.[32] Two classical analogues to Tamar have been suggested, the second of which shows Graeco-Roman interest in a woman's justifiable deception of a paternal figure to ensure elect offspring: Ann Engar sees in the women tricksters of the Old Testament—especially Rebekah, Rachel, Tamar, and Ruth—a positive resort to wit and intellect like that of Odysseus and his grandfather Autolycus, and William Shullenberger sug-

---

[30] That is the view of J. P. Fokkelman, writing on Genesis in *A Literary Guide to the Bible,* ed. Robert Alter and Frank Kermode (Cambridge: Belknap Press of Harvard Univ. Press, 1987), 40.

[31] See Bloom, *The Book of J,* 220.

[32] That is the opinion of Bloom, *The Book of J,* 220–23, and Ann W. Engar, "Old Testament Women as Tricksters," in *Mappings of the Biblical Terrain,* 148–50.

gests many points of similarity with the story of Myrrha in Ovid's
Metamorphoses.[33]

Milton's nonliterary allusions taken together with his literary plan
again display the three interests I have been examining. His literary
treatment exonerates Tamar, accepting the integrity of her decisive action and its gendered necessity. His earliest allusion, however, in *Animadversions . . . against Smectymnuus* polemically applies the story to a
sectarian issue in a way that utterly subverts the moral he gave for the
tragedy. Disputing the Remonstrant's suggestion that the prayer book
liturgy was mercifully and charitably intended to help Papists worship in
the Church of England, Milton writes: "It was Pharisaicall, and vain-
glorious, a greedy desire to win Proselites by conforming to them
unlawfully, like the desire of *Tamar,* who to raise up seed to her Husband sate in the common road drest like a Curtezan, and he that came
to her committed incest with her" (CPW 1:688–89). This ahistorical
and conventionally moralistic reading has some Reformation authority;
the Geneva Bible, for example, explains the struggle between the
unborn twins in her womb to be born first by noting "their heinous
sinne was signified by this monstruous birth." But polemic requires that
Milton reverse the moral he planned to draw when he highlighted
Judah's confession in Genesis that, "She is more righteous than I; for she
hath done it because I gave her not to Shelah my sonne" (Gen. 38.26).[34]

Milton's *Animadversions* polemic also runs counter to the historical
relativism he urged, most plainly referring it to Tamar's case in *Hirelings:*

Whatsoever was don in religion before the law written, is not
presently to be counted moral, when as so many things were
then don both ceremonial and Judaically judicial, that we need
not doubt to conclude all times before Christ, more or less

---

[33] See Engar, "Old Testament Women as Tricksters," 143, 149. Schullenberger suggests:
Ovid's Myrrha offers some broad and imperfect parallels.... (1) Myrrha tricks
and seduces her father; (2) her father's self-righteous condemnation of her is
undercut by hints of his complicity; (3) in the midst of other 'tragic women,'
Ovid renders her as the central character of the tale and initiator of action; (4)
she gives birth to a hero, Adonis, which, if not a dynastic parallel to the Tamar
/ Judah, has some interesting sacrificial resonances. (Letter written August 1991)
[34] The Trinity manuscript outlines for tragedy are usually assigned to the dates 1639 to
1642 (CPW 8:539, 550, n. 2). *Animadversions* is usually dated July 1641 (CPW 1:653).
Whichever treatment of Tamar came first, both coincided so nearly in time as to make their
distinctiveness of position noteworthy.

under the ceremonial law. To what end servd els ... the raising up of seed to the elder brother? (CPW 7:284)

Milton's imagination is caught by his last postdiluvian tragic woman of
Genesis, yet he is capable *at the same time* of reading her censoriously in
the interests of antiprelatical or sectarian polemic, against not only the
insights of his imagination but his own historical principles. *Animadversions* has on many occasions been criticized for its harshness, unfairness,
inconsistency, and insensitivity. Milton himself apologizes in advance for
its tone, or at least adjudges in his own case that he "cannot be blam'd
though [he] bee transported with the zeale of truth to a well heated fer-
vencie" (CPW 1:663). I would find it a straining after misogyny to discover in this polemical use a rooted male chauvinism; the sufficient
source is rooted anticlericalism.

What are we to conclude about the multivalence of Milton's biblical allusions, observed in the applications in his works of the stories of
these four women? As a scholar and theologian Milton sets out in
Christian Doctrine "the right method of interpreting the Scriptures," en-
dorsing linguistic, contextual, and hermeneutic care (CPW 6:582–83).
First he assures us, however, in a peremptory foreclosure to fend off
over-interpretation in the interests of a rational biblical faith, that "each
passage of scripture has only a single sense, though in the Old Testament
this sense is often a combination of the historical and the typological"
(CPW 6:581). In his own allusions, however, his assurance proves false;
again and again he draws out an equivocation in the text or offers
equivocal readings between the lines of, or filling in gaps within, biblical
texts with his own fictions.[35] I might propose a number of reasons why
this is so, from the general (the Bible is not the unitary text he thought
it was and all communications are more polysemic than he guessed) to
the specific reasons I have hoped to give (Milton experiences Genesis
while public and political tides of disinterest and interest ebb and flow
through his imagination, his reason, his experience, and his society).

But are we in a very different situation from Milton? Contemporary
theoretical discourse discourages monocausal and unitary explanations for
complex phenomena. For myself I am far from urging that either bad
faith or masculinism created Milton's politicizing ambivalence. Yes, he

---

[35] This move Fish, "Wanting a Supplement," 41–68, characterizes by reference to
Derrida, and Woods, "Elective Poetics and Milton's Prose," 193–212, by reference to elective
poetics.

both suppresses a psychosexual uproar in favor of a more archaeological interest (Lot's wife) and discerns a whorishness similiar to prelatical ecumenism in the adherence to Levirate law through which he planned to exonerate adultery (Tamar). Yes, he asks us at least to consider Abraham a superstitious zealot for being willing to cut his son's throat (through Sarah challenging the power structure of patriarchy) and proposes to make literary use of a tribal slaughter (Dinah) without elsewhere in his works either demurring at or apologizing for its barbarism. I conclude from the shimmer of his passionate allusiveness that Milton imitates and transumes from Genesis inconsistently, sometimes very freely and sometimes very conservatively, but always knowing scripture as it would be prudent in us to know it when reading him. It is as vain, however, to believe ourselves in possession of what Genesis "really means" as it is to doubt that Milton always found a single sense or unitary meaning in what he read there. Milton's adducing of biblical texts in *Christian Doctrine* is the closest in his works he comes to arriving at the single signification that Reformation hermeneutics endorses; often enough he conservatively reproduces there the very same texts chosen also by his sources Ames and Wolleb, "[his] contribution consisting for the most part in the collection of more proof texts" (CPW 6:20). But even in *Christian Doctrine,* the more independent his thinking, as in his treatment of mortalism or the Holy Ghost, the more equivocal or multiple his exegesis. While *Christian Doctrine* incorporates Milton's most conservative scripture exegesis, the antiprelatical tracts incorporate his most polemical.

Finally, is it possible to seek a single impulse under the forms of interest I have found Milton to take in the stories Genesis tells of tragic women—an interest in historical difference, in gender difference, and in making polemical use of the Bible's multiform applicability to later historical periods—on the one hand sometimes to support the paternalistic theocratic structures of power in his own society and on the other hand sometimes to challenge them? First, I would isolate Milton's contrary use of gender-distinctive materials from Genesis in order to further polemical ends from his other two interests. I think that any endorsement I might wish to make of Milton's nomination as proto-feminist would be unimpeached by such contrary polemical usage. Milton does not display sensitivity to the feminine by looking at the content of scripture through the same colored lenses throughout his works and at all times; I have not found his proto-feminism invariably content-linked. For me the affirmation of such a nomination would not rely upon the false supposition that he always reads the female characters of Genesis in a simple,

sympathetic, quasi-allegorical vein, conforming them to a single paradigm. My endorsement would lodge in the discovery of his two other
interests in gender-distinctive materials from Genesis: his historical relativism and his recognition of the distinctiveness of womanhood as gender integrated. As a historian, Milton reads scripture conscious of its
pastness and presence, seeing the women of Genesis not as prescriptive
models for the present but as absorbingly valuable instances of woman's
rich humanity coming to terms with difficult situations in the tract of
time. As a writer and reader of narrative, his literary experiences of the
Bible, like those of the classics, organize by gender as much as genre or
any other formal category.

Is it possible to seek, however, a single impulse under Milton's remaining two interests, his historicism and gender sensitivity? If there is
such a single impulse, its name is respect for difference. Contemporary
theorists argue that the perception of difference is a subtler discovery
than the perception of similarity. Increasingly, Miltonists have observed
that one of the most consistent of Milton's intellectual traits is a preoccupation with otherness in its various forms. Beneath the heterogeneity
of Milton's interests probably lies a unifying and abiding concern with
difference itself. The Bible provided him with materials strikingly reinforcing both his historical and gender relativism.

I began by hinting that my subject has a revisionary aspect. First, I
have hoped to show, without specifically arguing the point but merely
suggesting a possible direction in which to seek parallels to each biblical
woman among classical analogues, that biblical and classical narration are
neither competing nor hierarchical but simultaneous interests to Milton
so that our newer keenness to respond to the Hebraic Milton ought to
go hand in hand with richer comparativism. Second, I think that Milton
disliked and avoided typological interpretation more than we have fully
seen; I believe that over-Christianizing or under-Judaizing his way of
interpreting is nearly over with, even in my generation of Miltonists,
and I am glad of that, for it thinned the texture of his thought. Finally,
I understand the ambition to "leave something so written to aftertimes
that they should not willingly let it die" (CPW 1.810) as an ambition to
write towards change and substantive political reform, not an ambition
to write outside any age at all, an ambition to be timely by engendering
a society in which readers saw the needfulness of rereading the sacred
texts as endlessly relevant human documents.

CORNELL UNIVERSITY

Dayton Haskin

CHOOSING THE BETTER PART
WITH MARY AND WITH RUTH

WHEN EARLY IN 1642 JOHN MILTON DECLARED HIS AMBITION
to become "an interpreter & relater of the best and sagest things,"[1] he
could not have foreseen how soon he would experience the most significant discontinuity in his interpretive career. He had been accustomed to
crediting the familiar theory that the plain words of the Bible provide the
ultimate criterion for judgment in spiritual matters. In *Of Reformation*
(1641), he proclaimed that the scriptures "protest ... their own plainnes,
and perspicuity, calling to them to be instructed, not only the *wise*, and
learned, but the *simple*, the *poor*, the *babes*, foretelling an extraordinary effusion of *Gods* Spirit upon every age, and sexe" (CPW 1:566). Yet in the
first months after his marriage to Mary Powell, when the New Testament
passages concerning divorce threatened to entrap him in his misery, he
insisted that "there is scarse any one saying in the Gospel, but must be read
with limitations and distinctions to be rightly understood" (CPW 2:338).

   The startling change in Milton's career as an interpreter was effectively identified by Arthur Barker when he pointed out that in *The
Doctrine and Discipline of Divorce* "the proposed method of exegesis ...
bears a striking resemblance" to the methods that in the prolusions and
even as recently as in *The Reason of Church Government* Milton had rather
cavalierly dismissed.[2] Milton himself described his new method when

---

[1] *The Reason of Church Government*, in *The Complete Prose Works of John Milton*, 1:811–12.
All quotations from Milton's prose are from this edition, to which reference is made in the
text as CPW.

[2] Arthur Barker, *Milton and the Puritan Dilemma, 1641–1660* (Toronto: Univ. of Toronto
Press, 1942), 72.

he insisted that "Christ gives no full comments or continu'd discourses, but scatters the heavenly grain of his doctrin like pearle heer and there, which requires a skillful and laborious gatherer, who must compare the words he finds, with other precepts" (CPW 2:338; 1st ed.). Following up on Barker's observation, Stanley Fish has proposed that in the divorce tracts Milton relocated the "plainness" of scripture, which he had previously taken to be a property of the words themselves, projecting it into the intention of the author. This, Fish claimed, amounted to Milton's presuming to know the mind of God and implicated him in the sort of dangerous supplementation against which he had argued in the anti-prelatical tracts.[3]

Be that as may be, the enormous shift in Milton's interpretive practice made for new dispositions in his reading and for new inflections in his poetry. In this essay I want to relate that shift to the workings of a particular poem. But first, a word more about *The Doctrine and Discipline of Divorce*. The title page of the first edition had proclaimed that the author was guided by "the Rule of Charity" in recovering the "long-lost meaning" of "many places of Scripture." When the second edition appeared in 1644, it had a new title page, and the claim that "the Rule of Charity" had guided interpretation was omitted. In the new prefatory matter, however, Milton provided a much more subtle indication that he himself had only recently discovered the importance of applying scriptural teachings with charity, or compassion. He asked sympathy for the sort of bearer of burdens that he himself had ignored until recently:

> Indeed mans disposition though prone to search after vain curiosities, yet when points of difficulty are to be discusst, appertaining to the removall of unreasonable wrong and burden from the perplext life of our brother, it is incredible how cold, how dull, and far from all fellow feeling we are, without the spurre of self-concernment. (CPW 2:226)

This was an extraordinary admission, and it shows that to some extent Milton recognized his own bias in the discussion about divorce. He presented it as a bias that, on the grounds of personal experience, he had

---

[3] Stanley E. Fish, "Re-Covering Meaning: Intention and Interpretation in Milton's *Doctrine and Discipline of Divorce*," a paper read at the annual convention of the Modern Language Association, San Francisco, December, 1987; "Wanting a Supplement: The Question of Interpretation in Milton's Early Prose," in *Politics, Poetics, and Hermeneutics in Milton's Prose,* ed. David Loewenstein and James Grantham Turner (Cambridge: Cambridge Univ. Press, 1990), 41–68.

chosen and was willing to stand by. It entailed a disposition to interpret scripture with sympathy for the perplexed.[4]

The implications for Milton's poetry of the radical shift in his interpretive practice are already apparent in a sonnet thought to have been written between 1642 and 1645 but not ordinarily related to the new theory that he was devising about how to read the Bible with discernment and compassion. At least since the nineteenth century Sonnet 9 ("Lady that in the prime of earliest youth") has seemed to many readers a rather conventional poem in praise of a "lady" who is considered virtuous because she has accepted one of the traditional roles assigned to Christian women. Mark Pattison effectively damned the poem when he praised it for achieving "impressive" effects in spite of its "hackneyed biblical allusion" and "commonplace" thought.[5] Assuming that the allusions derive from a familiar repertoire and provide a stable field from which the poet offers moral advice, critics who have written on the poem have often directed their energies to attempting to identify a real-life woman who was the object of Milton's praise. Even in the hands of the New Critics, there was a curious reluctance to explore the complex network of language and imagery.[6] Brooks and Hardy urged readers not to inspect the "echoes" from the biblical story of Ruth too carefully: "we cannot insist that the reader be aware of [these echoes] or accept them as 'meant' by the poet." At best "they constitute a kind of symbolic coincidence." Where Pattison, bored with evangelical piety, missed all that is startling about the poet's assimilation of the wise virgins of the parable in Matthew (25.1–13) to the complex figures of Mary and Ruth, New Critics, in their concern to demonstrate unity in the poem, sought to cover up the potentially fascinating ways in which the texts to which the poem alludes jar with one another and challenge the reader to exercise more mature powers of discrimination than were formerly required of her. Far from relying on safely domesticated materials to prop up

---

[4] The lack of sympathy for women's experience shown in the divorce writings is palpable and notorious. For an excellent discussion of some biographical implications of this literature, see Annabel Patterson, "No meer amatorious novel?" in *Politics, Poetics, and Hermeneutics in Milton's Prose,* 85–101.

[5] Mark Pattison, *The Sonnets of John Milton* (London, 1883), 138.

[6] Cleanth Brooks and John Edward Hardy, eds., *Poems of Mr. John Milton: The 1645 Edition with Essays in Analysis* (New York: Harcourt Brace, 1951), 160. Cf. the attempt by the late Leo Miller to read the poem as addressed to Milton's seventeen-year-old bride-to-be, in "John Milton's 'Lost' Sonnet to Mary Powell," *MQ* 25 (1991): 102–7.

conventional praise for a woman who accepted silence, chastity, and
obedience as her duty, Milton brought into contact with another well-
known passage from Matthew (the one about taking the narrow path,
7.13–14) a variety of controversial texts which, when they are asked to
work in concert, sort oddly with one another.

Written in the epideictic manner of Jonson's poetry of praise,[7] yet in-
fused with a curious array of biblical references, Sonnet 9 makes a radical
revision in the kind of poem in which a poet typically puts his praise of a
woman for her beauty and virtue at the service of a request for her favor.
The diction of the opening lines ("Lady," "the prime," "earliest youth,"
"the broad way," "the green") invites comparison with poems of persuasion even as its thought separates it decisively from them. We can
compare Sonnet 6 in Daniel's *Delia,* in particular its opening lines:

> Faire is my loue, and cruell as sh'is faire;
> Her brow shades frownes, although her eyes are sunny;
> Her Smiles are lightning, though her pride dispaire;
> And her disdaines all gall; her fauours hunny.
> A modest maide, deckt with a blush of honour,
> Whose feete do treade greene pathes of youth and loue,
> The wonder of all eyes that look vppon her:
> Sacred on earth, design'd a Saint aboue.
> Chastitie and Beautie, which were deadly foes,
> Liue reconciled friends within her brow:
> And had she pittie to conioine with those,
> Then who had heard the plaints I vtter now.
> O had she not beene faire, and thus vnkinde,
> My Muse had slept, and none had knowne my minde.[8]

Milton demonstrates his own powers of discrimination as he swerves
away from the broad path worn down by Elizabethan sonneteers.

---

[7] On the affinities between Milton and the epigrammatic Jonson, see Judith Scherer
Herz, "Epigrams and Sonnets: Milton in the Manner of Jonson," *MS* 20 (1984): 29–41. My un-
folding of the reference to Ruth in what follows suggests that in this biblical figure Milton found
a model for relating creativity with political engagement. This shows that Sonnet 9 bears
significant affinities to the poet's more conspicuously political sonnets as discussed by Janel
Mueller, in "The Mastery of Decorum: Politics as Poetry in Milton's Sonnets," in Robert von
Hallberg, ed. *Politics and Poetic Value* (Chicago: Univ. of Chicago Press, 1987), 63–96.

[8] Samuel Daniel, *Delia with the Complaint of Rosamond* (1592): A Scolar Press Facsimile
(Menston, Yorks.: Scolar Press, 1969).

Instead of inviting the lady to come into the public eye and instead of providing a blazon that catalogues various facets of her beauty, he praises her for having actively chosen a path in which she must withstand scorn and unacknowledged jealousy. The trochees at the start of lines 2 and 6 reinforce the poet's emphasis on a wise choice:

> Lady that in the prime of earliest youth,
> > Wisely hast shun'd the broad way and the green,
> > And with those few art eminently seen,
> > That labour up the Hill of heav'nly Truth,
> The better part with *Mary* and with *Ruth,*
> > Chosen thou hast, and they that overween,
> > And at thy growing vertues fret their spleen,
> > No anger find in thee, but pity and ruth.
> Thy care is fixt and zealously attends
> > To fill thy odorous Lamp with deeds of light,
> > And Hope that reaps not shame. Therefore be sure
> Thou, when the Bridegroom with his feastfull friends
> > Passes to bliss at the mid hour of night,
> > Hast gain'd thy entrance, Virgin wise and pure.[9]

Despite the conspicuous presence of the past participle at the start of line 6, the choice of "the better part" cannot refer to something sealed up in the past, for "Chosen" forms part of a verb in the present perfect tense. By skillful manipulation of verb tenses, particularly in the last three and a half lines, Milton manages to represent choice (including God's choice, or "election") as a process, not as a discrete act.[10] (The implications of "hast shun'd" and "Chosen ... hast" are to be found in the iterative present tense of "attends" and in the forward-looking counsel of "be." Ultimately the syntax urges a future perfection in "Hast gain'd.") The whole utterance implicitly acknowledges that the passage of time alienates a past choice if it is not renewed, so that it comes to be experienced as an imposition. This implies a narrative sequence, the passage from what is imposed to what is accepted. It is a sequence which, as the emphasis on a future consummation in lines 12 and 13 suggests, cannot

---

[9] Quotations from Milton's poetry are from *The Works of John Milton,* gen. ed. Frank Allen Patterson, 18 vols. (New York: Columbia Univ. Press, 1931–38).

[10] On Milton's handling of tenses, see Edward Tayler, *Milton's Poetry: Its Development in Time* (Pittsburgh: Duquesne Univ. Press, 1979), 198–99.

issue into final closure before the end of time.

The choice of "the better part" engages what is problematic in this narrative sequence. The sonnet negotiates a problem encountered by young persons whose early decision for piety has precluded their passing through the period of sinful youth routinely rehearsed in popular conversion narratives of the period, according to examples thought to be found in the lives of Paul and Augustine and Luther. To ignore Milton's dissent from this paradigm is to make it seem that the poet is attempting to fix the lady in her choice and to close off the possibility of change, even that he is seeking effectively to curb her freedom by telling her that she must walk in the path she has set out on, and implicitly that she must now lie in the empty bed she has made for herself. Instead of making her feel that there is much to look forward to, such an utterance seems to hold out a long barren period through which she will be expected to do nothing but preserve her virginity. It is against just such an unsympathetic way of reading that the allusions to Mary and Ruth do their best work. In seventeenth-century England, Mary and Ruth were often thought to be complex figures of considerable experience, and the moral propriety of their conduct was disputed. It was not easy to assimilate these women to the wise virgins of Matthew's parable. Moreover, what Jesus had meant when he said that Mary had chosen "the better part" was the object of longstanding debate.

In the gospels there is a bewildering array of women named Mary, and readers have often sought to reduce the complexity by referring various portraits to the same woman. From early in the medieval period, the sister of Martha, who sat at the Lord's feet, had been conflated with the unnamed sinful woman who had anointed the Lord's feet in the house of Simon the Pharisee (Luke 7.36–50 was assimilated to John 12.1–11) and also with Mary Magdalen, "out of whom went seven devils" (Luke 8.2).[11] Authorized by the liturgical practice of reading the passage about the sinful woman on the feast of Mary Magdalen, the conflation of Marys continued to show up frequently in sixteenth- and seventeenth-century popular devotion, as illustrated in a poem of 1601, *Marie Magdalen's Lamentations*. Here, in the fourth of seven parts of the poem, "Marie bewailes the losse of that part which Christ promised her: when he said, Marie hath chosen the better part, which shall not be

[11] Compare John Donne's verse letter, "To the Lady *Magdalen Herbert*, of St. *Mary Magdalen*."

taken away from her."[12] Among those who thought that the truly elect went through a period of sinfulness before their conversion, this conflation had an apparent interpretive advantage for explaining Jesus's preference for Mary's way over Martha's. A few lines from a poem by Quarles show how the passage about "the better part" was interpreted by way of Jesus's explanation to Simon the Pharisee that the sinful woman was forgiven her sins because "she loved much" (Luke 7.47). The poem, titled "On *Martha* and *Mary*," associates Martha with the Pharisee to whom Jesus told the parable of two debters (Luke 7.40–43):

> 'Tis true; Our blessed Lord was *Martha's* Guest;
>   *Mary* was his; and, in his feast, delighted:
> Now which hath greater reason to love best,
>   The bountifull Invitor, or th' invited?
>   Sure, both lou'd well; But *Mary* was the detter,
>   And therefore should, in reason, love the better.[13]

When in Milton's sonnet the poet asked the Lady to think of herself as Mary, he was not by any means making an unproblematic comparison. He was alluding to a figure whose past may have been, from a conventionally moralizing point of view, badly tainted: a figure whose past qualified her to be the sort of sinner to whom grace abounds. In view of the manifest difference between the sinful woman praised by Jesus for having accepted forgiveness and the woman praised by the poet in

---

[12] [Gervase Markham], *Marie Magdalen's Lamentations for the Losse of her Master* (1601), in Alexander B. Grosart, ed., *Miscellanies of the Fuller Worthies' Library,* 4 vols. ([printed privately in England], 1871; repr. New York: AMS, 1970), 2:563. The words quoted here appear in Grosart entirely in capital letters; I have retained the spellings and other punctuation given by Grosart but have reduced most of the letters to lower case in conformity with modern usage, lest the passage have undue prominence in my text.

[13] "Divine Fancies" (1632), in Alexander B. Grosart, ed., *The Complete Works in Prose and Verse of Francis Quarles,* Chertsey Worthies' Library, 3 vols. ([printed privately in England], 1880–81; repr. New York: AMS Press, 1967) 1:102. Not everyone in the period accepted the traditional identification of Martha's sister with the sinful woman. The dispute was conducted on both scholarly and moral grounds. In a lengthy annotation on the sinful woman, Henry Hammond, seeking to disentangle the various female figures, argued that the "sister of *Lazarus* so beloved of *Christ* will be much injured in her story," if it is allowed to consider her to have been either "a *whore* or *Gentile*." Other interpreters, including Calvin, would not countenance the possibility that two or three of the biblical figures may have been referable to the same woman. See H[enry] Hammond, *A Paraphrase and Annotations upon all the Books of the New Testament,* 2d ed. (London, 1659), 214. Cf. John Lightfoot, *The Harmony, Chronicle and Order of the New-Testament* (London, 1655), 28–29, 47, 54.

Sonnet 9, Milton's allusion seems to involve a challenge to learn to "love much," without the curious benefit of having first sinned much.

In addition to its allusion to Mary, Sonnet 9 also involves a conspicuous allusion to another of Matthew's parables of judgment. Looking towards "the mid hour of night" as the time of reckoning,[14] the parable of the five foolish virgins, who did not keep on hand sufficient oil for their lamps, and the five wise virgins, who were prepared for the sudden coming of the bridegroom, provides a variation on the lesson of the parable of the talents. In fact, all three pericopes in Matthew 25 were frequently considered by commentators to concern both the General Judgment and the particular judgments of individuals, and they were said to be Jesus's means of promising an ultimate discrimination between hypocritical Christians, whose faith is merely temporary, and the truly regenerate, who will persevere to the end. In particular, the parable of the virgins was said to teach nothing about the fate of unbelievers but to show how Christ will expose the hypocrisy of a professing person who "is confident and thinkes well of himselfe" and lacks a proper fear of God.[15] This way of interpreting the parable suggests, incidentally, that the application derived from the parable that follows (the talents) by the initial speaker in Milton's sonnet "When I consider . . ." may ultimately dissolve. For he has been fearing not only that he is a victim prematurely punished for having failed to use his talent but also that he is one of the foolish virgins whose "light is spent."

In Sonnet 9 Milton projects the moment of decisive judgment into the future and encourages the Lady to find in the case of the wise virgins a "place" to assure her during the interim that she will finally enter into the master's joy. In this way he raises earlier in the poem the sort of question raised by the ending of "When I consider . . . ," namely, what constitutes proper waiting, or more practically, what to do while you have to wait. The problem of perseverance is the more acute for her just because she has made a difficult commitment early in life, while she was

---

[14] On Milton's interest in midnight as an hour of reckoning, see Albert R. Cirillo, "Noon-Midnight and the Temporal Structure of *Paradise Lost*," *ELH* 29 (1962): 372–95.

[15] See the commentary on Matt. 25 in Augustine Marlorate, *A Catholike and Ecclesiastical Exposition of the holy Gospel after S. Mattewe, Gathered out of all singuler and approved Devines*, trans. Thomas Tymme (London, 1570); *Annotations upon the Holy Bible*, vol. 2, *Being a Continuation of Mr. Pool's Work by certain Judicious and Learned Divines* (London, 1685). For the parable of the virgins in particular, see Marlorate, fol. 592; Edward Leigh, *Annotations upon All the New Testament Philological and Theologicall* (London, 1650), 67–68.

still "in the prime of earliest youth," whereas the time when her choice
is to be rewarded has been delayed indefinitely. In this respect the poem
offers the obverse of "When I consider . . .": instead of being tempted to
think that the judgment has come already, she will be tempted (as the
narrator of Bunyan's *Grace Abounding to the Chief of Sinners* claims he
was) to think that judgment has been deferred and may not come at all.

In face of the likelihood that she may become weary of the narrow
path on which she had resolutely begun her progress, the poet subjects
her to a repetition of biblical promises, especially when, alluding to
Romans 5.3–5, he challenges her to fill her lamp not only with "deeds
of light" but with "Hope that reaps not shame."[16] The phrase "deeds
of light" supplies a content to the parabolic figure of storing up oil. (It
is closely parallel to the content supplied by the considerer in the sonnet
about the talent, who, knowing that the parable teaches the obligation
of service, worries that his "light is spent.") The referent of "deeds of
light" becomes in turn a new object of interpretation, and it is defined
within the framework of the poem chiefly by reference to the Lady's
"labour[ing] up the Hill of heav'nly Truth" and by her having chosen
"the better part." These two controls on the meaning of "deeds of
light" reintroduce us to some submerged autobiographical implications.
They associate the poem with Milton's defense of his life of study in the
letter in the Trinity manuscript to an unknown friend. The poet who
justified his way of life as against that of more active and "timely-happy
spirits" had reason to know what difficulties followed after voicing a
commitment "in the prime of earliest youth."

Milton's "better part" accords with the best philological scholarship
of his day, which recognized that the Greek ἀγαθὴν μερίδα implied a contrast between Mary and Martha.[17] Still more to the point, the phrase
serves his purposes in a poem that calls for and celebrates the right use
of one's powers of discrimination and interpretation. In Luke's gospel,
the episode in which Martha complains to Jesus about her sister's failure

---

[16] In this way the poem bears out what Mary Ann Radzinowicz has said of Milton's
poetry of praise: that "for every grain of panegyric there will be a gram of advice." See
Towards Samson Agonistes: The Growth of Milton's Mind (Princeton: Princeton Univ. Press,
1978), 135.

[17] See *Synopsis Criticorum Aliorumque S. Scripturæ Interpretum*, 4 vols. in 5 (London, 1669–
76) 4,i: col. 1001; (1694 ed.: col. 942). Cf. both the Geneva Bible and the Authorized
Version, which render the Greek of Luke 10.42 as the "good part," in accord with Calvin's
rejection of the superlative (*optimam partem*) in the Vulgate.

to help her serve dinner follows the parable of the Good Samaritan. That parable, which is manifestly concerned with service, had long been made to answer questions about the supposedly competing claims of one's duties to God and neighbor. According to Luke, its telling was occasioned by "a certain lawyer," who sought "to justify himself" and tempted Jesus with a question that later became dear to predestinarian divines in England, who recommended reading the Bible for "experimental" knowledge: "What shall I do to inherit eternal life?" Jesus had answered, "What is written in the law? how readest thou?" He received the reply, "Thou shalt love the Lord thy God with all thy heart ... and thy neighbor as thyself." Then he went on to tell a parable that stands on its head the question, Who is my neighbor? The hated Samaritan shows what it means to act as a "neighbor." Reasonably enough, then, the passage about Mary and Martha came to be interpreted as a kind of corresponding parable about the service of God. Mary, who sits at the Lord's feet and attends to his words, is said to have chosen "that good part," while Martha, who frets and complains about her sister's conduct, is told that only "one thing is needful." These teasing phrases do not settle the issue. Rather they open up a range of interpretive possibilites. Given the stakes in the matter ("What shall I do to inherit eternal life?"), commentators often contested the sense of both phrases with a good deal of passion.

The passage about Mary and Martha had been an object of considerable controversy at least since the time of the magisterial reformers. Through the Middle Ages this text had been a Christian *locus classicus* useful for drawing a distinction between contemplation and action and thus complementing the Jewish stories about Rachel and Leah. Jesus's judgment about Mary's having chosen "the better part" was taken as proof for the superiority of the monastic way of life. Calvin sought to refute this "old error" held by the "Sorbonistes," that those who "withdraw themselues fro[m] the common trade of life ... imagined them selues to be like Angels." He sought to discredit this interpretation by tracing the idea back to a non-biblical source, Aristotle's belief that the highest good consists in contemplation. Calvin emphasized that Christians are called to action, to work for "the common wealth." He insisted that Christ's words to Mary not be used to justify "solytarines & idlenesse," which lead to "pride."[18] While Milton in the letter to a friend

---

[18] John Calvin, *A Harmonie Vpon The Three Euangelistes, Matthewe, Marke, and Luke*, trans. E[usebius] P[aget] (London, 1610), 371.

CHOOSING THE BETTER PART   163

of 1633 sought to refute the implication that his own life of study amounted to self-indulgent indolence, in Sonnet 9 he risked provoking a similar charge against the Lady when he brought together his praise for her "deeds of light" with the allusion to choosing "the better part" and the image of her "labour[ing] up the Hill of heav'nly Truth." In this poem Milton was already inviting his reader to work toward the redefinition of service with which the sonnet "When I consider . . ." would end: "They also serve who only stand and waite."

The redefinition turns on the phrase with which Jesus chastens Martha's impatience and introduces a preference for the way of Mary: "But one thing is needful." Some commentators, acknowledging that the Lord might be thought to be blaming Martha "for her too great sollicitude, and trouble to provide a Dinner," proposed the possibility that Jesus may have been saying something as simple as "We need only a single dish." This seemed "too low" a sense, however, to readers eager to search the scriptures for the way to salvation; and in any event there were poets who recognized in the phrase some intriguing metaphorical possibilities. There is a precedent for Milton's handling of the phrase, for instance, in Sonnet 99 of Henry Lok's second century. This poem fuses the story of Martha and Mary with the famous passage on charity from 1 Corinthians 13. Lok's speaker is like Paul in proposing many hypothetical accomplishments ("If I can speake . . ."), but instead of concluding with an explicit recommendation of "charity" as the virtue surpassing all others, he ends by turning the whole Pauline passage into an interpretation of the "one thing needful" for entrance into the eternal wedding feast:

> By all my trauell I no gaine shall win;
>   Although my paine shall proue to others blest,
>   But—as the symbal's sound doth to the rest—
> I might haps morne, when others mirth begin;
>   The feast but thin, would be vnto my share,
>   Though many dishes to the guests I bare.[19]

In this way all the hypothetical accomplishments enumerated in 1 Corinthians are seen to be the good works of Martha, while "charity" is the single but necessary dish which allows Mary her portion with the Lord.

To avoid seeing in the passage a justification for a "Life of Medita-

---

[19] Henry Lok, in Alexander B. Grosart, ed., *Miscellanies of the Fuller Worthies' Library*, 4 vols. ([printed privately in England], 1871; repr. New York: AMS, 1970), 2:236.

tion and Contemplation," protestants often interpreted the passage more "*generally,* concerning *the care of the Soul with reference to eternity.*" This left space, in view of Mary's having literally been listening to Jesus's words, to reintroduce the idea that the passage recommends study, and it focused that study specifically upon the scriptures. "Christ," comments Edward Leigh, "would not suffer *Mary* to be drawne away from an extraordinary exercise of the word, though there was much businesse by reason of his unlooked-for coming with his Disciples."[20] Among seventeenth-century protestants, it seems not to have been thought in any way to contradict the doctrine of salvation by grace alone to recommend the good work of studying the Word. In treating the training appropriate for ministers, Lancelot Andrewes taught that landed men had founded colleges in which "men of gifts" would be trained as their "*hæredes ex optimis,* heirs of the best choice."[21]

Blurring a customary boundary between gender roles, then, Milton gestured toward this line of interpretation in Sonnet 9 by embedding the phrase "the better part" in a context that suggests a life of study in preparation for active service. He had already used the word "part" in a specifically biblical sense in the *Animadversions* (1641). Arguing against the practice of promising young scholars "Bishopricks and Deaneries" to motivate them to study, Milton remarked that "young mercenary stripplings" will "have no part or lot in [Christ's] Vineyard," since their study is done out of "pride and ambition" (CPW 1:718). A still more helpful gloss on Matthew's "part" comes from the usage of the Authorized Version, where the word "portion," which serves to render the metaphorical "dish" (Septuagint, μερὶς), is joined to the word "lot": "The LORD *is* the portion of mine inheritance and of my cup: thou maintainest my lot" (Psalm 16.5). It is this set of connections that makes for subterranean linkages between Mary and Ruth and between Milton and the Lady. For Milton elsewhere called "labour and intent study" his "portion in this life" (CPW 1:810), and in the sonnet "How soon hath Time …"

---

[20] See [Poole's] *Annotations upon the Holy Bible,* 2 (1685): at Luke 10.42; Leigh, *Annotations.* Cf. Hammond, *Paraphrase and Annotations,* 225; Richard Baxter, *A Paraphrase on the New Testament, with Notes, Doctrinal and Practical* (1685), 3d ed. (London, 1701). Although all these commentaries postdate Milton's sonnet, they take up long-standing interpretive questions and regularly report on older interpretations.

[21] Lancelot Andrewes, *A Pattern of Catechisticall Doctrine* (London, 1630), 325.

spoke confidently of "that same lot" which would eventually be his.[22]

Because the phrase "the better part" belongs specifically to the story about Mary, Milton's line about choosing "the better part with *Mary* and with *Ruth*" invites a rereading of the book of Ruth to discern a basis for the various comparisons. Ostensibly set in the period of the Judges, the book is now widely thought to be a late addition to the Hebrew Bible, perhaps a post-exilic reworking of an older tale, designed to counteract the strict prohibitions against foreign wives enacted under Ezra and Nehemiah. In the Geneva Bible it was said to "set forthe the state of the Church which is subiect to manifolde afflictions," and to teach "vs to abide with pacience til God deliuer vs out of troubles." This linked it with the parables about learning to wait. With its emphasis on famine and female barrenness, the book is reminiscent of various tales found in Genesis and Exodus. Yet it is the interpretation placed on the women's plight by Ruth's mother-in-law, Naomi, that makes the story a kind of female version of the book of Job. Having lost her husband and two sons, living in exile without any "hope" (1.12) of offspring, Naomi tries to send her two daughters-in-law back home, to save them from further association with a woman whom the Lord has "afflicted" (1.21) and against whom He has lifted his hand (1.13). The most obvious basis of comparison of Ruth with Mary, the sister of Martha, arises when Ruth, unlike her sister Orpah, chooses to journey to Bethlehem. Yet to follow through the two women's stories is to see that, inasmuch as Ruth labored to support herself and her mother-in-law, Martha was more like Ruth than Mary was. Still, in the part of Ruth's story where she appears as a gleaner, the biblical language provides a conspicuous basis for connecting her with Mary's "better part."

When Ruth goes off to work, "her hap," the Authorized Version tells us, "was to light on a part of the field belonging unto Boaz," a kinsman of her dead father-in-law (2.3). Or, as the Geneva Bible has it, "it came to passe, that she met with the portion of the field of Boaz." The sense that the story involves the workings of divine providence, potentially lodged in the Authorized Version's "hap," was made explicit in various Renaissance commentaries.[23] It is the imagery of nourishment,

---

[22] The connection between the biblical word "portion" and a life of studious labor in a quest for "perfect faith" was prominent in John Preston's *The New Covenant, or The Saints Portion* (London, 1629), 175–76.

[23] See, for example, Joseph Hall, *A Plain and Familiar Explication, By Way of Paraphrase, of All the Hard Texts of the Whole Divine Scripture*, in *Works*, new ed., 12 vols. (Oxford, 1837), 3:110.

hinted at in Geneva's "portion," that becomes increasingly prominent in the subsequent narrative: Boaz protects Ruth from molestation and feeds her; he sends her back to Naomi with a surplus of barley; and finally he takes her as his bride and gives her, and (in accord with custom) gives Naomi as well, a male child, who becomes the grandfather of King David. So much for the story summarized from a point of view compatible with the idea that the Gentile Ruth was an honorary Jewish matriarch and a type of the Virgin Mary: she is modest, compliant, accepting of her lot. In the nineteenth century, Millet, in his great painting, Harvesters Resting, dressed her in blue, a hard-working peasant girl, reluctant to join Boaz and his feastful friends for a meal.[24]

There is in Millet's depiction of Ruth's reluctance (she is being prodded towards the reclining harvesters by a dog at her back) a hint that can help us see that Milton's sonnet invites interest in features of Ruth's behavior that distinguish her from Mary. As a Gentile, Ruth was a lost sheep. She was also a latecomer to the day's work. She had reason to consider herself (like the first speaker in George Herbert's third poem called "Love" in *The Temple*) unworthy to be served at the meal. Yet the whole book of Ruth is a marvelous story to illustrate that it is not too late: not too late for Ruth to gain entrance into the chosen people, not too late for Naomi to have a grandchild, and not too late for Boaz to experience the joys of marriage and fatherhood. "*For* thou hast showed more kindness in the latter end," Boaz tells Ruth, "than at the beginning, inasmuch as thou followedst not young men, whether poor or rich" (3.10). In this reversal of traditional roles—she has chosen Boaz—lies the defining characteristic of the title character, her compassion, expressed in Milton's rhyming Ruth with "ruth."

In Boaz's feeling that this foreign widow has shown him a great and unexpected kindness, there is still another basis for Milton's interest in Ruth. For this is Ruth not so easily assimilated with the Virgin Mary, or even with the Mary who sat patiently at the Master's feet listening to his words. This is Ruth more readily associated with Mary Magdalen, who even after the Resurrection, longed for contact with the Lord's body. This is Ruth as she appears when she boldly steals up to Boaz as he sleeps, uncovers his "feet," and positions herself near-by. When he wakes "at midnight" (3.8), already in the Hebrew Bible the hour of

---

[24] See Alexandra R. Murphy, *Jean-François Millet* (Boston: Museum of Fine Arts, 1984), 60–64, esp. n. 22.

reckoning,[25] she says to him, "spread ... thy skirt over thine hand-maid" (3.9). This Ruth was no model of compliant, submissive "Christ-ian" womanhood. She gave the commentators a good deal of trouble.

While I have not been able to find evidence that Christian com-mentators of the seventeenth century went so far as to speculate just what Ruth uncovered when she uncovered Boaz's "feet" (in Exodus [4.25] and Isaiah [7.20] the word seems to be a euphemism for the geni-tals), the rabbis had debated whether Boaz's discomfort was a matter of sexual excitement.[26] In any event, Ruth's astonishing sexual initiative in going to the place where he was sleeping and in asking him to spread his skirt over her was as troubling to many interpreters as the sinful woman's anointing of the Lord's feet is represented (in Luke 7.39) as having been to Simon the Pharisee. While many puzzled over what sort of status Ruth was seeking and whether she was referring to actual *copula carnali,* most agreed that she was using a figure of speech that indicated she wished to be made a concubine.[27] Naomi, who had advised her how to act until the very point when "he will tell thee what thou shalt do" (3.4), was censured by commentators for having been imprudent. Her plan was said to have involved a "manifold Irregularity" and to have gone against Modesty, Honesty, and Prudence, the shame being compounded by the action's being taken at night. Instead of seeing in the dynamics of the initiatives taken by Naomi, Ruth, and Boaz a won-derful representation of the subtle workings of grace, it was alleged that Naomi's "Clandestine proceeding" had "arisen from a distrust of Gods

[25] Jack Sasson gives a host of references to other passages in the Hebrew Bible, including ones about the slaying of the first-born Egyptians and Samson's hoisting of Gaza's gate. In connection with Milton's joining Ruth to the parable of the wise virgins who enter the wedding feast just after midnight, it is interesting to note that this modern commentator, who presumably knows nothing of Milton's sonnet, suggests that Matt. 25.1–13 throws light on Ruth 3.8. He treats the passage where Naomi advises Ruth to "Sit still . . . until thou know how the matter will fall" (3.18) under the rubric, "Nothing to Do But Wait." See *Ruth: A New Translation with a Philological Commentary and a Formalist-Folklorist Interpretation* (Baltimore: Johns Hopkins Univ. Press, 1979), 74ff. For a rich discussion of the "alternate possibilities" about what is to happen at the "mid-hour of the night," see Tayler, 198–99.

[26] See Étan Levine, *The Aramaic Version of Ruth,* Analecta Biblica, vol. 58 (Rome: Biblical Institute Press, 1973), 89; cited by Sasson. For a recent discussion, see James Black, "Ruth in the Dark: Folktale, Law and Creative Ambiguity in the Old Testament," *Literature and Theology* 5 (1991): 20–36.

[27] See Poole, *Synopsis criticorum,* 1 (1669): columns 1237–38.

Providence."[28] And yet, unprepared as they were by conventional notions of sexual morality adequately to acknowledge it, there was among some commentators a recognition that God was at work in Ruth's choosing Boaz. The story offers a profound illustration of the importance both of waiting *for* the right time and of acting *at* the right time. The biblical author had already associated Ruth with both Rachel and Leah (Ruth 4.11), traditional figures, respectively, of contemplation and action. This writer also likened her to the widow Tamar, who "played the harlot" to get her father-in-law to beget children (Gen. 38; Ruth 4.12). In the seventeenth century John Lightfoot suggested that Ruth was descended from Lot's daughters, who, after their mother was turned to salt, got their father drunk so that he would sleep with them and "preserve [his] seed" (Gen. 19).[29] The book of Ruth had, in short, many features to make it attractive to a writer who was already keenly interested in negotiating his own way between the apparently incompatible alternatives of study and action and who sought an authorized model for his trust in a God whose providence sees to bestowing fruitfulness after hard labor, skillful gathering, and long delays.

Some will see Sonnet 9, then, as carrying latent autobiographical implications with which one might reconstruct a narrative about an aspiring poet who seems to have been called "the Lady" at Christ's College. Others may think that the poem suggests a good deal about the sort of ideal partner Milton had in mind in the period when he was writing the divorce tracts. All speculation apart, however, what can be affirmed about this sonnet is that in it Milton rejected the poem of persuasion and revised the traditional poem in praise of female virtue. His poem sets into operation an idea of virtue that involves developing readerly habits of discernment and sympathy. Like the biblical parables of judgment, his poem points toward an ultimate separation of those who have stored up sufficient biblical knowledge to illuminate a subterranean interplay of its allusions from those whose confident familiarity with the Bible and deadening habits of reading reduce the utterance to merely conventional praise for the cloistered virtue of a virgin. The poem pays its addressee at least three subtle compliments. Besides inviting her to

---

[28] [Poole], *Annotations upon the Holy Bible:* gloss on Ruth 3.4.

[29] John Lightfoot, *The Harmony, Chronicle and Order of the Old Testament* (London, 1647), 97. On attitudes toward sexuality, see Theodore de Welles, "Sex and Sexual Attitudes in Seventeenth-Century England: The Evidence from Puritan Diaries," *Renaissance and Reformation*, n.s. 12, no. 1 (1988): 45–64.

hold in her consciousness a range of apparently incompatible alternatives, it shows a sympathetic understanding of the besetting difficulties experienced by one who has made an early commitment. Not least it tactfully acknowledges the danger that she may become dissatisfied with biblically mediated promises of a happy ending when, through the long course of life, they will often seem at odds with a belated consummation. Yet it also reveals the poet's trust that the lady—and other fit readers—will meanwhile enjoy turning their knowledge and considerable interpretive skills upon the surprising interplay of the biblical pretexts. In this way the poet's counsel serves at once to validate the hidden theme, to save the praise from degenerating into empty flattery, and to turn attention to a really decisive time yet to come. It is the lady's "care," her persistent activity and bent, that is said to be "fixt," not her achieved position.

Insofar as Sonnet 9 implies that interpreting scripture never issues into full consummation short of the Second Coming of the Bridegroom, the poem belongs to the hermeneutical climate into which Milton entered when he composed the first edition of *The Doctrine and Discipline of Divorce*. In this climate the scriptures, far from being plain and perspicuous and already domesticated, often seemed unsettling and even threatening. They were assumed, moreover, to be perpetually in need of intelligent, imaginative, and compassionate renegotiation, so that interpretation proves a complex and potentially pleasurable business. With its demanding array of biblical allusions, Sonnet 9 offered, then, the first fruits of a new attitude towards interpretive tasks that came eventually to inform Milton's representation of pleasurable labors in prelapsarian paradise. Having discovered that the Bible requires a skillful and laborious gatherer, Milton went along for more than a quarter century, as *De Doctrina Christiana* evinces, gathering and comparing biblical places. In the major poems of his maturity his assiduous sifting of places issued into a disciplined, imaginative fusing of carefully chosen pretexts. That, however, is another story; and it requires a much more entailed exploration.[30]

BOSTON COLLEGE

---

[30] See my *Milton's Burden of Interpretation* (Philadelphia: Univ. of Pennsylvania Press, 1994) which greatly expands the argument of the present essay.

Michael Wilding

"THIR SEX NOT EQUAL SEEM'D": EQUALITY IN *PARADISE LOST*

THE FIRST DESCRIPTION OF ADAM AND EVE IS A CRUCIAL passage for our understanding of *Paradise Lost:*

> ... but wide remote
> From this *Assyrian* Garden, where the Fiend
> Saw undelighted all delight, all kind
> Of living Creatures new to sight and strange:
> Two of far nobler shape erect and tall,
> Godlike erect, with native Honor clad
> In naked Majesty seem'd Lords of all,
> And worthy seem'd, for in thir looks Divine
> The image of thir glorious Maker shone,
> Truth, Wisdome, Sanctitude severe and pure,
> Severe, but in true filial freedom plac't;
> Whence true autority in men; though both
> Not equal, as thir sex not equal seem'd;
> For contemplation hee and valor form'd,
> For softness shee and sweet attractive Grace,
> Hee for God only, shee for God in him:
> His fair large Front and Eye sublime declar'd
> Absolute rule; and Hyacinthine Locks
> Round from his parted forelock manly hung
> Clust'ring, but not beneath his shoulders broad:
> Shee as a veil down to the slender waist
> Her unadorned golden tresses wore
> Dishevell'd, but in wanton ringlets wav'd
> As the Vine curls her tendrils, which impli'd

> Subjection, but requir'd with gentle sway,
> And by her yielded, by him best receiv'd,
> Yielded with coy submission, modest pride,
> And sweet reluctant amorous delay.
> Nor those mysterious parts were then conceal'd,
> Then was not guilty shame: dishonest shame
> Of Nature's works, honor dishonorable,
> Sin-bred, how have ye troubl'd all mankind
> With shows instead, mere shows of seeming pure,
> And banisht from man's life his happiest life,
> Simplicity and spotless innocence.[1]   (4.284–318)

Not surprisingly, this description is provocative, confrontational, argumentative, and fraught with ambiguity. How could it be otherwise? Twenty-five years ago Helen Gardner wrote of book 4, lines 296–99, "No lines have, I suppose, been more quoted and quoted against Milton than these. But all that is Milton's is the unequivocal firmness and clarity with which he states the orthodox view of his age."[2] Twenty years earlier, similarly troubled by the passage, Balachandra Rajan had resorted to a similar explanation: "It typified the deepest and most impersonal feelings of the time."[3]

Yet in so many of his beliefs Milton the revolutionary challenged "the orthodox view of his age" and "the deepest and most impersonal feelings of the time." Is it likely he so passively accepts them here? The male supremacist, anti-egalitarian, and absolutist sentiments are proclaimed with an extraordinary brusqueness, yet "the unequivocal firmness and clarity" ascribed to them by Helen Gardner are upon examination remarkably lacking. The passage is permeated with equivocation and uncertainty in its repetition of "seem'd" and "seeming":

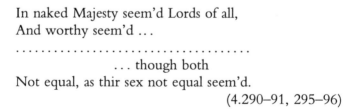

> In naked Majesty seem'd Lords of all,
> And worthy seem'd ...
>
> . . . .
>   ... though both
> Not equal, as thir sex not equal seem'd.
>   (4.290–91, 295–96)

[1] All quotations from Milton's poetry follow Hughes.

[2] Helen Gardner, *"A Reading of Paradise Lost"* (Oxford: Clarendon Press, 1965), 8.

[3] Balachandra Rajan, *"Paradise Lost" and the Seventeenth-Century Reader* (London: Chatto and Windus, 1947), 66.

The sense of false appearance in "seem'd" is reinforced by Milton's use of "seeming" in the clearly unambiguous sense of deceit only twenty lines on: "With shows instead, mere shows of seeming pure" (4.315). At so crucial a passage, why does Milton offer "seem'd"? Why not "as thir sex not equal was," if that was what he meant? Why is the unambiguous avoided?[4]

If "thir sex not equal seem'd" and if "seeming" is false, does that mean that their sex *was* equal? The uncertainties of "seem'd" spread elsewhere. To find Adam and Eve described as "seem'd Lords of all" makes us wonder whether they were really lords of all, and ask what weight does "Lords" carry from a revolutionary who had supported the abolition of the House of Lords. Is "Lords of all" the same as "Lords of the World" (1.32), or is it a more excessive version? Even stranger is the terse proclamation of "Absolute rule" (4.301) from an intransigent opponent of absolutism.

This first description of Adam and Eve is problematical, of course, because, as commentators have recurrently pointed out,[5] it is presented through Satan's perceptions:

> ... this *Assyrian* Garden, where the Fiend
> Saw undelighted all delight, all kind
> Of living Creatures new to sight and strange:
> Two of far nobler shape ...　　　　　　　(4.284–88)

Marcia Landy's reading is hence questionable when she writes "we are

---

[4] David Aers and Bob Hodge have noted the "seem'd"s but conclude "these doubts or equivocations are not dominant, and the passage basically supports a male supremacist reading" ("'Rational Burning': Milton on Sex and Marriage," *MS* 13 [1979]: 23). Julia M. Walker, "'For each seem'd either': Free Will and Predestination in *Paradise Lost*," *MQ* 20 (1986), examining Milton's use of "seem'd" in relation to free will and predestination in *Paradise Lost,* suggests:

> Throughout the poem, Milton uses "seems" in three different ways: first and most simply, "seems" is used to mean a false appearance, a seeming not an actual reality; second, and more ambiguous, "seems" is used as "appears" but without a clear judgment about reality; ... finally and most confusingly, "seems" is actually equated with some form of the verb "to be."

And she attributes "thir sex not equal seem'd" to his hypothetical "some form of the verb to be" (20). This is an unconvincing redefinition. Cf. also Stephen M. Fallon, "The Uses of 'Seems' and the Spectre of Predestination," *MS* 21 (1987): 99–101, and Julia M. Walker, "Free Will, Predestination, and Ghost-Busting," *MS* 21 (1987): 101–2.

[5] See for example Diane Kelsey McColley, *Milton's Eve* (Urbana: Univ. of Illinois Press, 1983), 40, and Gardner, 81.

told by the narrator, lest we misunderstand, that Adam and Eve are 'not equal, as thir sex not equal seem'd.'"[6] This is not something told us by the narrator, but something perceived by and mediated through Satan's prejudiced vision. His sight is darkened, "undelighted," and distortive; it "seem'd" that way to Satan. It would make sense that Adam and Eve "seem'd Lords of all" to Satan with his preoccupations about authority, that he should see their relationship as political and inegalitarian, that he should see Adam as absolutist, and that he should offer a political interpretation of the way Eve's hair

> . . . in wanton ringlets wav'd
> As the Vine curls her tendrils, which impli'd
> Subjection.   (4.306–8)

Again there is ambiguity. The image "implies," but does not clearly state. This is apt since the image of the vine and elm traditionally represents mutuality, reciprocity, and fertility, but not subjection, as Peter Demetz and Todd H. Sammons have scrupulously demonstrated.[7] If subjection is an implication it is a false one—one taken by Satan or the careless fallen reader. It is a suspect political authoritarian interpretation analogous to the way Adam's "fair large Front and Eye sublime declar'd / Absolute rule."[8]

If we take the description of Adam and Eve as recording Satan's interpretative vision, then we can suggest that Satan is projecting a political, hierarchical hell onto an Eden that is something other. At the beginning of book 4 we were told

> . . . for within him Hell
> He brings, and round about him, nor from Hell
> One step no more than from himself can fly
> By change of place.   (4.20–23)

---

[6] Marcia Landy, "'A Free and Open Encounter': Milton and the Modern Reader," *MS* 9 (1976): 17.

[7] Peter Demetz, "The Elm and the Vine: Notes Toward the History of a Marriage Topos," *PMLA* 73 (1958): 521–32; Todd H. Sammons, "'As the Vine Curls Her Tendrils': Marriage Topos and Erotic Countertopos in *Paradise Lost*," *MQ* 20 (1986): 117–27.

[8] Aers and Hodge, 22. "One might wonder whether 'declar'd' (4.300) undercuts the whole speech on male rule since these signs may only 'declare' absolute rule to the fallen Satan, who does not know what Raphael told Adam, 'that Great / Or Bright infers not Excellence'" (8.90–91). Nonetheless Aers and Hodge see "these doubts or equivocations" as "not dominant."

At the end of his encounter with Adam and Eve, Satan's soliloquy suggests just such a habit of projection, demonstrated in the opening words in which he literally projects hell onto Eden: "O Hell! what do mine eyes with grief behold" (4.358), and he goes on to relate to Adam and Eve in a political, hierarchical way, offering them "League" and a reception in hell of "all her Kings" (4.375,383).[9] That Satan's thinking is absolutist, tyrannical, Milton spells out explicitly in a voice unambiguously narratorial:

> So spake the Fiend, and with necessity,
> The Tyrant's plea, excus'd his devilish deeds.
>
> (4.393–94)

The vision of an inegalitarian, hierarchical, and absolutist paradise, then, we can interpret as a Satanic vision.[10] This is what Satan imports from hell, and this is what he turns paradise into. The perceived unequal relationships are not ideal but proleptic of the postlapsarian human condition. The seeming inequality, the seeming lordship, the declared absolutism, the implied subjection—these are all from hell and all to come on earth. But the true paradise is to be deduced from the opposite of Satan's vision, the paradise to come from the negation of the negation.[11] This reading can be supported both by significant absences and by explicit evidence in the poem.

The absences first—some already remarked by previous commentators. Aers and Hodge ask, " 'Absolute rule' for instance: does Adam really have that? To the horror of the orthodox he does not claim it in the crucial exchange with Eve before the Fall."[12] And Marcia Landy remarks of Milton's treatment of Adam and Eve's postlapsarian quarrels

---

[9] Michael Wilding, *Dragons Teeth: Literature in the English Revolution* (Oxford: Clarendon Press, 1987), 227.

[10] Dennis H. Burden's model of "the Satanic poem" contained within *Paradise Lost* is useful here. See his *The Logical Epic: A Study of the Argument of* Paradise Lost (London: Routledge and Kegan Paul, 1967), 57ff.

[11] "Milton's stridently masculinist 'Hee for God only, shee for God in him,'" as Mary Nyquist has categorized it, can perhaps now be resituated as *Satan's* stridently masculinist sentiment. It has worried readers as far back as Richard Bentley, who proposed emending it to "Hee for God only, shee for God *and* him." See Mary Nyquist, "The Genesis of Gendered Subjectivity in the Divorce Tracts and in *Paradise Lost,*" in *Re-membering Milton,* ed. Nyquist and Margaret W. Ferguson (New York and London: Methuen, 1987), 107; *Dr. Bentley's Emendations on the Twelve Books of Milton's* Paradise Lost (London, 1732), 15.

[12] Aers and Hodge, 22.

that "in spite of his psychological insight into the ways in which mental
conflict is acted out, he does not see their struggle as arising from the
stringent boundaries of hierarchy, with male dominance and female subordination, which make conflict inevitable."[13] Significantly, the absolutism and hierarchy are not features of the dramatized dynamic of
Adam and Eve's relationship.

We might have expected the alleged hierarchical relationship of
Adam and Eve to be spelled out in the authoritative account of creation
given by Raphael, but again it is most significantly absent:

> Let us make now Man in our image, Man
> In our similitude, and let them rule
> Over the Fish and Fowl of Sea and Air,
> Beast of the Field, and over all the Earth,
> And every creeping thing that creeps the ground.
> This said, he form'd thee, *Adam,* thee O Man
> Dust of the ground, and in thy nostrils breath'd
> The breath of Life; in his own Image hee
> Created thee, in the Image of God
> Express, and thou becam'st a living Soul.
> Male he created thee, but thy consort
> Female for Race; then bless'd Mankind, and said,
> Be fruitful, multiply, and fill the Earth,
> Subdue it, and throughout Dominion hold
> Over Fish of the Sea, and Fowl of the Air,
> And every living thing that moves on the Earth.
>
> (7.519–34)

Authority over fish, fowl, and beasts is spelled out here; but there is no
mention of "Lords of all" and no mention of "rule" or "dominion" by
mankind over mankind, or by one sex over another. Mary Nyquist remarks that the reference to Eve here is "meagre,"[14] as indeed it is. But
it is importantly non-discriminatory, unlike the Satanic observations of
book 4, and the meagerness, the very absence of comment, is in itself
significant. As the Diggers declared in *The True Levellers Standard* (1649),
"Man had domination given to him, over the beasts, birds and fishes;
but not one word was spoken in the beginning, that one branch of

---

[13] Landy, 23.
[14] Nyquist, 117.

mankind should rule over another. And the reason is this. Every single man, male and female, is a perfect creature of himself."[15] Domination is explicitly limited to "beasts, birds and fishes" here on the basis of absence in Genesis. Milton perpetuates that significant absence in Raphael's Genesis-based account, and reasserts the interpretation in Adam's comments on Nimrod:

> O execrable Son so to aspire
> Above his Brethren, to himself assuming
> Authority usurpt, from God not giv'n:
> He gave us only over Beast, Fish, Fowl
> Dominion absolute; that right we hold
> By his donation; but Man over men
> He made not Lord; such title to himself
> Reserving, human left from human free.   (12.64–71)

The model for human society is "fair equality, fraternal state" (12.26) which Nimrod has rejected for "Dominion undeserv'd / Over his brethren" (12.27–28). How then could Adam's "fair large front" legitimately declare "Absolute rule"?[16]

Marcia Landy acknowledged that Adam's assessment of Nimrod "might seem to argue for egalitarianism. It certainly argues against externally imposed dominion by king or overlord. Yet the equality of fraternity is qualified throughout *Paradise Lost* by the idea of merit."[17] Certainly there is a hierarchy of merit in *Paradise Lost,* but this is something very different from a fixed hierarchy of birth, rank, caste, or class, and in in no way conflicts with egalitarianism. The confusion of these different sorts of hierarchy has caused considerable problems in interpreting *Paradise Lost,* especially in those feminist readings that have too readily accepted the Satanic rigid hierarchy.[18]

---

[15] See Christopher Hill, ed., *Winstanley: The Law of Freedom and Other Writings* (Harmondsworth: Penguin, 1973), 77.

[16] Of course, when we turn back to book 4, "Absolute rule" is not explicitly applied to man ruling over woman: the context seems to imply it, but the expression is ambiguous and evasive. It is an appropriate Satanic suggestion, inexplicit, insinuating. It can always be plausibly denied and interpreted as applying only to "beast, fish, fowl"—though male supremacism is the prime Satanic implication.

[17] Landy, 9.

[18] Landy, passim; William Shullenberger, "Wrestling with the Angel: *Paradise Lost* and Feminist Criticism," *MQ* 20 (1986): 74: "The doctrine of woman's subordination is explicit

The hierarchy of birth, caste, rank, or class which rigidly fixes its components and allows little or no change, which is predetermined, is one that institutionalizes privilege, power, and inequality. Admiringly defined by C. S. Lewis, it is a system represented by Satan, a model for postlapsarian earthly dynasties, for monarchical, feudal, imperial, and class structures.[19]

The hierarchy of moral and spiritual development that Milton has Raphael describe in book 5 is entirely different. A "curiously fluid conception of hierarchy," as Barbara Lewalski characterizes it,[20] it is a dynamic model of alchemical circulation and continual refinement.[21] There is no fixed inequality. It is open to everything to ascend spiritually. This is the divine hierarchy, one of process and ascent, not rule and repression.

> To whom the winged Hierarch repli'd.
> O *Adam,* one Almighty is, from whom
> All things proceed, and up to him return,
> If not deprav'd from good, created all
> Such to perfection, one first matter all,
> Indu'd with various forms various degrees
> Of substance, and in things that live, of life;
> But more refin'd, more spiritous, and pure,
> As neerer to him plac't or nearer tending

in the text"; Virginia R. Mollenkott, "Milton and Women's Liberation," *MQ* 7 (1973): 101: "Milton treated the subject of female subordination in the most objective fashion possible, not with egotistical gratification but because his view of a hierarchical universe would allow no other concept"; Ricki Heller, "Opposites of Wifehood: Eve and Dalila," *MS* 24 (1988): 190. The hierarchical, gender-discriminatory model is, of course, endemic in non-feminist readings such as, for example, Joseph H. Summers, *The Muse's Method: An Introduction to "Paradise Lost"* (London: Chatto and Windus, 1962):

> The inequality of man and woman is imaged as clearly as is their perfection. It is not only modern ideas of the equality of the sexes which may make this passage difficult for us; the democratic assumption that ideally every individual *should* be self-sufficient and our tendency to define "perfection" as eternal self-sufficiency complicate our difficulties further (95).

[19] C. S. Lewis, *A Preface to "Paradise Lost"* (London: Oxford Univ. Press, 1942), 72–80.

[20] Barbara K. Lewalski, "Milton on Women—Yet Once More,"*MS* 6 (1974): 6.

[21] On the alchemical, see Alastair Fowler in *The Poems of John Milton,* ed. John Carey and Alastair Fowler (London: Longman, 1968), 704; and see also Michael Lieb, *The Dialectics of Creation: Patterns of Birth and Regeneration in "Paradise Lost"* (Amherst: Univ. of Massachusetts Press, 1970), 229–44.

> Each in thir several active Spheres assign'd,
> Till body up to spirit work, in bounds
> Proportion'd to each kind. So from the root
> Springs lighter the green stalk, from thence the leaves
> More aery, last the bright consummate flow'r
> Spirits odorous breathes: flow'rs and thir fruit
> Man's nourishment, by gradual scale sublim'd
> To vital spirits aspire, to animal,
> To intellectual, give both life and sense.
> Fancy and understanding, whence the Soul
> Reason receives, and reason is her being,
> Discursive, or Intuitive; discourse
> Is oftest yours, the latter most is ours,
> Differing but in degree, of kind the same.
> Wonder not then, what God for you saw good
> If I refuse not, but convert, as you,
> To proper substance; time may come when men
> With Angels may participate, and find
> No inconvenient Diet, nor too light Fare:
> And from these corporal nutriments perhaps
> Your bodies may at last turn all to spirit,
> Improv'd by tract of time, and wing'd ascend
> Ethereal, as wee, or may at choice
> Here or in Heav'nly Paradises dwell.   (5.468–500)

As Raphael makes clear, this is a dynamic, evolutionary process. It is a flowing scale of ascent, not a fixed hierarchy. It utterly subverts any fixed political or social or gender roles.[22]

Moreover, the unequivocal inapplicability of fixed gender roles is clear when we relate this passage to what we were told in book 1 about spirits:

> For Spirits when they please
> Can either Sex assume, or both.   (1.423–24)

---

[22] Cf. Marilyn R. Farwell, "Eve, the Separation Scene, and the Renaissance Idea of Androgyny," *MS* 16 (1982): 13: "Thus, anyone who at one point represents the natural and material world is not bound to remain at that level. Theoretically then, Eve has the potential to grow into more wisdom and spirituality."

Since Adam and Eve may "at last turn all to Spirit" and since "Spirits when they please / Can either Sex assume, or both," any assertion of gender hierarchy is ultimately unsustainable.

The concepts of sexual inequality and absolute rule are introduced so brusquely and indeed brutally into the portrayal of Paradise that the reader might expect they would be active concepts in the presented relationship of Adam and Eve in the events leading up to the Fall.[23] Strikingly, this is not so. Nor is equality an issue in Satan's temptation. His strategy is to flatter Eve, to suggest her unique superiority—"who shouldst be seen / A Goddess among Gods, ador'd and serv'd / By Angels numberless" (9.546–48), "no Fair to thine / Equivalent or second" (9.608–9). Only after Eve has eaten the apple does she raise the issue of equality, considering whether to share her knowledge with Adam

> ... and give him to partake
> Full happiness with mee, or rather not,
> But keep the odds of Knowledge in my power
> Without Copartner? so to add what wants
> In Female Sex, the more to draw his Love,
> And render me more equal, and perhaps,
> A thing not undesirable, sometime
> Superior: for inferior who is free?   (9.818–25)

"She is feeling inferior for the first time," Dorothy Miller remarks of these lines.[24] Eve only expresses this sense of any inequality when she is fallen. This suggests that inequality is a part of the fallen world, projected by Eve when she herself has fallen.[25]

---

[23] The sheer blatancy of the inegalitarian and absolutist ideas expressed in the vision of Adam and Eve in book 4 has inevitably shocked readers. And this very brusqueness and brutality may well be interpreted as Milton's strategy for shocking readers into reassessing their attitudes. Stanley Fish's model for reading *Paradise Lost* could well be applied here: "Milton consciously wants to worry his reader, to force him to doubt the correctness of his responses and to bring him to the realization that his inability to read the poem with any confidence in his own perceptions is its focus" (*Surprised by Sin: The Reader in "Paradise Lost"* [Berkeley: Univ. of California Press, 1967], 4).

[24] Dorothy Durkee Miller, "Eve," *JEGP* 61 (1962): 546.

[25] Oddly, Diane K. McColley puts it the other way: "Equality in any case is a fallen concept—the legal recourse of a race not much given to rejoicing in the goodness, much less the superiority, of others—needed to rectify injustices that no one in a state of sinless blessedness would consider committing" ("Milton and the Sexes," in *The Cambridge Compan-*

And now in the fallen world, confusions abound. Marcia Landy remarks, "The speech portrays the idea of equality as confused in Eve's mind with dominance. She errs, like Satan, in confusing hierarchy and equality of affection."[26] But Landy too readily accepts a pejorative account of Eve:

> By violating boundaries and moving to adopt more power through Satan's offers of equality, power, and authority, Eve identified herself as a deviant. In other words, her resistance to subordination is invalidated and stigmatized through its association with the archetypal subverter, Satan. Are we to consider Eve's rebellion and the rebellion of all women against subordination as evil?[27]

The issue is more tangled than that. Firstly, Eve undoubtedly errs in eating the apple. Secondly, equality is not an issue in her temptation: it is an explanation, a rationalization, that enters afterwards. Indeed, it can only enter later if, as I have suggested, inequality was not the reality of the paradisal relationship but rather something that "seem'd" the case in Satan's distorted and evil perception.

So although Eve in falling is stigmatized through her association with Satan, this in no way stigmatizes the egalitarian impulse. Once in the fallen, Satanic world the question "for inferior who is free?" is a valid one.

The complicating factor, of course, is that though Satan uses the rhetoric of egalitarianism in rousing supporters for his rebellion, his own motives are profoundly unegalitarian. As Joseph Wittreich puts it, "Satan's strategy is to employ a rhetoric of equality through which he would bring all creation under subjection."[28] Satan's handling of the issue of egalitarianism shows all his political and oratorical shiftiness:

> Will ye submit your necks, and choose to bend
> The supple knee? ye will not, if I trust

ion to Milton, ed. Dennis Danielson [Cambridge: Cambridge Univ. Press, 1989], 159).

[26] Landy, 21.

[27] Landy, 19. The parallels between Eve and Satan are stressed in Sandra M. Gilbert, "Patriarchal Poetry and Women Readers: Reflections on Milton's Bogey," *PMLA* 93 (1978): 368–82, and King-Kok Cheung, "Beauty and the Beast: A Sinuous Reflection of Milton's Eve," *MS* 23 (1987): 197–214.

[28] Joseph Wittreich, Jr., *Feminist Milton* (Ithaca: Cornell Univ. Press, 1987), 90–91. And see John M. Steadman, "Satan and the Argument from Equality," in his *Milton's Epic Characters: Image and Idol* (Chapel Hill: Univ. of North Carolina Press, 1959), 160–73.

> To know ye right, or if ye know yourselves
> Natives and Sons of Heav'n possest before
> By none, and if not equal all, yet free,
> Equally free; for Orders and Degrees
> Jar not with liberty, but well consist.
> Who can in reason then or right assume
> Monarchy over such as live by right
> His equals, if in power and splendor less,
> In freedom equal? . . .   (5.787–97)

Equality is a part—and only a part—of Satan's rhetoric, but never of his social practice. His rhetoric is a serpentine display of confusion and contradiction. Orders and degrees certainly do jar with liberty.[29] That is why those observations of "thir sex not equal seem'd," "Absolute rule," and "implied subjection" conflict with a true vision of Paradise and alert us that there is a Satanic rhetoric intruding. Satan plays hypocritically with a rhetoric of egalitarianism but acts as an absolutist monarch and sets up a patriarchal dynasty with Sin and Death. About this there are no ambiguities. The narratorial voice denotes him firmly as "Monarch" (2.467) and "Tyrant" (4.394). It is essential to stress, however, that Satan's use of the language of equality in no way discredits the concept of equality. Indeed, his lack of egalitarian practice serves to confirm egalitarianism as a good: "fair equality" (12.26). To reply at last to Marcia Landy, No, we do not have to consider the rebellion of all women against subordination as evil. But Satan is a bad model. Satan's "rebellion" was an attempt to establish tyranny, authoritarian rule. Human rebellion for the good is a rebellion against the Satanic authoritarian, an attempt to "Restore us, and regain the blissful Seat" (1.5) by following the way of Christ:[30] a model, indeed, that Eve does follow, her "On mee, mee only" (10.832) echoing Christ's speech (3.236). Social subordination is a Satanic practice introduced by the Fall. But it

---

[29]Satan's argument is hampered by the fact that he particularly wants to avoid equality among his own faction, and therefore has to turn aside for a moment to explain (789ff.) that "Orders and Degrees Jarr not with liberty." He is not very explicit on the subject, *et pour cause.* The passage is one of those where (rightly and inevitably) an element of grim comedy is permitted. (Lewis, 76) Mollenkott, however, writes, "It is . . . generally true that 'Orders and Degrees jar not with liberty'" (101).

[30] Wilding, 226; Fredric Jameson, "Religion and Ideology," in *Literature and Power in the Seventeenth Century,* ed. Francis Barker et al. (Colchester: Univ. of Essex Press, 1981), 329.

was not present before the Fall, nor does Milton present Eve as rebelling against it, for it is not shown as present.

The issues of equality and masculine rule are raised again in the judgment and punishment episode in book 10. Again, the passages are fraught with ambiguity. And it is this ambiguity I want to continue to stress. There is certainly a male supremacist, authoritarian, inegalitarian reading prominent in the poem, as numerous critical accounts testify; but at the same time the ambiguities and contradictions and cross-references serve to undermine and deconstruct this reading. They do not do so to the extent of utterly canceling it; but they certainly qualify and challenge it, demonstrating that there was a tension and a debate, which the poem embodies and expresses.

In the judgment there is a wavering between whether Adam treated Eve as his "superior, or but equal." Do we read these as alternatives, or as equally unacceptable parallels in God's view?

> To whom the sovran Presence thus repli'd.
> Was shee thy God, that her thou didst obey
> Before his voice, or was shee made thy guide,
> Superior, or but equal, that to her
> Thou didst resign thy Manhood, and the Place
> Wherein God set thee above her made of thee,
> And for thee, whose perfection farr excell'd
> Hers in all real dignity: Adorn'd
> She was indeed, and lovely to attract
> Thy Love, not thy Subjection, and her Gifts
> Were such as under Government well seem'd,
> Unseemly to bear rule, which was thy part
> And person, hadst thou known thyself aright.
>
> (10.144–56)

The floating possibility is that seeing Eve as superior was wrong, as opposed to seeing her as "but equal." If Adam had seen her as "but equal" then his own inner rationality should have allowed him to make a better judgment of what she proposed.[31] Again there is the "seem'd," complicated further by a play on "unseemly": "her Gifts / Were such as under Government well seem'd, / Unseemly to bear rule, which was thy part."

---

[31] Cf. Dennis Danielson, "Through the Telescope of Typology: What Adam Should Have Done," *MQ* 23 (1989): 121–27.

And what might seem a firm resolution of the ambiguity here, that Eve was "Unseemly to bear rule, which was thy part" dissolves again when we come to Eve's punishment:

> ... to thy Husband's will
> Thine shall submit, hee over thee shall rule.
>
> (10.195–96)

How is this a punishment, if it was already the case before the Fall? Nowhere does Milton say the husband's rule over the woman was re-iterated.[32] It is not presented as a reassertion, but as a punishment in parallel with "Children thou shalt bring / In sorrow forth" (10.194–95). And if submission to the husband's will is a punishment for eating the apple, then before the Fall such a submission of man to woman did not apply. In the paradisal state, man and woman, then, lived in equality. But why is it all so ambiguous? In a legalistic episode of judgment and punishment, we might have expected clarity and scrupulous unambiguity. Yet ambiguity permeates the episode, as it does the whole expression of sexual equality.

The assertion of women's equality was contentious in the seventeenth century as it is today. The moves towards freedom and equality for women had scandalized the ruling classes: Clarendon expresses his horror at women and the lower orders preaching in church.[33] But Milton is not only writing about gender equality. He is writing about something that was much more revolutionary and subversive: equality, human equality. This was a truly subversive doctrine, and its developing expression in the late 1640s had provoked the full repression of the bourgeois revolutionary state. The levellers, the diggers and such like were extirpated with a fervor never applied to extirpating royalists.

As Christopher Hill continues to remind us, "Milton wrote under censorship, and was himself a marked man, lucky not to have been hanged, drawn and quartered in 1660. Two of his books were burnt. So

---

[32] Cf. Maureen Quilligan, *Milton's Spenser: The Politics of Reading* (Ithaca: Cornell Univ. Press, 1983), 237: "Her punishment is not merely to bear children in pain, but to (re)submit to her husband's will"; and see also James Grantham Turner, *One Flesh: Paradisal Marriage and Sexual Relations in the Age of Milton* (Oxford: Clarendon Press, 1987).

[33] Edward Hyde, earl of Clarendon, *The History of the Rebellion and Civil Wars in England* (Oxford, 1704), 3:32.

he had to be very careful how he said things he wanted to say."[34] Assertions of egalitarianism could only be made carefully and obliquely. Like the assertion that Paradise was communist, that there was no private ownership, also in book 4, it can only be inserted glancingly, in passing, amidst other issues:

> Hail wedded Love, mysterious Law, true source
> Of human offspring, sole propriety
> In Paradise of all things common else.   (4.750–52)

The issue of common ownership emerges in a discussion of human sexuality. Similarly, the issues of sexual equality rapidly lead on to "sweet reluctant amorous delay" and "those mysterious parts" (4.311–12). Within one contentious issue, human sexuality, Milton involves another contentious issue, egalitarianism and common ownership.

This is not to undercut the issue of gender equality at all. It is not undercut in the poem. But it is firmly attached to that more inclusive and revolutionary aim of achieving total human equality, of restoring us to that still unregained blissful seat, of liberty without orders and degrees, without discrimination, with all things common.

UNIVERSITY OF SYDNEY

---

[34] Christopher Hill, "*Samson Agonistes* Again," *Literature and History,* 2d ser., 1 (1990): 24. For a full discussion of the topic, see "Censorship and English Literature," in *The Collected Essays of Christopher Hill: Writing and Revolution in Seventeenth-Century England* (Brighton: Harvester Press, 1985), 1:32–71.

John Leonard

MILTON'S VOW OF CELIBACY: A RECONSIDERATION OF THE EVIDENCE

RECENT YEARS HAVE SEEN THE REVIVAL OF AN OLD NOTION in Milton criticism: the notion that Milton in his youth made a "vow" of sacrificial celibacy. First proposed in 1925 by James Holly Hanford, and subsequently adopted by E. M. W. Tillyard and Ernest Sirluck, this idea has won new and vigorous support from J. Martin Evans, William Kerrigan, and others. As recently as 1988, Christopher Kendrick could confidently refer to Milton's "cult" of celibacy as "a biographical datum."[1] Resistance to this view of Milton has not been lacking, but it has too seldom been willing to engage with the details of the relevant texts.[2] This paper will attempt to redress this imbalance by reconsider-

---

[1] James Holly Hanford, "The Youth of Milton: An Interpretation of his Early Literary Development," *Studies in Shakespeare, Milton and Donne* (New York: Macmillan, 1925), repr. in *John Milton, Poet and Humanist: Essays by James Holly Hanford* (Cleveland: Western Reserve Univ. Press, 1966), 1–74. E. M. W. Tillyard, *Milton* (London: Chatto and Windus, 1930, repr. 1956), 374–83. Ernest Sirluck, "Milton's Idle Right Hand," *JEGP* 60 (1961): 749–85. J. Martin Evans, *The Road From Horton: Looking Backwards in "Lycidas,"* English Literary Studies Monograph Series, 28 (Victoria, B.C.: Univ. of Victoria Press, 1983). William Kerrigan, *The Sacred Complex: On the Psychogenesis of "Paradise Lost"* (Cambridge: Harvard Univ. Press, 1983), 22–72. Christopher Kendrick, "Milton and Sexuality: A Symptomatic Reading of *Comus,*" in *Re-Membering Milton: Essays on the Texts and Traditions,* ed. Mary Nyquist and Margaret W. Ferguson (London and New York: Methuen, 1988), 43–73.

[2] See e.g., William Haller, "Hail Wedded Love," *ELH* 13 (1946): 79–97. Haller assumes Milton's conformity with Puritan views of marriage. Rosemund Tuve in *Images and Themes in Five Poems by Milton* (Cambridge: Harvard Univ. Press, 1967) grounds her argument more closely on the poems, but never mentions Revelation 14 or the undefiled virgins.

ing one of the central claims of the celibacy critics: the claim that
Milton's early poems reveal a deep and personal preoccupation with the
144,000 virgins of Revelation 14.[3]

At Revelation 14.1–4, St. John tells how he heard a choir of male
virgins singing before the Lamb on Mount Zion:

> I heard the voice of harpers harping with their harps. And they
> sung as it were a new song before the throne, and before the
> four beasts, and the elders: and no man could learn that song
> but the hundred and forty and four thousand, which were re-
> deemed from the earth. These are they which were not defiled
> with women; for they are virgins.[4]

Numerous critics have believed that Milton pledged himself to celibacy
in the hope that he might join the undefiled virgins or at least acquire
special poetic gifts.[5] Most cite the following passage from *An Apology for
Smectymnuus* (1642) in which Milton answers the charge that he has fre-
quented brothels:

> a certain reserv'dnesse of naturall disposition ... was enough to
> keep me in disdain of farre lesse incontinences then this of the
> Bordello. Nor did I slumber over that place expressing such
> high rewards of ever accompanying the Lambe, with those ce-
> lestiall songs to others inapprehensible, but not to those who
> were defil'd with women, which doubtlesse meanes fornica-
> tion: For mariage must not be call'd a defilement.[6]

It is strange that critics should cite this passage as evidence for a vow of
celibacy when Milton is explicit that St. John's virgins may include

---

[3] The other major source of the celibacy theory is the Lady's speech on "the sage / And
serious doctrine of Virginity" in *A Mask* (756–800). Due to constraints of space, this essay
concentrates exclusively on the 144,000 virgins. I have written about the Lady's speech and
its alleged implications for Milton in "Saying 'No' to Freud: Milton's *A Mask* and Sexual
Assault," *MQ* 25 (1991): 129–40 (see pp. 135–36).

[4] King James (Authorized) Version. Unless otherwise stated, all biblical citations will be
from this translation.

[5] See esp. Hanford, *John Milton,* 60–64, Tillyard, *Milton,* 377–78, Sirluck, 749–85,
Kerrigan, 59, and Evans, 59–60. See also Edward Le Comte, *Milton and Sex* (London and
Basingstoke: Macmillan, 1978), 22.

[6] CPW 1:892–93.

married men.[7] Those who believe in the vow of course recognize this. Their answer is that Milton's opinions may have changed before 1642.[8] Arguing backwards from *An Apology for Smectymnuus*, the celibacy critics claim to have found earlier allusions to the 144,000 virgins that show that Milton did once see earthly marriage as a disqualification for singing at the marriage of the Lamb. The most commonly cited poems are "At a Solemn Music," *A Mask, Lycidas, Elegia tertia, Ad Patrem* and *Epitaphium Damonis*. I shall argue that all but the last of these are quite unconcerned with St. John's virgins. While Milton does make a special claim for virginity in *Epitaphium Damonis*, the claim he makes need not amount to a slur upon marriage.

Tillyard finds what he takes to be "an uncommon theory of virginity" in these lines from "At a Solemn Music":

> And the Cherubic host in thousand choirs
> Touch their immortal Harps of golden wires,
> With those just Spirits that wear victorious Palms,
> Hymns devout and holy Psalms
> Singing everlastingly.   (12–16)[9]

Arguing from the premise that "those just Spirits" are St. John's virgins, Tillyard infers a pledge of celibacy from Milton's desire to "rightly answer" them.[10] However, Milton's spirits are not the 144,000 virgins of Revelation 14. As Ernest Sirluck points out, the "just Spirits that wear victorious Palms" are taken from Revelation 7 where St. John draws a clear distinction between the precisely numbered 144,000, drawn from the twelve tribes of Israel, and a "great multitude, which no man could number," drawn from "all nations, and kindreds, and people" (7.4–9). It is the latter group who bear "palms in their hands" (7.9).

---

[7] I do not deny that Milton places an emphasis on sexual mores that would have seemed excessively literal to many seventeenth-century protestants. Joseph Mede had opted for an allegorical reading: "I understand it to be *A Description of the faithful and undefiled Company of Christ under the polluted times of the Antichristian Beast.* . . . By their Worship in praying and praising God, wherein they were undefiled *Virgins,* not polluting themselves with the Mother (or Metropolis) of Fornications" (*Remains on Passages in the Apocalypse* in *The Works of Joseph Mede D. D.,* 4th. ed. [London, 1677], 513). When Milton's interpretation is placed alongside Mede's, it is clear why his refined and delicate nature should have earned him the nickname "the Lady of Christ's." But this need not imply a vow of celibacy.

[8] Tillyard, *Milton,* 380. See also Sirluck, 766 and Evans, 60.

[9] All quotations from Milton's poetry are from Hughes.

[10] Tillyard, *Milton,* 378.

Milton's palm-waving spirits are the unnumbered "multitude," not the precisely numbered virgins. As Sirluck succinctly notes, "'At a Solemn Music' is certainly a religious poem in which the poet aspires rightly to answer the melodious noise made by the angels and the just spirits," but "sacrificial celibacy" has nothing "to do with hearing or answering this song."[11]

Tillyard's argument might survive Sirluck's critique were we to suppose that Milton himself confused the palm-waving spirits with the 144,000 virgins. But Tillyard's identification encounters a still greater obstacle when Milton voices the hope

> That we on Earth with undiscording voice
> May rightly answer that melodious noise;
> As once we did, till disproportion'd sin
> Jarr'd against natures chime, and with harsh din
> Broke the fair music that all creatures made
> To their great Lord.   (17–22)

The fact that "we on Earth" may hope to "rightly answer" the "just Spirits" shows that their melody cannot be the "new song" that "no man could learn . . . but the hundred and forty and four thousand." For Tillyard's argument to work, "we" would have to be identical with the virgins we are trying to "answer." It is clear that "we" are nothing of the sort. "We" are all the redeemed:

> O may we soon again renew that Song,
> And keep in tune with Heav'n, till God ere long
> To his celestial consort us unite,
> To live with him, and sing in endles morn of light.   (25–28)

"Consort" here plays on the senses "company of musicians" and

---

[11] Sirluck, "Milton's Idle Right Hand," 763. Since I have named Sirluck as one of the critics who believe in Milton's vow of celibacy, it might seem odd that I now enlist him against Tillyard. The difference between the two critics is one of dating. Sirluck argues that Milton's vow dates only from 1637. Ironically, Tillyard in a later study (ignored by Sirluck) had come to see 1637 as the year in which Milton abandoned his vow. Thus while Tillyard and Sirluck both believe in the vow of celibacy, Tillyard's evidence for it is Sirluck's evidence against it, while Sirluck's evidence for it is Tillyard's evidence against it. See E. M. W. Tillyard, *Studies in Milton* (London: Chatto and Windus, 1951), 82–99. By ignoring Tillyard's change of mind, Sirluck obscures the fact that there is not even one poem that the two critics can agree to see as evidence for the alleged vow of celibacy.

"spouse." Milton is not alluding to Revelation 14 and the song of the undefiled virgins; he is alluding to Revelation 19 and the marriage song of the Lamb.

I cannot emphasize too strongly the distinction between these songs, which are sung by different persons, in different places, at different times. The "new song" of the virgins is sung on Mount Zion by the virgins alone. The Lamb's nuptial song is sung "in heaven" by the whole church. Generations of Miltonists have nevertheless written as if these two songs were one and the same. It was James Holly Hanford who did most to ease this misreading of Revelation into Milton criticism. Two pages after citing St. John's vision of the virgins, Hanford tells us that their song "was connected with" the "mystic marriage of the soul with God," which Hanford equates with the marriage of "the Lamb and his eternal bride" (63). Sixty years after Hanford's seminal essay, even so scrupulous a critic as William Kerrigan is still arguing from the false premise that "the 144,000 virgins stand closest to the throne at the marriage of the lamb" (59). In fact, Revelation 14 does not mention the Lamb's marriage. Conversely, Revelation 19 does not mention the undefiled virgins. Let us attend, then, to what St. John does say about the marriage of the Lamb:

> And a voice came out of the throne, saying, Praise our God, all ye his servants, and ye that fear him, both small and great. And I heard as it were the voice of a great multitude, and as the voice of many waters, and as the voice of mighty thunderings, saying, Alleluia: for the Lord God omnipotent reigneth. Let us be glad and rejoice, and give honour to him: for the marriage of the Lamb is come, and his wife hath made herself ready. (19.5–7)

St. John says that the nuptial song is sung by "all" the Lamb's servants, "both small and great." The undefiled virgins presumably form one part of this choir, since the earlier chapter had told us that they "follow the Lamb whithersoever he goeth" (14.4). But nothing in Revelation supports the unscriptural superstition that virgins alone may celebrate the Lamb's marriage.

"At a Solemn Music" is not the only poem to have been ill-served by Miltonists confusing Revelation 14 and 19. Critics have repeatedly misinterpreted the following lines from *Lycidas:*

> With *Nectar* pure his oozy Locks he laves,
> And hears the unexpressive nuptial Song,
> In the blest Kingdoms meek of joy and love.
> There entertain him all the Saints above,
> In solemn troops, and sweet Societies
> That sing, and singing in their glory move,
> And wipe the tears for ever from his eyes.   (175–81)

As early as 1752, Thomas Newton identified "the unexpressive nuptial Song" as "the song in the Revelation, *which no man could learn but they who were not defiled with women*."[12] The same identification has since been made by Hanford, Tillyard, Sirluck, Le Comte, Evans, and Kerrigan—all of whom intuit a "pledge" or "vow" or "covenant" of celibacy from Milton's supposed allusion to Revelation 14.[13] It is to Evans's credit that he should at least quote (rather than merely paraphrase) St. John's words—but the manner in which he does so exposes the weakness of his argument:

> These are they which were not defiled with women; for they are virgins. These are they which follow the Lamb whithersoever he goeth. These were redeemed from among men, ...
> And I heard as it were the voice of a great multitude, and as the voice of mighty thunderings, saying Alleluia! for the Lord God omnipotent reigneth. Let us be glad and rejoice, and give honour to him: for the marriage of the Lamb is come, and his wife hath made herself ready.[14]

The flaw here is of course Evans's ellipsis which at one slight bound high overleaps five whole chapters of Revelation, transporting the unwary reader over the seven last plagues, the treading of the winepress of God's wrath, and the fall of the whore of Babylon. Most significantly, Evans must directly excise the tell-tale words "all ye his servants, and ye that fear him, both small and great" (19.5) before he can confidently conclude: "No one who has been 'defiled with women,' St. John appeared to confirm, could hope to sing the new song honouring the

---

[12] Thomas Newton, ed., *"Paradise Regain'd": a Poem in Four Books, to which is added "Samson Agonistes" and "Poems upon Several Occasions"* (London, 1752), 499.

[13] See Sirluck, 765: "he would have made a covenant with himself and given a pledge." See also Hanford, 63–64, Tillyard, *Milton,* 377, Le Comte, 22, Evans, 59, and Kerrigan, 59.

[14] Revelation 14.3–4 and 19.6–7, cited by Evans, 59.

heavenly bridegroom and his bride" (59). However deeply entrenched in Milton criticism, this reading is *not* confirmed by Revelation.

At this point someone might retort that Revelation is a book of prophecy and so not subject to the usual principles of fair quotation. More reasonably, someone might point out that Milton saw Revelation as "the majestick image of a high and stately Tragedy, shutting up and intermingling her solemn Scenes and Acts with a sevenfold *Chorus* of halleluja's and harping symphonies."[15] If we assume that Revelation, like most Greek tragedies, has a single chorus, my distinction between the 144,000 virgins and the unnumbered "servants" begins to look less stable. But this argument cuts both ways. If we must attribute all songs in Revelation to a single chorus, why must we assume that this chorus is synonymous with the 144,000 virgins rather than "all [the Lamb's] servants"? Milton in *Lycidas* directly echoes that "all" when he tells how Lycidas is entertained by "all the Saints" (178). The fact that Lycidas hears a "nuptial Song" also points toward Revelation 19 (not 14) as the dominant source text. The hypothesis of a single tragic chorus actually works against the celibacy critics, for it implies that the 144,000 virgins are subsumed within, rather than privileged above, the general host of the redeemed.

The all-inclusiveness of this moment in *Lycidas* is reinforced by "wipe the tears for ever from his eyes" (181) which is a direct borrowing from Revelation 7.17 and 21.4 ("God shall wipe away all tears from their eyes"). At Revelation 7, God wipes the eyes of the palm-waving multitude drawn from all nations. At Revelation 21 he brings comfort to all the redeemed as the New Jerusalem descends "as a bride adorned for her husband." Celibacy is quite simply irrelevant to these biblical verses and irrelevant to Edward King's apotheosis. Critics would appear to have been misled by "unexpressive," which they take to mean "inexpressible save by a virgin." It is simpler to suppose that "unexpressive" means "inexpressible in this poem." That, at least, is what the word means on the one other occasion Milton uses it.[16]

If Revelation lends no support to the notion that earthly marriage precludes marriage to the Lamb, where do Miltonists get this notion from? Those who have not lifted it straight from Hanford have presumably encountered a Roman tradition, dating from the third and fourth

---

[15] *The Reason of Church Government*, CPW 1:815.
[16] "On the Morning of Christ's Nativity" (116).

centuries (and gaining currency throughout the Middle Ages), in which nuns were seen as "brides of Christ."[17] The standard scriptural authority for this tradition is not Revelation but the Song of Songs. The seminal exegetical texts are Origen's *Commentary* and two *Homilies* on *The Canticle of Canticles*. At no point in his *Commentary* or *Homilies* does Origen even mention Revelation 19.[18] It is not difficult to see why. St. John's ecclesiological application of the *sponsa Christi* metaphor is at variance with Origen's emphasis on the individual virgin soul. As John Bugge remarks,

> in the pneumatic reading the virginity of the bride points directly to the asexuality of the soul and all that that implies in Christian gnosis about its sinless condition: its virginal status is the prerequisite for its acceptance by the Bridegroom. For practical purposes, the ecclesiological interpretation makes this concept irrelevant, as it does not stipulate that individual members of the virginal Church actually be virgins.[19]

It would appear, then, that Miltonists have taken a Roman tradition built around the Song of Songs and applied this tradition in an uncritical manner to the Book of Revelation, eliding chapters 14 and 19 in the process. In "At a Solemn Music" and *Lycidas* Milton employs the *sponsa Christi* metaphor in its ecclesiological rather than its pneumatic sense.

Let us now turn to the promised marriage of Cupid and Psyche at the conclusion of *A Mask:*

> But far above in spangled sheen
> Celestial *Cupid* her fam'd son advanc't,
> Holds his dear *Psyche* sweet entranc't
> After her wand'ring labors long,
> Till free consent the gods among
> Make her his eternal Bride,

---

[17] For an excellent study of asceticism in the early Church, see Peter Brown, *The Body and Society: Sexual Renunciation in Early Christianity* (New York: Columbia Univ. Press, 1988). See esp. chap. 13. See also John Bugge, *Virginitas: an Essay in the History of a Medieval Ideal*, International Archives of the History of Ideas, Series Minor 17 (The Hague: Martinus Nijhoff, 1975), see esp. chap. 3, "*Sponsa Christi:* Virginity and Epithalamian Mystery" (59–79).

[18] Origen, *The Song of Songs: Commentary and Homilies*, trans. R. P. Lawson, Ancient Christian Writers 26 (Westminster, Md.: Newman Press, 1957).

[19] Bugge, *Virginitas*, 65–66.

> And from her fair unspotted side
> Two blissful twins are to be born,
> Youth and Joy; so *Jove* hath sworn.   (1003–11)

Critics frequently identify Cupid as Christ and Psyche as the soul of an undefiled virgin.[20] I agree that the "Celestial *Cupid*" is Christ. The fact that "Psyche" means "spirit" would also suggest that Milton is here thinking primarily of the individual soul. But we need not suppose that Psyche enjoys marriage in heaven because she rejected marriage on earth. As Apuleius tells the story, Psyche had been Cupid's mortal bride before she became his "eternal Bride" among the gods.[21] Even when christianized, the myth of Cupid and Psyche does not denigrate earthly marriage. Milton actually pays a most delicate tribute to it. To appreciate his point, we must recognize his biblical allusion, which is not to Revelation 14 but to Ephesians 5.25–28:

> Husbands, love your wives, even as Christ also loved the church, and gave himself for it; that he might sanctify and cleanse it with the washing of water by the word, that he might present it to himself a glorious church, not having spot, or wrinkle, or any such thing; but that it should be holy and without blemish. So ought men to love their wives as their own bodies.

Milton directly echoes the words "not having spot" when he writes of Psyche's "fair unspotted side." For Kerrigan, these words "signal the flesh's escape" from "contagious matter".[22] I should rather say that Milton affirms the spotless dignity of marriage whether in heaven or on earth. Psyche is the soul, yes; but she is also the church as bride, setting the pattern for all earthly brides. I must not overstate my case by insist-

---

[20] Hanford, 63, Kerrigan, 60–61. See also A. S. P. Woodhouse, "The Argument of Milton's *Comus*," *University of Toronto Quarterly*, 11 (1941): 46–71. Woodhouse agrees with Hanford that the promised marriage is a reward for celibacy, but where Hanford locates this reward in heaven, Woodhouse locates it "here and now" (69).

[21] *Metamorphoses* (*The Golden Ass*), 5.4–5, 6.23–24.

[22] Kerrigan, 61. Kerrigan is here referring to Milton's conscious meaning, which he believes is undermined by an oedipal subtext. Present space does not permit a discussion of Kerrigan's psychoanalytic speculations, which are built upon the premise of Milton's vow of celibacy.

ing that the 1637 epilogue is a pointed vindication of matrimony.[23] Milton's compliment to earthly marriage is casual rather than central to his concerns at this moment. But a casual compliment is all that is needed to discredit the view that the Attendant Spirit denigrates sexuality as defilement and contagion. Milton's allusion to Ephesians implies continuity between marriage in heaven and marriage on earth. As for the 144,000 virgins, I cannot see that they have any relevance for the masque's epilogue.

Evans finds yet more allusions to the 144,000 virgins in *Elegia tertia* and *Ad Patrem*. *Elegia tertia* does echo Revelation 14.13 in inviting Lancelot Andrewes to "rest from his labours," but this particular verse in Revelation is not concerned with celibacy. The choir which greets Andrewes is in any case a choir of angels, not a choir of virgins "redeemed from the earth" (Rev. 14.3).

The lines from *Ad Patrem* are no more hospitable to the celibacy theory, despite the fact that Tillyard cites them as "proof" of the theory. Tillyard thinks that the "inenarrabile carmen" ("indescribable song") of *Ad Patrem* is indescribable because only a virgin can sing it.[24] Once again, Milton's actual meaning is that the song is indescribable in the poem we are reading:

> Spiritus et rapidos qui circinat igneus orbes
> Nunc quoque sidereis intercinit ipse choreis
> Immortale melos et inenarrabile carmen.   (35–37)

> [Even now the fiery spirit who flies through the swift spheres is singing his immortal melody and unutterable song in harmony with the starry choruses.]

Whatever "Spiritus" means in these lines—whether it is the World Soul, the sun, Milton's own disembodied spirit, or (as one recent commentator suggests) a more general reference that "includes Milton, his father, and any bard reading the poem"[25]—there is no justification for Tillyard's assertion that these lines allude to the 144,000 virgins. Here as in "At a Solemn Music," Milton employs a generous "we" to assert that all

---

[23] Here I differ from Tillyard, who, in *Studies in Milton* (95) argues that the Attendant Spirit counsels the Lady to marry. I have argued elsewhere that the Lady never denies herself the possibility of marriage. See above, n. 3.

[24] Tillyard, *Milton*, 377.

[25] M. N. K. Mander, "The *Epistola ad Patrem*: Milton's Apology for Poetry," *MQ* 23 (1989): 158–66 (162).

the redeemed will sing in heaven:

> Nos etiam, patrium tunc cum repetemus Olympum,
> Aeternaeque morae stabunt immobilis aevi,
> Ibimus auratis per caeli templa coronis,
> Dulcia suaviloque sociantes carmina plectro,
> Astra quibus geminique poli convexa sonabunt. (30–34)

> [When we return to our native Olympus and the everlast-
> ing ages of immutable eternity are established, we shall
> walk, crowned with gold, through the temples of the skies
> and with the harp's soft accompaniment we shall sing
> sweet songs to which the stars shall echo and the vault of
> heaven from pole to pole.]

As Polly Mander has recently noted, *Nos* "emphatically joins [Milton]
with his father, as sharing the one vocation of bard."[26] The fact that
Milton's father was a father makes it unlikely that his son would place
him in a choir of virgins—unless Milton is anticipating his own later insistence that "mariage must not be call'd a defilement." If that is the
case, then these lines just might glance at St. John's undefiled virgins.
But such an allusion, far from supporting Tillyard and Evans, would
undermine their whole argument. The subversive presence of a husband
and father in a choir of nominal virgins would require such a radical redefinition of virginity as to place *Ad Patrem* squarely alongside *An
Apology for Smectymnuus* as a Puritan celebration of the married state.
Celibacy, then, is as irrelevant to the "inenarrabile carmen" of *Ad Patrem*
as it is to the "unexpressive nuptial Song" of *Lycidas* or the "melodious
noise" of "At a Solemn Music." Critics have coarsened these poems by
taking any reference to any kind of choral singing as a personal pledge
of lifelong sexual abstinence.

One remaining instance is more difficult to dispose of. In *Epitaphium Damonis* Milton does state that Charles Diodati will be rewarded for
his virginity:

> Quod tibi purpureus pudor, et sine labe iuventus
> Grata fuit, quod nulla tori libata voluptas,
> En! etiam tibi virginei servantur honores!

---

[26] Ibid., 161.

Ipse, caput nitidum cinctus rutilante corona,
Laetaque frondentis gestans umbracula palmae,
Aeternum perages immortales hymenaeos,
Cantus ubi, choreisque furit lyra mista beatis,
Festa Sionaeo bacchantur et Orgia Thyrso.   (212–19)

The image of Diodati holding palm leaves recalls "At a Solemn Music"
and the palm-waving "multitude" of Revelation 7. The "immortal marriage rite" ("immortales hymenaeos") is the heavenly marriage of Revelation 19. But here Milton does say that "virginal honours are reserved"
for Diodati ("tibi virginei servantur honores"). This would appear to be
an allusion to the 144,000 virgins. What are we to make of this? A critic
of Hanford's persuasion might cite these lines as evidence that Milton
himself confused the song of the virgins with the marriage song of the
Lamb. Such a critic might then try to smuggle St. John's virgins into *Lycidas* through the back door of Milton's unconscious. A more plausible
explanation would be that *Epitaphium Damonis* exalts celibacy though
the other poems we have considered do not. Let us suppose, for the
moment, that Milton in this poem does mean to present marriage to the
Lamb as the peculiar privilege of sexually inactive persons. One can
entertain this hypothesis and still resist the theory that *Epitaphium Damonis* voices a personal program of inaction. After all, Milton is mourning
the death of his close friend, Charles Diodati, who had had the misfor-
tune to die unmarried at the age of twenty-nine. It is only natural that
the grieving poet should seek some kind of consolation; St. John's vision
of the undefiled virgins provides a particularly apt consolation in the circumstances. In short, the fact that Diodati died a virgin does not show
that either he or Milton planned to live a celibate life. Had Diodati
lived, he might have married. Milton too could be open to the possibility of marriage, even though he makes the tactful decision to celebrate
virginity in this poem.

The case can be made more strongly than this, for Milton's Latin is
not so clear-cut as English translations suggest. Hughes renders the lines
as follows:

Because you loved the blush of modesty and a stainless youth
and because you did not taste the delight of the marriage-bed,
lo! the rewards of virginity are reserved for you. Your glorious
head shall be bound with a shining crown and with shadowing
fronds of joyous palms in your hands you shall enact your part
eternally in the immortal marriage where song and the sound

of the lyre are mingled in ecstasy with blessed dances, and where the festal orgies rage under the heavenly thyrsus.

Hughes's "because you did not taste the delight of the marriage-bed" is a dubious rendering of "quod nulla tori libata voluptas" (213). Hanford, Bush, Shawcross, and Carey all translate *torus* as "marriage bed" or even "marriage." *Torus* actually means "couch" and can refer to any bed of pleasure, licit or illicit.[27] Here it is instructive to turn to Ovid's *Amores*, where Corinna and the poet frequently engage in sexual adventures on a *torus*. Ovid's *torus* is not a specific term for Corinna's violated marriage-bed. In the most notoriously explicit of the *Amores*, Corinna pays the poet an unexpected visit and makes love to him on his own pallet:

> Aestus erat, mediamque dies exegerat horam
>   adposui medio membra levanda toro.
> pars adaperta fuit, pars altera clausa fenestrae,
>   quale fere silvae lumen habere solent,
> qualia sublucent fugiente crepuscula Phoebo
>   aut ubi nox abiit nec tamen orta dies.
> illa verecundis lux est praebenda puellis,
>   qua timidus latebras speret habere pudor.
> ecce, Corinna venit. . . .

> [Siesta time in sultry summer.
> I lay relaxed on the divan.
> One shutter closed, the other ajar,
> made sylvan semi-darkness,
> a glimmering dusk, as after sunset,
> or between night's end and day's beginning.
> the half light shy girls need
> to hide their hesitation.
> At last—Corinna. . . .][28]

Corinna's *pudor* is a kind of bashfulness quite different from Diodati's *purpureus pudor* (212), but Ovid's *torus* could well have more in common with Milton's than critics have recognized.

---

[27] Had Milton meant "marriage-bed," one would expect him to use *thalamus* rather than *torus*. Alternatively, he could have spoken of a *torus genialis*. Cf. Apuleius, *Met.* 10.34.

[28] *Amores* 1.5.1–9. Text and translation from Ovid's *"Amores,"* trans. Guy Lee (London: Murray, 1968), 14–15. For other occurrences of *torus* as a bed of illicit pleasure, see *Amores* 2.4.14, 2.4.34, 2.11.8, 2.11.31, 2.17.24, 2.19.42, 3.5.42, 3.7.4, 3.7.78, and 3.14.32.

Milton's translators, confident that Milton is drawing a sharp antithesis between two kinds of marriage, have translated *torus* as "marriage bed" or "marriage" so as to make this antithesis more clear. But *Epitaphium Damonis* does not say that Diodati is rewarded with marriage in the next world because he avoided it in this one. Milton might mean nothing more than that the unmarried Diodati had led a blameless youth ("sine labe iuventus," 212) by keeping his virginity unsullied by fornication. Such a reading would be entirely consistent with Milton's later pronouncement that *defiled with women* "doubtlesse meanes fornication: For mariage must not be call'd a defilement."

We should not suppose that a compliment of this kind would be insulting to Diodati. Redundant compliments were quite proper in the seventeenth century. Jonson in "To Penshurst" comments on Lady Sidney's chastity with a bluntness that few dignitaries would now appreciate:

These, *Penshurst,* are thy praise, and yet not all.
      Thy lady's noble, fruitfull, chaste withall.
His children thy great lord may call his owne:
      A fortune, in this age, but rarely knowne.[29]

However unseasonable to modern ears, Milton's exaltation of Diodati's premarital chastity accords with the decorum of his age. It also accords with the values we know Milton shared with Diodati. In *Elegia sexta* (addressed to Diodati) Milton had stated that the aspiring epic poet must lead a "chaste youth" ("casta iuventus") if he is to accomplish great things (63). In *Prolusion VI,* while reflecting on his nickname "the Lady," he taunts his undergraduate audience with the possibility that he is so called because he does not share their enthusiasm for brothels (CPW 1:284). Although it is my whole purpose in this essay to discredit the celibacy theory, I have no doubt that premarital chastity always mattered to Milton, nowhere more so than in the early poems. My objection to the celibacy critics is that they repeatedly blur the distinction between celibacy and premarital virginity.

I shall conclude with two examples of such blurring. Kerrigan in *The Sacred Complex* draws attention to two inscriptions that Milton placed beneath his name in the guest book of the Cerdogni family in Geneva toward the end of his travels abroad. The first reads: *Coelum non animum muto dum trans mare curro* ("I do not change my mind with my

[29] *The Complete Poetry of Ben Jonson,* ed. William B. Hunter, Jr., The Stuart Editions (New York: Doubleday, 1963).

skies as travel across the sea"). The second inscription consists of the last words of *A Mask:* "if virtue feeble were / Heaven itself would stoop to her." Kerrigan conjectures that both inscriptions refer to Milton's virginity (37). The hypothesis is not implausible, but it matters that Milton voices his commitment (which is not quite the same thing as a "vow") in the context of foreign travels and the notorious temptations of Italy. Neither inscription implies a determination to remain unmarried.

The second instance of a blurring of celibacy with premarital virginity occurs in Martin Evans's otherwise fine comment on the following lines from *Lycidas:*

> Alas! What boots it with uncessant care
> To tend the homely slighted Shepherd's trade,
> And strictly meditate the thankless Muse?
> Were it not better done as others use,
> To sport with *Amaryllis* in the shade,
> Or with the tangles of *Neaera's* hair? (64–69)

I wholeheartedly agree with Evans when he rejects the view of "several recent critics that Amaryllis and Neaera stand for no more than the composition of love poetry." As Evans notes, Milton is not considering "the writing of a different kind of poem"; he is considering "the living of a different kind of life" (46). One can nevertheless accept this point without accepting Evans's conclusion that Milton's swain rejects marriage when he rejects the nymphs. Amaryllis and Neaera represent the temptation of premarital sex. (Why else should there be *two* nymphs?) I do not deny that some part of Milton feels attracted to the temptation he resists. I take it that "as others use" is an envious glance at those who scorn to "live laborious days" of premarital strictness. As these examples from Kerrigan and Evans show, the belief in Milton's vow of celibacy can vitiate even the most intelligent Milton criticism. I have tried to show that the case for Milton's vow is weaker than is sometimes supposed. Milton may not have "slumbered" over Revelation 14 ("nor did I slumber over that place"), but the same cannot be said for those critics who have made the 144,000 virgins a shibboleth in Milton criticism. It is of course finally impossible either to prove or to disprove the case for Milton's vow of celibacy, but if (as George Santayana has said) "scepticism is the chastity of the intellect," some scepticism might be especially appropriate to this topic.

UNIVERSITY OF WESTERN ONTARIO

Donald M. Friedman

DIVISIONS ON A GROUND:
"SEX" IN *PARADISE LOST*

I HAVE PUT QUOTATION MARKS AROUND THE WORD "SEX" because, like and unlike Milton calling upon Urania, I want to summon not only the meaning, but also the name, or word, itself. What follows is an inquiry into the implications of the several and differing uses of the word in the poem, particularly in its relations to other, associated terms that both define and differentiate the physiological, social, and spiritual realities that are engaged in any meditation on the sexual institutions of an imagined world.

Most of the meanings to be found under the sigla of the *Oxford English Dictionary* for the word "sex" were available to Milton, in that they were in fairly common currency during his lifetime (and earlier), even the relatively new sense (sb. 3) which the *OED* characterizes, with exquisite precision, as "the sum of those differences in the structure and functions of the reproductive organs on the ground of which beings are distinguished as male and female," and, more generally, "the class of phenomena with which these differences are concerned." One can well imagine that class to be fairly extensive; and it is not surprising that the first citation of this usage is found in Donne's *Songs and Sonets*. What is surprising is that the example given there is Donne's remark that if his prophetic primrose should have six petals his not impossible she may prove to "Be more than woman," and that therefore "she would get above / All thought of sex."[1] Donne's meaning here seems to hew

---

[1] John Donne, *Complete English Poems,* ed. A. J. Smith (Harmondsworth: Penguin Books, 1978), 74.

closely to the idea of "sex" as either the set of all women of that sex, or to the idea of sex as an identifying marker for both men and women. In "The Ecstasy," by contrast, his meaning draws closer to later (and modern) usage when, in commenting on the power of the lovers' souls' out-of-body "negotiation," he claims that in the ecstatic clarification of "what we love," "We see by this, it was not sex."[2] In insisting that what each loved and drew each to other was not sex, Donne is eliding the general notion of definitional characteristics and the specific forces of attraction generated by them. His phrase also begins to suggest, almost hypostatically, an entity in some sense separable from its constitutive manifestations, an entity that can be contemplated in itself, possessed of agency, and in its exercise of power both implicated in and transcendent of its binary forms.

This use appears rarely in Milton, possibly only once in *Paradise Lost;* again, we are not likely to be surprised to find that it is uttered by Satan during his "glozing" temptation of Eve in book 9. There, to demonstrate the height of exaltation which he has experienced after eating the forbidden fruit, he recalls his earlier existence as one of the "beasts that graze," "of abject thoughts and low" like the "trodden herb" by which he nourished himself in that state. The sign of his abjection is that he "nor aught but food discerned / Or sex, and apprehended nothing high."[3] Sex is equated implicitly with appetites appropriate to beasts,[4] and even though it remains an essential mode of distinguishing among things, in Satan's perspective the purpose of such discerning is "nothing high." What Satan actually knows about the nature of beasts is unclear; either he is endowed angelically with an intellectual penetration equal to Adam's own or in this passage he is, as always, revealing the lineaments of his imagination and, as always, debasing the nature of his subject and the purposive design of which it is part and exemplar.

Nothing in what we have learned in the poem to this point corre-

---

[2] Smith, 53ff., lines 30–31.

[3] *Paradise Lost,* 9.571–74, in *The Poems of John Milton,* ed. John Carey and Alastair Fowler (London: Longman, 1968). All quotations of Milton's poetry are taken from this edition; passages from *Paradise Lost* are identified in the text by book and line numbers.

[4] It is characteristically Satanic to regard those appetites that preserve and produce life as "low." If neither Raphael's discourse on angelic alimentation nor his description of the food-chain of being (5.404–33) suffices to make the contrary point, the analogy of knowledge and food that pervades *Paradise Lost* should make clear that the desire for sustenance, whatever the dangers of overindulgence, is normative, essential, and "good" in Milton's design.

sponds to or sustains Satan's vision. Raphael's description of the days of creation presents the animals in emblematic fashion, their distinctive forms mimed by their behaviors, and all of them responding to the divine imperatives of abundance and ontological plenitude. Only those fish that live in "pearly shells" are shown to be concerned with food, as they "attend / Moist nutriment" (7.407–408); and the "female bee" solicitously "feeds her husband drone / Deliciously" (7.490–91). But that is all Adam hears about the bestial desire for food or sex. Even the serpent, last in the parade of beings that passes before Adam's inner eye, is sketched in impressive, superlative, mainly visual phrases: "huge extent," "brazen eyes," "hairy mane terrific." That he is "subtlest" is qualified to Adam by his also being "not noxious, but obedient at thy call" (7.496–98), so that his powers of discernment are made to seem parallel to human intelligence, not the agents of appetite to which Satan reduces them in his speech to Eve.

Moreover, the proper discrimination between the orders of creation in the matter of appetite has been addressed in several ways in book 8, before we (or Eve) encounter Satan's revisionary account of what moves the animals in their quest for physical and spiritual sustenance. Remembering how he mingled supplication and protest in asking for a mate, Adam tells Raphael that he named the creatures, at God's behest, while or because he "understood / Their nature"; a moment earlier he noticed that "each bird and beast" approached him "two and two" (8.349–53), and although he does not claim to have discerned the marks of sexual differentiation, the implication is clear enough that "two by two-ness" is somehow essential to "their nature." More remarkably, he perceives intuitively that this principle applies to him as well, albeit he has been given dominion over the beasts, and is to this extent superior to them. The dialectic with God moves in stages, however, beginning with Adam's questions: "In solitude / What happiness, who can enjoy alone, / Or all enjoying, what contentment find?" (8.364–66), and moving to his counterargument to God's disingenuous proposal that Adam find company among the other creatures: "Among unequals what society / Can sort, what harmony or true delight?" (8.383–84).

Adam thus realizes that he is both like and unlike the animals whose nature he has so immediately understood. Solitude is not simply a matter of being sole; solitude is the absence of an equal, not merely the absence of another. From this understanding arises Adam's consciousness of his defects (8.419), and his discovery that the cause of human desire is this consciousness, with its concomitant drive to "help

... or solace" his "deficience" with "conversation with his like" (8.416–18). Although the word "conversation" occurs here only in *Paradise Lost,* we know from the argument of *The Doctrine and Discipline of Divorce,* as well as from other writings, what value and emphasis Milton placed on the range of acts and functions he included in the concept, discourse and intercourse of all kinds. It is typical of his usage to dissolve the boundaries between physical and intellectual interchange, while acknowledging their hypostatic union in the word itself. It is also, perhaps, typical that in the same speech to God (8.412–36)—Adam's plea for the necessary satisfaction of the desire for conversation—the word's semantic range is itself converted into a part of his argument. To converse is at the same time to turn (something) about and to stay in the same place, to dwell and to change, to learn by continued acquaintance and to transmute by virtue of superior knowledge. As Adam reminds God, while the creator can "raise" his creatures by will, Adam "by conversing cannot these erect / From prone" (8.432–33); conversation cannot convert that which is not already conversant, change can operate only on a base of the unchanged, the equivalent, the same. Thus, while Adam has realized that he is like other creatures in needing another like himself, he is aware that his field of perception has not discovered such a one. The shape of that ideal of likeness is formed by his understanding of the difference that lies between him and the creatures, a difference he can nevertheless conceptualize in his discourse with God (and later with angelic—i.e., superior—intellects). To "solace his defects" (8.419) he calls for "conversation with his like" (8.418), an action and experience he has not known, but is moved to imagine by his powers of inference. Moreover, those powers are the sign of his rationality, the faculty that at the same time distinguishes him from both the lesser creatures and from his superhuman guides and mentors, and defines both his links with them and his own differentiated identity.[5]

---

[5] As might be expected, Milton dwells most frequently on the vocabulary of equality among creatures, and its problematics, in the several tracts on divorce. For example, in *Tetrachordon* he argues a comparison between Moses' accommodation to "hardness of heart" in his commandments concerning divorce, and God's "suffering" all manner of injustices to exist because of "our imperfect and degenerat condition." But at the same time Milton recalls that "prime Nature made us all equall," referring only to human beings, who are "equall coheirs by common right and dominion over all creatures"(2.661). Equality is here defined implicitly as holding common status within the ontological hierarchy; and yet it inevitably carries with it some flavor of other of its connotations, such as "fair," "just,"

Milton allows, or creates, an ambiguity in Adam's formulation of his request to God for a "help"; he names as "the cause of his desire" (8.417) either the degree of his "deficience" in contrast to God's being "absolute, though one" (8.421), or his yearning for "conversation." Both explanations, of course, are the same, although they appear to be different. Although Adam has not yet seen his image, and thus has not discovered the equal that will nevertheless appear as his "not equal" (4.296), he knows that what he desires cannot be found among the creatures with whom he shares both the need for "two-by-twoness" and the appetites which govern the processes of survival and procreation. In order to achieve "his image multiplied," to "beget / Like of his like," he "requires / Collateral love, and dearest amity," found in "Social communication" (8.424–29). In short, that which distinguishes him from the creatures who have instructed him by appearing "two and two," is the power to imagine the essential ability to "participate / All rational delight" (8.390–91), the idea of a "society" that cannot exist "Among unequals" when to be equal means to be "fit" to "converse" (8.384–96).

If God seems satisfied with his creature's understanding of this matter, Raphael, at least, is skeptical; for he reacts to Adam's "confession" that in the presence of Eve "transported I behold, / Transported touch" (8.529–30) by severe admonition:

> But if the sense of touch whereby mankind
> Is propagated seem such dear delight
> Beyond all other, think the same vouchsafed
> To cattle and each beast; which would not be
> To them made common and divulged, if aught
> Therein enjoyed were worthy to subdue
> The soul of man, or passion in him move.   (8.579–85)

The angel seems not to have noticed that Adam does not speak of himself as subjected to Eve's "outside," as he puts it, but as transported, moved, from within his prior understanding toward a new and disturbing view of the way things are. Adam understands "well" that Eve is "in the prime end / Of nature . . . inferior, in the mind / And inward facul-

---

"impartial," and the like—in other words, the qualities that entitle men and women (which the word "equall" does not differentiate in this context) to "common right and dominion." All quotations of Milton's prose are taken from *Complete Prose Works of John Milton*, ed. Don M. Wolfe et al. (New Haven: Yale Univ. Press, 1953–82), and cited as CPW followed by volume and page number.

ties"; and he understands as well that she only "seems" "so absolute
... And in herself complete" because of his approach to her "loveliness." But it is not seeming that Adam finds in Eve's ability "to consum-
mate all" (i.e., to bring to perfection by completion); it is, rather,
"Greatness of mind and nobleness" that build their seat in her, an assertion that is as clear and categorical as is Adam's self-aware account of his
reaction to Eve's beauty, in which he grasps surely that her appearance
of completeness is a product of his passion and "Commotion strange"
(8.531–57). Raphael has attended to only part of what Adam has said;
and it is plausible that the angel's easy and assured disjunction between
"heavenly love" and "carnal pleasure" (8.592–93) derives from his own
ignorance of the sense of touch, its powers to transport, and its role in
human "conversation." In Raphael's mind, Adam's subjection to the trans-
muting force of Eve's beauty is simply a sign of his descent to a level of
experience he shares with beasts—that is, sexual excitation. But Adam has
never been so deluded or misguided; his original sense of the meaning of
desire was based on the perception of his difference from the creatures.
His concern is rather with the puzzling relations of his equal with her
differences from him—in other words, with the web of meanings that
define and differentiate "inward" and "outward show"[6] (8.538).

We recall that it was Satan (and Donne) for whom the word "sex"
refers primarily to that complex of organs and functions that separate and
attract men and women; Milton's use of the word is both more various
and more problematic, at least in *Paradise Lost.* In *Samson Agonistes,* for
example, and perhaps understandably in view of its dramatic imperatives,
the word "sex" appears always in connection with the female, and in a
sense that almost approaches the cant locution of "the sex" to mean
women as a group. Somewhat similarly in the prose, Milton means
"sex" to indicate generic groupings of male and female, almost exclusively. But in the epic the word and its denotative purposes move more ob-
scurely from physical attributes to gender identities to profound and inward essences; and it is among these meanings that Adam, Eve, and the

---

[6] Although notions of the bestial are, in Milton's prose, most often associated with the
beast of Revelation, it is again in the divorce tracts that he explores what it is that distinguishes human creatures from the beasts. Lust is of course differentiated from love, but
primarily on the grounds of what in *The Doctrine and Discipline of Divorce* is called "a bestiall
necessitie," a Pauline "bestial burning" (CPW 2.259–60; 269) that erodes rational choice and
overwhelms conversation. That which "can give a human qualification to that act of the
flesh, and distinguish it from the bestial" (CPW 2.606) is the mysterious union of like with
like that Milton hymns in book 4 as Eden's "sole propriety."

supernatural creatures maneuver as they attempt in their various ways to stabilize themselves and their societies.

The history of the word in the poem begins as Milton explains the transformations and persistence of the fallen angels throughout human history. Their substance is of course immortal, but the fact that they have appeared as both "Baalim and Ashtaroth; those male, / These feminine" (1.422–23) rests on the angels' ability to "either sex assume," and this in turn because "so soft / And uncompounded is their essence pure, / Not tied or manacled with joint or limb, / Nor founded on the brittle strength of bones, / Like cumbrous flesh" (1.424–28). They can take "what shape they choose," so long as it allows them to "works of love or enmity fulfil" (1.428–31). For spirits, then, sex is a matter of "shape" or appearance, which to them is infinitely variable because not "manacled" to the instrumentalities of body; from this perspective the strength of bones is but a "brittle strength."[7] What seems to guide these lines is a complex of feeling in which the elusiveness of fallen spirituality is associated with the blurring of sexual lines of differentiation, and in which, also, Milton's lifelong wrestling with the desire for inner, unconstrained freedom appears in the light of his acknowledgment of the structural inevitability of defined and differentiated sexes. It is not only the paradox of likeness in unlikeness that gravels him, but also the necessity of acknowledging visibly differing shapes as signifiers of the otherness that is the remedy for "single imperfection" and "unity defective" (8.423, 425).

That acknowledgment reveals itself, both explicitly and by analogy, in the innumerable polarities by which and through which the poem proceeds; Mary Ann Radzinowicz, for instance, glossing the "male and female light" of the sun and the moon, says simply, "hence active and passive, rational and animal, mental and physical,"[8] assuming quite reasonably that such a string of comparisons will appear obviously pertinent and Miltonic. Indeed, the passage she is glossing, part of Raphael's astronomical exposition in book 8, displays a polarity—or at least an internal division—of its own as it proposes to order knowledge of the heavens by an argument of subjection to earthly concerns. Adam has asked, with suitable humility, why God has made the stars to move about "this earth a spot, a grain, / An atom" (8.17–18). Rather ambivalently, Raphael tells him first

---

[7] Compare Marvell's play on the same trope in "A Dialogue between the Soul and Body": "manacled in Hands."

[8] See her edition (with David Aers) of *Paradise Lost: Books VII-VIII*. The Cambridge Milton for Schools and Colleges (Cambridge: Cambridge Univ. Press, 1974), 135.

that God has kept secret from men the truth about heavenly and earthly motion, but then goes on to correct his misapprehension that "great / Or bright infers ... excellence" (8.90–91). His point is that the earth may in fact be more excellent than the "bright luminary" the sun because the latter shines "barren," working no "virtue on itself" "But in the fruitful earth," where "His beams, unactive else, their vigour find" (8.94–97). The communication of vital force is figured unmistakably as an act of fertilization; but in keeping with Milton's exploration of the mysteries of reciprocity it is the male symbol, the sun, which is described as "barren," the "vigour" of its presumably and traditionally potent beams "found" only in the "fruitful earth." The deliberate confusions of the analogies of light and potency are maintained as Raphael goes on to consider the question of the earth's several possible motions by moving from a vision of the shifting illumination of the earth by sunlight to contemplation of the earth's reflected light illuminating the moon, "Enlightening her by day, as she by night / This earth" (8.142–44). The angel's purpose is to bring before Adam the possibility that the earth itself provides procreative light to a world in the moon, and thence to suggest that

> ... other suns perhaps
> With their attendant moons thou wilt descry
> Communicating male and female light,
> Which two great sexes animate the world.   (8.148–51)

It is clearly the case that "male and female light" refers to the light of sun and moon, direct and reflected light, and that these are arranged hierarchically in a conventional way. But it seems equally clear that the laws of procreation have been recast in this passage to allow for a degree and kind of reciprocal authority that belies that apparent hierarchical disposition. Just as Milton has Raphael say that the sun's beams would be barren without their intercourse with the fructifying earth, so here the angel tells Adam that it is the function of the *two* great sexes to "animate the world." The slight but considerable difference is to shift the paradigm from the active, masculine sun impregnating the receptive, female earth to a process in which the communication of male and female creates life in the world, which otherwise would be "desert and desolate," "in nature unpossessed / By living soul" (8.153–54). In short, both sun and earth, male and female, active and passive, in Milton's revisionary sexual dispensation, are lifeless and unproductive in themselves; the "living soul" is the product of their mutual conversation.

But there remains the difficulty of identifying the mutuality that underlies sexual difference. I say "sexual difference" in part because although "gender," the word and the concept, were available to Milton, he rarely made use of them except in his *Accedence Commenc't Grammar*. The reason may be suggested by the familiar passage in book 4 where we first see Adam and Eve; I say "we" despite the equally familiar assumption that we see Eden and its inhabitants first through Satan's eyes. If the fiend "Saw undelighted all delight" (286), that is patently not the mood in which "the loveliest pair" are described in lines 287–324. It is not that Satan is incapable of understanding that "in their looks divine / The image of their glorious maker shone, / Truth, wisdom, sanctitude severe and pure" (291–93); indeed, he is better able than they—or we, for that matter—to recognize how clearly they resemble the "image of their . . . maker." It is, rather, that his knowledge would not have produced the climactic definition of the meaning of what he sees, the filial freedom which is the source of "true authority in men." That is, Satan is at best capable of perceiving and reporting what he *sees;* his capacity falls short of understanding its meaning, as is consistently the case with him. Thus we are presented with the image: "though both / Not equal, as their sex not equal seemed," an image defined almost entirely by negation or difference, and yet relying on the detailed visual description that follows and the specification as well of "those mysterious parts" which are not concealed. That the outward signs of their sexuality are not the same hardly needs emphasis; but that is not Milton's point, just as "equal" does not mean simply "identical." What is "not equal" between them are their functions and purposes, as these are expressed by the obvious physical differences in the way they have been "formed." When Adam later tells Raphael about his dream of Eve's creation he will remember watching "the shape still glorious before whom awake I stood" and seeing that "Under his forming hands a creature grew, / Manlike, but different sex" (8.463–64, 470–71). Thus in book 4 we are instructed that the outward signs reveal that he is for "valour formed" and she "for softness . . . and sweet attractive grace" (4.297–98). Nevertheless, these are outward signs only, and must be *read* in order for their meaning to be properly constructed and grasped.

In the unfallen state, this passage suggests, signs and their meanings enjoy a relatively untroubled interconnection; the fallen mind disrupts these correspondences, as for example when Eve, thinking to "add what wants / In female sex," plans to make herself "more equal" (822–24), thus yielding to the belief that differences can be levelled and that a state of equivalence can be transcended. Like the Satan who "trusted to have equalled the most high," Eve plots to wipe out the distinctions which keep true identity in place. Milton perceives, I think, the same absurdity

in the attempt to constrain the nature and import of sexual difference
within the outward signs and groupings that are taken as markers of
"the two great sexes." As Adam probes the depths of his despair and
disgust in book 10, he laments that God has decreed the sole "Way to
generate / Mankind," which he characterizes as "strait conjunction with
this sex" (10.898). Sex is equated with "this sex," "conjunction" replac-
es "conversation," and the human condition is defined as the straitness
of being joined to the other sex. In other words, the union that lies
within communion is perceived, and thus experienced, as an enforced
yoking of incompatibles, rather than the interdependence of different essences. One consequence of the fall is that those meanings of "sex" that
attach themselves to outward and visible signs, the "letter" of sexual difference, come to replace the spirit of sexuality, in which mutuality and
the exchange of potency and fertility are the inward signs. *Paradise Lost,*
even as it opens out finally into the world we inherit of constrained sexual differentiation, preserves a visionary memory of the universe of the
"two great sexes" as they existed in their freedom from exclusive definition and the tyranny of appearances.[9]

UNIVERSITY OF CALIFORNIA, BERKELEY

---

[9] The critical literature concerned with Milton's treatment of issues of gender and sexuality
is considerable, and continues to grow more extensive. Contemporary discussions took major
impetus from Marcia Landy's essay, "Kinship and the Role of Women in *Paradise Lost,*" in *MS,*
4 (1972), and eventually involved Barbara K. Lewalski, Sandra Gilbert, and Joan Webber, among
others. In 1983, Diane McColley, in *Milton's Eve* (Urbana: Univ. of Illinois Press), William Kerrigan, in *The Sacred Complex: on the Psychogenesis of "Paradise Lost"* (Cambridge: Harvard Univ.
Press), and Christine Froula in "When Eve Reads Milton: Undoing the Canonical Economy,"
in *Critical Inquiry* 10, added valuably to the developing conversation. More recently, essays by
Mary Nyquist, particularly those published in *Re-Membering Milton: Essays in the Texts and the
Tradition,* ed. Nyquist and Margaret W. Ferguson (New York and London: Methuen, 1987) and
in *Post-Structuralism and the Question of History,* ed. Derek Attridge, Geoffrey Bennington, and
Robert Young (Cambridge: Cambridge Univ. Press, 1987), have advanced our understanding.
Milton and the Idea of Woman (Urbana: Univ. of Illinois Press, 1988), a collection of essays by
several hands edited by Julia Walker, may also be consulted with profit.

Part III

POETRY AND POLITICS

Balachandra Rajan

BANYAN TREES AND FIG LEAVES: SOME THOUGHTS ON MILTON'S INDIA

SCHOLARSHIP ON MILTON'S INDIA IS NOT VOLUMINOUS AND the student in search of understanding cannot proceed very far beyond the Milton encyclopedia article on the subject. The general disposition is to treat the handful of references to India as unrelated excursions into the exotic, part of an encyclopedic epic's obligation to be encyclopedic in its naming of places. If the references are taken together, their most conspicuous characteristic is that nearly all of them occur in infernal or postlapsarian contexts. They can then be regarded as collectively proposing the satanization of the Orient in a way becoming familiar to Milton's time. Milton's contemporaries were not unanimous on the matter and Dryden's *Aureng-Zebe,* performed a year after the second edition of *Paradise Lost* was published,[1] seems to turn an Islamic fundamentalist into a model of magnanimity, an example for European princes to emulate. For the biblical imagination, however, Egypt was an abomination and anything east of it was likely to be worse.

The first book of *Paradise Lost* is indeed heavily laden with pejorative references to the Orient. Both the catalogue of false gods and the building of Pandemonium provide rich opportunities for moral invective. The opportunities, though seized with characteristic energy, remain sufficiently routine for Broadbent to observe that "the oriental similes place the building as a citadel of barbaric despotism."[2] It is to be noted that Babylon forms the eastern limit of these similes almost as if the true

---

[1] Dryden's play was first performed at Drury Lane on 17 November 1675.
[2] J. B. Broadbent, *Some Graver Subject* (London: Chatto and Windus, 1960), 101–2.

heart of darkness has been set apart for deeper castigation. Nevertheless, Pandemonium is not totally oriental. Its facade reflects the Mediterranean world with Doric pillars that may be designed to remind us of the colonnade that Bernini built for St. Peter's. The bee was the emblem of Pope Urban VIII who consecrated St. Peter's and Milton duly provides us with a bee simile that deflates the stature of the fallen angels and embroils the papacy in oriental viciousness. We are now in the outer chamber of Pandemonium and a reference to pygmies beyond "the *Indian* mount" (1.781)[3] seems designed to advise us that the center of evil is about to be entered. The great hall of Pandemonium is for the democratic multitude. "Farr within" is the council chamber for the "secret conclave" of the power elite. The first book ends poised on these lines and as we turn the page, the imagination opens the door to the interior.

> High on a Throne of Royal State, which far
> Outshone the wealth of *Ormus* and of *Ind,*
> Or where the gorgeous East with richest hand
> Showers on her Kings *Barbaric* Pearl and Gold,
> Satan exalted sat, by merit rais'd
> To that bad eminence.   (2.1–6)

Ormuz was once the emporium of the Orient and Marvell's deluded voyagers to the Bermudas dream appropriately of "jewels more rich than Ormuz shows." By the time Milton wrote *Paradise Lost,* this legendary splendor was becoming a thing of the past. Ormuz's fortunes declined after its capture from the Portuguese in 1622 by an Iranian expedition with British naval support. On the other hand, the wealth of Ind was very much a matter of the present and was commented upon by every traveler to India, including English emissaries such as Roe and Hawkins. The "throne of royal state" could well be the Peacock Throne. Since 1634, when Shah Jehan moved the Mogul capital to Delhi, the throne had stood in the Hall of Public Audience, a structure six hundred feet in length and three hundred and seventy in width, which might have suggested the outer court of Pandemonium. Tavernier, the French jeweler, had examined the throne in 1665 and though his detailed description was only translated after the second edition of *Paradise Lost* was published, reports about the throne would have been widespread in a London where the

---

[3] All quotations from Milton's poetry follow Hughes.

East India Company had been in existence for two-thirds of a century. The throne with its pearl-fringed canopy supported by golden pillars was the epitome of the "gorgeous East" in its opulence.[4]

When *Paradise Lost* was published, the monarch on the Peacock Throne was Dryden's hero, Aureng-Zebe. He could be said to have been raised to his eminence by merit if by merit we mean the successful killing off of every other claimant. History supports the impression of such barbarity, but Milton may not have been aware of this appropriateness. It is tempting to think that he was aware of the inscription four times repeated in letters of gold, in Shah Jehan's white marble Hall of Private Audience which corresponds to the council room of Pandemonium. As a comment on Satan's situation its layered irony must be deemed Miltonic:

"If there be Paradise on earth, it is this, it is this, it is this!"

The direct application is obvious but the statement becomes more interesting read against the grain, with the triple repetition compounding the force of the *if*. Paradise can be not native but alien to the earth, won laboriously against the earth's resistance. Shah Jehan built in this way and his achievement has become identified with one matchless building demonstrating that death is the mother of beauty. The proud hedonism is really not in conflict with another description to be found over the Victory Gate in Akbar's abandoned palace at Fateh pur Sikri:

The world is a bridge, pass over it but do not build upon it.
He who hopes for an hour may hope for eternity. The world
is but an hour; spend it in devotion, the rest is unseen.[5]

Pandemonium has been built and the two statements put before us both the elation and the vanity of building. The mind is its own place but can only be its own place by installing itself on the Peacock Throne of the self. The throne is in the inner chamber and is thus a statement of identity as well as a public announcement, a tacit disclosure of the weakness to be found in its strength.

So far, the movement to the center through the precincts of Pandemonium and through a corresponding geography of vainglory and os-

---

[4] The phrase is used by Shakespeare in *Love's Labor's Lost*, 4.3.218–21, though not with the associations with which Milton invests it.

[5] As quoted in Waldemar Hansen, *The Peacock Throne* (Delhi: Banarsidass, 1972), 68.

tentation seem to assign India a decisive place at the heart of the evil empire. The proposition is staged with sufficient persistence to persuade us that no other proposition needs to be made. The moral imagination can be discouragingly simplistic; but Milton is fortunately not a simple writer. At first it may seem that in the spice trade simile, Milton is once again presenting India as one of the primary sites of infernality:

> As when far off at Sea a Fleet descri'd
> Hangs in the Clouds, by *Equinoctial* Winds
> Close sailing from *Bengala,* or the Isles
> Of *Ternate* and *Tidore,* whence merchants bring
> Thir spicy Drugs: they on the Trading Flood
> Through the wide *Ethiopian* to the Cape
> Ply stemming nightly toward the Pole. So seem'd
> Far off the flying Fiend.   (2.636–43)

Ternate and Tidore are spice islands in the Moluccas but the phrase is also an alliterative remembrance of the *Lusiads;* and Satan's voyage, the ancestor of all voyages, is being placed in relationship to Vasco da Gama's voyage to India of which Camoëns' poem is the epic celebration. Milton's treatment of Camoëns is heavily revisionary,[6] as is his treatment of Vergil whom Camoëns imitates zealously, notwithstanding the ten book structure of his poem. Camoëns writes a poem about religion and empire in which religion is by no means foregrounded. "Honor, dominion, glory and renown," Satan's repeated manifesto, might well be the charter under which Vasco's sailors set forth, with "dominion" inexorably the central objective on which the other three are made contingent. Milton, one might say, is writing a poem on religion versus empire, a poem the impact of which is not fully clarified until *Paradise Regained,* when Christ refuses the kingdoms of the world.

The purpose of Vasco's voyage was to end the Venetian monopoly of the spice trade, and by opening up the passage round the Cape, to break the Arab stranglehold on the trade routes by which the "spicy drugs" of Asia came to Europe. Milton's re-alignment can be approached by noting that Bengal was not on the spice trade route and

---

[6] On Milton's revisionary treatment of Camoëns, see James H. Sims, "A Greater than Rome: The Inversion of a Virgilian Symbol from Camoëns to Milton," in *Rome in the Renaissance: The City and the Myth,* ed. P. A. Ramsey (Binghamton, N.Y.: Medieval & Renaissance Texts & Studies, 1982), 333–44 and esp. 339, 342.

that European trade with Bengal was not in spices. The detour through
Bengal may have been made to include within the scope of the simile
the East India Company, for which the Bay of Bengal had been a principal theater of operations ever since the founding of Madras in 1640;
but the geographical expansion is also designed to advise us of an expansion in the scope of the term, "spicy drugs." As G. V. Scammell, a
leading historian of early European imperialism observes:

> ... spice was a vast and ill-defined generic which also em-
> braced perfumes like incense and musk, medicines and drugs
> (the galingales of China and the aloes of Socotra), dyes, and the
> exquisite manufactures of the East, ranging from Chinese silk
> and porcelain to the carpets and tapestries of Persia. To those
> were added the products, as we shall see of the Middle East—
> the glassware for example of Damascus. . . .[7]

The term is in fact a synecdoche for the entire range of conspicuous
consumption, and conspicuous consumption had been an issue with
Milton ever since 1634 when Comus produced a bizarre ecological
argument in its favor.[8] Thrift needed to be part of the protestant ethic
if the middle class was to be instrumental in capital formation. At this
point in the poem, "spicy drugs" anticipates Adam's and Eve's transgres-
sion and the hallucinogenic qualities of the forbidden fruit. It also links
original sin to all subsequent excesses in consumption ("Greedily she en-
gorged without restraint" [9.791]), and inscribes the Satanic voyage
within subsequent voyages of exploration and commerce as the tainted
origin from which they may need to be rescued. In the process attention
shifts from the Orient as a primary site of evil to the Orient as supplier
to a clientele who have discovered it and made use of it to pamper the
weakness within themselves. It is notable that the fleet described in the
simile is en route to Europe, laden with profits of the spice trade, even
though Satan is en route to Asia.

In looking at Milton's similes, we have to pass by their most important characteristic, namely the extraordinary completeness with which
the similes translate what they purport to resemble. We have to restrict
ourselves to how India is perceived within the translation. It is already

---

[7] G. V. Scammell, *The World Encompassed* (Berkeley: Univ. of California Press, 1981),
101–2.

[8] See *Comus, A Mask Presented at Ludlow Castle*, ed. Hughes, 705–35.

clear that there can be more than one perception, depending on the course of action, or the religious or moral imperative to which the construction of India is annexed. The next reference to India occurs when Satan alights on the outer shell of the "pendent world"—an outer shell where limbo is derisively located and which is compared in its desolation to the central Asian plateau:

> As when a Vultur on *Imaus* bred,
> Whose snowy ridge the roving *Tartar* bounds,
> Dislodging from a Region scarce of prey
> To gorge the flesh of Lambs or yeanling Kids
> On Hills where Flocks are fed, flies toward the Springs
> Of *Ganges* or *Hydaspes, Indian* streams;
> But in his way lights on the barren Plains
> Of *Sericana,* where *Chineses* drive
> With Sails and Wind their cany Waggons light:
> So on this windy Sea of Land, the Fiend
> Walk'd up and down alone bent on his prey.
>   (3.431–41)

The crucial element in this compendious simile is the pun which joins Tartar to Tartarus. Milton did not invent the pun; it is attributed to Pope Innocent IV in response to Tartar invasions which, by 1241, had extended into Hungary and Germany. In further response to those invasions Pope Innocent's successor, Pope Alexander IV, issued the following warning to the princes of Christendom:

> There rings in the ears of all, and arouses to vigilant alertness those who are not befuddled by mental torpor, a terrible trumpet of dire forewarning which, corroborated by the evidence of events, proclaims with so unmistakable a sound the wars of universal destruction wherewith the scourge of Heaven's wrath in the hands of the inhuman Tartars, erupting as it were from the secret confines of Hell, oppresses and crushes the earth that is no longer the task of Christian people to prick up their ears so as to receive surer tidings of these things, as though they were still in doubt, but their need is rather for admonition to take provident action against a peril impending and palpably approaching. . . .[9]

---

[9] As quoted in *Marco Polo: The Travels,* trans. R. E. Latham (London: Penguin Books, 1958), 11.

The similarities between the papal bull and Milton's poem written over four centuries later do not need to be labored. Particularly important is the connection between the Tartar invasions and the opening lines of book 4 where the poet wishes that Adam and Eve had been shocked into attention by that "warning voice," that "terrible trumpet," as the papal bull has it, foretelling the "wars of universal destruction" envisioned in Revelation 12.7–12. The conspicuous difference is that the pope's concerns are limited to the penetration of Europe by the Tartars. India is not even on the horizon of calamity. In Milton's simile, on the other hand, India is central. It is the destination to which the vulture flies, leaving an inhospitable and barren habitat in search of a more fertile environment where he can "gorge the flesh of Lambs or yeanling Kids." It is true that the vulture seeks the sources of the Jhelum (Hydaspes) and the Ganges, rather than the plain which those great rivers irrigate and which future invasions of India were to ravage. But his flight, Satan's journey and the Tartar *débouchement* into India run parallel courses, brought together all the more evocatively because the earthly paradise was reputed to lie where the Ganges had its beginnings. In the opening lines of the seventh canto of *The Lusiads* all India is hailed as lying in proximity to this paradise (see also 4.74). More than one ancient Father followed Josephus in making the Ganges one of the rivers of paradise.[10]

In linking India to paradise and the vulture's flight to the Satanic journey, Milton now presents India not as the site of infernality but as its victim. It is a construction reinforced by "Lambs or yeanling Kids," which, apart from its religious overtones, cannot but suggest the exposure of inexperience and helplessness to the onslaught of power and cruelty. Tamerlane sacked Delhi in 1398 and is said to have slaughtered 80,000 of its inhabitants, leaving pyramids of skulls to mark the milestones on the city's highways. The Great Mogul on the Peacock Throne when Milton wrote his poem proudly affirmed his descent from the house of Timur. Milton's immediate reference is to the Tartars but the reference can be extended to all those invasions which the snowy ridge of Imaus could not contain and which erupted into India along a much traveled route of conquest. We can even read the "windy Sea of Land" which so felicitously materializes the indeterminate nature of limbo, as

[10] See John Drew, *India and the Romantic Imagination* (Delhi: Oxford Univ. Press, 1987), 166; cf. *PL* 9.76–82 and the comment in *The Poems of John Milton*, ed. John Carey and Alastair Fowler (London: Longman, 1968), 860.

pointing to a windy sea not of land, which was to become the route of further conquests. Milton obviously did not intend to say this but poems have a life beyond their boundaries.

In the fifth book Raphael descends to Paradise not to blow "a terrible trumpet of dire forewarning," but to "bring on discourse" and thereby instruct Adam and Eve on their place in the order of things. He approaches the Edenic pair through a wilderness of "flow'ring Odors," a "spicy Forest" which invites us to reflect on the misappropriations of the spice trade (5.291–99). Dinner is served with an international menu in which India is prominently though vaguely featured. The emphasis is not on indiscriminate variety but upon "Taste after taste upheld with kindliest change" (5.336). There is no gorging on the "flesh of Lambs or yeanling Kids." The meal is vegetarian and the three partake of it in order to suffice and not to burden nature (5.451–52).

Commenting on the meal, Fowler detects a "grim irony." Pontus was notorious as a source of poisons and Punic figs were best known for the threat to Rome which Plutarch made them symbolize.[11] Good things can be directed to evil uses as is apparent even from the pre- and postlapsarian connotations of words such as "errant" and "wanton." Milton is at pains to advise us that when the right order of things existed it was eloquent about itself even in such matters as serving an appropriate meal to a visiting angel. But the right order of things can no longer be presumed to exist pristinely behind the masks of misappropriation. We can seek to arrive at it inferentially from the wrong constructions but these are usually only known to be wrong by the manner in which they have not worked out in history. Progress by trial and error can be costly and the cost is all too frequently offered as proof of the progress. Shifting depictions of India do not necessarily lay bare an essential India which lies beyond and is uncontaminated by the depictions. Even in their "corrective" efforts they may only succeed in putting into place and thus making possible a critique of those assumptions which the next construction of India must avoid.

These entanglements must be borne in mind as we proceed to the proliferations of the banyan tree passage, which, of all Milton's images of India, is the most compelling and also the most evasive (9.1099–1118). Before doing so we need to consider Satan's activities in the interval between his expulsion from paradise by Gabriel and his assistants, and his

[11] See Carey and Fowler, 695.

second entry for the successful temptation. Satan has circled the earth three times in an east-west and four times in a north-south direction. The purpose of these peregrinations is not merely to survey his kingdom while he awaits another opportunity but also with "inspection deep" to consider which among the world's creatures might best "serve his wiles." His last stop is the "land where flows / Ganges and Indus" and his final choice, "after long debate" is "The Serpent subtlest Beast of all the Field" (9.81–82, 86–87). It is more than arguable that the infernal potentiality of India is once again being underlined and that India as victim or as prime provider of a repast fit for angels has receded into the background.

Satan now enters paradise but not with his earlier exuberance when with "one slight bound" he leaped over the garden's protective barrier (4.181). This time he makes his entry via one of the rivers of paradise, fortunately not the Pison which was identified with the Ganges, but the Tigris which shoots into an underground gulf at the foot of paradise and emerges as a fountain by the tree of life. Satan emerges in the rising mist of the fountain "involv'd" with the primordial fluidity, as if inextricably part of the elemental nature of things (9.69–76).

The choice of India as the last stop before paradise and of the serpent with which India is strongly associated as the fittest vehicle for the original sin might be regarded as appropriate preliminaries to the choice of the banyan tree for the original cover-up. Milton's emphatic dismissal of alternatives seems designed to pave the way for the cumulative infernalization of India. The subtlety and deviousness of which the serpent is the symbol and the comprehensive concealment afforded by the banyan tree are invested in Paradise Lost with the authority of origins. Those propositions were soon to be engraved in imperial rhetoric as routinely part of India's representation.

Paradise Lost is a scholarly poem, and when Milton in choosing his tree waves aside "that kind for Fruit renown'd" (9.1101), he reminds us of an earlier gesture. In the fourth book the possibility that paradise may lie at the summit of Mount Amara, "under the Ethiop Line / By Nilus head" is mentioned to be dismissed. It is, Milton tells us, "by some suppos'd" (4.281–83). In fact, it is hard to find anyone who confidently upholds this possibility, though every discussion of the location of paradise raises it. The citation count is extensive but the acceptance count approaches zero. Milton is very much in the majority here, tilting at a windmill in the robust fashion of scholarship. In the ninth book, on the other hand, he may be in an insubstantial minority, proceeding as if determined to take issue with nearly every available commentary on Genesis.

Reasons for setting aside precedent can always be found and are most persuasive when they can be shown to be part of the imaginative logic of the poem. If the choice of the banyan tree is innovative, so too is the readiness to make paradise a site for postlapsarian lust. That "God attributes to place / No sanctity, if none be thither brought" is Milton's justification for the destruction of paradise (11.836–37). The desecration of sanctity which Milton's departure from precedent serves to underline deepens the original shame and calls for a more comprehensive cover-up. The connections are plausible but we still need to argue that an innovation is not justified by referring it to another innovation that need not have been made.

Another view might be that the infernalizing of India has always been part of the poem's agenda, and that the more benign presentations we have explored merely mean that the infernalization is not total. "The proliferating tree is a tree of error," Fowler tells us categorically. "It is an objective correlative of the proliferating sin that will ramify through Adam's and Eve's descendants."[12] If true, this conclusion is a virulent desacralization of a tree that has always been holy to Indians, that is both the site and the subject of Upanishadic instruction, a tree which Southey in a poem not particularly sympathetic to India approaches with respect as a temple of nature.[13]

Milton's similes invite straightforward readings by their sustained correspondences between tenor and vehicle. But his language can also circumvent and retreat from the dominant momentum which it nourishes. The tree "spreads her arms" in an encompassing gesture reminiscent of the crucifixion. The "Daughters grow / About the Mother Tree" (9.1105–6) and the gesture can be read as bringing together and protecting the human family rather than as bringing about the confusion that Gerard describes in his Herball, "the first or mother of this wood or desart of trees, is hard to be knowne from the children."[14] The "Pillar'd shade" which the daughter trees provide suggests a composed

---

[12] Ibid., 920.

[13] See Robert Southey, The Curse of Kehama, 13.5, in Poems, ed. Maurice H. Fitzgerald (Oxford: Oxford Univ. Press, 1909), 161. Moore similarly refers to the "sacred shade" of those "holy trees, whose smooth columns and spreading roofs seem to destine them for natural temples of religion." Thomas Moore, Lalla Rookh, in Poetical Works, ed. A. D. Godley (Oxford: Oxford Univ. Press, 1915), 342, 412.

[14] Carey and Fowler, 920.

architecture rather than a wilderness of reflections. Yet Milton in putting forward his representation always seems aware of another representation that may be the normal reading and that the turns of his language are not prepared to reject. The pillared shade recalls the Corinthian pillars of Pandemonium, and their "High overarch't" formations take us back to the Vallombrosa simile where the infernal angels were compared to leaves fallen from the tree of life into the valley of the shadow of death (1.302–4). The "Etrurian shade" of the Vallombrosa trees was "imbowered," as if turned in on itself. The bower of concealment is similar and is in designed contrast to the nuptial bower of book 4, lines 690–708. Yet when Svendsen describes the recesses of the tree as a "deep interior sanctuary,"[15] he is not proceeding against Milton's language. The tree serves for shelter though it can be used for concealment. It permits withdrawal into meditative depths. It also encourages absorption in a narcissistic coma. Its "echoing walks" can be self-imprisoning; but they can also prolong the cadences of voices that need to be heard (4.680–85).

The contesting interpretations of itself which the spreading tree puts forward allow its proliferations and decentrations to be read as an expanding assault upon hierarchic order. Its leaves are not really as "broad as Amazonian targe" and if bodily concealment were the objective, other trees in India would have served the purpose better. But other trees would not have lent themselves to the emblematization delighted in by Renaissance herbalists and compilers of dictionaries. The Amazons are introduced not so that a passing reference can be made to the size of their shields, but as a further source of hierarchic disturbance with which readers of book 5 of *The Faerie Queene* would have been familiar. They go well with the role reversal that has been prominent in Milton's version of the Fall and with the feminization of the tree which, blessed exclusively with daughters, compounds by its generative wantonness the destabilization of structure and design.

As we trace the echoing walks of this particular passage, many of the echoes lead us back through the history of the poem into occasions or images of the infernal. The lines are all the more disturbing because the tree's natural attributes lend themselves so easily to demonic appropriation. In addition, Milton compounds the discommoding effect by gestures towards scientific accuracy, reminding us that the Fall was history to him even though it may be mythology to us. "Columbus found

---

[15] Kester Svendsen, *Milton and Science* (Cambridge: Harvard Univ. Press, 1956), 135.

the American so girt," he tells us, decisively. Primitive societies are closer to the source, and the characteristics of the source can be discerned more clearly in them.[16] The land that was mistaken for India justifies its erroneous identification by indicating how the resources of the true India were used. The banyan tree is "at this day to Indians known." Any official of the East India Company can inspect it and verify that there was no better way for Adam and Eve to cope with the sudden problem of their nakedness.

It is against the passage's traversals of itself and the received interpretations it accepts and circumvents that we need to consider the figure of the herdsman. Fowler is less than tactful in arguing that "The Indian herdsman is put in because he is primitive and pagan."[17] He is put in to point out to us that though his responsibilities are far more limited than those of the faithful herdsman in *Lycidas,* he observes these responsibilities, unlike the corrupt clergy whom Milton excoriates and unlike Adam and Eve at this moment. He "tends his pasturing herds" and if he seeks the protection of the tree and cuts loopholes through the "thickest shade" of its foliage, it is not to conceal himself but to perform his task more efficiently and with less likelihood of being incapacitated by sunstroke. Other revealing images offer themselves as we contemplate the figure of the herdsman. Adam and Eve like him are hidden in the tree's recesses; but it is the flock that is now hidden, not the shepherd. The shepherd seeks refuge from the heat of the sun's rays. Adam and Eve seek refuge from the "blaze / Insufferably bright" (9.1083–84) of the Son's presence. The Son is the shepherd, offering a protection symbolized by the tree's outstretched arms, which the guilty pair unknowingly invoke in using that very tree to avoid the Son's gaze. In its dense entanglements the passage works powerfully to persuade us that appropriation is not simply a matter of channeling the properties of the tree to infernal uses. The tree is reinvented by the perspective in which it is installed. And the perspective cannot be said to be optional. It is largely responsible for inventing those who use it.

The final reference to India is in the panorama of the world's empires which Adam sees from the highest hill of paradise. The *Aeneid* (6.741ff.) is being remembered with Milton's typical distancings from

---

[16] In fact Columbus did not find the American "girt" at all but clad in "native honor" (4.289) as Adam and Eve were before taking refuge in the banyan tree.
[17] Carey and Fowler, 920.

that seminal text. The vision is seen from a hill and not foretold in the underworld; it is concerned with all empires, not one; and it turns from those empires to "nobler sights" (11.411), from the sequence of secular pomp to the meaning of sacred history. Camoëns, laboriously Vergilian in his machinery, can be seen as intermediate between Vergil and Milton. Like Vergil he is concerned with a single nation's imperial destiny. Like Milton his hero is shown the future from a mountain top. But it is a future in which empire building is glorified, not questioned. Adam looks at the havoc to which his actions will lead. Vasco da Gama looks at the fulfillment of his mission in a future that is only possible because of his heroic accomplishment. The splendors of the Portuguese empire are elegantly displayed to him gift wrapped in the layers of the Ptolemaic universe.[18]

Vergil associates the Roman destiny with ancestral statements of the white man's burden, with bringing justice and the rule of law to barbarians. Camoëns is less concerned with such refinements and shows us the face of imperialism more candidly. Those who chafe under Portugal's light yoke will be made to pay dearly for their insolence. Ironically, the example chosen is Ormuz which was to pass out of Portuguese hands forever, half a century after Camoëns published his poem.

The mountain top prophecy, the panorama of empires and the roll call of place names form multiple lines of connection between *Paradise Lost* and the *Lusiads*. The connections are enforced by the second of Milton's alliterative remembrances—"*Mombaza,* and *Quiloa,* and *Melind*" (11.399). Melind was Vasco's last port of call before setting off on the final stage of his audacious voyage to India under the helpful guidance of an Indian pilot.

The overlap in the view from the two mountain tops is extensive. One might argue that some attention has been paid to making it extensive. To connect the two poems is to become pointedly aware of the sudden blaze and swift extinction of the Portuguese imperial dream. That recognition finds its way back into Milton's poem as a general comment on the transience of empires. What we see from the mountain top in the first place is the peripheral turbulence and pandemonium of history, not the inner theater of clarified engagement where the forces shaping history are exposed.

Much has changed in the descent from Vergil, and Vergil's Rome

[18] See *Lusiads* 10.40–41.

is among the empires dismissed. From an Iraqi mountain top, Rome and
"*Agra* and *Lahor* of great *Mogul*" (11.391) are approximately equidistant;
"great *Mogul*" designates not simply the dynasty but a diamond of unprecedented size (the Kohinoor) presented to Shah Jehan. Stereotypes of
oriental opulence are reinforced, taking us back in one of the poem's
many circularities, to the wealth of Ind and Satan's throne of royal state.
But Rome was also a center of ostentatious excess as *Paradise Regained*
makes clear, and so far there has been nothing in the poem to suggest
that Asia surpasses Rome in moral turpitude. We can even conjecture
that if Milton had known of it, the Augustinian inscription at Fatehpur-
Sikri would have appealed to him more than any Roman text.

The inner theater of significance, surrounded by an otherwise
meaningless periphery of empires dramatizes the proposition that the
only true kingdom is the kingdom of God. The nature of things in their
purity does not permit the rule of one people by another:

> . . . Man over men
> He made not Lord; such title to himself
> Reserving, human left from human free.   (12.69–71)

Unfortunately, we are dealing not with the nature of things, but with
their fallen nature. In such circumstances

> Tyranny must be,
> Though to the Tyrant thereby no excuse.   (12.95–96)

The argument does not condone tyranny but it does suggest that
attempts to overthrow tyranny will only reinscribe it unless they are accompanied by a radical change in the structure of the self. One can accept this as an argument but it needs to be pointed out in reply that
Milton unbalances his critique of dominance by too strong an insistence
that subjected people deserve their own misfortunes. In the England of
a failed revolution this insistence may have been proper to the poetics of
the moment. On a less localized scale we have to observe that phrases
such as "tyranny must be" amount to a *de facto* acquiescence in tyranny.
Tyrants are seldom deterred by the observation that their behavior cannot be excused.

The failed revolution and the need to justify its failure continue to
be present in Milton's thought as the temptation of Rome is offered. In
Paradise Regained, Satan accompanies his offer with the hyperbolical
statement that not merely India, but Sumatra and the Malay peninsula

render obedience to "Rome's great emperor" (*PR* 4.73–76).[19] Christ
does not contest this exaggeration. Presumably he has more important
things on his mind. He points out predictably that Romans have earned
their fate by their degeneracy. "Peeling thir Provinces," already exhausted by lust and rapine, and carried away by the "insulting vanity" of their
triumphs, they are luxury-loving, cruel, greedy, and "from the daily
Scene effeminate" (*PR* 4.136–42). That last and climactic epithet used
extensively by the Romans in the denigration of Egypt was to be much
used again in marginalizing India. Originating in Michael's rebuke to
Adam (*PL* 11.634), it becomes the final touch in the conqueror's inward
enslavement to the other he constructs for his contempt.

Milton's description of Rome's degeneracy is not surprising, but his
prelapsarian characterization of the Romans as just, frugal, mild, and
temperate (*PR* 4.133–34) seems to invoke Christian rather than classical
heroism. The choice of virtues becomes clearer when we turn to the
Second Defence: "to be free is precisely the same as to be pious, wise, just,
and temperate, careful of one's property, aloof from another's, and thus
finally to be magnanimous and brave" (CPW 4:684). A parallel between
Rome and seventeenth-century England is clearly in the making and
perhaps it is the pursuit of this parallel that leads Milton to observe that
the Romans "conquer'd well, / But govern ill" (*PR* 4.134–35). Government by conquest can never be good government. Human was "left
from human free" by the divine edict and a relationship between
peoples based on dominance can never be other than deformed. Difference turned into confusion and conversation into the failure to communicate when the original tower of dominance was built. Milton's language moves away at this point from an egalitarian recognition which
his own previous language has inscribed. In an age when empires were
materializing on the horizon and India was beginning to assume its glittering shape as the most coveted of imperial prizes, he cannot quite say
that the pursuit of empires can only be destructive and that there is no
people that can "conquer well." In addition, his concentration on an inner theater where the principles of a single wisdom are made manifest

---

[19] See Carey and Fowler who note (1139) that G. W. Whiting (*Review of English Studies*
13 [1937]: 209–12) has produced evidence to indicate that Taprobane usually meant Sumatra.
However, in the *Lusiads* (10.107), Taprobane is identified with Sri Lanka. Since Taprobane
is mentioned in conjunction with the Malay Peninsula ("golden Chersoness"), Sumatra is
indicated. "Indian isle" may seem to suggest Sri Lanka but Sumatra was part of "further
India" and "utmost" is less effective if Sri Lanka is intended.

by their performance in history reduces other wisdoms to peripheral status. At best the periphery can only reflect the center or be the shadowy
type to the center's truth. The design of understanding is potentially imperial. Other designs which are less lofty and humane will sustain themselves on the same geography of privilege.

UNIVERSITY OF WESTERN ONTARIO

J. Martin Evans

MILTON'S IMPERIAL EPIC

IN HIS COMPREHENSIVE STUDY OF THE NORTH ATLANTIC
world, K. G. Davies remarks that "no major English literary work of the
seventeenth century comes to mind that breathes an Atlantic air or takes
the American empire for its theme."[1] The purpose of this essay is to
suggest that *Paradise Lost* constitutes at least a partial exception to
Davies's generalization. Milton's epic, I believe, interacts continuously
with the deeply ambivalent feelings which the conquest of the New
World generated in seventeenth-century English culture. Like its closest
classical model, the *Aeneid*, *Paradise Lost* seems to me to be, among other
things, a poem about empire.[2]

Certainly, there were many reasons for pondering the colonization
of America as Milton turned his attention back to his long-delayed plans
for an epic poem in the mid-1650s. The Commonwealth's war with
Spain had rekindled anti-Spanish sentiment, and writers in tune with the
mood of the times were busy turning out works based on the so-called
"black legend" of Spanish brutality in South America—Milton's nephew
John Phillips, for instance, translated Las Casas' *Brevissima relacion de la
destruycion de las Indias* into English in 1656, and in 1658 Sir William
Davenant, the erstwhile governor-designate of Maryland, catered to prevailing English taste with his sensational play on the same subject, *The*

---

[1] K. G. Davies, *The North Atlantic World in the Seventeenth Century* (Minneapolis: Univ.
of Minnesota Press, 1974), 325.

[2] The word echoes and re-echoes throughout the text of *Paradise Lost*. See: 1.114; 2.296,
310, 315, 327, 378, 446; 4.145, 390; 5.724, 801; 7.96, 555, 585, 609; 10.389, 592; 12.32, 581.

Cruelty of the Spaniards. Still more to the point, Cromwell's "Western Design" and the conflict with Spain it precipitated served as a vivid reminder that England, too, was a major colonial power. Indeed, the crucial first phase of English empire-building in the New World coincided more or less exactly with Milton's lifetime. The year before he was born the first English settlers dispatched by the Virginia Company of London arrived in Chesapeake Bay. The establishment of the Plymouth colony took place when he was eleven, the widely publicized Virginia massacre when he was thirteen, and the great Puritan migration to Massachusetts Bay while he was in his twenties. He was thirty-five when the second Virginia massacre occurred, forty-six when Cromwell acquired Jamaica. By the time he had reached his fifties, England was the dominant colonial power in North America with between twenty-five and thirty thousand settlers in New England and thirty-six thousand or so in Virginia.[3]

What is more, by the time he began to work on *Paradise Lost* Milton had come into contact with numerous men who had promoted or emigrated to the colonies. Ralph Hamor, the author of *A True Discourse of the Present State of Virginia*, grew up in the house next to the Milton family home on Bread Street. Several of his Cambridge contemporaries emigrated to New England, and his longtime friend Samuel Hartlib produced a treatise on the Virginian silk-worm. Sir Henry Vane, to whom Milton addressed an admiring sonnet in 1652, was a former governor of Massachusetts. And Roger Williams, the notorious champion of religious liberty and Indian property rights, gave him conversation lessons in Dutch in the early 1650s.[4] It is hardly surprising, then, that Milton's writings are liberally sprinkled with references to the colonization of the New World.

Not that Milton needed large numbers of close friends and acquaintances actively involved in the settlement of America in order to be vividly aware of its progress. For "this glorious business," as William Crashaw called it,[5] was deeply imprinted in the national consciousness of seventeenth-century England, inscribed there by dozens of promotional pamphlets, controversial tracts, personal histories, and economic analyses. From 1609 to 1624 the London bookstalls were inundated

---

[3] Davies, 63.

[4] See W. R. Parker, *John Milton: A Biography* (Oxford: Clarendon, 1968), 1.53, 410; 2.698, 1008.

[5] William Crashaw, Preface to Alexander Whitaker's *Good Newes from Virginia* (London, 1613), A2ʳ.

with sermons and treatises either prophesying or proclaiming the success of the English plantation in Virginia. Beginning with the publication of *Mourt's Relation* in 1622, there followed a steady stream of works recording the early history of New England, detailing the political and religious controversies going on there, and asserting the progress of the gospel among the Indians. Then in the mid-1650s came a spate of tracts reporting on the power struggle between the Catholic proprietor Lord Baltimore and his Puritan adversaries in Maryland. Whether or not he had a personal stake in the success of the American colonies, Milton could hardly avoid being aware of events taking place on the other side of the Atlantic.

With the exception of a handful of works by New England dissidents like Samuel Gorton and John Child, most of the literature I have just mentioned took a wholeheartedly positive view of England's transatlantic activities. Yet just beneath the surface of even the most optimistic evaluations of England's settlements in the New World there runs a powerful undercurrent of barely repressed anxiety concerning the entire colonial enterprise. For over and over again the promoters complain that Virginia and New England have been unjustly slandered by various unnamed detractors.

Few, if any, of these reported slanders were ever printed—like the heresies of the early Christian church they owe their preservation to the writers who endeavored to refute them—but they clearly constituted a powerful critique of England's activities across the Atlantic. As a result, whether they are excusing the failure of the New World to live up to expectations in some regard, or defending Virginia and New England against some allegedly unjustified criticism from their detractors, seventeenth-century English descriptions of America are relentlessly defensive. From Daniel Price's *Saul's Prohibition Staide ... with a reproofe of those that traduce the Honourable Plantation of Virginia* (London, 1609) to John Hammond's *Leah and Rachel... With a Removall of such Imputations as are scandalously cast on those Countries* (London, 1656) justification is the keynote.

Nor is it difficult to understand why a seventeenth-century English protestant might have harbored deeply ambivalent feelings about his country's American colonies. To begin with, their history had hardly been a happy one. After a disastrous beginning, which cost many of the adventurers their investments and hundreds of planters their lives, Virginia had sided with the king during the civil war and only with the very greatest reluctance had accepted the authority of the Common-

wealth commissioners dispatched by Cromwell. As John Hammond put
it, England's first plantation was "whol for monarchy, and the last
Country belonging to England that submitted to obedience of the
Common-wealth of England."[6] Maryland, despite several attempts to
reverse Lord Baltimore's policy of religious toleration, was still a haven
for English Catholics, "a receptacle for Papists, and Priests, and Jesuites"
as one writer called it.[7] New England, riven by internal disputes in the
1630s and 1640s, was regarded in many quarters as "a Nursery of
Schismatickes,"[8] and had in any case lost a great deal of its ideological
raison d'être now that the reform of the church had been accomplished in
England. And finally, as the century wore on, English protestants were
becoming increasingly concerned about the question of native American
property rights and the failure of the English missionaries to convert the
Indians to the reformed religion.

For all these reasons, then, the colonization of America stirred
deeply ambivalent feelings in the collective consciousness of seventeenth-century England. *Paradise Lost*, I now want to suggest, not only
registers many of these ambivalences, but plays them out in mythic form
by reenacting on the cosmic stage many of the central events in the
conquest of the New World. The argument is a complex one to which
I am in the course of devoting an entire book, but in this brief "pro-
spectus" I may be able to illustrate my general thesis by discussing the
way in which Milton treats the central figure in the colonial drama, the
colonist himself. He appears in *Paradise Lost* in various guises: most obviously as Satan, the diabolic deceiver who enslaves the inhabitants of the
New World by cheating them out of their territory and replacing them
with his own destructive plenipotentiaries; but also as Raphael, the divine missionary who brings to Adam and Eve the authentic word of
God and instructs them in the history of the ancient rivalry of which
their world is the focal point; then as Adam, the indentured servant
placed in the paradisal garden by "the sovran Planter" (4. 691) and destined for release from his labors after a fixed period of obedient toil; and
finally as Michael, the representative of imperial authority who drives the
rebellious natives out of their original home into the alien wilderness.

To begin with Satan, during the course of his triumphant speech in

---

[6] *Leah and Rachel* (London, 1656), 22.
[7] Anon., *Virginia and Maryland* (London, 1655), 199–200.
[8] John White, *The Planter's Plea* (London, 1630), 37.

book 10 announcing the conquest of Eden, the devil sounds at times very much like Amerigo Vespucci reporting back to Lorenzo Pietro di Medici on his latest voyage to the New World. The echoes are probably accidental, but the general resemblance is not, for of the various roles that Satan plays in *Paradise Lost* none is more richly elaborated than his impersonation of a Renaissance explorer. It has often been noticed, for example, that Milton arranges the early part of the story so that we experience it as a diabolic voyage of discovery. Just as Columbus and his contemporaries heard rumors of the New World long before its existence had been confirmed, so we learn from Satan in book 1 that "a fame in Heav'n" has spread stories of "new Worlds" (650–51) elsewhere in the universe. In books 2 and 3 we then accompany him on the perilous "voyage" (2. 426, 919) across the "gulf" (2. 441) of chaos to "the coast of Earth" (3. 739). And at the beginning of book 4 we finally see the terrestrial paradise at least partially through the Devil's consciousness.

The motives which impel Satan on his voyage replicate, in turn, virtually all the social and political arguments advanced in favor of England's colonial expansion in the late sixteenth and early seventeenth centuries. The first of them emerges in Beelzebub's speech at the end of the infernal debate in book 2. After mentioning the rumors circulating in Heaven about the creation of the world, he proposes that even though

> Heav'n be shut,
> . . . .
> . . . this place may lie expos'd
> The utmost border of his Kingdom, left
> To their defense who hold it: here perhaps
> Some advantageous act may be achiev'd
> By sudden onset. . . .   (2. 358–64, Hughes edition)

This bears a startling resemblance to the political rationale for Elizabethan attacks on Spanish possessions in the New World a century before.[9] Indeed, Beelzebub's proposal momentarily transforms Satan into a demonic Sir Francis Drake setting off to singe God's beard. On one level, at least, the assault on Eden will be a daring naval raid by an infernal buccaneer.

The second motive for undertaking the journey across chaos is disclosed by Satan himself in his parting speech to his followers in Pande-

---

[9] See, for example, Hakluyt's *Discourse concerning Western Planting* (1584), chap. 5.

monium. Oppressed by God's vengeance, he tells them, "I abroad / Through all the Coasts of dark destruction seek / Deliverance for us all" (2.464–65). In a diabolic parody of the pilgrims on the *Mayflower* he presents himself as the ultimate separatist, a victim of religious persecution in search of a new home where he and his fellow dissidents can practice their infernal rites in peace—in heaven, we have already been told by Mammon, the angels were constrained by "Strict Laws impos'd" to celebrate God's throne with Laudian ceremoniousness, worshipping their "envied Sovran" with "warbl'd Hymns" and "Forc'd Halleluiahs" (2.242–44). Like the faithful and freeborn Englishmen who, in Milton's words in *Of Reformation* "have bin constrained to forsake their dearest home, their friends and kindred, whom nothing but the wide Ocean, and the savage deserts of *America* could hide and shelter from the fury of the Bishops,"[10] the Devil claims to be seeking refuge from the oppression of a tyrannical power.

As Satan approaches the garden of Eden, however, a third motive makes its appearance. His underlying purpose, he now confesses, is territorial expansion. By raiding this vulnerable outpost of the heavenly kingdom he hopes to share at least "Divided Empire with Heav'ns King" (4.111). Hence the extraordinary scene in book 10 when Sin greets her triumphant parent at the foot of the "wondrous Pontifice" (348) which she and her son have constructed across chaos "by wondrous Art / Pontifical" (312–13). Henceforth, she declares, let the Creator "Monarchy with thee divide / Of all things, parted by th'Empyreal bounds" (379–80). Cued by Milton's anti-papal puns, we seem to be witnessing a grotesque reenactment of Alexander VI's division of the western world between the Spanish and the Portuguese, a cosmic *inter caetera*.

During the course of the poem, then, Satan rehearses virtually all the major roles in the repertoire of English colonial discourse. By turns buccaneer, pilgrim, and empire-builder, he embodies not only the destructive potential of imperial conquest but its glamour and energy as well. It may well be no accident that the critical glorification of Milton's devil took place during the heyday of England's imperial power while his descent from hero to fool coincided with its decline.

Satan is not the only figure in the poem who embodies the colonial quest, however. God's emissaries, too, function as agents of imperial au-

---

[10] CPW 3:49–50.

thority. Indeed, Raphael has in some ways even more in common with the explorers than his diabolical antagonist. For the extraordinary scene in which the archangel is greeted by two naked human beings as a "Native of Heaven" (5.361) reenacts an encounter which had been described in countless Renaissance descriptions of the discoverers' arrival in the New World. Like the ideally submissive and subservient Indians of those early narratives, Adam welcomes his "god-like" (351) visitor "with submiss approach and reverence meek" (359). Unquestioningly he agrees that he possesses the garden of Eden "by sovran gift" (366) from Raphael's divine master. Then he and Eve proceed to entertain the "Heav'nly stranger" (316, 397) in their "Silvan Lodge" (377) with all the bounty their world has to offer.

Unlike Columbus and his successors, of course, Adam's visitor really has come from heaven. As the "Empyreal Minister" (5.460) of the Almighty, his function is to instruct Adam and Eve in the indispensable colonial virtues of loyalty and obedience, to give them a brief lesson in the recent political history of the cosmos, and most important of all to alert them to the existence of an unfriendly rival power at large in the universe (5.233–41). In place of the Indians' tragic misconception of their future oppressors, the poem thus offers us an authentic encounter between man and angel, an encounter in which the problematic territorial and political claims of Spain and England have given way to the Creator's legitimate authority over his creation. In *Paradise Lost* the anxiety attaching to the discoveries has been relieved by the simple device of re-writing the scene as if the Indians and the Spanish had both been right. This visitor really does come from heaven, as the Indians believed, and the sovereign he represents really does own the land, as the Spanish, and later the English, insisted.

Thanks to Milton's revision of the primal imperial encounter, Adam and Eve are consequently spared the violent aftermath of Columbus's arrival in the New World. Unlike the Indians, they do not experience the horrors of Renaissance warfare at first hand; they learn about such murderous inventions as gunpowder only at second hand from their heavenly instructor. The appalling butchery and violence which characterized the Spanish conquest of America is thus projected onto Satan's campaign against his Maker.

When the natives do eventually rebel against their master, they receive a second visitor from heaven, with orders to drive them forth "without remorse" (11.105) from their terrestrial paradise into the wilderness beyond it. Michael's mission in books 11–12 thus recapitulates in mythic form not only Spain's campaigns in Mexico and Peru—Adam is shown the seats of Montezuma and Atabalipa (11.407–9)—but England's more recent dispossession of the Indians in New England and Virginia. The image of the colonist as a ruthless invader is too powerful to exclude entirely, and although Milton insists that the garden will remain empty once Adam and Eve have vacated it (11.101–3;123–25), their expulsion by a force of "flaming Warriors" (11.101) could hardly have failed to summon up in the minds of Milton's readers disquieting memories of the final act of the colonial drama.

The colonial figures we have considered so far were all, for one reason or another, eager to cross the Atlantic. A significant portion of the early emigrants to England's colonies, however, had to be actively recruited as indentured servants. Essentially indentured service was a mechanism which permitted potential emigrants to be shipped to America at the expense of a colonial landowner to whom they were subsequently bound as servants for a fixed term of years, usually four or five. In return for their transportation across the Atlantic and their food, lodging, and clothing in the colony, they worked on their master's property without wages until their term of service expired, at which time they received enough cash, provisions, and land to set up as independent smallholders themselves.[11]

Seen in this general context, Adam's situation in *Paradise Lost* resembles nothing so much as an idealized form of indentured servitude. Placed in an earthly paradise by the "sovran Planter" (4.691), he is destined to serve out a fixed term of "pleasant labor" (4.625) at the end of which, "by long obedience tri'd" (7.159), he may be given the status of an angel and allowed to dwell permanently in the terrestrial or the celestial paradise (5.500). His biblical counterpart, of course, had long been regarded as a paradigm of the colonial settler. In 1612 Robert Johnson, for example, commended "that most wholesome, profitable and pleasant work of planting in which it pleased God himself to set the first man and most excellent creature Adam in his innocencie."[12] But in *Paradise Lost* the current of correspondence between the two figures is reversed: the colonist doesn't resemble Adam so much as Adam resembles the

---

[11] For this account I have relied principally on: Abbott E. Smith, *Colonists in Bondage: White Servitude and Convict Labor in America 1607–1776* (Chapel Hill: Univ. of North Carolina Press, 1965), chap. 1; Carl Bridenbaugh, *Vexed and Troubled Englishmen 1590–1642* (New York: Oxford Univ. Press, 1968), chap. 11.

[12] Robert Johnson, *The New Life of Virginia* (London, 1612), 17.

colonist. The result is a vision of prelapsarian man unlike any other in the history of the Genesis myth. To take just one example, the concept of indentured labor may well be responsible for the quite unprecedented significance which Milton gives to Adam's daily toil in *Paradise Lost*. As I have shown elsewhere,[13] in no other version of the biblical story is the necessity of cultivating the garden so emphatically asserted.

When Adam and Eve eventually break the terms of their contract, moreover, they behave at first like run-away servants—they hide from their master and blame him for their disobedience. Adam, in particular, makes it sound as if he had been kidnapped by a "spirit," as the agents of the colonial landowners were called, and forced to work against his will on God's plantation:

> . . . did I solicit thee
> From darkness to promote me, or here place
> In this delicious Garden?   (10.744–46)

In spite of the care with which the system of indentured labor has been purged of its most flagrant abuses—in Milton's definition of the human situation the master is benevolent and just, the servants are well fed and well lodged, the labor is strenuous but not backbreaking—a residue of uneasiness is still detectable in Adam's protest. He may admit that "then should have been refus'd / Those terms whatever, when they were propos'd" (10.756–57), but the lawyerly debating point cannot entirely dispose of the underlying objection. For when Adam was presented with the conditions of his contract, his existence was already a *fait accompli*. Like the convicted criminals who were beginning to be shipped to the New World in ever greater numbers as the seventeenth century wore on, Eden's original colonist had only two choices: indenture or death.

As these examples may suggest, Milton not only divides the role of colonist among the various characters in his poem. He associates the characters in his poem with different colonial roles at different points of the narrative. In some episodes, we have seen, Adam resembles the English settlers laboring in indentured servitude on a royal plantation; in others, he has more in common with the Indians welcoming Columbus to their American paradise. Clearly these contradictions and disjunctions do not permit a naive, uniplanar interpretation of the poem—we cannot

---

[13] "Native Innocence" in *"Paradise Lost" and the Genesis Tradition* (Oxford: Clarendon, 1968).

simply equate God with James I, Eden with Virginia, and then read the poem as a straightforward political allegory about the conquest of America. My point is both simpler and more complicated. Milton's epic, I believe, not only breathes an Atlantic air but expresses in all their bewildering complexity the radically divided attitudes towards the American empire which existed in seventeenth-century English protestant culture.

STANFORD UNIVERSITY

Gary D. Hamilton

PARADISE REGAINED AND THE
PRIVATE HOUSES

IN THE VARIOUS ATTEMPTS TO DEFEND OR MODIFY ANY GIVEN
construction of the later Milton, *Paradise Regained* has come to occupy
a central place. Whether one regards this work as the key or the problem to be explained away when delineating the shape of the final chapter of a career once passionately committed to changing the nature of
society's public institutions, the task at hand has inevitably involved for-
mulating the implications of the poem's intense focus on the privacy and
interiority of religion. As Earl Miner has noted in one of the most ap-
preciative descriptions of Milton's achievement, *Paradise Regained* is a
work in which "the public mode has been made completely inward, and
man's soul becomes the issue in the most public of forms, the heroic
poem."[1] If some readers have responded to this presentation by finding
in it confirmation that the later Milton was a contemplative artist who
had retired from politics—a figure, in other words, not unlike the otherworldly knight-hermit of "Il Penseroso" who would be turning "old
experience" into "prophetic strain"—others have plausibly argued that
the poem's emphasis on interiority need not signal any Miltonic devalua-
tion of action in the public world.[2] It is toward an expansion and

---

[1] Miner, *The Restoration Mode from Milton to Dryden* (Princeton: Princeton Univ. Press,
1974), 507.

[2] Blair Worden, "Milton's Republicanism and the Tyranny of Heaven," *Machiavelli and
Republicanism*, ed. Gisela Bock, Quentin Skinner and Maurizo Viroli (Cambridge: Cambridge
Univ. Press, 1990), 224–25, emphasizes that "By the time of *Paradise Regained*," Milton's
"retreat from politics is complete." In contrast, Christopher Hill, *Milton and the English
Revolution* (London: Faber and Faber, 1977), 460, 417, 466, emphasizes "the this-worldliness

refinement of this latter argument that I shall be directing my efforts in this essay.

For at least two reasons, it is indeed odd that the poem's depiction of the Son's rejection of the things of the world should in itself be taken to signal a Miltonic withdrawal from political involvement. First of all, the notion of the inwardness of religion was clearly a presence in Milton's writing long before he became a political exile in Restoration England. Secondly, and of more central concern to this essay, such a belief in the privacy and interiority of religion was not simply a private matter. Throughout the time period in which Milton lived and wrote, and nowhere more so than in the Restoration, it was a pressing political issue as well. This historical fact, however, has had little bearing on most critical readings of this work. Rather than undertaking an expanded new reading of the poem, therefore, my task is to present a specific context in which we might more fully describe the implications of the poem's "otherworldly" emphasis, a description which will involve responding to the poem more as a public event, that is, more as a rhetorical gesture directed toward a Restoration audience, than as a reservoir of biographical clues concerning the poet's own private vision of the place and obligations of humankind in the world. Thus, at the core of my argument is an acknowledgment of the politics of inwardness at the time when *Paradise Regained* was first published; and in the context of that politics, I would suggest that the central figure in that poem might better be described as a nonconformist hero than as an otherworldly one. Central to a delineation of this perspective on the poem is an account of the contemporary political suggestiveness of the Son's insistence on remaining a private person, an insistence which fully manifests itself at the end of his wilderness trial, when he "Home to his Mother's house private return'd" (4.639).

The politics of inwardness, as it relates to *Paradise Regained* and its first audience, is intricately tied up with the issue of the illegality of conventicles, often referred to by contemporaries as "private houses."[3] Of

---

of [Milton's] thought," finds in this poem no more than a caution against "pre-mature or ill-conceived political action," and acknowledges that "*Paradise Regained* renounces some of" the kinds of political activity in which Milton had earlier engaged but argues that "we must not exaggerate the renunciation." For another attempt to move away from an "otherworldly" reading of *Paradise Regained,* see Joan Bennett, *Reviving Liberty: Radical Christian Humanism in Milton's Great Poems* (Cambridge: Harvard Univ. Press, 1989), 161–202.

[3] The commonplace lexical substitution of "private house" for "conventicle" in seventeenth-century polemical writings had firm grounding in the *Constitutions and Canons*

direct relevance here is the Conventicles Act of 1664, along with its successor, the Second Conventicles Act of 1670. Enacted on the premise that "private Meetings, or Conventicles [were] the seed plots of faction, and seditious practises" where republicanism thrived, this legislation sought to curtail the ill effects of the "Contagion and Deformity of private Ministers."[4] Aimed at punishing those who neglected, or supplemented, public worship in the Church of England by attending conventicles that "demolish in private, what we build in publick,"[5] the 1664 Act against such meetings sanctioned fines and imprisonment for those who gathered in a private house with more than five adults, and it specified a fine of 100 pounds or deportation to America on the third offence. It authorized village officials to disrupt meetings and permitted justices to break into suspected houses to gather information about them. When Parliament approved these punitive measures, it regarded

Ecclesiastical (1604), reprinted in _Homilies and Sermons,_ 4th ed. (Oxford, 1846), 552–53, which stated, in section 71, that "No minister shall preach, or administer the Communion, in any private House," and "that houses are here reputed for private houses, wherein are no Chapels dedicated and allowed by the Ecclesiastical Laws of this Realm"; see also section 73, which states that "no Priests, or Ministers of the Word of God, or any other persons, shall meet together in any private house, or elsewhere, to consult upon any matter . . . which may in any way tend to the impeaching or depraving of the doctrine of the Church of England, or of the Book of Common Prayer." For examples of the widespread royalist practice of playing up the conspiratorial associations of this substitution, see Henry Ferne, _A Reply unto severall Treatises Pleading for the Armes now taken up by Subjects in the pretended defence of Religion and Liberty_ (London, 1643), 45, who speaks of "private houses, where those few contrivers held their close meetings"; and George Seignior, _God, the King, and the Church_ (London, 1670), 52, 178, 180, who condemns those who are guilty of "neglecting public assembly to betake themselves to private houses," where they substitute "their private hypothesis for the standard of publick truth" and "forget rebellion and disobedience to be a sin."

    [4] _The Anti-Quaker_ (London, 1676), [dedicatory preface] To the most Judicious . . . High Court of Parliament; John Gauden, _Considerations Touching the Liturgy of the Church of England_ (London, 1661), 13. In his 10 March 1670 letter to Mayor Tripp, Andrew Marvell, _The Poems and Letters of Andrew Marvell,_ ed. H. M. Margoliouth, 3rd ed. (Oxford: Clarendon Press, 1971), 2:101, quotes, from the recently passed statute, the official rationale for the Second Conventicles Act: "because seditious Sectaryes, under pretense of tender consciences do contrive insurrections at their meetings." Writing shortly before the passage of the Second Conventicles Act, [Simon Patrick], the author of _An Appendix to the Third Part of the Friendly Debate_ (London, 1670), 94, focuses on the anti-royalist disposition of dissenters by noting "that the Conventicles, which are so frequent and numerous on other dayes, are observed to be so few, if any, upon the day of this Kings Return, or upon the day of the former Kings Death."

    [5] [John Hinckley], _Pithanalogia, Or a perswasive to Conformity_ (London, 1670), 8; W[illiam] B[asset], _Corporal Worship Discuss'd and Defended_ (London, 1670), 27, also charged that conventicles were "undoing in private, what we endeavour in publick."

them as temporary, stipulating that the act should lapse three years after the end of the session in which it had been passed.[6] With the expiration of this period, on 1 March 1669, came an intensification of the ongoing national debate over whether this act should be reinstated. On 9 March 1670, after lengthy discussion, and upon the third reading, the "Bill of Conventicles" was passed by the House of Commons "upon division 138 against 78 & sent up to the Lords & voted their concurrence."[7] "One of the most bitterly resented of the penal statutes,"[8] the Second Conventicles Act was severer than the first in two significant ways: (1) it put heavier penalties on preachers and on owners of houses; and (2) it authorized heavy fines on village officers and justices who did not seek out and punish the offenders.[9]

The effect of this parliamentary action was that nonconformist communities were once again at the mercy of the whims of local officials who might or might not prosecute them,[10] and they had to find ways to survive in the face of such uncertainties. Craig Horle, in his important study of how the Quaker community resisted the imposition of penalties under this law, argues that by the mid-1670s and onward, this

---

[6] 16 Car. II, c. 4 (The Conventicles Act, 1664), *Statutes of the Realm*, 5:516–20.

[7] Marvell, *Poems and Letters*, 2:102, in his 10 March letter to Mayor Tripp. On the various efforts between 1668 and 1670 to renew the Conventicles Act, see *The Diary of John Milward esq.*, ed. Caroline Robbins (Cambridge, 1938), 214–22, 277–83, for accounts of the House of Commons debates of 11 March and 24 April, 1668; Clayton Roberts, "Sir Richard Temple's Discourse on Parliament of 1667–1668," *Huntington Library Quarterly*, 29 (1957): 140; Richard Davis, "The 'Presbyterian' opposition and the emergence of party in the House of Lords in the reign of Charles II," *Party and Management in Parliament, 1660–1784*, ed. Clyve Jones (Leicester, 1984), 11–12; Anthony Fletcher, "The Enforcement of the Conventicle Acts 1664–1679," *Persecution and Toleration*, ed. W. J. Sheils, *Studies in Church History*, 21 (Oxford, 1984), 236–37; Tim Harris, *London Crowds in the Reign of Charles II* (Cambridge: Cambridge Univ. Press, 1987), 86–87 ; and Ronald Hutton, *Charles II: King of England, Scotland and Ireland* (Oxford: Clarendon Press, 1989), 256, 266–70.

[8] Tim Harris, " 'Lives, Liberties and Estates': Rhetorics of Liberty in the Reign of Charles II," *The Politics of Religion in Restoration England*, ed. Tim Harris, Paul Seaward, and Mark Goldie (Oxford: Blackwell, 1990), 225.

[9] 22 Car. II, c. 1 (The Conventicles Act, 1670), *Statutes of the Realm*, 5:648–51. For brief accounts of how this Act differed from the 1664 Act, see: *The Stuart Constitution 1603–1688*, ed. J. P. Kenyon, 2d ed. (Cambridge: Cambridge Univ. Press, 1987), 357n, 359n; Fletcher, "Enforcement," 236; and Harris, " 'Lives, Liberties and Estates,' " 224–25.

[10] On the issue of the enforcement of the conventicle acts, see Fletcher, "Enforcement," 235–246; Clive Holmes, *Seventeenth-century Lincolnshire* (Lincoln, 1980), 220–34; and Paul Seaward, *The Cavalier Parliament and the Reconstruction of the Old Regime, 1661–1667* (Cambridge: Cambridge Univ. Press, 1989), 60–61.

most persecuted of all dissenting groups was becoming quite adept at intervening in the judicial process.[11] My own research shows that resistance to imposition of penalties was already in place by the mid-sixties, where it took the form of printed instructions to justices and potential jurors on how to interpret the law in question. For example, a 1664 anonymous pamphlet, *The Jury-man charged,* urged jurors to find all persons charged under the law "not guilty." The court, it explained, could not be sure of the motives of defendants:

> Suppose the Witness say, they were met together at a private house, and prayed together … but did not reade … their Prayers … out of a Book called the Lyturgy …, can you hereupon pawn your Soul … that they are guilty according to the Indictment?[12]

Richard Farnworth adopted another tactic when he argued, also in 1664, that the Conventicles Act actually meant the opposite of what the government said it did. At the crux of its meaning was a proper understanding of the *true* church. Utilizing a rhetoric of inwardness that would be at the center of many subsequent defenses of nonconformity, he emphasized that

> They … in whom all carnal affections do die, and all things belonging to the Spirit do live … are the people of God allowed by the Liturgie so to be, and may meet upon the account of Religion and Worship of God, to the number of five and above.[13]

In *A Tolleration Sent down from Heaven to Preach,* printed a year after the Conventicles Act had gone into effect, Farnworth shifted the grounds of his argument from semantics to history, explaining that "the manner of Christian Religious Meetings, in other places then in Parish Churches and Chappels, is allowed by the *Liturgie*" because

---

[11] Horle, *The Quakers and the English Legal System, 1660–1688* (Philadelphia: Univ. of Pennsylvania Press, 1988), 163–244. Horle's account of the Quakers' confrontational style and shrewd manipulations of the law provides a significant alternative to the perspective of Hill, *Experience of Defeat,* 315, on "the post-1661 Quaker position of pacifism and abstention from politics," from which he insists that the politically active Milton must be dissociated.

[12] *The Jury-man charged; or A Letter To a Citizen of London Wherein is shewed the true meaning of the Statute, Entituled, An Act to prevent and suppress Seditious Conventicles* (London, 1664), 14.

[13] Farnworth, *Christian Religious Meetings Allowed by the Liturgie* (n.p.,1664), 20.

it is apparent and evident that Christ and his Apostles, did meet
and assemble with the primitive Christians, and such as came
to hear the word of God preached, in private Houses, and
upon Mountains, and by the Sea side as well as other places.[14]

Such arguments were abundantly answered by government apologists, whose purpose was invariably to increase pressure on local officials
to prosecute offenders rigorously. One of these works, appearing in
1664 and called *Cabala, or the Mystery of the Conventicles Unveiled,* complained both of the tactics and the rhetoric of dissenters. Puzzling over
how conventiclers could continue to meet "when the Law is so severe,"
the writer of this tract noted, "They have private houses whereinto the
Entries are dark, and from which there are several passages into other
houses ... Those that meet are invited to a Feast, and if you surprize
them, the table is laid and they go to dinner." Though conventiclers
often met secretly, they could be readily identified, this author claimed,
by their "canting notions of indwelling, enlightning, soul-saving, heart-
supporting," and by their "sermons of inward sincerity against outward
conformity, the Sabbath against Holidays, and a pure heart instead of the
Surplice."[15] Amidst new pressures to enforce the Second Conventicles
Act, in 1670, George Seignor published a sermon in which he confronted the historical argument for private houses by constructing even the
first Christians as religious conformists:

nay, not only the Jewish temple and Synagogues were freqen-
ted by the Apostles upon all occasions ... they did not abstain
from the Jewish rituals and service, though by the bringing in
of a better hope those things were already abolished.[16]

Surely one of the most important government apologists for the
Conventicles Act was Samuel Parker, whose treatise, *A Discourse of Eccle-
siastical Politie,* bore the date "1670" on a title page that claimed, "The
Mischiefs and Inconveniences of Toleration are Represented And all
Pretenses Pleaded in Behalf of Liberty of Conscience are fully an-
swered."[17] Already enjoying a third edition in 1671, when *Paradise Re-*

[14] Farnworth, *A Tolleration Sent down from Heaven to Preach* (n.p.,1665), 18–19.

[15] [David Lloyd], *Cabala* (London, 1664), 59, 57.

[16] Seignor, *God, the King, and the Church* (London, 1670), 55–56.

[17] Parker was Archbishop Sheldon's chaplain from 1667 to 1670 (see *DNB*, 15:272), and
the first printing (in London) of Parker's *Discourse* might have been a part of Archbishop

gained appeared, Parker's work offered a comprehensive rationale for en-forcement of the Conventicles Act. Claiming to write on behalf of a church "savagely worried by a Wild and Fanatique Rabble" and by "Principles of Irreligion [which] unjoynt the Sinews and blow up the very foundations of Government," Parker set out to answer one of his political opponents' main arguments, that enforcement of the Conventi-cles Act was contrary to the example of Christ and the apostles.[18]

At stake for both Parker and opponents of the Act was the basis on which "the Ecclesiastical Jurisdiction of Princes" was to be established. For Parker, the example of Christ was irrelevant. This jurisdiction was "not derived from any grant of our Saviours but from the natural and antecedent Rights of all Sovereign Power."[19] Grounding his own posi-tion on the role of fathers in families, Parker noted that "All the ways our Saviour has appointed in the Gospel for the advancement and propa-gation of Religion, were prescribed to Subjects, & not to Gover-nours."[20] "Christ and his Apostles could not use any coercive Jurisdic-tion," he noted, "because they acted in the capacity of Subjects ... In the First Ages of the Christian Church God supplied its want of Civil Jurisdiction by immediate and miraculous Infliction from heaven" with the same effect that "temporal Punishment" would have on later Chris-tians. But the ideal situation existed "when the Emperours became Christian," and "the Ecclesiastical Jurisdiction was annext to the Civil Power."[21]

Were we to relate *Paradise Regained* to Parker's treatise *without* tak-

Sheldon's campaign to rally support for the Conventicles Bill, just as the printing of subse-quent editions might be seen as promoting the enforcement of the 1670 Act. Although the printer dated the work "1670," it was entered in the Stationers' Register in September 1669; and in that year there appeared in print at least two answers to it: John Owen's *Truth and Innocence Vindicated* (London, 1669), and John Humfrey's *A Case of Conscience* (London, 1669). W[illiam] B[asset], the author of *Corporal Worship*, writes, in 1670, in defense of Parker's treatise.

[18] Parker, *A Discourse*, iv, xxii. See especially 39–48 for Parker's discussion of the irrelevance of Christ's example.

[19] Ibid., 3.

[20] Ibid., 40–41; see 29–31 for the argument from paternal authority.

[21] Ibid., 3–4, 48. See John Marshall, "The Ecclesiology of the Latitude-men 1660–1689: Stillingfleet, Tillotson and 'Hobbism,'" *Journal of Ecclesiastical History* 36 (1985): 425, for a discussion of the manner in which Parker's treatise "highlights the authoritarian possibilities inherent in Hobbes' work." See also Richard Ashcraft, *Revolutionary Politics & Locke's Two Treatises of Government* (Princeton: Princeton Univ. Press, 1986), 48–53, for a treatment of Parker's "complicated" relationship to Hobbes.

ing account of the rhetorical situation which they address, it would not
be hard to find points of agreement. When Parker, for example, asserts
that

> the power, wherewith Christ intrusted the Governours of his
> Church in the Apostolical age, was purely Spiritual; [and that]
> they had no Authority to inflict temporal Punishments, or to
> force men to submit to their Canons, Laws and Penalties,[22]

he seems quite compatible with Milton's Son. But it would be rather
strange to discuss Parker's ideas on this matter apart from their rhetorical
function. For we easily recognize them as a part of a strategy whereby
the writer grants the opponents' point only to assert that it is no obstacle
to his argument. Indeed, by casting the spiritually minded Son as the
obedient private person, Parker appears to have used his opponents' arguments against them. "And this is indeed certain," he emphasizes, "that
no private person can have any power to compel men to any part of the
Doctrine, Worship, or Discipline of the Gospel."[23]

My own argument is that by taking notice of Parker's language we
can clarify ways to situate *Paradise Regained* in relation to the political discourses that constituted the debates on the Conventicles Act and its enforcement. When considered within this context, the most interesting aspect of relating Milton to Parker is surely not the points of similarity in
their portraits of Christ but the radically different uses to which these
images can be put. Whereas Parker's picture serves a full blown Erastian
view of church-state relations compatible with his interest in the forcing
of consciences, Milton's portrait provides the kind of critique of that
view most useful to the nonconformist cause. A simple way of putting
the matter, as it might pertain to the penal laws then in effect against non-
conformists, would be to say that, while Parker's world-denying Christ is
constructed so as to remove a problem that could impede the enforcement
of these laws, Milton's world-denying Son is constructed so as to feature
the problem of their enforcement in order to make the problem known.

Perhaps the easiest way of illustrating my point is to recall Parker's
treatment of Christ as obedient subject and to notice how Milton com-
plicates this issue. Parker deals with his opponents' objections by keeping
Father and Son separate. In assuming power over ecclesiastical matters,

---

[22] Parker, *A Discourse,* 43.
[23] Ibid., 41.

the magistrate takes up the role of Father, and the bishop himself acts as the Magistrate/Father's agent. The subject, however, models his conduct on the Son, who as a private person renounces the use of force. Milton, on the other hand, deals with *his* opponents' argument by presenting the Son not only as a private person but also as a king, thereby highlighting the notion that those who assume ecclesiastical jurisdiction stand in Christ's stead. In defining his office as king, that is as head of the church, the Son insists on remaining a private person. It is Satan who holds Parker's position that "king" and "private person" are opposites. Throughout the poem Milton emphasizes the need to separate civil power from church matters by insisting on the distinction between the two states in which the Son's kingship will be manifested, the "then" and the "now," what Milton in *Christian Doctrine* called the kingdom of glory and the kingdom of grace. Time will come when the Son will rule over the earth as well as the church—when civil and ecclesiastical jurisdictions will be joined—but not now. Milton hereby puts constant pressure on the problem of civil magistrates' forcing consciences by earthly means, identifying the temptation to do as that which the Son, the head of the Church, withstood. According to the logic of Milton's Son, non-enforcement of penal laws is Christlike. Succumbing to enforcement is giving in to Satan.

If the publication of *Paradise Regained* in 1671 can be seen as an intervention into the government campaign of pressuring magistrates to enforce penal laws against nonconformity, it can also be read as an encouragement to nonconformist communities under the threat of this enforcement. If Milton's young Quaker friend, Thomas Ellwood, was in any way justified in his claim that he prompted Milton to write this poem, I suspect that it was his imprisonment for his religious principles, more than his query about where was "Paradise Found," that provided the motivation to write it. Indeed, *Paradise Regained* celebrates an exemplary epic action for Milton's time, the story of a head of a community whose trials consist of standing up for those principles which the most beleaguered of the nonconformist communities held dear. Milton shapes his account of the Son in the wilderness so that it can also tell the Revelation story of the woman in the wilderness, an account, in other words, of the church under persecution. What makes Milton's version a truly contemporary one is his emphasis throughout the poem on the role of the Spirit. Beginning with the descent of the Spirit, the epic presents a hero who makes the presence of the Spirit the central term in all of his rejections of Satan's carnal means. In a quakerly fashion that might have made Ellwood beam, the Son interprets scripture not by the letter but by the living oracle now in him, and he evaluates his qualifications to lead the church not by his university degrees but by the Spirit in him. Most significant of all, he assesses his future plans according to the Spirit.

Too little has been said in Milton studies of the striking manner in which the poet departs from tradition at the conclusion of his story. The traditional version is that Christ's wilderness experience is a preparation for his public ministry. But Milton's Son will remain a nonconformist hero to the end. Instead of entering the public ministry—an act that many dissenters in 1671 regarded as equivalent to selling one's soul to the devil—he will go home to his private house, where, we can assume, he will continue to act as the Spirit moves him. He thereby provides "the example and practise" that Farnworth claimed was "ordained of Christ Jesus," who commanded his disciples

> to wait at *Jerusalem,* for the promise of the Father ... but they were not commanded by Christ to wait in the Temple at *Jerusalem,* nor in a Parish Church ... but rather in a private House ... and the place where they were when they received the holy Ghost; was neither a Parish Church nor a Chapel, but a private House.[24]

Concluding *Paradise Regained* as he does, Milton thus lends support to the position of Farnworth and others, that it was among the dissenters, not in the public temples, that the Spirit of God now dwelt.

UNIVERSITY OF MARYLAND AT COLLEGE PARK

---

[24] Farnworth, *A Tolleration Sent down from Heaven to Preach,* 20–21.

Peter Lindenbaum

THE POET IN THE
MARKETPLACE: MILTON
AND SAMUEL SIMMONS*

IF AN EGREGIOUS PUN MIGHT BE FORGIVEN ME, SAMUEL SIM-
mons, the printer and publisher of the first three editions of *Paradise
Lost,* never has had a good press. From the mid-eighteenth century on,
he has been mentioned, if at all, primarily as the man who underpaid
Milton for his epic. His moment of perhaps greatest fame was also his
moment of greatest obloquy, and on that occasion he was not even
honored with a name. For he was the "bad printer" whom Richard
Bentley accused of collaborating with an even "worse editor" in violat-
ing ("defoedating" was Bentley's term) Milton's text to such an extent
that it made necessary Bentley's own "judiciously corrected" edition of
1732. But the contentious and self-serving Bentley of course had it
wrong, as Jacob Tonson, in possession of the manuscript of book 1 at
the time, pointed out in a private letter to his nephew. The comparison
of the manuscript with Simmons's printed edition showed Tonson what
most modern editors and critics have been quick to agree with, that
Simmons in fact did well by Milton's text, that the text of the 1667
Paradise Lost was by seventeenth-century standards rather good, carefully

* It is a pleasure to acknowledge the considerable help of D. F. McKenzie, Professor of
Bibliography and Textual Criticism at Oxford University, who not only answered an endless
number of questions but kindly allowed me to read the manuscript of his as yet unpublished
Lyell lectures, "Bibliography and History: Seventeenth-Century England," presented at
Oxford in 1988. My debt to those lectures, and to much else of McKenzie's work, will be
evident throughout my essay. Another version of the present essay appeared as "Milton's
Contract," in the *Cardozo Arts & Entertainment Law Journal* 10 (1992): 439–54.

prepared and well presented, neatly printed and without major errors.[1]

Simmons did well by *Paradise Lost* in other ways as well. He made arrangements with six different booksellers to assure proper distribution of the poem's first edition, a relatively high number for the time and perhaps motivated by a desire to share the risk of the undertaking, but an act which would plainly benefit Milton's poem as well. The addition of bookseller Henry Mortlack, evidently in mid-1668 with the distribution of those copies bearing the fourth title-page, is particularly significant. Mortlack's shop was in Westminster Hall and with such an outlet, Milton's poem could have more direct access to a potential audience surrounding the court. In any case, it was with that issue, the evidence of surviving copies suggests, that the work began to sell in earnest.[2] And it was with that issue also that the preliminary material—the argument for the ten books, Milton's defense of blank verse, and an errata list—was included for the first time, and evidently at Simmons's urging. Accompanying that material is a note from Simmons to the courteous reader announcing that he, Simmons, had obtained the argument "for the satisfaction of many that desired it." Simmons would appear, then, to be responding conscientiously to what his booksellers and their customers were telling him, in an effort to boost sales.[3]

---

[1] See R. G. Moyles, *The Text of "Paradise Lost": A Study in Editorial Procedure* (Toronto: Univ. of Toronto Press, 1985), 28, 31. Stuart Bennett, "Jacob Tonson: An Early Editor of *Paradise Lost*?" *The Library*, 6th ser., 10 (1988): 249, remarks that Tonson "probably felt, as indeed must any modern editor, that the standard of printing of the first three editions of *Paradise Lost* was exceptionally high judged by comparison with the manuscript." The text of Tonson's letter to his nephew, which accompanies the manuscript of book 1 now in the Pierpont Morgan Library, is included in the introduction to Helen Darbishire's edition of *The Manuscript of Milton's Paradise Lost Book I* (Oxford: Clarendon Press, 1931), xi–xv.

[2] See William Riley Parker, *Milton: A Biography*, 2 vols. (Oxford: Clarendon Press, 1968), 2:1111. Thirty-eight copies of the issue with the first state title-page survive, 35 copies of the second, 24 copies of the third, and 82 of the fourth. And for the two issues of 1669, the numbers are 109 and 51 respectively. I follow Parker's version of the chronology of the six title-pages of the first edition rather than that of Hugh Amory ("Things Unattempted Yet: A Bibliography of the First Edition of *Paradise Lost*," *Book Collector* 32 [1983]: 41–66) both for clarity of reference and because I happen to find Amory's account of the chronology of the different title-pages unconvincing. Moyles, *The Text of "Paradise Lost*," 4, thinks that the second title-page is a mere variant of the first and hence that there are only five distinct title-pages, one dated 1667, two of 1668, and two of 1669.

[3] Moyles, 12–15, records that there are a few copies with a 1667 title-page which contain the argument and defense of blank verse, but agrees with the scholarly consensus that the preliminary material was printed up for copies bearing the second 1668 title-page (the

But if we take that prefatory note to the reader as evidence of business acumen or sagacity on Simmons's part, we have to admit that it is one of the few bits of such evidence we can find in Simmons's career. For while there is every indication that Simmons was indeed a good printer, there is much to suggest that he was *not* a very good business-man.[4] As it happens this evidence of what we might call Simmons's weaknesses as a stationer turn out to be just as important as his strengths, if not so much for the text of *Paradise Lost*, at least for that text's author and the way that author might look upon himself, and the way we ought to look upon him.

Any statement we make about Samuel Simmons, however, has to be made with a great deal of caution. For Simmons was a rather shadowy figure, both in his own time and ever since. That relative obscurity is in part a function of the single most important fact we need to keep in mind about him, and that is that Simmons, unlike the more famous members of the seventeenth-century book trade and those whose names are well known to students of the trade today—for instance, Humphrey Moseley, Henry Herringman, and Jacob Tonson—was primarily a printer rather than a bookseller (although he did some bookselling as well). As the many petitions by printers attest and complain from the end of the sixteenth century on, it was the booksellers who were rising steadily to positions of prominence in the Stationers' Company and to financial dominance in the trade generally, at the expense of both printers and book-binders.[5] Yet even when we have allowed for this major distinction between printer and bookseller, we still have to acknowledge that Samuel Simmons's career in the book trade was far from brilliant or striking. For there were printers about who can be said to have made a bigger immediate impact upon the trade—most notably perhaps and very close to

---

one with Mortlack's name on it). In the case of those few aberrant copies, the preliminary material was presumably inserted late, just before these copies bearing an earlier title-page were bound.

[4] This is the conclusion that D. F. McKenzie comes to as well, in his "Milton's Printers: Matthew, Mary, and Samuel Simmons," *MQ* 14 (1980): 87–91, esp. n. 10.

[5] See Cyprian Blagden, *The Stationers' Company: A History, 1403–1959* (London: George Allen and Unwin, 1960), 90, 122, 149–52, and documents such as *A Brief Discourse Concerning Printing and Printers*, published by a "Society for Printers" in 1663.

home, Samuel's own parents, Matthew and Mary Simmons.[6]

D. F. McKenzie has recorded Matthew Simmons's name on some 433 imprints in a printing career that spanned twenty years from 1635 to an early death in 1654, an average then of 21.7 items per year.[7] The name of Mary Simmons, who took over the business upon her husband's death and who bore sole responsibility for the shop until 1662 when son Samuel completed his apprenticeship and, evidently, prime responsibility for some time thereafter, is to be found on some ninety-one items over the seven-year period from 1655 to 1661, or an average of thirteen items a year. Oddly, once Samuel finishes his apprenticeship and his name begins to appear on imprints along with Mary's and there are now two people who presumably can conduct business for the firm, the number of Simmons imprints goes *down:* for the period from 1662 until 1678 (the last year Samuel's name appears on a title page), there are fifty-eight items, or an average of 3.4 imprints a year. And once Mary's name ceases to appear on imprints altogether (after 1670) and only Samuel's name is on new imprints, when it would appear that Mary has gone into partial or full retirement, the average number of imprints decreases farther yet, to fewer than three items a year (twenty-three new imprints in the eight years from 1671 to 1678). Now as McKenzie also demonstrates, the number of acknowledged imprints by no means represents the total output of a printing house's work: for instance, 54% of the items published in 1668 and still extant do not carry a printer's name.[8] The three new Simmons titles for that year listed in Wing could have supplied, McKenzie calculates, little more than six weeks' work for the firm's two proprietors, five workmen, one apprentice, and two

---

[6] I take it as now settled that Samuel Simmons was the son of Matthew and Mary, not the nephew (as was assumed by Harris Fletcher, William Riley Parker, and John T. Shawcross); see McKenzie, "Milton's Printers." To the evidence that McKenzie provides—for instance, the entry in the Stationers' Company Apprentice Book declaring Samuel to be both Matthew's son and freed by patrimony—I can add the fact that on 22 December 1671 Samuel took receipt of Mary's English Stock dividend for that year, signing the Dividend Book "Samuel Simmons, for My Mother."

[7] These and the following figures on imprints are from the appendix to the fourth of McKenzie's Lyell lectures, "Simmons."

[8] McKenzie, "The London Book Trade in 1668," *Words: Wai-Te-Ata Studies in Literature* (Wellington, N. Z.) 4 (1974): 81. In his fourth Lyell lecture of 1988 (pp. 10–11), McKenzie notes that similarly in 1644 only 46% of the items published and still extant carry a printer's name and only 32% a bookseller's; in 1688, the corresponding figures are 31% for printers and 32% for booksellers.

presses.[9] There must, then, have been considerably more anonymous work printed in the shop, if the shop were to proceed at anything like its full capacity (and remain open for business the next year). But even if we take into account that—to assume the trade average—there must have been at least an equal number of unacknowledged works printed in Simmons's shop in the years from 1662 to, let us say, 1680, it is still difficult to see how Samuel Simmons could have been earning a decent living. Either he was not doing so very well, or he was an extraordinarily self-effacing figure in his trade. I suspect both.

If we look at the particular works that bear Samuel's name as printer, we are, I think, driven to much the same conclusion. In a printing career extending from 1662 to perhaps 1680 (when he sold the rights to *Paradise Lost*), Samuel's name appears, either with his mother's or alone, on only eleven different works, although some of them in several editions or differing versions. Of these eleven items, four were continuations of ventures that one or both of his parents had printed before him;[10] four we can identify as printing jobs for other stationers;[11] and,

---

[9] McKenzie, 1988 Lyell lectures, no. 4, "Simmons," 6. The number and names of the workmen in the Simmons shop are provided on a list drawn up on 29 July 1668; this list is to be found in the State Papers Domestic, Charles II, vol. 243, no. 181, and is discussed by McKenzie in "Milton's Printers," 89.

[10] (1) John Speed's *A Prospect of the Most Famous Parts of the World* was printed with Mary in 1662, the early date suggesting that Mary was the main impulse behind its publication; she had earlier, on 18 October 1656, entered in the Stationers' Register a work entitled "A New Geographical and Accurate Description of the Whole World" (no longer extant or never printed), the entry revealing that a geography was part of her long-term plans for the Simmons printing house. (2) John Mennes's *Witts Recreations* (also appearing in its alternate title, *Recreation for Ingenious Head-peeces*), printed with Mary in 1663 and by Samuel alone in 1667 (in two different editions), had been published earlier by Matthew Simmons in 1650 and 1654; the Stationers' Register records Matthew acquiring the rights to the work from Humphrey Blunden on 3 June 1654. (3) Thomas Shelton's *Tachygraphy or Short-writing*, published by Samuel in 1671 and 1674, had been published earlier by Mary in 1660 and 1668, Matthew having obtained partial rights to the work on 25 January 1649/50 and Mary having purchased Samuel Cartwright's original share on 19 April 1659. (4) Joseph Caryl's *Exposition . . . upon the Book of Job:* several parts of Caryl's *Job* were published by Samuel alone (1664, chapters 1–3; 1671, chapters 15–18) and by Samuel and Mary together (1666, chapters 38–42), and Samuel published the complete Caryl *Exposition* in a two-volume folio edition in 1676–77; but early parts of the *Exposition* had been published by Matthew as far back as 1650. When the parts of Caryl's work first began to appear in 1643, copyright was shared by several different stationers; the Stationers' Register reveals Matthew and then Mary buying up the shares of those other stationers from the 1650s through the 1670s: in 1651 Matthew acquired John Rothwell's and a portion of Giles Calvert's shares in parts 1–4; in 1656/57

at best, only three can be said to be entrepreneurial efforts undertaken by Samuel himself, works that he alone went out and sought (or which sought him out), these last three being *Paradise Lost,* Hugh Davis's *De Jure Uniformitatis Ecclesiasticae,* and Milton's *Accedence Commenc't Grammar.*[12] If we look at the seven items that involved some thought on

Mary took over the rest of Calvert's share of the rights to parts 2–4; and on 15 November 1672 she purchased the shares to various parts from Nathaniel Ranew, Jonathan Robinson, Lodowick Lloyd, and Andrew Crooke. By the end of 1672 she evidently owned all rights to all twelve parts, whereupon she signed them over to Samuel on 5 May 1673. When Samuel came to publish the complete Caryl in 1676, he would (all going well) be following upon, and benefitting from, the earlier efforts and perhaps vision of his parents.

[11] (1) Thomas Goodwin's *Patience and Its Perfect Work* (1666) was, the title page tells us, "Printed by S. Simmons for Rob. Duncan," who had entered the work in the Stationers' Register on 21 February 1666/67. (2) Thomas Lye's *The Child's Delight* was printed in 1671 for Thomas Parkhurst, who had entered the work in the Stationers' Register on 1 March 1669/70. (3) Peter Heylyn's *Theologia Veterum* was printed in 1673 "for A. S.," who is presumably the widow Anne Seile whose husband Henry had published the first edition in 1654. (4) Robert Clavel's *Catalogue of All the Books Printed in England Since the Dreadful Fire of London in 1666, to the End of Michaelmas Term, 1672,* printed in 1673 "by S. Simmons, for R. Clavel, in Cross-Keys Court in Little Britain," was plainly an advertising venture (and thus not in need of the copyright protection that entry in the Stationers' Register would provide) by Robert Clavel, who would simply hire a printer for the task; it is of some interest that Clavel did not stay with Simmons for the 1674 version of the *Catalogue,* switching to Andrew Clarke instead (and then to Samuel Roycroft for the 1680 version).

[12] Simmons entered *Paradise Lost* in the Stationers' Register on 20 August 1667 and Davis's *De Jure Uniformitatis Ecclesiasticae or Three Books of the Rights Belonging to an Uniformity in Churches* on 9 October 1668. There is no entry for *Accedence Commenc't Grammar.* I am assuming that it was Simmons rather than bookseller John Starkey (who was later to enter *Paradise Regained* and *Samson Agonistes*) who is the publisher of the *Grammar,* that is, the person who took the financial risk in having it printed and thus the one who ordinarily *would* have entered the title in the Stationers' Register. The information on the two different title-pages of the work seems to point to that role for Simmons: the first title-page reads "Printed by Samuel Simmons next door to the Golden Lion in Aldersgate Street," the inclusion of the address implying that Simmons is selling the work from his shop (which he, being a printer rather than a bookseller, ordinarily does not do for other stationers' copy); the other title-page reads "Printed for Samuel Simmons and to be sold by John Starkey at the Miter in Fleet Street, near Temple Bar." The phrase "printed for . . ." (particularly when a bookseller is also mentioned) is ordinarily, but not always, used to identify the copy holder.

As to why there was no Stationers' Register entry for the work, the reason may be simply that the work did not appear to be of the type that would prove popular enough to need the copyright protection that such an entry would provide. But there is an order in Court Book D of the Stationers' Company, for 5 February 1666/67, stipulating that "the copie Intitled Accedence Commenc'd Grammar Disburdened &c be not entered into the Register of this companie as the proper copie of any person" until the work has been subject

Simmons's and his mother's part, that is, printing jobs for which there would not be immediate payment and therefore for which there was some monetary risk involved (the first and third categories just mentioned), we find a reasonably varied list: two prose works of a religious nature, one religious epic poem, an anthology of light verse, two instructional works (Shelton's book on shorthand and Milton's grammar), and one geographical survey. The list is suitably varied even if it does lean towards the religious (although much less so than a similar list we might construct for Samuel's father, Matthew). But the list remains undeniably short.

Simmons's career is alas all too easily summed up—for good and for ill—in his edition of the complete Joseph Caryl *Exposition with Practical Observations upon the Book of Job,* the individual parts of which seem to have been among the mainstays of the Simmons printing house for over twenty years and thus among the works handed on to Samuel by his parents. It is a magnificent two-volume work, running to more than 2400 folio pages. Simmons put it forth as a subscription edition, partaking of that new method of marketing that was to prove increasingly popular and profitable in the next century.[13] And, in promoting it, Simmons reveals some flair for advertising. He announced the venture

to the perusal of Mr. Roger Norton. If this order in fact refers to Milton's *Grammar,* it may denote that Simmons (or Starkey) did try to enter the work and the work was subject to some kind of objection (perhaps another work with the same title?), which proved unfounded once Norton had examined the text, whereupon Simmons was allowed to go ahead with the printing and the formal entering of the work in the Stationers' Register was waived or forgotten.

It should be acknowledged as well that, given Milton's earlier association with Matthew Simmons in the 1640s, the two Milton titles on Samuel's list might also be considered mere continuations of earlier interests of his parents and thus rightfully belonging in the first category of items I have mentioned.

[13] It is an early example of such a venture but not necessarily to be viewed as a groundbreaking one. See the list of such projects in F. J. G. Robinson and P. J. Wallis, *Book Subscriptions Lists: A Revised Guide* (Newcastle-upon-Tyne: Book Subscriptions List Project, 1975). Robinson and Wallace provide, though, the titles of only those works which included a published list of subscribers along with the text (which Simmons's edition of Caryl did not); they list four such works before 1676. Sarah Clapp, "The Beginnings of Subscription Publishing in the Seventeenth Century," *MP* 29 (1931): 199–224, records 54 instances of subscription publishing from 1617 to 1688; see too Clapp's "The Subscription Enterprises of John Ogilby and Richard Blome," *MP* 30 (1933): 365–79. Using the work of Robinson/Wallis and Clapp, as well as John Feather, *English Book Prospectuses* (Newtown, Pa.: Bird and Bull Press, 1984), I count twelve examples of subscription ventures prior to 1676 and two more in that year, in addition to the Caryl *Job* (several others—for instance, an Oxford University Press Bible in the 1670s—were attempted but did not materialize).

in the Michaelmas 1673 *Term Catalogue,* claiming that the true value of the work when completed and bound would be four pounds and would in fact be sold at that price in the future. But those who subscribe now would pay only fifty shillings for the work in quires, twenty-five shillings now ("it being a work of great charge") and twenty-five for the second volume upon delivery of the first. Those who subscribe for six copies would get a seventh free. The *Term Catalogue* for Hilary Term 1676 announces the publication of volume 1 and that for Michaelmas Term 1677 announces the appearance of volume 2. But in this latter announcement Simmons acknowledges that he has run into some difficulty in his venture, that the project has been "long a doing ... to the great vexation and loss of the Proposer." To his great injury he has been subject to unjust carping against the text, some critics motivated by "malicious prejudice, others simply subject to imprudent mistake." And unfortunately, Simmons appears to have made other miscalculations as well, since three years after his death the Trinity 1690 *Term Catalogue* announces that the work is being remaindered. What Simmons originally announced would be worth four pounds and which he was selling for only fifty shillings, now could be purchased for thirty shillings in quires, forty shillings bound, at W. Marshall's at the Bible in Newgate.

It could very well be that, as Harris Fletcher suggested in 1945, the Caryl venture drove Simmons to virtual bankruptcy.[14] Or the miscalculations attendant upon that venture may have been more a symptom than the cause of what we have to see finally as an undistinguished and relatively quiet, probably even failing, career as a printer. It is possible, of course, that Simmons, like others in his trade, developed other business interests besides printing and bookselling. But as a stationer at least, as printer and publisher, he does not separate himself from number.

Now what I think we can conclude from even this brief examination of Simmons and his career is that when John Milton entered into his contract with him for *Paradise Lost,* the poet was by no means in the hands of a "sharper" (Dryden's label for his publisher Jacob Tonson, the poet being in a fit of pique over the financial arrangements for his

---

[14] Harris Francis Fletcher, ed., *John Milton's Complete Poetical Works, Reproduced in Photographic Facsimile,* 4 vols. (Urbana: Univ. of Illinois Press, 1943–48), 2:109.

Virgil).[15] Simmons is simply not the sort of figure to make a fast pound, either at an author's expense or indeed in any other way. And in view of the fact that Simmons reveals little of the entrepreneurial spirit of the more successful stationers of his time nor even the market aggressiveness of his parents (there is no sign, for instance, of his buying up the copy of other stationers' successful imprints, as his parents did), we are probably safest in assuming also that it was Milton who sought out Simmons rather than vice versa, and presumably because of the long-standing relationship Milton had established with the Simmons family in the 1640s when Matthew printed a number of Milton's prose tracts. We have no idea, of course, whether Samuel Simmons would have been Milton's first or fourth choice as publisher, but what we have to assume is a relationship between relative equals, in which neither author nor printer/publisher comes before the other with cap in hand.[16]

We get much the same impression from the contract between the two for the publication of *Paradise Lost,* a document which might best be viewed against a background of contemporary trade practice and of the rest of Simmons's own career in the trade. The details of that contract have long been known, but the document itself has not always been interpreted correctly. Milton was to receive five pounds from Simmons immediately, five more at the end of the first impression (the impression or edition considered completed when 1300 copies were sold off to "particular reading Customers"), and then five more pounds at the end of each of the second and third editions (these, too, considered to be completed when 1300 copies were sold). The contract stipulated further that none of the three editions was to run more than 1500 copies. Milton on his part agreed to give up to Simmons all future "benefitt proffitt & advantage" arising from the copy or manuscript of the poem

[15] For Dryden's comment on Tonson, see his letter to the bookseller of December or January 1695/96: "Upon triall I find all of your trade are Sharpers & you not more than others; therefore I have not wholly left you." *Letters of John Dryden,* ed. Charles E. Ward (Durham, N.C.: Duke Univ. Press, 1942), 80.

[16] There has been much speculation about Milton's possible dissatisfaction with Simmons as a publisher, since the poet did not return to Simmons with his later two volumes of poetry, the *Paradise Regained/Samson Agonistes* volume and the 1673 *Poems &c. upon Several Occasions.* But the spottiness of Simmons's career, the very evidence that prompts one to conclude he was not likely to take advantage of the blind, out-of-favor fifty-nine year-old poet, suggests further that Simmons himself may not have been greatly interested in publishing more of Milton's poetry (or indeed any poetry), or more simply that Simmons was not an obvious figure in the trade for Milton to return to.

and Simmons was to have rights to all future impressions after the third without let or hindrance from Milton.[17]

That much we know; what we don't know is precisely what to make of those sums mentioned. John Dryden is reported to have received twenty pounds (in borrowed funds) from Jacob Tonson for the manuscript of that author's *Troilus and Cressida* in 1679, but the source of that report is Edmond Malone, writing in 1800.[18] Richard Baxter was paid ten pounds in 1649 by his printers Thomas Underhill and Francis Tyton *after* the publication of his *Saints Everlasting Rest,* and thereafter, the two printers paid him ten pounds each for every subsequent impression of the work through 1665, thus evidently bringing Baxter a total of £170 for that one work over a thirteen-year period—all in all, a rather good sum.[19] On the other hand, in 1633 George Herbert's widow seems to have received no payment at all upon the posthumous publication of *The Temple,* and about the same time William Prynne received thirty-five or thirty-six copies of his *Histriomastix* to dispose of as he saw fit, either by sale or as presentation copies.[20]

Such evidence, sparse as it is, is plainly not enough upon which to base a judgment as to whether Milton was adequately or fairly remunerated. But the other provisions of the contract, often overlooked in the focus on the sums, provide more definite help. For putting an upward limit of 1500 copies on each impression—an apparently odd or inconsequential stipulation, at first glance—ensures that Simmons's profits do not increase inordinately in relation to the amounts Milton was to receive. And further, the contract contained the stipulation that Milton could demand an accounting of sales at reasonable intervals, with any failure on Simmons's part to provide the same obligating him to pay the

[17] The text of the contract is to be found in J. Milton French, *The Life Records of John Milton,* 5 vols. (New Brunswick, N.J.: Rutgers Univ. Press, 1949–58), 4:429–31. The original is British Museum Additional MS 18,861.

[18] Edmond Malone, "Some Account of the Life and Writings of John Dryden," in Malone's edition of *The Critical and Miscellaneous Prose Works of John Dryden,* 3 vols. (London, 1800), 1:522–23.

[19] *Reliquiae Baxterianae* (London, 1696), part 3, appendix 7, 117. Baxter also reports in that same letter that Dr. William Bates received above £100 for his *Divine Harmony* (i.e., the *Harmony of the Divine Attributes* [1674]) and "yet reserving the power for the future to himself."

[20] On Herbert, see Daniel W. Doerksen, "Nicholas Ferrar, Arthur Woodnoth, and the Publication of George Herbert's *The Temple,* 1633," *George Herbert Journal* 3 (1979–80): 22–44; and on Prynne, see W. W. Greg, *A Companion to Arber* (Oxford: Clarendon Press, 1967), 277–78, who quotes from State Papers Domestic, Charles I, vol. 231, art. 77.

five pounds for the whole impression as if it were due. Such stipulations imply that the five-pound installments were definitely not viewed as mere tokens by either party in the contract, and indeed that such sums seem to be about right. And if the ten pounds for the first edition and the twenty pounds altogether for three editions are in fact just or normal payments for the time, what I think we must consider as most significant about the payment to Milton is not so much the sum agreed upon as that it was agreed upon by means of a formal document between author and publisher. For in that alone we see an author who is fully acknowl-edging the condition of authorship, viewing himself as the possessor of property that gives him definite rights (for instance, the right to demand an accounting of sales), even as he lives and writes at a time when copy-right is granted only to stationers through entry in the Stationers' Com-pany Register. This is not the off-hand agreement of, let us say, some-one affecting to be an amateur or a gentleman-poet, anxious to avoid the stigma of print, a figure using poetry for advancement in some other, non-literary, realm.[21]

How in fact Milton ought to appear before us in that transaction is

[21] My phrasing here is designed to call to mind J. W. Saunders's innovative studies of the 1950s and 1960s: "The Stigma of Print: A Note on the Social Bases of Tudor Poetry," *Essays in Criticism* 1 (1951): 139–64; "Milton, Diomede and Amaryllis," *ELH* 22 (1955): 254–86; and *The Profession of English Letters* (London: Routledge and Kegan Paul, 1964). Saunders recorded the move from a Renaissance literary system based on patronage in which poets write as ama-teurs, using their poetry as means of advancement in other realms, to a system in which the writer emerges as an independent professional. But unfortunately, thrown off by the Milton-Simmons contract's reference to an upper limit of 1500 copies per edition while payment was to be provided Milton when 1300 copies were sold, Saunders placed Milton incorrectly in his scheme. Saunders assumed that 200 copies of each impression were put at Milton's disposal as presentation copies. Were that true, Milton would indeed be the poet Saunders envisions, a con-tinuing participant in the patronage system, writing if not for a social elite, at least for a *cultured* "fit audience . . . though few." But William Riley Parker located 343 extant copies of the first edition's original 1300 (or 1500), or approximately one in four from that edition (see *Milton: A Biography*, 2:1109–12); if 200 of the original copies were presented to friends or potential patrons by the author, we would expect some 50 of those copies to have survived, perhaps more, since it is fair to assume that a recipient of such a copy (or his or her heirs) would be more likely than the regular buyer to save it, particularly after the poem came to be recognized as a classic. But there does not seem to be any reliable evidence in *any* extant copy of it having been such a gift (Parker, 2:1116), that is, no evidence such as we have on the title-page of John Morris's copy of the *Pro Populo Anglicano Defensio* of it being "ex dono authoris." We have to assume, then, that the number of presentation copies was very small and that Milton was farther removed from conditions of earlier Renaissance authorship and closer to those of the eighteenth-century profes-sional than Saunders suggested.

highlighted if we glance back at what we can construct of Milton's relations with the publisher of his first volume of poetry, the bookseller Humphrey Moseley, who brought out the *Poems of Mr. John Milton* in 1645. If
Simmons was rather diffident and retiring among printers, Moseley was
nothing if not flamboyant among booksellers. He plainly thrived in his
trade, finding numerous opportunities for self-display, ranging from prefaces in which he praised himself, to service in high offices in the Stationers'
Company (Stockkeeper, Renter Warden, Under Warden), to a will in
which he left the Company ten pounds to buy a standing bowl or cup.[22]
Moseley made no secret of his royalist sympathies in the period from 1641
to 1660 and even in his book lists gives us something of himself. In the
latest such catalogue I have seen, one listing 363 items and evidently from
1659 or 1660, he announces a final category of "Books I Purpose to
Print, Deo Volente," thus positing not simply a potential clientele but
one perhaps interested in Humphrey Moseley himself.[23]

Moseley was by no means necessarily a sharper either, but an entre-
preneur he certainly was, with a good eye for what is likely to impress
a reader. He states in his preface to Milton's *Poems* that he has been so
encouraged with the reception of Waller's late choice pieces among
most ingenious men that he has been prompted to venture forth once
again in search of "ever-green and not to be blasted Laurels" such as
follow in the present volume. As part of the presentation of Milton's
poems, he provides not only that self-congratulatory preface, but a letter
of commendation on *Comus* from Sir Henry Wotton (duly mentioned in

---

[22] For Moseley's will, a brief biography, and a comprehensive list of books he published,
see John Curtis Reed, "Humphrey Moseley, Publisher," *Oxford Bibliographical Society
Proceedings and Papers* 2, part 2 (1928): 55–142.

[23] This list is inserted into a Bodleian Library copy of Waller's *Poems* (shelf no. Don.f.144),
published in 1645 but evidently not sold and bound until 1659 or 1660 since the inserted list
provides titles from those years. For evidence of Moseley's royalism, see the prefaces to his
editions of Arthur Lake's *Ten Sermons on Several Occasions* (1641), Beaumont and Fletcher's
Comedies and Tragedies (1647), and Suckling's *Last Remains* (1659). That political-religious bias
is to be seen as well in the nature of the religious works he published; for instance, in a list
of 1650–51, included in the British Library copy of Robert Stapylton's translation of Famianus
Strada's *De Bello Belgico* (shelf no. 9415.b.1), items 69 to 83 are grouped under the heading
of "Several Sermons, with Other Excellent Tracts in Divinity, Written by some most Eminent and Learned Bishops and Orthodox Divines" and include one work by someone who
turned out to be of strong Puritan tendencies (Nicholas Darnton), one by a moderate
conforming Puritan (Richard Sibbes), and the vast majority by what we might call conservative, high church figures, for instance, Donne, Andrewes, Bishop Arthur Lake, Edmund
Reeve, Thomas Reeve, etc.

the preface), letters and poems of praise from Milton's Italian friends, and a dedicatory letter, again for *Comus,* from Henry Lawes to Viscount Brackley, heir apparent to the earl of Bridgewater. It is possible of course that Milton originally volunteered such letters without any prompting, but they look more like responses on Milton's part to requests for such items by Moseley; or if not that, in view of the fashionable appeal of Moseley's other volumes, what Milton assumed Moseley and his projected readers would like to see gracing the pages of a Moseley volume.

Warren Chernaik has suggested rather wittily that in the 1645 *Poems,* Moseley kidnapped Milton and made a royalist out of him, much against the poet's will.[24] Richard Helgerson earlier pointed to the similar way in which Milton's, Carew's, and Shirley's volumes of poems appear next to each other in Moseley's book lists and with virtually the same title, variations upon *Poems with a Masque.*[25] We are informed on the title-page of Milton's *Poems* that "Mr. Henry Lawes, Gentleman of the Kings Chappel, and One of His Maiesties Private Musick," set the songs to music, and we are given similar information on the title-pages of the works of Waller, Carew, and William Cartwright as well, and on the second title-page of Suckling's *Fragmenta Aurea.* We know from the Greek verse added at the bottom of the frontispiece of his *Poems* that Milton did not think highly of William Marshall's artistry; Moseley on the other hand evidently did, since Marshall's engraved portraits appear as frontispieces for the poems of Milton, Shirley, and Suckling, and for prose works of Robert Stapylton, Edmund Gregory, and no doubt others. The works of Milton, Waller, Carew, Shirley, Suckling, and Cartwright are by these various means made to look like part of a series: Moseley's English Poets. Marshall even succeeded in making Milton and Shirley *look* alike. We know nothing at all of possible payments Moseley might have made to his various authors, but what his prefaces, his standardized format and frontispieces, and his various appeals to a common (and mainly royalist) audience did was to make these authors *his* authors.

What happened in the move from Humphrey Moseley to Samuel Simmons was that Milton the poet gained greater leverage in his dealings with his representative in the marketplace, a change which is epito-

[24] Chernaik, "Books as Memorials: The Politics of Consolation," *Yearbook of English Studies* 21 (1991): 210.

[25] Helgerson, *Self-Crowned Laureates: Spenser, Jonson, Milton, and the Literary System* (Berkeley: Univ. of California Press, 1983), 272.

mized by a contract guaranteeing Milton recompense and rights in his manuscript. And this greater leverage marks the emergence of Milton as a rather new kind of author in a newly developing market-oriented literary system. The very same critics and biographers who, I would argue, misread the contract Milton signed with Simmons help us to see that. In 1725 Elijah Fenton complained about the small sum *Paradise Lost* brought its author: "So unreasonably may personal prejudice affect the most excellent performances"; and in 1749 the future bishop Thomas Newton, discussing the conditions of the Milton-Simmons contract, narrowed the attack from one upon the age to one upon publishers, remarking "how much more do others get by the works of great authors, than the authors themselves."[26] In mounting such attacks, these writers were plainly viewing Milton as an unfairly-treated author of their own eighteenth-century sort. Despite the fact that Milton had enough inherited wealth not to *need* to make a living from his pen, and even despite the fact that his recourse to Samuel Simmons may well have been brought on by political change and his own fall from favor rather than a self-conscious assertion of political and economic independence, Milton has claim to be our earliest modern professional author.[27]

INDIANA UNIVERSITY

[26] Elijah Fenton, "Life of Milton," prefacing his edition of *Paradise Lost* (London, 1725), xxiii; Thomas Newton, "The Life of Milton," in his edition of *Paradise Lost,* 2 vols. (London, 1749), 1:xxxvii.

[27] Shortly after completing this essay, I came upon Dustin Griffin's "The Beginning of Modern Authorship: Milton and Dryden," *MQ* 24 (1990): 1–7, which is concerned with many of the same issues I have raised. Griffin argues that our definitions of authorship for the seventeenth century are not flexible enough, that we need better terms than those of amateur and professional, as used for instance by J. W. Saunders (see above, n. 21). Griffin concludes with the exhortation: "We need to pay more attention to the material circumstances of writing, and how these circumstances helped shape the way writers perceived their working world and constructed their place in it" (6). I hope that the present essay, along with Griffin's, may be seen as helping to achieve such a goal.

Janel Mueller

CONTEXTUALIZING MILTON'S NASCENT REPUBLICANISM

STUDENTS OF MILTON HAVE LATELY BEEN STRUGGLING WITH a settled critical tendency to approach him in more or less lonely eminence. We are renewing efforts to locate him within one or more of his contemporary contexts. In the process, what we take to be relevant and revealing contexts for discussing Milton are proving quite interestingly varied.[1] The challenging theoretical questions that arise from postulating a text/context relationship—for example, clarifying the nature and implications of this binary distinction, defining operative senses of "context," relating these to considerations of authorial agency and cultural determination—cannot be given anything like their due within the brief scope of the present discussion.[2] For my purposes here, I will simply assume that "context" denotes a meaning-bearing connection which can be argued to hold between a specifiable textual feature—say, a term, an articulated

---

[1] They range, notably, from Richard Helgerson's "literary system" defined by the professional constraints and opportunities that confronted successive generations of English writers (*Self-Crowned Laureates* [Berkeley: Univ. of California Press, 1983]) to Christopher Hill's notion of a coffee-house subculture that fostered a radical idea-matrix in mid-seventeenth-century London (*Milton and the English Revolution* [New York: Viking Press, 1977]).

[2] I proceed here on the assumption that certain extratextual features can manifest a bearing on the text which, if not perhaps fully self-evident, does allow of their being handled as evidence in my argument for their pertinence. However, the language of contextualizing does appear more generally vulnerable to demands that the utterance which performs the act of contextualizing should itself be contextualized (i.e., my understanding of 'evidence' and 'argument' requires its own interpretive framing and placing), thus entailing upon the method a potentially infinite regress. For thoughtful reflection on this problem, see Dominick La Capra, *Rethinking Intellectual History* (Ithaca: Cornell Univ. Press, 1983), chap. 2.

concept, a rhetorical or polemical stance—and discourses in circulation, other texts known to be accessible to the author while writing, or events in train at the time the text was being written. I realize that I run a risk by contextualizing on such a heuristic basis, but I am willing to do so because it permits me to apply my attention on another front. This is the matter of our quite complacent sense, overall, of Milton as a figure in intellectual history. While we have recently been doing more to contextualize Milton, we have held to a sense that we already have the larger picture of his religious or political or social thought, and that attending to contexts may refine our grasp of details but probably not any basics of interpretation. In what follows I hope to contribute to the surprise as well as the enterprise of contextualizing Milton by bringing some pressures of discursive and experiential connections to bear on our standing assumptions about him as a political thinker.

Milton is typically recognized as robust, fearless, and independent-minded, but nonetheless both unoriginal and reactive in his political thought—possessed of excellent reflexes perhaps, but still reactive. The evolutionary narrative that we owe largely to Arthur Barker, Don Wolfe, and the prefaces to the Yale edition of the prose categorizes him as some kind of monarchist, though never a divine-rightist, from the beginning of his prose writings right up to January 1649.[3] Then, in writing *Tenure of Kings and Magistrates,* Milton—so the stock tale runs—first showed his colors as a republican. This self-identification is traced to the ringing words in which Milton declares it

> manifest that the power of Kings and Magistrates is nothing
> else, but what is only derivative, transferr'd, and committed to
> them in trust from the People, to the Common good of them
> all, in whom the power yet remaines fundamentally, and
> cannot be tak'n from them, without a violation of thir natural
> birthright.... And indeed ... since the King or Magistrate
> holds his autoritie of the people, both originaly and naturally
> for their good in the first place, and not his own, then may the
> people as oft as they shall judge it for the best, either choose

---

[3] Arthur Barker, *Milton and the Puritan Dilemma, 1641–1660* (Toronto: Univ. of Toronto Press, 1942; repr. 1956); Don M. Wolfe, *Milton in the Puritan Revolution* (New York and London: Nelson, 1941; repr. 1963); Don M. Wolfe, gen. ed., *Complete Prose Works of John Milton,* 8 vols. (New Haven: Yale Univ. Press, 1953–82), hereafter cited as CPW with volume and page number placed in parentheses after the quoted text.

him or reject him, retaine him or depose him though no Tyrant, meerly by the liberty and right of free born Men, to be
govern'd as seems to them best. (CPW 3:202, 206)

Such an identification quite straightforwardly contextualizes the term
"republican" by defining it in the increasingly well understood and current mid-seventeenth-century English sense of an advocate for parliamentary supremacy in government.[4] But we then proceed to insert this
identification into a picture of a reactively political Milton who, upon
witnessing the civil war and the Rump's trial and conviction of Charles
I on capital charges, shifted from king to Parliament the locus of sovereignty in the mixed polity of the English state.

I want to contest this picture on two counts: (1) the date and (2)
the circumstances of Milton's first manifestation of republicanism in his
published writing. By "Milton's republicanism" I too will always mean
his vesting of supreme political authority in Parliament. My dual challenge is staked on a single salient stretch of text—a passage from *Of Reformation,* Milton's first antiprelatical tract, published in May 1641. But
the significance of the challenge broadens considerably by way of the contexts that can be sketched for this passage. In this regard let me acknowledge at the outset the invaluable help I have received from a study that I
cite frequently, Michael Mendle's *Dangerous Positions.*[5] When the passage
I have targeted in *Of Reformation* is contextualized within what may be
called the discourse of the estates in sixteenth- and earlier seventeenth-
century England and Scotland, it raises political implications that are new,
I believe, in regard to Milton. At least I know of no Milton scholarship
that addresses them.[6] These implications locate Milton in the forefront,
not in the wake, of a nascent English republicanism for England, and they

---

[4] Pertinent literature on this topic abounds. See especially chaps. 11 and 12, both of
which bear the title "The Anglicization of the Republic," in J. G. A. Pocock's *The Machiavel-
lian Moment: Florentine Political Thought and the Atlantic Republican Tradition* (Princeton:
Princeton Univ. Press, 1975).

[5] Michael Mendle, *Dangerous Positions: Mixed Government, the Estates of the Realm, and the
Making of the "Answer to the xix propositions"* (University: Univ. of Alabama Press, 1985).
Subsequent references, abbreviated "Mendle," are incorporated parenthetically within my
text.

[6] I include my own discussion in "Embodying Glory: The Apocalyptic Strain in Milton's
Of Reformation," in David Loewenstein and James Grantham Turner, eds., *Politics, Poetics, and
Hermeneutics in Milton's Prose* (Cambridge: Cambridge Univ. Press, 1990), 30–33, which
predates the understanding of Milton's passage that I develop here.

do so by evoking in turn a context of events that predate by a considerable stretch the king's execution and the advent of the English Commonwealth.

My focal passage from *Of Reformation* picks up with the positive turn that Milton finally gives to his attack on the institution of episcopacy and the abuses of both spiritual and temporal power that bishops have committed through the ages down to the immediate present in England. This positive turn takes the form of an answer to a linked pair of anticipated (though rhetorically long deferred) questions in the tract. What would be so good about an England rid of its bishops? What would such an England look like? Milton undertakes to answer both questions at once in this extended passage:

> Because things simply pure are inconsistent in the masse of nature, nor are the elements or humors in Mans Body exactly *homogeneall*, ... the best founded Common-wealths ... have aym'd at a certaine mixture and temperament, partaking the severall vertues of each other State. ...
>
> There is no Civill *Government* that hath beene known, no not the *Spartan*, not the *Roman* ... more divinely and harmoniously tun'd, more equally ballanc'd as it were by the hand and scale of Justice, then is the Common-wealth of *England*: where under a free, and untutor'd *Monarch*, the noblest, worthiest, and most prudent men, with full approbation, and suffrage of the People have in their power the supreme, and finall determination of highest Affaires. Now if Conformity of Church *Discipline* to the Civill be so desir'd, there can be nothing more parallel, more uniform, then when under the Soveraigne Prince *Christs Vicegerent* using the *Scepter* of *David*, according to *Gods Law*, the *godliest*, the *wisest*, the *learnedest* Ministers in their severall charges have the instructing and disciplining of *Gods people* by whose full and free Election they are consecrated to that holy and equall *Aristocracy*. And why should not the Piety, and Conscience of *Englishmen* as members of the Church be trusted in the Election of Pastors to Functions that nothing concerne a *Monarch*, as well as their worldly wisedomes are priviledg'd as *members* of the *State* in suffraging their Knights, and Burgesses to matters that concern him neerely? ... What a blindnesse to thinke that what is already Evangelicall as it were by a happy chance in our *Politie*, should be repugnant to that which is the same by divine com-

mand in the Ministery? Thus then wee see that our Ecclesiall, and Politicall choyses may consent and sort as well together without any rupture in the STATE, as Christians, and Freeholders. (CPW 1: 599–600)

I begin contextualizing by noting that the vocabulary of "a certaine mixture," "each other State," and "the Common-wealth of England" in this passage identifies England as a mixed state compounded of so-called estates. By Milton's time the senses of the term "estate" had become highly charged. In England as in Europe, the older, general, and deepest-lying sense was that of a constituent order of society, as in the three estates: those who fight, those who work, those who pray.[7] In a more specific and more recent sense, one going back to sixteenth-century humanists and protestants who construed the government of Henry's or Edward's or Elizabeth's England as that of the king- (or queen-) in-Parliament, the "states" or "estates" were those political entities out of which their own mixed state was compounded: the king, the Lords, the Commons.

The immediately pertinent fact about this Miltonic passage, printed in May 1641, is that public discussion of the estates in England had been prohibited as treasonous since 1606, early in James's reign, and that the subject of the estates had indeed all but vanished from English political discourse until 1640 (Mendle, 111). In that year, not the treason ordinance but the climate changed with the convening of the Short and then the Long Parliament in the immediate aftermath of the Bishops' Wars waged by Laud and Charles in Scotland. Viewed, then, in temporal context, Milton cannot be said to be merely joining current "root-and-branch" agitation in the estates passage of *Of Reformation*. He has put himself in the vanguard of those addressing long forbidden questions linking the composition of English society with the government of the English state. Here, then, is a risky step taken in public by this new participant in the hyperactivity of current polemical pamphleteering, one in which political self-consciousness combines daring with circumspec-

---

[7] The importance of the estates as cultural categories has been argued by Georges Dumézil in "L'idéologie des trois fonctions dans les épopées des peuples indo-européens," part I of his *Mythe et épopée* (Paris: Gallimard, 1968), by Jacques LeGoff in *Pour un autre Moyen Age: Temps, travail et culture en Occident*, trans. Arthur Goldhammer as *Time, Work and Culture in the Middle Ages* (Chicago: Univ. of Chicago Press, 1982), and by Georges Duby in *Trois Ordres*, trans. Arthur Goldhammer as *The Three Orders: Feudal Society Imagined* (Chicago: Univ. of Chicago Press, 1990).

tion. Milton does not put his name to what he says in *Of Reformation*.

The sense of Milton's political self-consciousness intensifies, moreover, when account is taken of the textual echoes that link the foregoing passage to two contiguous entries under the heading KING in his *Commonplace Book,* compiled mostly between 1640 and 1644 to fill out a core of material collected between 1631 and 1639.[8] Both entries, from Sir Thomas Smith's *De republica Anglorum* (1565, published 1583), are deliberations on the scope and definition of kingship in language more explicit than that of the passage from *Of Reformation* yet exactly of a piece with it in key vocabulary and concepts. Identical in the first entry are the mixed elements in nature and commonwealth that prevent a king's power from being "pure," that is, absolute; identical in the second entry are the people's good will as a condition on rule and the people's well-being as the concern that will uniformly characterize a king (thus distinguishing the king from the tyrant):

> whether monarchy be a power absolute. Sr Tho. Smith answereth. that neither it nor any other kind of common wealth is pure an absolute in his kind, no more then the elements are pure in nature, or the complexions, and temperatures in a body but mixt with other, "for that nature ... will not suffer it." com-wealth Eng. c[hapter] 6 and in the 9 c[hapter] that the act of a k. "neither approved by the people, nor establisht by act of parliament" is "taken for nothing either to bind the k., his successors, or his subjects."
>
> ....
>
> definition of Sr Tho. Smith is. "A K. is who by succession or election commeth with good will of the people to his goverment, and doth administer the com-welth by the laws of the same and by equity, and doth seeke the profit of the people as his owne." and on the contrarie, "he that coms by force, breaks laws at his pleasure, maks other without consent of the people, and regardeth not the wealth of the commons, but the advancement of himselfe, his faction, and his kindred" he defines for a tyrant. c[hapter] 7. See Arist. eth. [Book] 9. c[hapter] 10. "The tyrant seeks what benefits himself, the king what benefits his subjects." (CPW 1:442, 443)

---

[8] Thus Ruth Mohl ranks and dates the two principal periods of Milton's activity in compiling his *Commonplace Book* (CPW 1:348–49).

In turn, as cued by the Aristotle citation in the excerpt above, the intertextual link to the *Nicomachean Ethics* and to thematically consonant passages in the *Politics* points to the intense Renaissance interest in these works as sources for political theory—a further context that had an energizing influence on the discourse of estates. Aristotle analogized between the human body and the body politic, claiming that health in both cases resulted from a mixture of discrete elements that tempered extremes. In the case of the body politic, the discrete elements were the One, the Few, and the Many, which, if allowed to run to any single extreme, could respectively end in the diseases—the unjust conditions—of tyranny, oligarchy, or mob rule. Milton's physiological terminology and his reference to "*Spartan . . . Civill Government*" bespeak this Aristotelian connection. Aristotle's formulations, moreover, occasioned the recurrent volatility of Renaissance estates discourse: its easy slippage from a descriptive *is* to a normative *should* in describing the constitution of a political order and its straightforward treatment of all the elements as being of equal standing. Just such slippage is evident in the concepts and terms that link the *Of Reformation* passage with the Smith excerpts in Milton's *Commonplace Book*. It is easy to see that such language collides head-on with absolutist or divine-right conceptions of monarchy, and indeed this was a major reason for James's ban on it. The royal prerogative was ranked among the estates instead of being set over and above them, the king complained in his *Basilikon Doron,* published in Scotland in 1598 and in England in 1603 (Mendle, 94, 107). Accordingly, Don Wolfe's footnote to my quotation from *Of Reformation* remarks on "Milton's implicit rejection of divine right in this passage" (CPW 1: 599). In fact, this rejection is hardly implicit.

By May 1641, the publication date of *Of Reformation,* the volatility of the language of estates had heightened well beyond the mere denial of divine-right monarchy. The gradual but inexorable process by which this language became volatile is mainly a Scottish rather than an English story until its final chapters. By and large, earlier sixteenth-century English writers, ranging from Sir Thomas Elyot in *The Book of the Governor* (1531) to William Harrison in the prefatory "Description of England" contributed to Holinshed's *Chronicles* (1577) to Smith in *De republica Anglorum,* tapped into this language for laudatory purposes and applied it in glowing generalities. They wrote of a mixed state composed of a triad of monarch, lords, and commons that had insured good order and political well-being in England since time immemorial. Since these writers envisioned no jostling whatever for supremacy in their early discourse of the estates, there is also no evidence whatever that this discourse was repugnant to the English Crown (Mendle, 42–59). When these writers did on occasion use the term "supremacy," they applied it not to the increasingly powerful legislative function of Parliament under the Tudors but rather to its time-honored judicial function, and they meant by it "the court of last resort, the place of highest appeal" from any other of the realm.[9]

In the 1570s and 1580s the laudatory glow began to fade from estates language in England when Presbyterians like Walter Travers and Thomas Cartwright applied it to the analysis of church rather than civil government. They equated the normatively balanced and healthily mixed state with the Calvinist system they sought to impose upon the Church of England: in their formulation, the constituent elements were Christ as king, an aristocracy of ministers and lay ruling elders, and a democracy of membership in a congregation. Cartwright also took the further portentous step of analogizing explicitly to the civil estates of the English polity from the prescriptive form of church government that he found laid down in scripture. "The church," he wrote in his *Reply* to John Whitgift's *Answer to the Admonition* (1574),

> is governed with that kinde of government whiche the Philos-
> ophers that wryte of the best common wealthes affirme to be
> best. For in respecte of Christe the heade, it is a Monarchie;
> and in respecte of the auncientes [elders] and pastoures that
> govern in common and wyth like authoritie amongste them
> selves, it is an Aristocratie, or the rule of the best men; and, in
> respect that the people are not secluded but have their interest
> in churche matters, it is a Democratie, or a populare estate....
> An image whereof appeareth also in the pollicie of thys realme,
> for, as in respect of the Queene hir majestie, it is a Monarchie,
> so in respect of her most honorable councill, it is an
> Aristocratie; and having regarde to the Parliament, whych is
> assembled of all estates, it is a Democratie.[10]

---

[9] Charles H. McIlwain, *The High Court of Parliament and Its Supremacy* (New Haven: Yale Univ. Press, 1910), 119–37.

[10] Thomas Cartwright, *A Replye to an Answere made of M. Doctor Whitgifte, agaynste the Admontion to the Parliament* (London, 1574), 35. For discussion, see Brian Manning, "Puritanism and Democracy, 1640–1642," in *Puritans and Revolutionaries: Essays in Seventeenth-Century History Presented to Christopher Hill*, ed. Donald Pennington and Keith Thomas (Ox-

Cartwright provides an excellent example of just how volatile English estates language both could get and would not get, so long as it was confined within a purely English frame of reference. On the one hand, Cartwright would incur Whitgift's vehement reproaches for a claim he couched in a long-remembered image, that the civil order ought to match the ecclesiastical order "even as the hangings to the house" (Mendle, 67). In the passage I have just quoted, by contrast, Cartwright clearly skirts any revisionary implications regarding the status quo of governance in Elizabethan England: he refers blandly to "the Parliament . . . assembled of all estates" (who are further unparticularized), to the queen's council, and to the queen's majesty. This last reference to the queen might even be read as consistent with divine right, since it functions as the target term in an analogy whose source term is "Christ the head."

But such neatly equivocal suspension would not characterize key references in English estates language much longer. Nor would the concept of Parliament's supremacy much longer remain limited to its judicial powers without extension to its legislative powers. In 1587 this language was stretched to an extreme by Job Throckmorton (the likeliest author of the Marprelate pamphlets) in a series of three speeches in the House of Commons urging the execution of Mary Queen of Scots. Denying that such action should be left to princes, Throckmorton contended that the action properly lay with Parliament, which he immediately identified with the lower house that he was addressing. "Under warrant of God's law what may not this house do?" he demanded of his fellow members in Commons. "I mean the three estates of the land," he continued. "To deny the power of this house, you know is treason. . . . The thing is lawful to be done, and this house hath absolute power to do it" (quoted in Mendle, 76). That a Scottish issue triggered Throckmorton's ascription of "absolute power" not to the English Crown but to Parliament—and specifically to the House of Commons— would prove, in the event, far from fortuitous.

For it was in later sixteenth-century Scotland that the discourse of the estates solidified the radical connotations that made it anathema to the James VI who would become England's James I. Two singular features of the Scottish context conduced to this radicalization. First, unlike the two houses of England, the Lords and Commons, Scotland had a unicameral Parliament that was itself conceived as an assembly of the three traditional estates under the king. The three Scottish estates were understood to comprise, respectively, the bishops and abbots; the higher and lower nobility—that is, the barons and shire commissioners; and the representatives of the city and town corporations—that is, the burgh commissioners (Mendle, 68). Notably the king himself did not figure as an estate in the Scottish conceptual scheme. (Thus Throckmorton's startling identification of the power of the estates with the House of Commons is most plausibly explained, it seems to me, as an importation by this English Calvinist of the peculiar Scottish sense of the term "estates"—namely, a unicameral Parliament.)

Secondly, the strength of Presbyterianism in Scotland by 1574 gave ascendancy to the militant James Melville and his theory of the two kingdoms, for which there was no English counterpart at this period. In his widely adopted *Second Book of Discipline* (1578), Melville drew a strict institutional divide between state and church: the king and other great personages would have no special voice in the kirk, while the clergy and elders, the officers of the Presbyterian polity, would have nothing to do with the state. One increasingly strongly spelled-out implication of Melvillean Presbyterianism, however, was to eliminate bishops both as ecclesiastical and as political entities: as they could find no legitimation as an estate separate from ministers in the church order, so they could have no legitimate claim to parliamentary membership among the Scottish estates. Forced to bear with these developments during his minority, James VI ultimately sought to check them in the so-called Black Acts of 1584, which made it treason to attack or in any way "impugn" the traditional estates of the realm (Mendle, 68–75). In defining this capital offense James simultaneously took action on his own behalf, laying claim to something like the English royal supremacy in state and church, and took action on behalf of the bishops, reaffirming their civil and ecclesiastical place (which they now directly owed to royal behest).

In due course this originally Scottish linkage between the king's supremacy over the estates and the king's guarantee of the bishops as a parliamentary estate was extended to England in the remark ascribed to James at the Hampton Court Conference of 1604: "No bishop, no king." It was here that the issues and the ideology pretty much stood still—blocked under Charles as well as James—until Laud's campaign to impose conformity to the English prayer book in Scotland triggered the swearing there of the National Covenant against popery and superstition in 1638 and the upheaval that brought Milton back from the continent in 1639. Agitation in Scotland reopened the question of the estates, particularly when the Glasgow General Assembly proclaimed itself the supreme religious authority, as the Scottish Parliament was the civil authority, and did away with the institution of episcopacy in late 1638. Melville's two-kingdoms theory revived with this abrupt translation into practice, and with it also revived the smouldering issues of the identity and political entitlement of the Scottish estates. The Edinburgh Parliament of 1639–1640 declared its mind despite a six-month prorogation engineered by Charles: the "true estates" of Scotland for the purposes of constituting Parliament were the nobles, barons, and burgesses (Mendle, 115–22).

In contrast to Scotland, in England it remained axiomatic that the king was to be counted as one of the estates. In April 1640 the Short Parliament took up the now fiercely politicized debate over the three estates and their parliamentary representation. The House of Lords resolved that the bishops held place there as lords temporal, just like the other lords; in no case did the bishops figure as a separate (ecclesiastical) estate. The upper house recorded its resolution with this significant comment: "There is the king, the barons, the commons; the bishops then would make four states, or exclude the king" (cited in Mendle, 127). The Lords' rhetoric on this occasion dispensed with one of the most venerable props of medieval social theory, representing what they had done as an elementary and self-evident piece of arithmetic. They denied the ancient rights of the clergy as a political estate in order to keep the king in the count—but at the additional cost to the king of being at best *primus inter pares,* the highest among the three estates.

Henry Parker, the leading political pamphleteer of the parliamentary cause in 1640–1642, took the rapidly advancing debate over the estates to a wider audience in *The Case of Shipmoney* (1640). In the furor over whether the king could impose tonnage and poundage and other arbitrary taxes for the upkeep of the army and navy without Parliament's consent, Parker saw a new crisis but an old and specifically English struggle. Other countries have monarchs of diverse kinds and powers, but the royal prerogative in England is limited by laws and charters which have been obtained through a long and sometimes bloody history of resistance to encroachments by the Crown. "Though the king is the highest civil officer, bound to act in time of national danger, he is by right neither the sole judge of danger nor the means of combating it. If the nation needs ship money to meet an emergency, the king should have the advice and consent of Parliament."[11] Parker's tract enlarges at length on the fallibility of previous English kings and on the danger of tyranny when a king sets himself up as "a controlling power over all Law, and knowes no bounds but [his] owne will." In the situation at hand he decries the malignant influence of the bishops (the Laudian party) as royal counsellors, denying that they can have any true claim to representation in Parliament. The bishops, says Parker, have confirmed their place among those "noted factions" who remain both "adverse to parliaments" and "hateful to parliaments": "the papists, the prelates, and court parasites." He warns Charles against "that mischiefe which makes all mischiefes irremediable, and almost hopelesse in England at this day, ... that Parliaments are clouded, and disused, and suffered to be calumniated by the ill boding incendiaries of our State."[12] If the English Parliament were to fight in defense of its powers, this in Parker's opinion would accord with the "custome of all Europe almost," since "for the most part now adayes the world is given to republistes, or to conditionate and restrained forms of government."[13] In this openly republican vein Parker appears to be going beyond any warrant provided by his English context alone.[14] Accordingly, *The Case of Shipmoney* retells from Livy Menenius's fable of the belly in a fashion that situates the king a good deal less gloriously than as the head of the body politic.

For the enterprise of contextualizing, there are important thematic and formal anticipations of Milton's *Of Reformation* to be found in this tract of Parker's from the preceding year. Broader correspondences between the two works include the rehearsal of material from English constitutional history to point the moral of safeguarding rights by limiting royal prerogative, the use of the fable of the belly to emphasize this moral, and the structuring of a sustained *ad hominem* attack on the bishops under tripartite headings—respectively, Milton's "Antiquitarian," "Libertine," and "Polititian" prelates, and Parker's prelates, parasites, and court flatterers who hate and are hated by Parliament. Most significantly

---

[11] Don M. Wolfe summarizing Parker's tract (Introduction, CPW 1:59).

[12] [Henry Parker], *The Case of Shipmony Briefly Discoursed, According to the Grounds of Law, Policie, and Conscience. And most humbly presented to the Censure and Correction of the High Court of Parliament, Nov. 3. 1640* (London, 1640), 38–39.

[13] *The Case of Shipmony*, 37, 7.

[14] Mendle, 131, hints at the influence of Virgilio Malvezzi, from whose *Romulus and Tarquin* Parker made a large unacknowledged borrowing in his next pamphlet of 1641.

CONTEXTUALIZING MILTON'S NASCENT REPUBLICANISM 275

of all, both Parker and Milton ascribe supremacy to Parliamentary government at the expense of kingly power. But at this point the dynamics
of the two texts begin to contrast. While Parker is content to multiply
his warnings to Charles, remaining inexplicit about how kingly power
accommodates institutionally to the supremacy of Parliament, he is explicit about the kind of government this is, "republiste." Milton does
not voice his republicanism as such, but the implications of the language
he uses in the representation of the English political order which he develops both in its own terms and on analogy with an English Presbyterian
ecclesiastical order can end only in republicanism as defined at that time.

Let us return for a closer look at the language of the focal passage
from *Of Reformation*. The first thing to notice is that Milton considers
the estates in the larger of their two senses as the constituents of English
society, not merely as the elements of the English form of government.
That Milton is working with "estates" in this larger sense is confirmed
by the analogy he proposes with the national church as an alternatively
all-inclusive organization of English society: as here the people entrust
their governance to an elected Parliament, so there the people will
entrust their governance to their elected ministers. Parliamentary governance—"the supreame, and finall determination of highest Affaires"—is
conducted "under a free, and untutor'd *Monarch*" but significantly not by
him. Milton minces no words in specifying that "supreame" power to
govern devolves on "the noblest, worthiest, and most prudent men" as
conferred "with full approbation and suffrage of the People." Because
the local discursive context is the entire body politic, the "estates" in
their inclusive sense, these specifications must be serving to enlarge on
Milton's understanding of the "certaine mixture and temperament" that
characterizes "the best founded Common-wealths," "partaking the
severall vertues of each other State." In England's true and proper form
of government, the rule of the Few (a supreme Parliament) moderates
and mediates between the One (the monarch) and the Many (the people
whose representatives Parliament is). The trace elements of Aristotelian
political reasoning in this formulation, as in the *Commonplace Book*
excerpts from Smith that lie behind this passage, are both revelatory and
characteristic of the humanist connections that show recurrently in the
texture of Milton's polemical prose.

But what is Milton saying or implying about the role of the king as
"a free, and untutor'd *Monarch*" in such a mixed polity? At this juncture
my contextualizing can avail itself of the recent computer-produced
Concordance to Milton's Prose, which enables "free" and "untutor'd" to be

defined by comparison with other occurrences in the early tracts. "Free" occurs abundantly throughout these and later tracts, thirteen times in *Of Reformation* alone, where its connotations run predominantly to the negative sense of freedom from someone or something that controls, hinders, or binds the exercise of some faculty or option. "Untutor'd" has only one other occurrence in Milton; both connote a lack of surveillance or supervision, good in *Of Reformation,* bad in *Of Education.*[15] Moving from the paradigmatic axis of definition to the syntagmatic axis of the words "free, and untutor'd" in their *Of Reformation* context, we can infer without difficulty that Milton images an English king free from the inveiglements of Laud, the bishops, and other evil counsellors. Given his extreme virulence in this tract against evil counsellors to Charles and other English kings, I think it possible that Milton envisages a king without a Privy Council—or without a *Stuart* Privy Council whose workings, legislative in their contribution to royal proclamations and judicial in the proceedings of Star Chamber, so directly challenged Parliament's exercise of its legislative and judicial powers. But, if Milton's monarch is freed from vicious and vitiating associates, is there anything he is left free to do? What positive powers might be left in 1641 for a king to whom not only an absolute prerogative has been denied but under whom "the supreme, and finall determination of highest Affaires" has been accorded to Parliament?

Milton does not expressly declare himself on this question, but there is an answer to be pieced out of two of the contexts that I have claimed for this passage. One such context is the definition of a king in the second of the excerpts from Smith in the *Commonplace Book,* as one "who by succession or election commeth with good will of the people to his goverment, and doth administer the com-welth by the laws of the same and by equity, and doth seeke the profit of the people as his owne." In copying out and reechoing Smith, Milton by implication credits the king with an administrative role, that of equitable enforcement of the laws, and apparently also with a kind of executive role, that of seeking the people's well-being as he would his own. (We recall that this same feature makes for the definitional contrast between a king and a tyrant.) I say "a kind of executive role" because nothing here is specified enough to point toward the eventual, later modern conception

---

[15] *A Concordance to the English Prose of John Milton,* ed. Laurence Sterne and Harold H. Kollmeier (Binghamton, N.Y.: Medieval & Renaissance Texts & Studies, 1985), 525, 1398–99.

of an executive power—the authority to act in cases for which legislation has not provided, because of loopholes or unforeseen emergencies, and in circumstances that cannot await the due process of the courts or the due assembly of a legislative body summoned into session. What Milton surely does not credit to the king are the earlier modern analogues of executive power: enforcing a royal proclamation without legislative warrant or dispensing with the force of some law (residual in our notion of "executive clemency").[16] The former of these was exactly what made ship money a *cause celèbre,* the latter was just then emerging as a null choice in the trial and capital sentencing of Charles's intimate, the earl of Strafford.

The other context that bears on answering the question of the role Milton envisages for the king is the analogy between civil and ecclesiastical institutions that this passage proceeds to develop. In the church "there can be nothing more parallel, more uniform, then when under"—again, that preposition "under"—"the Soveraigne Prince *Christs* Vicegerent using the *Scepter* of *David,* according to *Gods Law,* the *godliest,* the *wisest,* the *learnedest* Ministers in their severall charges have the instructing and disciplining of *Gods people* by whose full and free Election they are consecrated to that holy and equall *Aristocracy.*" The king here, once again, has a clear and clearly limited administrative role: to use his scepter according to God's law. Like "the supreame, and finall determination of highest Affaires" which is in the power of Parliament, "the instructing and disciplining of *Gods people*" are immediately specified as "Functions that nothing concern a *Monarch.*" Milton's appositives make a further point: "the Soveraigne Prince *Christs* Vicegerent" is sovereign insofar as he is a place-holder, a figurehead for Christ, who is the Church's real head.

Taken altogether, Milton's eulogizing of the English constitution, his reckoning of the king among the estates, and his assertion of parliamentary supremacy combine to place him not only in an identifiably English line of estates discourse but, more precisely, on a trajectory of nascent republicanism that Parker a year earlier had declared the coming European thing. As with Throckmorton's strikingly early (and, in his case, isolated) access to republican language through ostensibly Scottish connections, Milton's location with regard to the Scottish line of estates discourse is too complex a question to be handled adequately here. I

---

[16] See McIlwain, 318–20, for pertinent historical commentary.

can, however, note certain differences and similarities. The emphatic prominence of the analogy which Milton sustains between the English body politic and the English body ecclesiastic in this passage from *Of Reformation* declares him no adherent—not, at least, in May 1641—of Melville's two-kingdoms theory. The pointed directionality of this same Miltonic analogy—which credits the English state with realizing norms that still await realization in the English church—also sets him apart from all of the Presbyterian clergy, Scottish and English, who address the organization of church and state. These Presbyterian clergy always argue from the opposite direction for Calvinist theocracy by positing church government and their own clerical roles as both primary and paradigmatic. Milton's is an emphatically lay perspective within estates discourse, as lay as it is Parliamentary. However, in this regard, *Of Reformation* evinces a strain that passed quickly and enthusiastically from Scotland to England; Mendle (115) refers to the "menacing laicism" that had come to characterize the Presbyterian movement in 1638–1641.

As we have already seen, the "People" in Milton's *Of Reformation* passage are not to be identified with the House of Commons, as in the English tradition of estates discourse, but rather with the citizen electorate, as in the Scottish tradition. Nevertheless, he departs from the Scottish tradition's emphasis on popular sovereignty. Milton's own emphasis falls on the *"Aristocracy"* of the ministry "by full and free Election ... of *Gods people"* in an ostensibly Presbyterian church polity and on "the supreame, and finall determination of highest Affaires" exercised by "the noblest, worthiest, and most prudent men, with full approbation, and suffrage of the People"—that is, on the parliamentary sovereignty that makes him a definitional instance of an English republican. Even so, the Miltonic character given the English Parliament appears oddly unitary. Does the unicameral Scottish Parliament stand behind this eulogistic representation of the English Parliament with what, in Milton's eyes, is a more ideal form? Although the possibility cannot be ruled out (I know of no direct evidence either way), I do not incline to this explanation for the character of the English Parliament that Milton presents in May 1641. At this point I propose to contextualize in a different line, by moving from books and ideas to the action in the London streets and on the floor of Parliament as Milton was writing *Of Reformation*.

April and May of 1641 saw the earl of Strafford's trial, the bishops' exclusion bill in both houses of Parliament, and the introduction of the root-and-branch bill in the Commons. By that turbulent time, crowd politics had become an established feature of the Westminster scene. Equally well established, so it seemed, was the tendency of these street demonstrations to focus narrowly on religious and ecclesiastical issues. However, April and May 1641 witnessed a significant redirection of the focus of crowd politics, in threats and pressure aimed at Queen Henrietta Maria, at her visiting mother, Marie de Médicis, and at the House of Lords. People massed outside the royal residence at St. James's; riots that claimed two lives broke out in that vicinity on 11 and 18 May, while the latter day also saw a hysterical millenarian libel posted near the Parliament, which the Lords interpreted as a threat of violence to the bishops who were then still in their midst. The Lords decided in advance for adjournment if they could not get assurances that the crowds would be controlled. But when the upper house appealed to the Commons for assistance, they received a studiously guarded response. The Commons appointed two of its most radical members, Henry Martin and Arthur Goodwin, to confer with the Lords. Martin's and Goodwin's message was that the Commons were uncertain about being able to suppress the tumults in the vicinity of Charles's French Catholic queen and mother-in-law and thus thought it best if the latter left England as the crowds demanded, for the good subjects' "jealousies" about her popish entourage were well founded. The Commons themselves also applied continuous pressure on the Lords throughout May to vote to exclude the bishops from their parliamentary seats, exhorting the upper house to what the lower house termed "good correspondency"—that is, agreement with the Commons and by implication, if inchoately, with their far more numerous constituency in the London streets (Mendle, 156–58, 163).

I suggest that the events and proceedings that center in the agency of the House of Commons in May 1641 serve as contextual referents for the idealized character of the Parliament in *Of Reformation,* published by Milton late that same month. The lower house can be heralded in the contemporary London context of that date as a body of "the noblest, worthiest, and most prudent men" who indeed seem to "have in their power the supreame, and finall determination of highest Affaires" as well as the "full approbation, and suffrage of the People." However, even if my argument for Milton's self-identification as a parliamentary supremacist in May 1641 is plausible, other major questions immediately arise. When and where, for example, does Milton next confirm his republicanism? And how might his republicanism make a difference to our understanding of the polemical agendas of his prose after *Of Reformation* but prior to *Tenure of Kings and Magistrates*? I have no full answers to these important questions, but I do have some concluding remarks to offer in the direction of eventual answers.

I believe that Milton's specifications of audience and issues in his prose tracts of the 1640s will prove a more significant index to the articulation of his politics than has yet been realized. The republicanism in *Of Reformation,* addressed "To a Friend" not further identified, is explicit enough, but this republicanism also finds voice in the implicit context of a private letter. In the four subsequent antiprelatical tracts, published between July 1641 and April 1642, Milton addresses a "Reader" or "Readers" whom he sometimes credits but sometimes enjoins to be of his mind regarding Presbyterianism as both a scripturally mandated and an inherently optimal church order. In July 1641 the Lords' rejection of the Commons' bill for the exclusion of bishops from Parliament was the great topic of public interest in England. The subject here is exactly the one that, as we have seen, made Scottish estates discourse a treasonable offense. To strike at the political or ecclesiastical roots of the episcopal system was to strike hard at monarchy by curtailing the potent prerogative of creating and sustaining institutionalized extensions of royal authority—a prerogative that had seen such large advances under the Tudors. Milton's antiprelatical tracts certainly strike hard at English episcopacy, but in doing so they leave their implications for English monarchy as unspecified as they do their readership.

On the textual evidence Milton appears uncertain about the manner and degree of accommodation to be struck between the One and the Few empowered by the Many in the English context of 1641 and early 1642—or, in his now familiar phrases, how "the noblest, worthiest, and most prudent men, with full approbation, and suffrage of the People" are to "have in their power the supreme, and finall determination of highest Affaires ... under a free, and untutor'd *Monarch.*" He does, however, get clearer with himself on his own necessarily secular identity as a citizen and political writer, as attested in the famous preface to the second book of his penultimate tract against the bishops, the *Reason of Church-Government,* published in January or February of 1642.

Charles's own actions in the spring of 1642 relieved Milton of any practical necessity to theorize an accommodation between the English monarchy and the exercise of supreme power by an English Parliament. In mid-March 1642 the king, in what became a permanent removal from the capital, left Whitehall and established himself at York. Six months later, on 22 August 1642 at Nottingham, Charles divided the country into the two parties of royalists and parliamentarians by raising the standard of civil war. Effectually now, and not just by ascription, the power of "the supreame, and finall determination of highest Affaires" in England was the power of Parliament. Correspondingly, after the outbreak of civil war, Milton makes a crucial departure from his earlier unspecificity in addressing a readership. He steadily and repeatedly names Parliament as his desired readership, and he does so explicitly because Parliament has sovereign disposition of the public concerns that exercise Milton in the tracts of the mid-1640s. Although the first edition of the *Doctrine and Discipline of Divorce* (August 1643) figures as a last vestige of Milton's unspecificity in positioning himself rhetorically and politically, the second edition in February 1644 sharply reverses this course in its long prefatory address "to the Parlament of England, with the Assembly" of Divines, itself the creation of Parliament (CPW 2:222). The two subsequent divorce tracts that advocate legislative redress for the scandal of marital incompatibility—*The Judgment of Martin Bucer* (July 1644) and *Tetrachordon* (March 1645)—renew Milton's direct addresses "to the Parlament" (CPW 2:430, 578).

In the event, it is *Areopagitica* (November 1644) and not any of the divorce tracts that gives Milton's republicanism its fullest and most precise articulation in the interval between *Of Reformation* and the *Tenure of Kings and Magistrates*. In *Areopagitica* Milton not only posits a deep situational analogy between his own address to the "Lords and Commons of *England*" and Demosthenes's address to the Areopagus, which Milton styles "the Parlament of *Athens*" (CPW 2:487,489). Milton opens by specifically addressing the English Lords and Commons as "High Court of Parlament" (CPW 2:286). The contrast between the discursive specificity of this phrase in prior English contexts and its capaciousness of reference when Milton uses it in late 1644 sheds a good deal of light on the antecedents and the content of Milton's republicanism at that date. McIlwain's *The High Court of Parliament and Its Supremacy,* subtitled "an historical essay on the boundaries between legislation and adjudication in England," makes the repeated point that the earliest (fourteenth century) and most enduring use of the "High Court of Parliament" nomenclature referred to its judicial role. The oldest ascribed function of English parliaments was to resolve, at the king's behest, disputes which he entrusted to it with judgments from which there was to be no appeal. Accordingly, the earliest meaning of parliamentary supremacy was a judicial one too. In McIlwain's representation, down through the entire course of the sixteenth century and into the seventeenth, polemical writers who addressed themselves to "the high Court of Parlia-

ment"—as, for example, Thomas Wilcox and John Field do to open
their *Admonition to the Parliament* (1570), as Thomas Cartwright does to
open the *Second Admoniton* (1572), as Henry Parker does in the full title
of *The Case of Shipmoney* (see my note 12)—were invoking Parliament's
final power of judicial redress for illegal wrongs. McIlwain also concedes, however, that the English Parliament had been accruing great *de
facto* legislative powers in exactly this period, so that within a short while
after the convening of the Long Parliament it becomes impossible to
distinguish surely between judicial and legislative connotations of the
supremacy attributed in the phrase "the high Court of Parliament."
McIlwain's candidate for the pivotal text clearly attesting the transfer of
lawmaking power from the king to Parliament is William Prynne's *Soveraigne Power of Parliaments and Kingdomes* (1643), which undertakes to
justify Parliament's authority to annul any commission or proclamation
of the king, as well as its recent act depriving the king of power to
adjourn or prorogue Parliament.[17] It will be obvious how closely on
the heels of this tract of Prynne's follows Milton's own explicit ascription
of legislative supremacy to Parliament in his arguments for repeal and
reenactment of respective licensing orders in *Areopagitica* that only
recently lay within the scope of royal prerogative—that is, the power of
the now abolished Star Chamber.

   If my various approaches by way of context have succeeded in
energizing some significant aspects and implications of the passage from
Of Reformation on which I have focused attention here, we will need to
rethink and redate Milton's embrace of parliamentary supremacy in
government along with a lay position in his society as he staked his
opposition to major elements of Crown policy in the early 1640s. We
will need to redraw our picture of the political Milton and ascribe to
him more features of a vanguard revolutionary at a considerably earlier
point than we have hitherto been inclined to recognize.

UNIVERSITY OF CHICAGO

[17] Ibid., 154–55. Cf. the identical time frame proposed by Ernest Sirluck for the ascendancy of conflict over "supremacy in the state" (CPW 2:11, 130).

Achsah Guibbory

CHARLES'S PRAYERS, IDOLATROUS IMAGES, AND TRUE CREATION IN MILTON'S *EIKONOKLASTES*

THE VERY TITLE OF *EIKONOKLASTES* ANNOUNCED MILTON'S engagement in the battle over images and idolatry fought during the English Civil War. His earlier polemical prose had attacked the pagan idolatry and outward formalities of worship that Puritan reformers believed characterized the Church of England under Charles I and Laud, but *Eikonoklastes* offers Milton's most extended consideration of the problem of idolatrous images. In refuting *Eikon Basilike,* the enormously successful piece of royalist propaganda purporting to be the king's last work, Milton aligns himself with Parliament, which had ordered the destruction of all "images" and "monuments of idolatry." Milton the "iconoclast" undertakes the desecration and destruction of *The Pourtraicture of His Sacred Majestie* (as the subtitle calls the book).[1]

---

[1] See, for example, ordinances of 12 June 1643 (in John Rushworth, *Historical Collections,* vol. 5 [London, 1721], 337), 26 Aug. 1643, 9 May 1644, and 27 May 1648 (*Acts and Ordinances of the Interregnum,* ed. C. H. Firth and R. S. Rait, 2 vols. [London, 1911], 1:265–66, 425–26, 1143). On Milton's iconoclasm, see Ernest B. Gilman, *Iconoclasm and Poetry in the English Reformation: Down Went Dagon* (Chicago: Univ. of Chicago Press, 1986), chap. 6; Florence Sandler, "Icon and Iconoclast," in *Achievements of the Left Hand: Essays on the Prose of John Milton,* ed. Michael Lieb and John T. Shawcross (Amherst: Univ. of Massachusetts Press, 1974), 160–84; David Loewenstein, *Milton and the Drama of History: Historical Vision, Iconoclasm, and the Literary Imagination* (Cambridge: Cambridge Univ. Press, 1990), chap. 3; Lana Cable, "Milton's Iconoclastic Truth," in *Politics, Poetics, and Hermeneutics in Milton's Prose,* ed. David Loewenstein and James Grantham Turner (Cambridge: Cambridge Univ. Press, 1990), 135–51; and Julia M. Walker, "Eclipsing Shakespeare's Eikon: Milton's Subversion of *Richard II,*" *JEGP* 90 (1991): 51–60. On iconoclasm and the Protestant Reformation, see also John Phillips, *The Reformation of Images: Destruction of Art in England, 1535–1660* (Berkeley and Los Angeles: Univ. of California Press, 1973).

Milton's attack on idolatrous images shows how the intense religious conflict over images and ceremonial worship involved radically different understandings of history. As it responds to *Eikon Basilike* chapter by chapter, *Eikonoklastes* articulates the conflict between the "Puritan," reforming ideology, which insists on disruption and discontinuity in history, and the "Anglican" ideology, which values continuity and constructs history as a continuous, seamless whole in which the present gains its value from its connection with the past.[2] Milton, as reformer, identifies with the iconoclastic Greek emperors who disrupted the "long tradition of Idolatry in the Church ... and broke all superstitious Images to peeces," prophetically anticipating the iconoclastic acts of reformation in sixteenth- and seventeenth-century England.[3]

The Reformation distrust of images, founded on the Biblical commandment against "graven images" (Exodus 20.4–5), was directed towards pictures, statues, and spectacle, which were associated with the Roman Catholic church and worship, but it was not necessarily restricted to visual art. Words inscribed on paper could be "graven" images, for the word "graven," according to the *OED,* derived from the verb "to grave," meaning not only "to form by carving, to carve, sculpt" but also "to engrave (an inscription, figures, etc.) upon a surface," or "to engrave (a surface) with letters" (*OED* III.4 and 6). Moreover, print culture, which made multiple copies of texts available and gave them an appearance of greater physical permanence than the spoken word, intensified

---

[2] One finds this distinctively Anglican argument of continuity throughout the works of Laud and other defenders of his ceremonial worship, such as John Cosin and Peter Heylyn. The 1640 Root and Branch Petition might serve as an example of the Puritan emphasis on the necessity of disrupting the continuity of history. See Michael Walzer, *The Revolution of the Saints: A Study in the Origins of Radical Politics* (1965; repr. New York: Atheneum, 1973), for a discussion of Puritanism as "the earliest form of political radicalism" (vii), which necessitates opposition and the destruction of traditional order. Despite the well-recognized limitations of the terms "Anglican" and "Puritan," I follow historians Sears McGee (*The Godly Man in Stuart England* [New Haven: Yale Univ. Press, 1976], 9–10), John F. New (*Anglican and Puritan: The Basis of their Opposition, 1558–1640* [Stanford: Stanford Univ. Press, 1964]), and Peter Lake (*Anglicans and Puritans?* [London: Unwin Hyman, 1988], introduction) in using these terms provisionally to distinguish between two distinct ideologies.

[3] *Eikonoklastes,* in CPW 3:343. For Milton's poetry I quote from Hughes. Loewenstein, in his fine reading of *Eikonoklastes,* remarks that iconoclastic destruction of images was "tantamount to pulling down the past" (63), and rightly argues that Milton's iconoclasm expresses his dynamic sense of history and counters Charles's valorization of historical stability. See also my discussion of Milton's idea of history and his sense of the need to break with the past, in *The Map of Time* (Urbana: Univ. of Illinois Press, 1986), chap. 6.

the idolatrous potential of written texts. Milton's attack on the popular, widely disseminated *Eikon Basilike* as an "idol" reveals a keen awareness of this dangerous potential of published texts.

The conflict over images, so intense during the Civil War period, posed problems that were crucial for Milton as a poet. If the creation of graven images is potentially idolatrous, what space, if any, is left for literary art? How can one create non-idolatrous images? or distinguish between true and false ones?[4] As Thomas Corns has definitively shown, *Eikonoklastes* signals a lasting change in Milton's prose to a more sober, plainer style, a change which seems clearly tied to his Puritan distrust of images and imagination.[5] I would further argue that the terms in which Milton presents his iconoclasm and attacks the idolatrous image-making of Charles and the prelates show Milton struggling with these questions about artistic creation. Milton's text suggests tentative answers that anticipate his representation of poetic inspiration in *Paradise Lost*. Moreover, his differentiation between true and idolatrous creations constitutes a definitive rejection of the "Anglican" reading of history, with its emphasis on tradition and continuity.

Milton attacks not just the "conceited portraiture" (CPW 3:342) of William Marshall's famous frontispiece but also the text itself, the words, arguments, and prayers of *Eikon Basilike*. Refuting the royalist text chapter by chapter, Milton literally as well as symbolically breaks into pieces the verbal image of the king, fragmenting whole chapters, paragraphs, even sentences. Perhaps Milton, in his iconoclastic attack on the king's book, might be considered guilty of the very destruction of books that he had passionately warned against in *Areopagitica*:

> unlesse wariness be us'd, as good almost kill a Man as kill a good Book; who kills a Man kills a reasonable creature, Gods Image; but hee who destroyes a good Booke, kills reason it selfe, kills the Image of God, as it were in the eye. (CPW 2:492)

---

[4] Gilman discusses Milton's view of the differences between good poetic images and idols, as he surveys Milton's "agon as over the course of his career he confronts the baits and seeming pleasures of his own pictorial forms with the obligations, over and above, of writing as a militantly reforming Christian" (*Iconoclasm and Poetry,* chap. 6; quotation, 150). But more still needs to be said about Milton's discrimination between idolatrous and non-idolatrous creation.

[5] Thomas N. Corns, *The Development of Milton's Prose Style* (Oxford: Clarendon Press, 1982), 57–65.

But, as this passage itself implies, Milton believed there is a difference between good books and bad, and this crucial distinction implicitly left the door open for the destruction of "bad" books, which, lacking reason and truth, are decidedly not the image of God. Milton's defense of freedom of the press in *Areopagitica* was aimed at the attempt to license and hence regulate the publication of books. Though his arguments against pre-publication censorship could be extended to include any censorship, Milton himself insisted that, once published, a book should be judged— even, like a person, punished if it is guilty of crimes. It is necessary to "have a vigilant eye how Bookes demeane themselves, as well as men; and thereafter [after publication] to confine, imprison, and do sharpest justice on them as malefactors" (CPW 2:492). Before the Inquisition, books were freely allowed to be published but they were also held accountable: "if [a book] prov'd a Monster, who denies, but that it was justly burnt, or sunk into the Sea" (CPW 2:505). Such remarks about the legitimacy of executing judgment on books after they appear in print, which anticipate Milton's defence of the execution of Charles for tyrannical acts, suggest Milton's acceptance of the legitimacy—even necessity—of violence in the cause of truth. As he argued in *Reason of Church-Government,* the church cannot be reformed without the "fierce encounter of truth and falshood," a "violent" "jousting" which demands that idolatry in all its forms be punished and destroyed (CPW 1:796). In the holy wars of truth, the judicious reader has an obligation to sort out good and evil, to confute and destroy those books that are false, idolatrous images—if not by burning them (though Milton leaves open this possibility), certainly through the analytic power of reason.

Milton describes *Eikon Basilike* as an idol, published by the King's friends who "almost ador[e] it," admired by the "Vulgar audience" who "set it next the Bible, though otherwise containing little els but the common grounds of tyranny and popery, drest up, the better to deceiv, in a new Protestant guise, and trimly garnish'd over" (CPW 3:342, 340, 339). As these comments suggest, much of Milton's attack on Charles's book is couched in aesthetic terms.

Charles uses what Milton calls "faire and plausible words" (CPW 3:343) which, for all their external beauty, are false and hollow, disguising evil deeds and motives. Charles's "fiction" is so "smooth and cleanly" that Milton sarcastically suggests that "the whole Book might per-

haps be intended a peece of Poetrie" (CPW 3:406).[6] Charles's words
are the fair bait of art, used to catch or entice the undiscerning vulgar
"People" who are "prone ofttimes, not to a religious onely, but to a
civil kinde of Idolatry in idolizing thir Kings" (CPW 3:343). But what
Milton gives particular attention to as he "breaks into pieces" the text of
Eikon Basilike is the fact that Charles uses the words of others. Unable to
invent his own words and prayers, he resorts to borrowing them, usually
without acknowledging the debt.

The first instance occurs at the end of Charles's (and Milton's) first
chapter, where the king's "verbal Devotion" (marked by the absence of
"sutable deeds") is "model'd into the form of a privat Psalter" composed
of different pieces, "clapt together, and quilted out of Scripture" (CPW
3:360). Milton here condemns Charles's prayers as bad art, much as in
Lycidas he had described the corrupt priests as grating on "Pipes of
wretched straw" (line 124). The implication in both works is that good
prayers are also good art. Charles's religious devotions are "counterfet"
(CPW 3:361) in two senses: the piety is mere pretence, and the words,
stolen from others, are passed off as the real thing. Milton compares
Charles not only to Richard III, that "deep dissembler" of religion
(CPW 3:362), but also to the tyrant Andronicus Comnenus, who "incorporated the phrase & stile of ... [Paul] into all his familiar Letters" so
that "the imitation seem'd to vie with the Original" (CPW 3:361). But
Charles goes beyond these tyrants in impiety, using for his devotions
Pamela's prayer in Sidney's *Arcadia,* "borrowing to a Christian use
Prayers offer'd to a Heathen God" (CPW 3:362). Even Andronicus had
known to discriminate between pagan and Christian, but Charles, with
no sense of the inappropriateness, used "a Prayer stol'n word for word
from the mouth of a Heathen fiction praying to a heathen God" (362)
and "offer[ed] it to God" (CPW 3:364).[7] What I want to stress here is
not just Milton's Puritan sense of the clear division between pagan and
Christian but his indictment of Charles for literary theft.

Throughout *Eikonoklastes* Milton repeatedly attacks Charles as a

---

[6] Stevie Davies, in *Images of Kingship in "Paradise Lost"* (Columbia: Univ. of Missouri
Press, 1983), remarks that Milton attacks Charles for his "fiction" and "fraudulent imagery"
(17–18).

[7] Laud's breviary, which Milton mentions, was similarly indicted by Prynne at Laud's trial
for mingling pagan idolatry and Christian devotion (see William Prynne, *Canterburies Doome*
[London, 1646]).

plagiarist.[8] In stealing from the *Arcadia,* Charles has violated Sidney's rights: Milton insists that "every Author should have the property of his work reserved to him after death" (CPW 3:365). Charles's spiritual poverty—his inability to create his own prayers—is shown by his borrowing from others. The fact that he did not borrow from his own priests or from the church liturgy is an indictment of the poverty of their prayers as well, for both the liturgy and the prelates' "honycomb" devotions (CPW 3:366) are themselves, Milton suggests, a patchwork of stolen phrases. Milton's reiterated attack on Charles's "miserable indigence" is a nice glance at the king's many shifts to raise revenue; it also exposes his lack of a creative spirit. As Milton says, "he who wants a prayer to beseech God in his necessity, tis unexpressible how poor he is; farr poorer within himself then all his enemies can make him" (CPW 3:366).

It is by borrowing and stealing the words of others that Charles fashions the image of himself as a saint-like martyr. In chapter 2, Charles repents of complying with Strafford's execution "with the same words of contrition wherwith *David* repents the murdering of *Uriah*" (CPW 3:373). His imitation is lifeless since it presents the "words" of David, without his "spirit and conscience" (CPW 3:381–82). As a form without an animating soul, it is a dead image, an idol. Milton thinks Charles's repetition of David's psalms in chapter 23 is "more tolerable" than his use of Pamela's prayer, but it is still a "theft" since there is no creative reworking of the original: "such kind of borrowing as this," Milton says, "if it be not better'd by the borrower, among good Authors is accounted *Plagiarie*" (CPW 3:547). But the most criminal theft occurs when Charles repeats the words of Christ "*That God would forgive the people, for they know not what they doe*" (CPW 3:447). Sacrilegiously identifying himself with Christ and appropriating his words, Charles presents an image of himself as a fit object for the people's reverence and worship. Milton thus exposes Charles as an idolater—a king who has fashioned himself as a god and now presents his image to be worshipped—and as a bad artist, incapable of originality.

I would suggest that imitation and repetition are the appropriate literary modes for royalist Anglicans who value continuity, tradition, and the preservation of ties with the past. Conservative ideology (both

---

[8] Cable briefly suggests that Milton's attack on Charles's plagiarism is part of *Eikonoklastes'* attack on the idolatry of words (148), but the full significance of the charge of plagiarism has not been examined.

political and religious) and literary conservatism go hand in hand. Thus Milton rejects both servile literary imitation of past models and the idea of hereditary kingship, with its lineal succession (CPW 3:486–87). Both exemplify the continuity that, for Milton, inhibits excellence. Charles's plagiarism, his derivativeness, finds its counterpart in the behavior of his royalist supporters and in the ceremonial service of the Laudian church—both perpetuate the mode of imitation. Those closest to the king were, appropriately, "Courtiers and Prelates; men whose chief study was to finde out which way the King inclin'd, and to imitate him exactly" (CPW 3:350–51). The same mode of repetitive imitation characterizes "set prayers" and the liturgy of the church. "Model'd" on "the old Mass" (CPW 3:504), the liturgy ties us to the past; its words are regularly repeated. This criticism of the liturgy recalls Milton's anti-prelatical pamphlets, which attacked the liturgical repetition of prayers as a "rote-lesson" that puts the congregation to sleep, and mockingly compared ministers who need the help of "set forms" to school children relying on "loitering books, and *interlineary* translations."[9] *Eikonoklastes* insists that "sett formes" are lifeless, immobile images (CPW 3:505–7)— precisely what Milton says Charles hoped to turn his subjects and readers into (CPW 3:422, 417). Like the liturgy, Charles's words are intended to "charm us to sit still" (CPW 3:422), much as Comus charms the Lady and fixes her in her seat in Milton's *Mask.*

It is in this context that we should understand Milton's criticism of Charles's book for its repetitiveness—a sign that it is sloppy writing and also dangerous, seductive art. In answering chapter 22 ("Upon the Reformation of the times"), Milton accuses Charles of repeating himself: this chapter, he says, "presents us with nothing new"; the king's "exceptions against Reformation [are] pittifully old, and tatter'd with continual using." Indeed, Milton worries that he cannot refute this chapter "without more repetitions then now can be excusable" (CPW 3:533). He fears that he will fall into the same sin of imitation and repetition simply by answering Charles's argument chapter by chapter (a time-honored method, as Milton's editor Merritt Hughes notes). "To be ever answering fruitless Repetitions, I should become liable to answer for the same my self" (CPW 3:547). Should Milton repeat and answer Charles's objections to extempore prayer, he fears he "would turn my answers into *Responsories,* and begett another Liturgie, having too much of one already" (CPW 3:551).

---

[9] *Animadversions* and *An Apology against a Pamphlet,* in CPW 1:682, 691, and 937.

In contrast to the idolatrous images of Charles and his church, Milton seeks to define true "invention" and creativity. If the bad image, or idolatrous "invention," is repetitious, imitates the past and thus represents the continuity at the heart of what Milton sees as oppressive Anglican ideology, good creations—and true religious worship—will have distinctly opposite characteristics. And just as Milton describes idolatrous religion in terms of bad, imitative art and its connection with the past, so he will identify good religious worship with true creativity and the iconoclast's radical break with the past.

In discussing Charles's penitential meditations (chapter 25), Milton echoes Jonson's distinction in *Timber* between servile and true imitation as he distinguishes between Charles's borrowing from the Bible and true creativity, where the author makes the words his or her own: "It is not hard for any man, who hath a Bible in his hands, to borrow good words and holy sayings in abundance; but to make them his own is a work of grace onely from above" (CPW 3:553). Jonson, too, had condemned the literary thief, contrasting him with the "true" imitator who transforms his borrowed materials. Milton's attack on Charles's imitative prayers and his definition of true creativity in part draws on the classical and Renaissance notion of *imitatio,* which insisted that the poet/maker must transmute his models into something new and better and which thus allowed for an element of individuality.[10] But the conventional idea of *imitatio* is insufficient to explain Milton's stance, for he goes well beyond Jonson and traditional ideals of imitation in his distrust of models altogether. Whereas Jonson values the author's ties to past models, affirming a strong sense of lineage and succession even as he seeks to outdo his predecessors, Milton's commitment to originality involves a distinctive sense of discontinuity with the past that is part of his iconoclasm. Milton's feeling of historical discontinuity is the culmination of "the estrangement of the past"—the sense of the present's difference and division from the past—that Anthony Kemp has argued was the "historical revolution" effected by the Protestant Reformation.[11] But whereas the earlier reformers, wanting to return to an earlier purity, posited a

---

[10] See G. W. Pigman, III, "Versions of Imitation in the Renaissance," *Renaissance Quarterly* 33 (1980): 1–32, and Richard S. Peterson, *Imitation and Praise in the Poems of Ben Jonson* (New Haven: Yale Univ. Press, 1981), esp. 1–20. Peterson's discussion of Jonson's attempts to distinguish theft from true imitation is particularly relevant.

[11] Anthony Kemp, *The Estrangement of the Past: A Study in the Origins of Modern Historical Consciousness* (New York: Oxford University Press, 1991).

time in the history of the church with which the present was to be connected, Milton has a more radical sense of separation from the past, which never (for him) provides a perfect model. This profound sense of discontinuity even affects his understanding of the relation between Old and New Testaments. In rejecting the Anglican defense that episcopacy is modeled on the example of the Old Testament, he insists that the Gospel (our true source of church government) "does not ... imitate the law": she "lectures to us from her own authentick hand-writing, and command, not copies out from the borrow'd manuscript of a subservient scrowl, by way of imitating" (*Reason of Church-Government*, CPW 1:764). Authenticity would seem to require not simply a deviation from the past (even the past word of God) but a decisive break that makes past models irrelevant.

What in *Eikonoklastes* distinguishes true prayer, which is true "invention," is that it is both individualized ("his own") and the product of God's grace. Hence, the creation is not an idolatrous "humane invention" or an object of what Puritans called "will-worship." Rather than merely repeating the past, one is obliged to improve on it (anything borrowed must be "better'd by the borrower" [CPW 3:547]), even to create something entirely new. Whereas Charles lacks any creative spirit—"it [is] not in him to make a prayer of his own" (CPW 3:367)— Milton describes an ideal of prayer which is also, importantly, an ideal of original, artistic creation that looks forward to his invocations of the muse in *Paradise Lost*. Prayer is the "Gift" of God, who "every morning raines down new expressions into our hearts" (CPW 3:505–6). Unless we have God's spirit in us, the words are only dead images.[12] God's "sanctifying spirit" puts "filial words" into us, giving us "plenty" and "variety." These "new expressions" or prayers mark a decisive break from the past, and they cannot be "hoarded up" or, like manna, they will "*breed wormes and stink.*" True prayers are always new beginnings. Because they are never fixed or given permanent form, they avoid the statue-like qualities of permanence and immutability that, for Puritans, characterized the idolatrous image. Neither our prayers nor "the Divine Spirit of utterance that moves" us should be "imprison[ed] ... into a

---

[12] Cable observes that Charles is criticized for "spiritual laziness," whereas for Milton the "*effort* of original prayer ... at least partially constitutes prayer's worth" (146–47). Loewenstein points out the contrast between Milton's characterization of Charles's *Eikon Basilike* as a "dead image" and the ideal expressed in *Areopagitica:* a true book is alive, an animated spirit.

Pinfold of sett words" or bound to an endless round of repetition—they must be free like the spirit of God and godlike human beings (CPW 3:505–6). Milton's language suggests that prayers are alive and unique. In the definition of true prayer, we see his model for legitimate creativity, which privileges originality and individuality. No two prayers, or creations (literary or biological), will ever be the same; each will have its own distinct identity.

A fascinating metaphor of reproductive generation underlies Milton's description of prayer. Prayer is "conceav'd in the heart" (CPW 3:504, and cf. 507). The heart must be receptive (not stony) when God "raines down new expressions" (CPW 3:505)—an allusion to God's giving manna to the Israelites, and to Zeus's visiting Danae in a golden shower. The heart of the believer is thus like a woman, open to the impregnating spirit but also actively contributing to the creation of prayers with fertile "matter, and good desires" (CPW 3:504). Milton here appropriates the female capacity to give birth, but his metaphor gives an importance to the woman's contribution in generation that is unusual in the Renaissance when thinking about reproduction was still dominated by Aristotelian/Galenic traditions.[13]

Finally, this ideal of prayer in *Eikonoklastes* looks forward to the opening invocation of *Paradise Lost* where Milton asks the spirit of God, who hovered over the waters at creation, to inspire his sacred song:

> And chiefly Thou O Spirit, that dost prefer
> Before all Temples th'upright heart and pure,
> Instruct me, for Thou know'st; Thou from the first
> Wast present, and with mighty wings outspread
> Dove-like sat'st brooding on the vast Abyss
> And mad'st it pregnant: What in me is dark
> Illumine, what is low raise and support.   (1.17–23)

Poetic creation is analogous to the original creation of the world, and both are understood in generative, gendered terms. Like the female

---

[13] On Renaissance ideas of reproduction, see Ian Maclean, *The Renaissance Notion of Woman* (Cambridge: Cambridge Univ. Press, 1980), chap. 3; Thomas Laqueur, "Orgasm, Generation, and the Politics of Reproductive Biology," *Representations* 14 (1986): 1–41; and Laqueur's *Making Sex: Body and Gender from the Greeks through Freud* (Cambridge: Harvard Univ. Press, 1990). Milton's contemporary, William Harvey, offered a new understanding of generation that emphasized the contribution of the female far more than even Galen, who had diverged from Aristotle in according women "semen."

abyss, Milton will be visited by the seminal spirit of God which will make him "pregnant," able to bring forth his vital creation.[14] In *Paradise Lost* as in *Eikonoklastes,* God's participation in the creative process both enables the poet's originality and absolves him from pride in his invention.

By discriminating precisely between the idolatrous image (the object of Puritan attack) and legitimate human creations, Milton defines a safe, privileged place for human art, thus provisionally resolving the dilemma created for him as an artist by the Puritan attack on "graven images." Recent scholars, insisting that the truth or falsehood of icons and images did not actually reside in their external characteristics, have reminded us that the iconoclast as well as the image-lover used images, thus testifying to their power.[15] While we may thus recognize a certain absurdity in the iconoclast's claims for an ability to discern idolatrous images, we should not forget that Milton and his contemporaries believed they could make such distinctions. By paying closer attention to the terms in which they attacked idolatrous creations, and to their assumptions, we gain a better understanding of what they *thought* constituted the idolatrous image. This endeavor is important, since the conflict over images and ceremonies is an index to major disjunctions between Puritan and Anglican ideologies that fueled the English Civil War. For Milton, Charles's creations, like Satan's in *Paradise Lost,* are paradoxically both

[14] Cf. the prayer for illumination at the opening of book 3. Milton's special emphasis on the woman's role in reproduction is also evident in *Eikonoklastes* as he refutes the King's view of Parliament, turning upside down Charles's gendered language, which implicitly compared the King to the masculine sun and Parliament to the feminine earth, unable to bring forth anything without his influence:

> So that the Parliament, it seems, is but a Female, and without his procreative reason, the Laws which they can produce are but wind-eggs. . . . He ought then to have so thought of a Parlament, if he count it not Male, as of his Mother, which, to civil being, created both him, and the Royalty he wore. (CPW 3:467)

On the gendered, sexual metaphoric import of Milton's decription of his poetic inspiration in *Paradise Lost,* see Stevie Davies, *The Feminine Reclaimed* (Lexington: Univ. of Kentucky, 1986), 195–96, and Michael Lieb, *The Dialectics of Creation* (Amherst: Univ. of Massachusetts, 1970). See also William Kerrigan's discussion of Milton's "feminine identification" (*The Sacred Complex* [Cambridge: Harvard Univ. Press, 1983]), 50 and passim. Though, as Davies well recognizes, both the muse and the poet are in this passage somewhat androgynous, the emphasis is on the inseminating (masculine) power of God's spirit and the receptive, child-bearing (feminine) quality of the poet.

[15] See Gilman, 161–66; Cable, 135–36. Loewenstein in *Milton and the Drama of History* has further argued that Milton's iconoclasm was itself an imaginative, creative act.

self-generated and derivative, sterile imitations.[16] Tied to the past, they inculcate servile conformity in the name of community. In contrast, the new kind of creative invention that Milton celebrates, fresh and individualized yet always proclaiming its debt to God, is particularly suited for a progressive, radically Puritan ideology that insists on the need for new beginnings, for breaking from the past. *Eikonoklastes* registers in 1649 Milton's realization that political and religious reformation demands a new order of literature and a new conception of literary authority.

UNIVERSITY OF ILLINOIS AT URBANA–CHAMPAIGN

---

[16] On the connection between Milton's treatment of Charles in his prose and Satan in *Paradise Lost*, see Joan S. Bennett's "Satan and King Charles: Milton's Royal Portraits," originally published in *PMLA* (1977), and reprinted as chapter 2 of *Reviving Liberty: Radical Christian Humanism in Milton's Great Poems* (Cambridge: Harvard Univ. Press, 1989), and Davies, *Images of Kingship* (n. 6 above). Bennett shows "resemblances in metaphor and characterization" between Milton's Charles and Satan (43), arguing that Milton treats the king as a "fictional character" (35). Davies aptly recognizes that the idolatrous image of false kingship associated with Satan in *Paradise Lost* is similar to the Stuart image of kingship represented in *Eikon Basilike* (49).

Wyman H. Herendeen

MILTON'S *ACCEDENCE COMMENC'T GRAMMAR* AND THE DECONSTRUCTION OF "GRAMMATICAL TYRANNY"

Account might be now givn what addition or alteration from other Grammars hath been here made, and for what reason. But he who would be short in teaching, must not be long in Prefacing: The Book it self follows, and will declare sufficiently to them who can discern.

THESE ARE THE CONCLUDING SENTENCES OF THE ADDRESS "TO THE READER" of the *Accedence Commenc't Grammar.* Milton calls attention to the changes he has made "from other Grammars," but offers no particulars; he simply gives us "The Book it self."[1] He is not usually so reticent in matters didactic. Perhaps we should not be too suspicious when he suggests that the changes and his reasons for making them are self-evident "to them that can discern," but his phrasing is teasingly tautological. Change, "alteration," was important for Milton, and his preface alerts us to its importance without elaborating on it. As those who have worked on the *Accedence* have made amply clear, neither the changes nor the reasons for them are obvious.[2] Whatever the rationale for Milton's restraint—and it is a quality that pervades the work as a

---

[1] John Milton, *Accedence Commenc't Grammar,* introd. David P. French, in *Complete Prose Works of John Milton,* ed. Maurice Kelley (New Haven: Yale University Press, 1982), vol. 8: TO THE READER. References to the *Accedence* and to French's introduction are to this text. I am grateful to Gordon Campbell and John Shawcross for their responses to an earlier draft of this essay.

[2] In addition to David P. French's introduction, the major criticism of the *Accedence* consists of J. Milton French's "Some Notes on Milton's *Accedence Commenc't Grammar,*" *JEGP*

whole—the fact is that the *Accedence* is problematic in its relation to other grammars and to Milton's development. In this contribution to the heated cause of educational reform, Milton makes quite clear that to understand his "alteration[s]" is to begin to appreciate what he has done in his work. Virtually all of the criticism of the *Accedence* has implicitly responded to the first of his challenges, to identify how Milton used other sources, although not to the second, "for what reason."

This said, there has not been much study of the *Accedence Commenc't Grammar*. As J. Milton French said in 1961, it is still "without much doubt ... [Milton's] least read and least known book."[3] But the major work that has been done on it, by J. Milton French, David P. French, and Gordon Campbell, has done much to identify the "additions or alterations" that "hath been made from other Grammars." Their work reassures the reader that these changes are indeed not self-evident, and that Milton's *Accedence Commenc't Grammar* is neither a temporary lapse into ingenuousness, nor merely a mercenary venture prompted by the hard times of the 1660s.[4] All of the studies share a primary concern for Milton's pedagogy, and J. Milton French and David P. French in particular emphasize that the *Accedence Commenc't Grammar* is above all a response to William Lily's two-part grammar consisting of the *Shorte Introduction of Grammar* and the *Brevissima Institutio*. Lily's grammar was part of the shared cultural experience of English students and masters throughout the Renaissance; according to its recent editor, it went through two hundred editions between 1513 and 1595, the final revision of 1567 providing the text for the next century.[5] Known as the

---

60 (1961): 641–50, and Gordon Campbell's "Milton's *Accedence Commenc't Grammar*," *MQ* 10 (1976): 39–48. Campbell, too, finds Milton's reference to his use of other grammars puzzling, calling it "infuriatingly imprecise" (43).

[3] French, "Notes," 641; to this, David French, in CPW 8: introduction, 14, adds that it is also the "least popular."

[4] This financial need is one common explanation for Milton's late publication of the work.

[5] Vincent J. Flynn, ed., *A Shorte Introduction of Grammar* together with *Brevissima Institutio seu Ratio Grammatices Cognoscende* (New York, 1945), vi; a single edition, such as that of 1587, would often be as large as 10,000 copies (x), thus reflecting how the authorities swamped the market, and also the high financial stakes involved. For the pervasive presence of Lily in Tudor schools, see Foster Watson, *The English Grammar Schools to 1600: Their Curriculum and Practice* (London: Frank Cass, 1908), 243–75, and Thomas W. Baldwin, *William Shakespeare's Small Latine and Lesse Greeke* (Urbana: Univ. Illinois Press, 1944), appendix 2. Studies tend to concentrate on the Tudor period when Lily's influence was

"royal grammar," Lily's was the authorized, official Latin grammar text prescribed for school use, and so it was a presence that the author of any new grammar had to contend with. It provided Milton with a formal paradigm for his work and, according to both Frenches, with significantly more than sixty percent of the grammatical and syntactic illustrations.[6]

J. Milton French gets down to the nuts and bolts of differentiating between the two grammars by identifying the specific appropriations and additions. The Yale editor, David French, sharing his predecessor's preoccupation with sources, builds on the foundation of his scholarship, and examines larger, structural changes by which "Milton set out to revise the royal grammar into a more usable text for young schoolboys," and in the process he locates Milton's work in the tradition of Renaissance grammars.[7] His final evaluation of the *Accedence* is made in terms of Milton's success in creating a better grammar text by borrowing from and adding to Lily:

> Though he clearly intends to displace Lily, he does not hesitate to found his whole work on the received grammar, whose order of presentation he follows and whose very lists and catalogues he appropriates.... Though much of the *Accedence* appears also in Lily, in general Milton improves whatever he alters.[8]

The considerable scholarship is turned to assessing the pedagogical success of Milton's text in relation to Lily's grammar.

It is really Gordon Campbell who begins to consider further-reaching intellectual contexts for *why* Milton does what he does in his grammar:

> The question of Milton's motivation in adding another Ramist treatise on grammar to the list of those already published must be confronted. Did he write a Latin grammar simply to satisfy the humanist's urge to write on all topics, or did he have a more philosophical purpose in mind?[9]

---

consolidated. In the next century, Milton's, Lily has a rather different, more problematic history, although he remains at the core of the education system, and editions identifying their work as the "royal grammar" were published as late as 1688 and 1695.

[6] French, "Notes," 645; David French, CPW 8: introduction, 82.

[7] CPW 8:63.

[8] Ibid., 79.

[9] Campbell, 42.

Still exploring the question of the "addition or alteration from other Grammars," he shows how Milton extended Ramist methods of language instruction beyond what was being done by contemporary educators. Indeed, the very brevity that distinguishes the *Accedence* is part of its Ramism, and Campbell shows how Milton's deviations from other grammars reveal Milton to be truer to the principles of Ramist logic than Ramus's own grammar was.[10] The implications of this Ramist connection for Milton are considerable and not only expand our appreciation of the work itself, but suggest other philosophical and political motives behind its creation and design which, when explored, give the grammar an important place in Milton's development.[11] Ramus had long before been appropriated by protestant writers to countenance religious and political reform, and we want to remember that men working in the Ramist tradition of language training, such as Comenius and Hartlib, thought of themselves first as social reformers. It is appropriate at this point to ask if Milton's austere, even bland grammar, which has been viewed so apolitically, in fact shares this political self-awareness, and if so, how?

Although some "account" has now been given to the question of how Milton has used other grammars in the *Accedence Commenc't Grammar,* we are, nevertheless, left with serious questions about his larger intentions for the work. It is well to remember the inherently controversial nature of such a project. For Milton and his contemporaries, to undertake the reform of grammar was to destabilize one of the triple pillars of education, and the political implications of this were deeply felt by

---

[10] Ibid., 43–45.

[11] Concerned as he is with Ramist logic and grammar, Campbell's focus places the *Accedence* within a highly suggestive context. For the larger implications of Ramus in the intellectual trends of the Renaissance, see W. J. Ong, *Ramus: Method and the Decay of Dialogue* (Cambridge: Harvard Univ. Press, 1958). Ramus's role in the transformation of grammar theories and reactions against scholastic traditions is given generous historical scope in G. A. Padley's study, *Grammatical Theory in Western Europe 1500–1700. The Latin Tradition* (Cambridge: Cambridge Univ. Press, 1976), esp. 77–96; Padley (94) notes that Ramism found particularly fertile ground in protestant and later puritan England. Campbell (39–40) orients his argument around the publication date of 1669 for the *Accedence.* To focus more sharply on its place in Milton's development, I work from the generally accepted date of composition, sometime between 1640 and 1646 (see William Riley Parker, *Milton: A Biography,* 2 vols. [Oxford: Clarendon Press, 1968], 1:259, 293–94, and French, in CPW 8: introduction, 33–35). The date thus emphasizes the direct parallels with *Of Education* (see French, "Notes," 642) and its affinity with other works from the period.

that generation of reformers. In Stuart England, where the content and method of instruction were prescribed, such an undertaking was at the very least an infringement on royal prerogative, and during the Commonwealth it was viewed by many as part of the necessary process of political reformation. Samuel Hartlib, Milton's friend and the man who commissioned *Of Education,* explicitly links the need for language reform with a call for ongoing political and religious reformation: dedicating *The Latin Tongue* (1654) to Francis Rous, member of the Protector's Council and of the committee reviewing the issue of kingship, he says "*Mr.* Speaker, Although the Designes of this Age do tend ... to a thorough Reformation; yet ... hitherto we cannot see much more then the Overthrow and Deformation of former Establishments: partly, because there is much rubbish to be removed."[12] Among the institutions needing to be razed in order to be reformed is that of language instruction. His purposefully turned tropes convey his awareness of the interconnectedness of political and linguistic structures: "And because it is no small difficultie and hazard to venture upon the contradicting of a Custome so Universally received, as is the Grammatical Tyranny of teaching Tongues ... I am willing to make an Appeal, and seek out an Eminent Patron for this bold attempt" (A3).

Hartlib's Ramism manifests its attack on grammatical rules and precepts in terms of rebellion, an assault on tyranny, the defense of liberty against custom. His figures of speech which treat aspects of language with metaphors of power and the abuse of power are both commonplace and apt in the context of English instruction; in the mid-seventeenth century their self-referentiality assumes additional resonance. Ten years before, Milton, in the treatise he prepared for Hartlib, used similar tropes to express the political timeliness of language reform when he described the effects of pernicious methods of teaching, where "court shifts and tyrannous aphorismes" pass for expressions of wisdom.[13] Indeed,

---

[12] Hartlib, *The True and Readie Way To Leame the Latine Tongue* (London, 1654; Menston, Yorks.: Scolar Press, 1971), A2; page references will be provided parenthetically in the text. Hartlib's dedicatory letter is far more politically presumptuous than are the three essays on language that he prints in the book.

[13] *Of Education,* ed. Donald C. Dorian, in *Complete Prose Works of John Milton,* ed. Ernest Sirluck (New Haven: Yale Univ. Press, 1959), 2:375. Military and combative figures of speech permeate the essay, revitalizing the Renaissance commonplace that education is intended to prepare virtuous men for lives of action. However, the political dimension that is also part of the essay's idiom gives it a subversive quality.

the contrast that he draws between the enslaved language of the court and that of the free citizen is precisely that which Daniel Javitch identifies in the Tudor period, between a Ciceronian style associated with republicanism and an indirect courtly style that emerged in response to monarchic absolutism.[14] One is the language of engagement, the other one of indirection, and Milton and his fellow educators respond to these political implications of language reform. Like Hartlib's, Milton's metaphors pull the reader not in the direction of his subject, in this case a critique of the teaching of rigid rules of style, but away from it, to his "vehicle," servitude and the tyranny of arbitrary law. Figures of speech used to speak of figures of speech are often political in this way, and in *Of Education* Milton uses them frequently and self-consciously. In the very austere *Accedence Commenc't Grammar,* the "praxis" complementing the theory of *Of Education,* he does not. This, however, does not mean that the grammar lacks the political sensibility present in its companion piece.[15] Clearly, grammars were perceived as politically sensitive documents, and in the language used by both Milton and Hartlib, for example, we see the combative idioms of the political and religious controversy of the 1640s—language and ideas familiar to Miltonists from *Of Reformation in England* and *Of Prelatical Episcopacy* (1641), *The Reason of Church-Government Urg'd against Prelaty* (1642), and *Areopagitica* (1644). Milton shares in the political awareness of the educational and grammar reform movement, but he is careful of his place in it, and rejects traditional "Scholastick[s]" as well as the utopianism and theoretical rhetoric of the "modern *Janua's* and *Didactics.*"[16] The question remains, then, precisely how does *The Accedence Commenc't Grammar* figure in this spirit of reform?

To begin to answer this question we need to keep three things in mind. First, we need to consider Milton's use of Lily from perspectives

---

[14] Javitch, *Poetry and Courtliness in Renaissance England* (Princeton: Princeton Univ. Press, 1978), 32–33. Javitch, in studying the specific links between the court and poetry, sees changes in the political milieu as influencing the shift from a Ciceronian to a courtly and poetic rhetorical mode. A similar pattern of political instability existed in the middle of the next century when Milton and his peers foster a shift in the other direction: from a courtly to a Ciceronian style.

[15] See *Of Education,* CPW 2:373; here Milton provides the rationale for the kind of minimalist text that he provides in the *Accedence.* Not only is the *Accedence* the methodological (Campbell) and pedagogical (French, "Notes") complement to *Of Education,* but it is a political one as well.

[16] *Of Education,* CPW 2:364.

other than pedagogy. As we have seen, Lily's *A Shorte Introduction of Grammar* was the paradigmatic grammar text. But to appreciate Milton's achievement, we must also be aware of the evolving place of Lily's work in the political environment of grammar and its reform during the period up to 1646, a probable outside date for the creation of Milton's work. We need also to consider more particularly how grammars were used and regarded during that period, and what Milton's contacts were with others working on the reform of language instruction. In what follows, I will look briefly at these concerns to suggest that the *Accedence* is more expressive of Milton's political intentions than his critics have suggested.

The most striking feature of the *Accedence Commenc't Grammar* is its spareness. "Brevity" and "clearness of method" are its organizing principles just as they are part of its Ramism and its pedagogical method: "the long way [of learning Latin] is much abbreviated," Milton says to the reader, so that the "labour of understanding [may be] much more easie." It is also the quality that distinguishes the work from its sources and contemporaries, and we must not take it for granted: simplification of a text is as much a critical act as explication is. Milton drastically cuts explanatory material, compresses illustrations, and removes prayers and other religious material. As Campbell points out, he goes further than Ramus in dropping whole sections normally contained in grammars, such as the *orthographia* and the *prosodia*.[17]

Most of this material comes directly from Lily. David French dismisses it as innocuous because of its peripheral relationship to the pedagogy,[18] but it is an identifying aspect of the royal grammar and its offshoots, and must be weighed in the assessment of Milton's alterations. I will return to these alterations to suggest that Milton's radical surgery on his sources is a crucial part of his larger design of political and religious reform as reflected in other of his prose works of the period. Milton's method of revision is largely one of deconstruction and simplification of Lily's royal grammar: not only is his goal to improve upon and replace the royal grammar (as David French stresses), but also, in the process, to improve upon education in England.

---

[17] Campbell, 43–44.

[18] French, CPW 8: introduction, 50, describes much of this material as "somewhat perfunctory and easily expendable," and sees it as pedagogically unnecessary but otherwise inoffensive.

Before we can appreciate exactly what it meant for Milton to put the ghost of Lily to rest, we need to accept the inescapable political dimension of the grammar during the Reformation and Renaissance. To do this we might deal briefly with those two other related concerns— how grammars were regarded during the period, and what some of Milton's contacts were with contemporary grammarians. The fact that grammars were recognized as tools of profound political importance will not be lost on postmodern readers. Through their selection of illustrative material, grammars establish the intellectual canon, define "politically correct" texts and modes of thought, and influence the ideology of a generation of learners. Henry VIII, Edward VI, and Elizabeth I, their political advisors, and the Puritan reformers all knew the power of the subliminal as well as any psycholinguist. The grammar school system that used the Latin catechism for language training, as England's did, is concerned with matters other than syntax and a pure classical style. For Tudors and Stuarts alike, the desirability of universal and uniform religious texts was directly linked with the need for uniform grammar texts. Controlling the media was recognized as a means of behavior control.[19]

The details of the regulations concerning the creation and use of grammar and religious texts are well enough known, but the impact of this centralization of schools, information, and the canonization of thought and language on generations of students has hardly begun to be assessed, although it figures large in Milton's views on freedom of thought and expression.[20] For our purposes, the point is that grammars

[19] There have been useful and full histories of educational and religious reforms, mainly for the Tudor period, and the relation between the two has been surveyed; see, for example, Norman Wood, *The Reformation and English Education: A Study of the Influence of Religious Uniformity on English Education in the Sixteenth Century* (London: George Routledge & Sons, 1931). The extent to which the control of information and media was part of the strategy of Renaissance politicians of the sixteenth and seventeenth centuries, and how it affected the dynamic of social change and controversy, have only begun to receive proper attention. One perceptive reassessment of the subject in the Tudor period is Joan Simon's *Education and Society in Tudor England* (Cambridge: Cambridge Univ. Press, 1967). For Alexander Nowell's creation of the Latin and English catechism as a school text for use at Westminster, and its appproval in the Canons and adoption for universal use, and for Nowell's service to Elizabeth and Burghley as advisor in religious and educational reform, see Ralph Churton, *The Life of Alexander Nowell, Dean of St. Paul's* (Oxford: Oxford Univ. Press, 1809), 80–85, 107–9, 162–63, 185–90.

[20] See Watson, *Grammar Schools,* and Wood, *The Reformation,* for detailed accounts of and documents pertaining to the uniformity of text and the nature of protestant reform of the school system.

were a recognized part of the political and religious power structure that was being established during the Reformation and that was being challenged in the years leading up to the Civil War. While David French and Harris Fletcher place the proliferation of grammars in the context of the "Puritan victory" and the effort to break the "royal monopoly," they depoliticize the form and content of Renaissance grammars, and this is to depoliticize Milton's *Accedence*.[21] But in evaluating any new text and its deviation from the royal grammar (meaning Lily), we must remember that the road to the oath of conformity (the end of Renaissance education) begins with the encounter with educational uniformity in the grammars. Efforts to revise Lily, or to establish an alternative, were ideologically problematic, and until after the Restoration, the struggle for a voice in the school curriculum, where the political and religious tenets of the protestant state were entrenched in the instructional texts, was waged overtly in the grammars themselves.

The education statutes and edicts of the ecclesiastical canon that endorsed the royal grammar that Milton grew up with still pertained at the time of the probable composition of the *Accedence*.[22] They embodied an authoritarian hierarchy that would have been deeply repugnant to the man who was then lamenting "the Tyranny of *Prelates*," regretting the Elizabethan compromise that derailed the Reformation and created an "Episcopacy" admired (he says ironically) by the "wisest *Statesmen*," hoping at least for the reform of the bishoprics, and working for the reform of an education system that fettered thought through "tyrannous aphorismes."[23] The regulations behind the education statutes incorporate the infernal triad of episcopacy, monarchism, and arbitrary law:

> None [shall] ... teach Schoole without Licence.... No man shall teach either in publicke Schoole, or private house, but such as shall bee allowed by the Bishop of the Diocesse ...

[21] CPW 8: introduction, 64–65; French sees the growth of new grammars very broadly as "in part stem[ming] from the victory of Puritanism with its ardent interest in schooling." How the grammars, including Milton's, are part of the political and revolutionary process is not explored. Harris Francis Fletcher, too, in *The Intellectual Development of John Milton*, 2 vols. (Urbana: Univ. of Illinois Press, 1956), 1: 129, also sees Milton's grammar within the current of change but not as part of it.

[22] Watson, *Grammar Schools*, 258–59, Fletcher, *Intellectual Development*, 1: 169–70.

[23] The phrases are from the contemporary tracts, *Of Reformation ... in England* (1641), from *The Prose of John Milton*, ed. J. Max Patrick [Garden City, N.J.: Doubleday, 1967], 83), and *Of Education* (1644), CPW 2:375.

being found meete ... for his learning & dexteritie in teaching
... and also for right understanding of Gods true Religion.... All Schoolemasters shall teach in English or Latine
... the larger or shorter Catechisme heretofore by publike
authoritie set foorth ... and they shall teach the Grammer set
forth by King HENRY the eight, and continued in the times of
King EDWARD the sixt, and Queene ELIZABETH of noble
memorie, and none other.[24]

The passage from the statutes for 1604 is cited by Fletcher in the
context of Mulcaster's dismissal from St. Paul's, without any reference to
its political implications for Mulcaster or Milton, and it is a good example of how these documents tend to be depoliticized. Renaissance writers and teachers were directly affected by these statutes; they had to live
with the political ramifications of the educational statutes and texts, and
saw ecclesiastical, educational, and political reform as interrelated. Not
only can we see this to be the case in the careers of educators closer to
the Reformation, in men such as John Colet, William Lily, and Alexander Nowell, but it is also true of Milton's older contemporaries in the
second age of reform, men such as Alexander Gill, Ben Jonson, Thomas
Farnaby, John Comenius, and Samuel Hartlib, for example.[25] Like
their predecessors, they too were aware of the political context of their
work, and offer insights into how grammars were viewed and used
during Milton's generation. All of them were involved in one way or
another with educational reform and wrote or influenced the writing of
grammars. Jonson is particularly interesting not only because of his place
in Milton's literary patrimony, but also because of what he reveals about
the competitive market for grammars. He designed his *English Grammar*
after Lily's in the hope of securing its international reputation, and in his
choice of illustrative material he attempted to define a vernacular style

[24] Fletcher, *Intellectual Development,* 1:169–70.
[25] For Nowell, for example, working in conjunction with Burghley on combined
education and religious reform, see Churton, *Life of ... Nowell;* Lily's grammar begins as part
of Colet's humanist reform and is appropriated by Henrician protestantism; see Wyman H.
Herendeen, "*Coletus Redevivus:* John Colet, Patron or Reformer?" *Renaissance and Reformation*
24 (1988): 163–88. For Gill and other educators associated with Milton, see vol. 1 of
Fletcher's *Intellectual Development.* G. A. Padley's *Grammatical Theory ... The Latin Tradition*
and also his *Grammatical Theory in Western Europe 1500–1700: Trends in Vernacular Grammar
I* (Cambridge: Cambridge Univ. Press, 1985) place many of these figures within the movement of grammar reform as it evolves through the century.

that would supplant the courtly Petrarchanism found in his rival, Alexander Gill's *Logonomia Anglica* (1619).[26] As part of the artistic and political antagonism between the two, the *English Grammar* reflects the deep conservatism that we see in Jonson's late plays. In his search for a representative English idiom, Jonson reaches back to the Henrician reform and provides his readers with an authoritarian voice confronting political challenges. Born of his efforts to sustain his place in the Stuart court, the *English Grammar* shows us Jonson attempting to canonize a national literary repertory consistent with his own literary and political self-image.

In its right, Gill's *Logonomia Anglica* was itself deeply original, as Fletcher shows,[27] and it shares the spirit of radical reform that inspired Colet when he first commissioned Lily to write the Latin grammar. Sharpening the contrast with Jonson and giving an additional political edge to their rivalry, Gill's *Logonomia* advocates an intellectual independence that is consistent with his and his son's reputation as free thinkers. The Gills' intellectual heritage was the tradition of reform associated with St. Paul's, and it is their influence that Fletcher describes as instrumental in Milton's decision "not to enter either the academic life or the Anglican priesthood."[28]

These are but two early works that express their authors' political sensibilities in ways of importance for our appreciation of Milton. A wealth of grammars emerged during this period of increasing political crisis. Many of their political affinities are clarified by their relationship to Lily, the royal model. One, for example, was Thomas Farnaby's *Systema Grammaticum*, a reworking of Lily that was commissioned by King Charles; it appeared once only, in 1641. In the same year there appeared

---

[26] For Jonson's *English Grammar* and its place in his political sensibility and artistic contretemps, see Wyman H. Herendeen, "Ben Jonson and the Play of Words," in *Craft and Tradition: Essays in Honour of William Blissett*, ed. H. B. de Groot and A. Leggatt (Calgary, Alberta: University of Calgary Press, 1990), 123–36. Padley, in *Trends in Vernacular Grammar*, 57–74, shows Jonson's grammatological differences from Gill and places them both within the Lily-Ramus matrix.

[27] Fletcher, in *Intellectual Development* 1:174–81, emphasizes Gill's originality as an educator as well as the joint influence he and his son exerted on the young Milton. Aubrey's account of the elder Gill's encounter with authority, when he was arrested in 1628 for toasting the health of Buckingham's assassin, adds a political edge to their reputation.

[28] Fletcher, *Intellectual Development* 1:181. For the tradition of reform at St. Paul's, see Herendeen, "John Colet"; and for the school, its founder and first master as sources for the growth and diffusion of the tradition of humanist grammar in England, see Padley, *Latin Tradition*, 24–27 and 38–43.

306 WYMAN H. HERENDEEN

An English GRAMMAR *or, a plain Exposition* OF LILIES GRAMMAR *In English, with easie and profitable Rules for parsing and making Latine;* its author was probably Ralph Robinson, later bishop of Auckland. Meant to explicate Lily, the work is a good example of what Milton's *Accedence* is not, and for that reason warrants a brief examination.

An English GRAMMAR *or, a plain Exposition* OF LILIES GRAMMAR contains all the apparatus by which "clearness of method ... [is] clog'd with Catalogues ... or [with] too much interruption between Rule and Rule."[29] It adopts Lily's apparatus, amplifies it, and englishes it; having sections on prosody and orthography, and charts of various sorts, it boasts having what Milton is at pains to omit. However, its loyalty to the royal grammar is more than adherence to a pedagogical model, and it further illustrates the political awareness of seventeenth-century grammars. For example, it contains a section on parsing that is illustrated by an extended lesson on "THE SUMME OF CHRISTIAN DOCTRINE OUT OF NOWELL" (154). This explication of the "lex divina" was firmly associated with Henrician establishment of the uniformity of Anglican worship and educational texts; Alexander Nowell, former dean of St. Paul's, was one of the most influential of Elizabeth's and Burghley's domestic advisors and one who did much to bring educational and religious reform together through royal statute and charter.[30] This is all material that Milton carefully deletes from his secularized grammar.

Robinson's explication of Lily has a subtle, persistent royalist and Anglican subtext running through it. For a reader in 1600, it would probably have passed unnoticed as part of the decade's rhetoric. But read against its context in the 1640s, and against the austere rhetoric of grammars like Milton's, its adherence to Lily becomes more suggestive. Its "ADVERTISEMENT To the READER," exhorting the instruction of children in Latin grammar "to the great advantage of Learning, and to the unspeakable good both of the Church, and of the Commonwealth," has a much more pointed message in 1641 than it would have had in 1600. This theme of patriotic obedience to prince and prelate is present throughout, and is reiterated through paradigms and lessons that give the

---

[29] From Milton's *Accedence,* TO THE READER. For R[alph] R[obinson]'s *An English* GRAMMAR (1641), I have used the Scolar Press edition, ed. R. C. Alston (Menston, Yorks., 1972).

[30] Nowell was recognized as a man whose influence extended into virtually every aspect of Elizabethan religious and educational policy; see in particular Izaak Walton's appraisal of his importance, recorded in Churton, *Life of Nowell,* 81.

grammar its particular tone. Consider, for example, the opening lesson on orthography (a section that Milton omitted from his grammar):

> Letters are written two waies, with greater characters, and with smaller. With the bigger, sentences are begun: as, *Deum time:* Feare God. *Regem honora:* honour the King. (1)

Another lesson, on the parenthesis, is englished: "The Prince (because the enemies do threaten wars) doth fortifie the cities with soldiers and weapons" (5). The third concord on the agreement of the relative with its antecedent is illustrated with the sentence "Who is a good man? ... He which keepeth the statutes of his fathers, and their laws & ordinances" (110). Compounds of the verb "to be" requiring the dative case are cogently illustrated by the sentence: "a godly King is an ornament to the Commonwealth" (127).

Anyone who has worked with grammars knows how many hundreds of examples they contain and how treacherous it is to draw conclusions about authorial intention from them. On the same page with "a godly King is an ornament to the Commonwealth" are constructions for "I lie," "I smell somewhat," and "I object." Generalizations are risky. But the rhetoric of a grammar develops rather like that of a book of epigrams, and different grammars have different tones. In some, like Milton's, phrases about "godly kings" are weeded out, while in others, such as Robinson's, there is a dense texture of such phrases having political and religious resonance. In his *English Grammar* of 1641, Robinson teaches the king's Latin with the help of the king's English. It was not reprinted.

With this context for the seventeenth-century grammar in mind, we can return to Milton's *Accedence* and its "alteration[s] from" Lily's grammar. Harris Fletcher, in reviewing the grammars that Milton might have encountered, says, completely erroneously I think, that the "controversial material" had been removed from the later redactions of Lily.[31] In fact, even the hypothetical texts he imagines Milton to have used, while they may be free of vestigial Catholic material, have all the sections and illustrative apparatus that we have seen in Robinson's grammar and that announce its episcopal and royalist pedigree. More to the point, Lily's *A Shorte Introduction of Grammar,* endorsed by the Canons Ecclesiastical of 1604 and with authorized status still enforced in 1640,

---

[31] Fletcher, *Intellectual Development,* 1:129.

continued to be the only legal grammar text for schools.[32] Among the
arsenal of pedagogical tools that indicated its royal patronage and role as
a religious text were exercises using the Apostles' Creed, various prayers,
the Decalogue, or Ten Commandments, and sections on Baptism and
the responses to Holy Communion, and a verse meditation by Lily having strong political and religious elements.[33] The second part of the
volume, the *Brevissima Institutio seu Ratio Grammatices,* reiterates its royal
privilege, and contains sections on orthography, etymology, syntax,
prosody, the *De Rationi Studii* of Erasmus, various homiletic exhortations
for dutiful behavior from master to student, and appropriately dutiful responses, prayers, and further responses by the student before and after
Communion.[34] Although there are some gestures towards modern pedagogical methods, the format emphasizes memorization of formulaic responses, and reinforces its teaching methods through rigidly defined
hierarchic, authoritarian relationships (between Christ, monarch, priest,
master, and the student) that are ultimately political in nature.

The proliferation of grammars that we have witnessed is part of a
quiet struggle between those who would entrench the royal grammar
and those who would be free of it.[35] In their own way, they assumed
the idioms of political controversy and reform, and in their fidelity to or

[32] Flynn, *A Shorte Introduction,* x, Watson, *English Grammar Schools,* 258, Fletcher,
Intellectual Development, 1:169–70.

[33] The 1567 edition represents the last major revision and was the one that was authorized for use through the next century (Flynn, *A Shorte Introduction,* xi), although it varies
relatively little from earlier editions. Its divisions show a careful balance of political, religious,
and educational elements. The major sections of *A Shorte Introduction of Grammar* include: (1)
greetings from the Queen authorizing its use, with reference to precedent by Henry VIII,
Edward VI, and Mary; (2) address to the reader stressing learning by reason rather than by
rote; (3) list of vowels and consonants; (4) "precatio" requesting wit to learn "as well in good
lyfe as doctryne"; (5) the eight parts of speech; (6) "Guiliemi Lilii ad suos discipulos monita
paedagogica, seu *Carmen de Moribus";* (7) "Symbolum Apostolorum"; (8) "Decalogus"; (9)
"Baptismus"; (10) "Coena Dominica" with responses for the student before and after.

[34] The *Brevissima Institutio seu Ratio Grammatices* is part two of Lily's grammar, having its
own title-page, and containing the following sections: (1) reiteration of royal patronage,
"praescripta, quam solam Regia majestas"; (2) "orthographia"; (3) declensions and concords;
(4) conjugations; (5) syntax containing figures of speech and prosody; (6) Erasmus's *De rationi
studii;* (7) a series of exercises including: (a) homiletic address of master to student; (b)
student's response, invoking Christ as model; (c) student's responses before and after Communion; (d) "oratio matutina"; (8) index.

[35] Watson, *English Grammar Schools,* 276–89, characterizes the reform of the period as a
"grammar war."

deviation from Lily's model they addressed questions about the place of custom and the nature and desirability of change in human affairs. With Lily as the model, those seeking to "diversify" texts sought license in the name of liberty; those wedded to custom and authority feared change and retarded reform. Perhaps not exactly the trumpets of revolution, the grammars are part of the larger conflict, and have their own political rhetoric, as we have seen in Samuel Hartlib's idealistic exhortation to be free of "custom" and overturn "grammatical tyranny."

Milton's *Accedence Commenc't Grammar* also takes its stand in the face of custom and authority, but more subversively and aggressively than Hartlib does in 1654. Reversing the strategy of the royalist grammarians who built on and explicated Lily, Milton works directly to dismantle the body of the king's grammar. With this in mind, we can see how the "Book it self," with its "alteration[s] from other grammars," is a more radical transformation of the authorized texts than is usually noted.[36] Milton's "brevity" in combining the accedence and the grammar and in reorganizing Lily is also a process of removing language from structures of authority. Language is unfettered by ideologically weighted contexts. He has taken out the usual prayers and other religious material used for language training, removed the usual references to Henry VIII, Lily, Nowell, Erasmus, the "bonae literae," and all gestures to the humanist tradition that gave added authority to the official grammar. Structures by which lessons were then tested and reinforced by expressions of piety and loyalty—in the Decalogue or the Cathechism, or the responses to the priest at Holy Communion—are abandoned. For example, one crucial stage in Milton's Ramist design occurs at the point where in some earlier texts the move from the parts of speech to the concords is mediated by syntactic paradigms presented as "Godly lessons for Chyldren."[37] Milton deletes those aphorisms extolling obedience and piety in youth, and begins part two of his work, the *Syntaxis,* starting with the "concords," effectively removing the conjunction of grammar lesson and prescriptive ethics. His treatment of the concords themselves continues this process of strategic tightening of the text. He retains much of the material illustrating the concords which is found in earlier texts—but not

---

[36] French, CPW 8: introduction, 41, and Fletcher, *Intellectual Development,* 1:133–35, both conclude that Milton's work is essentially a conservative document; in this instance, grammatical "conservatism" does not imply political conservatism.

[37] Many of Milton's examples are identical to those found in the 1549 edition of Colet's and Lily's *A Short Introduction of Grammar* (Menston, Yorks.: Scolar Press, 1969).

all. Within a cluster of appropriated examples he retains sentences such as "Praeceptor praelegit, vos vero negligitis," but drops "Venit ne rex?" and "Rex & Regina beati."[38] Examples using the word "rex" are consistently removed while other, perhaps less politically hierarchic language—"praeceptor" and "pater" for example—is retained. On one rare occasion where Milton uses the word, he is *adding* a very ambiguous phrase—"Ingentis Rex nominis," or "a king of great (or monstrous) name"—to a section of otherwise borrowed material.[39] Thus, at the structural level and at the level of specific linguistic examples, Milton strategically dismantles his models, generally removing political and authoritarian structures and idioms.

In effect, he has unthroned the royal grammar and secularized it, deconstructing both monarch and episcopacy in the process. The austerity of Milton's grammar is exactly the eloquence that identifies his Ramism and his rebellion against the tyranny of grammarians. It makes no concession, in form, theory, or in the rhetoric of isolated examples, to the ideology couched in the major contemporary rival grammars that cling close to their royal mandate. Nor, it should be noted, does he give room to the utopian idealism of the "modern *Janua's* and *Didactics,*" or, for that matter, to his own idealistic view of the role of education in "repair[ing] the ruins of our first parents."[40] Learning is best pursued outside the turbulence of controversy, action is sometimes most effective when not accompanied by debate. Milton's grammar is an attempt to remove language—and the student—from controversy and scholastic rigidity. The student leaving *those* "Grammatick flats & shallows" with "unballasted wits" for the "fadomless and unquiet deeps of controversie," is utterly unprepared.[41] The language Milton gives his student in his *Accedence Commenc't Grammar* is the language of action and liberty, disengaged from either extreme in the prevailing storms of controversy. We tend to take the neutrality of grammars for granted; however, com-

---

[38] *Accedence,* CPW 8:113; the 1549 text has the same Latin text and provides the English translation: "The mayster readeth, and ye regarde not" (Cvi^v); while most of the examples of concords in the 1549 text appear in Milton (113–14), these other two sentences, englished as "Dooeth not the king come?" and "The kyng and the queene are blessed" (Cvi^v and Cvii) are dropped.

[39] *Accedence,* CPW 8:115; the parallel 1549 text to which Milton's phrase is added appears at Cviii^v.

[40] *Of Education,* CPW 2:366–67.

[41] Ibid., CPW 2:375.

ing to Milton's grammmar from other examples of the genre, we find
that his compact, high-performance text is in fact striking and extreme.
Anything but conservative, it reflects a characteristically Miltonic disin-
terested commitment to action and reform.

This silent but effective disestablishment of royal and episcopal authority is part of Milton's alteration of "other Grammars." In his "addition[s]" I would suggest that there is a subtle but assertive tone in the
Accedence Commenc't Grammar that complements his silent structural
design. Listening to the rhetoric of Milton's grammar—comparing it
with that of Farnaby or Robinson, for example—we can hear a distinctive rhetoric that emerges from the illustrations crowding the text. Some
objective sense of this can be gained from J. Milton French's data on
Milton's illustrations, although he himself warns that it is incomplete. He
shows that Milton borrows more than sixty percent of his material from
Lily, and that he usually selects passages from Cicero (rather than from
poets or religious material). Material not derived from another grammar-
ian, material which, in French's words, "may perhaps give a better clue
to his interests or his prejudices," tends to be still more Cicero.[42]

French draws no conclusions about what these "interests or ...
prejudices" might be, and any attempt to do so must be tentative. But
a general pattern can be identified. First, from my experience, no other
grammar resorts so consistently to Cicero, and secondly, nowhere else in
Milton do we see such an obsession with the exiled spokesman for political rights, liberties, independence, political integrity, and reform. The
contexts of the passages from Cicero are not altogether lost; in a few
pages from the Syntax we hear from the *Pro Cluentia,* the *Pro Quinctio*
(eight times), the Verrine orations (at least seven times).[43] These are
major documents in the struggle for justice and social reform, and
against corruption—he has not taken rhetorical texts from the *De oratore*
and the *De inventione*. Passages that Milton has chosen from *Pro Publio
Quinctio,* for example, deal explicitly with the defence of civil rights in
the face of oppressive power and privilege. One illustration of how certain adverbs govern the verb—"Nam quid hoc iniquius dici potest,
Quam me qui caput alterius fortunasque defendam, Priore loco dice-
re"—addresses the way that the corrupt judicial system favors the rich
and privileged Naevius and traduces the "honour" and "civil rights" of

---

[42] French, "Notes," 647.
[43] See *Accedence,* CPW 8: 123–26 and 117–19.

Cicero's client.[44] Others as well point to inequities and arbitrariness in law and governance, and to the struggle for individual rights and integrity, so that the lesson on adverbs constitutes a web of passages dealing directly and indirectly with aspects of social corruption and reform in a republican community.[45]

Thus, through his choice of texts Milton trains the student ear to hear Cicero's voice exhorting action in defense of social justice and reform, much as he recommends in *Of Education*.[46] The republican Cicero, then, establishes a rhetorical strain that consistently courses through the grammar, insinuating its political ideology in the place of Lily's royalism. Throughout the *Accedence Commenc't Grammar,* there is a consistency of vision which, one can say, has been consciously created to replace the tone of conformity and the hierarchic relationships that reinforce the language training in Milton's principal model. In his grammar, Milton constructs a Latin very different from his rivals', be they royalist or puritan. Far from being innocuous illustrations, they identify the language of the civil libertarian, the language of action rather than the rhetoric of idealism. Thus, in giving his *Accedence Commenc't Grammar* a form and voice of its own, Milton silenced the prelatical and monarchist "grammatical tyranny" by deconstructing the royal grammar.

UNIVERSITY OF WINDSOR

---

[44] Ibid., CPW 8:125. The passage is from *Pro Publio Quinctio* 2.8. For full text and translation, see *Cicero: the Speeches*, trans. John Henry Freese (Cambridge: Harvard Univ. Press, 1956), 14–15: "For can anything more iniquitous or more scandalous be spoken . . . than the fact that I, who am defending the civil rights, the good name and fortunes of the other party, should have to plead my cause first"; see p. 14, note *a*, on Cicero's use of the word "caput" for "civil rights."

[45] Other of Milton's passages from the *Pro Publio Quinctio* (*Accedence*, CPW 8:125) can be identified and further illustrate his choice of passages dealing with "civil rights" and individual liberties. For Milton's "Conturbatus discedit neque . . . ," see *Pro Pub. Quinct.* 9.31 (Cicero, 36–37); for his "Docui quo die hunc," see *Pro Pub. Quinct.* 28.86 (Cicero, 96–97); for Milton's "Dici vix potest . . ." see *Pro Pub. Quinct.* 17.54 (Cicero, 62–63). The emphasis on such passages from Cicero further suggests the applicability of Javitch's argument to our reading of Milton's view of grammar instruction.

[46] In *Of Education* Milton recommends Cicero for his moral training (CPW 2:396–97), for his political acumen, and for the "spirit . . . vigor" and eloquence of the orations, which, it is suggested, the student might memorize (401).

Ken Simpson

"THAT SOVRAN BOOK": THE DISCIPLINE OF THE WORD IN MILTON'S ANTI-EPISCOPAL TRACTS

CRITICS AS DIFFERENT IN METHOD AS ARTHUR BARKER AND Stanley Fish have concluded that Milton's doctrine of church discipline in the anti-episcopal tracts is poorly developed but essentially Presbyterian.[1] The acceptance of this thesis by later readers has led to the view that the tracts are of rhetorical interest only; that they are empty but colorful outbursts expressing the "straight Presbyterian party line."[2] Without denying the importance of the rhetorical dimensions of Milton's early prose, I would at least like to re-open the question of his position on church discipline by suggesting that it is more coherent than has been previously represented: since Milton's main purpose is to discredit the bishops, no systematic proposal is formulated; rather, as rhetorical occasions permit, alternatives to episcopacy are suggested, some of which support the Smectymnuans and many others which do not. This lack of agreement should not be surprising since in the early 1640s nothing resembling a unified Presbyterian party existed for those who sought more local autonomy for the church through government by lay

[1] Arthur Barker, *Milton and the Puritan Dilemma* (Toronto: Univ. of Toronto Press, 1942), 17; Stanley Fish, *Self-Consuming Artifacts: The Experience of Seventeenth-Century Literature* (Berkeley: Univ. of California Press, 1972), 270. The author gratefully acknowledges the assistance of the Social Sciences and Humanities Research Council of Canada.

[2] Keith Staveley, *The Politics of Milton's Prose Style* (New Haven: Yale Univ. Press, 1975), 29. Although she draws different conclusions, see also Lana Cable, "Shuffling Up Such a God: The Rhetorical Agon of Milton's Antiprelatical Tracts," *MS* 21 (1985): 3–33.

elders elected by the congregation.[3] Moreover, the principle of interpretation upon which Milton's discipline is based clearly distinguishes
him from the Presbyterians he is supposed to be defending: while the
Smectymnuans argue that the church, led by the ordained ministry, is
the final authority in matters of interpretation, Milton insists that each
individual, guided by the Holy Spirit, needs only the Word for salvation. Since, for Milton, the words of scripture, are inseparable from
Christ, they are the elements of a verbal sacrament of "Divine inter-
cours, betwixt *God,* and the Soule" (*Ref,* CPW 1:520) which frees each
Christian, as "God's living temple" (*CG,* CPW 1:843), to worship according to conscience.[4] Church discipline, then, includes more (or less!)
than ecclesiastical censure, church government, liturgy, and applications
of doctrine; for Milton, discipline refers to self-discipline or "likeness to
God" (*Ref,* CPW 1:571), the measure and proportion of action as the
Word becomes incarnate in daily life.

At least since 1572, the year of the *Admonition to Parliament,* reformation of church discipline according to an apostolic model was a goal
of many English reformers, but even at this early stage of the debate
"discipline" could be used in a variety of ways.[5] In its ecclesiastical context, "discipline" could refer to church government and worship generally or, more specifically, to the rules used to maintain order in the
church, especially as they related to the censure and excommunication
of wayward members of the congregation.[6] For English Presbyterians,
this power was prescribed by Christ to rest in ministers and lay elders

---

[3] William B. Hunter, "Milton and the Presbyterians," in *The Descent of Urania: Studies in
Milton, 1946–1988* (London and Toronto: Associated Univ. Presses, 1989), 93–95. I am
indebted to Professor Hunter for bringing this article to my attention at the Vancouver
Milton Symposium and discussing it in subsequent correspondence. Without implicating
Professor Hunter in my mistakes, I think I can say that, although we approach Milton's
discipline from different directions, we arrive at the same conclusion: that Milton's "Presbyte-
rianism" is general enough to be shared by Congregationalists and "Independents" within the
Church of England in the early 1640s. See also the following: George Yule, *The Independents
in the English Civil War* (Cambridge: Cambridge Univ. Press, 1958), 12; C. G. Bolam and
Jeremy Goring, *The English Presbyterians* (London: Allen and Unwin, 1968), 40; Murray
Tolmie, *The Triumph of the Saints: The Separate Churches in London, 1616–1644* (Cambridge:
Cambridge Univ. Press, 1977), 116.

[4] Unless otherwise stated, Milton's prose is quoted from *The Complete Prose Works of John
Milton,* ed. D. M. Wolfe et al., 8 vols. (New Haven: Yale Univ. Press, 1953–82).

[5] For a concise analysis of church discipline in the Jacobean and Caroline period see J. P.
Somerville, *Politics and Ideology in England, 1603–1640* (London: Longman, 1986), 189–240.

[6] OED, s.v. discipline.

and was independent of civil authority. In contrast, for Richard Hooker, unlike Bishop Hall who defended episcopacy by divine right, discipline was not prescribed in scripture but was a "thing indifferent" to salvation and, therefore, was determined by tradition and historical context.[7] In the case of England, this meant that the king was not subject to church censure and that bishops, as the king's representatives, could use civil power to enforce the judgments of ecclesiastical courts such as the High Commission. When, during the 1630s, theological differences between Arminians and Calvinists, constitutional differences between the king and Parliament, and liturgical differences between Laudians and Puritans developed in addition to differences between Presbyterians and Episco-palians, the result was the kind of polarization indicated by the conflict-ing demands of the Canons of 1640, on the one hand, and the Petition of London (1641), on the other.

"Discipline" was also used in an ethical context to refer to orderly conduct, moderation, and self-government. In practice, this sense of the word was never far below the surface of its ecclesiastical use because the purpose of discipline in most reformed churches was to strengthen the church as a witness to Christ by excluding from communion those who did not have discipline in the ethical sense.[8] Thus, the possibility of conflating the ecclesiastical and ethical meanings was available even before Milton turned in this direction in 1641. In *The Reason of Church Government*, for example, Milton associates discipline with the circum-scribed limit or measure that is inherent in each creature: God has "cast his line and levell upon the soule of man which is his rationall temple ..." (*CG*, CPW 1:758). Without a "reason of the measure," however, discipline would be groundless: for Milton, the reason of the measure is the Word as the sacrament in which God continues to speak.

Milton's doctrine of the Word as sacrament makes the protestant

---

[7] Joseph Hall, *Episcopacie by Divine Right Asserted* (London, 1640), 2:4; Richard Hooker, *Of the Laws of Ecclesiastical Polity, Preface, Books I–IV*, ed. Georges Edelen, *The Folger Library Edition of the Works of Richard Hooker*, 5 vols. (Cambridge: Belknap Press of Harvard Univ. Press, 1977–90), 1 (1977): 212; bk.3, chap.3, pt.4.

[8] See John Calvin, *Institutes of the Christian Religion*, trans. F. L. Battles, ed. J. T. McNeill, 2 vols. (Philadelphia: Westminster Press, 1960), 2:1232. For Calvin, church government and worship were not prescribed by Christ nor was discipline a sign of the visible church, but because the church was essential for salvation, discipline was still needed to maintain order in the church in the absence of a valid spiritual authority. See Calvin, *Institutes*, 2:1023, 1205, 1229–30.

conviction of salvation by faith, grace, and scripture alone the basis for
worship and communion with God. Even though in theory Milton and
other reformers regarded the Lord's Supper and Baptism as the only sac-
raments, or visible signs of grace appointed by Christ, in worship the
Word became a "de facto sacrament."[9] Not only were the liturgy of
the Word and ante-communion services more frequent than full celebration of the eucharist, but the Word was regarded as a purer means of
God's communication to believers since, especially when heard, but also
when read, communicants were led by the spiritual, invisible meaning
of the Word to ascend to God rather than "to drawe downe ... the
very shape of *God* himselfe, into an exterior, and bodily forme" (*Ref,*
CPW 1:520) of images, ceremonies, and sacramental signs. It is a short
step, therefore, to a view of the Word, and words in the service of the
Word, as sacramental: through words the presence of the Word is com-
municated to the listener or reader by the Holy Spirit, just as, once
consecrated, the signs of the Lord's Supper and Baptism unite the com-
municant to Christ's body and church. To read the Bible and interpret
a sermon correctly, then, is to receive Christ through the power and
testimony of the Holy Spirit. The authority of the Word derives from
the reader's experience of the Spirit's persuasive force as God speaks
through and in his Word.

The authority of the Word in matters of doctrine was taken for
granted by protestants in 1641, but just as important was the consequence that words became the medium of sacramental experience.[10]
The identification of words and the Word was encouraged by the wide
range of connotations of "Word" in Christian vocabulary. Thomas Wilson, for example, cites at least eleven, ranging from the pre-existent Son,
the incarnate Word made flesh, and the gospel, to the holy scriptures as
a whole, and the lexical word.[11] In addition, prelapsarian language was
often described as a convergence of words and the Word, of names and
essences. John Wilkins suggested that "the first language was con-created
with our first Parents, they immediately understanding the voice of God
speaking to them in the Garden"[12] while Robert Greville makes pre-

---

[9] Georgia Christopher, *Milton and the Science of the Saints* (Princeton: Princeton Univ. Press, 1982), 6.

[10] Ibid., 7.

[11] Thomas Wilson, *A christian dictionarie* (London, 1611), 544.

[12] John Wilkins, *Essay Towards a Real Character and a Philosophical Language* (London, 1668), 2.

lapsarian language more politically charged by claiming that the bishops "doe more than Adam did: He gave Names to Things according to their Natures; they will give Names according to their owne fancies."[13] In a similar way, though he invokes a different biblical archetype, William Prynne contrasts the confusion of words and titles used to enlarge "the Tower of Babel, for which the Prelate hath so laboured" with "one small breathe of the mouth of God in his word breathed by one poore Minister."[14] It was within this context that the Smectymnuans attacked the innovations of episcopacy in lexical terms, recalling a time in the church when words and things were united in the immediacy of the Word:

> We finde that the late innovations which have so much disturbed the peace and purity of our Church, did first beginne with the alteration of words; and by changing the word Minister, into the word Priest; and the word Sacrament into the word Sacrifice, have endeavored to bring in the popish Masse. . . . Let us keep our fore fathers words, and we shall easily keepe our old and true faith of the first Christians.[15]

Because of the sacramental relationship between words and the Word, any innovation or change from "the old and true faith," here defined as Presbyterian discipline, was a violation of the gospel and of the sacrament implied in reading. On this point, Milton agreed with the Smectymnuans: the sufficiency of the gospel was such that "no tittle of his word shall fall to the ground, and if one jot be alterable it is as possible that all should perish" (*Of Prelat,* CPW 1:652).

At the same time, Milton's combination of three scriptural passages from different contexts into a meaning wholly his own in this sentence, illustrates his method of interpreting according to "the quickning power of the Spirit" and anticipates conflict with those of any denomination who "scan the *Scriptures,* by the Letter" (*Ref,* CPW 1:522) and worship

---

[13] Robert Greville, *A Discourse Opening the Nature of That Episcopacie Which Is Exercised in England* (London, 1642), 14.

[14] William Prynne, *Lord Bishops none of the Lords bishops* (London, 1640), 66–67. For the suggestion that Henry Burton is the author see W. M. Lamont, "Prynne, Burton, and the Puritan Triumph," *Huntington Library Quarterly* 27 (1964): 103–13.

[15] Smectymnuus, *An answer to a book entitled An humble remonstrance* (London, 1641), 82.

external signs.[16] In this instance, the bishops were particularly guilty of
distorting words and the Word: the "scandalous misnaming" of sects
(CG, CPW 1:788), the mistranslation of presbyter into bishop (Of Prelat,
CPW 1:625), the invention of "a new Lexicon" (Of Prelat, CPW
1:632), and "the Abcie of a Liturgy" (Animadversions, CPW 1:685) were
all examples of "their Slavish approach to Gods behests by them not
understood" (Ref, CPW 1:522). He also defends his own "vehement"
style in An Apology Against a Pamphlet by citing the decorum of the
Word rather than the decorum of human authors, declaring that "the
Spirit of God who is purity it selfe, when he would reprove any fault
severely, or but refute things done or said with indignation by others,
abstains not from some words not civill at other times to be spoken"
(CPW 1:901–2). In a style which answers to the Word rather than to
the decorum of customary expectations, words reveal and embody the
Word rather than distort and hide things under false names and human
traditions. The author of A Modest Confutation, according to Milton, fails
to meet the standard of the decorum of the Word: his "lukewarme-
nesse," "specious antiquity," and "barbarous Latin" reveal him to be a
"Carnal Textman" who "makes sentences by the statute" according to
the letter of human invention rather than the Spirit of God and his
Word (Apology, CPW 1:868, 872, 874, 951, 873). Inappropriate style as
well as mistranslation, misnaming, and set prayers are all distortions of
the sacramental relationship of words and the Word. The Word as
sacrament was possible, however, only because Milton believed that
scripture was clear and sufficient in all matters of salvation.

The protestant doctrine of "scriptura sola," when carried to its logical extreme, helped to shift authority from the church itself to the congregation of individuals who constitute it. For Milton, like Calvin, the
only authority needed to prove that scripture was the "authentick hand-
writing, and command" (CG, CPW 1:764) was the Holy Spirit, but unlike Calvin, this led Milton to the view that the traditions of the church
were subordinate to the freedom of conscience of each Christian. The
main argument in Of Prelaticall Episcopacy, for example, is that episcopacy, as an order above the presbyter, has no scriptural foundation or
reliable testimony; it is a human invention and, therefore, can be
changed by free subjects. Not only is there no distinction between

presbyter and bishop in scripture, but the testimony of early Christians is inconclusive: Ignatius's texts are corrupt; Eusebius admits uncertainty; Tertullian expounds scripture unreliably, and even "Antiquity it selfe hath turn'd over the controversie to that sovran Book which we had fondly straggl'd from" (*Of Prelat*, CPW 1:631). Instead of worshipping the Fathers and church traditions we should make "wary usage" of them; otherwise, we "forsake our owne grounds, and reasons which led us at first to part from Rome, that is to hold to the Scriptures against all antiquity . . ." (*Of Prelat*, CPW 1:650).

The Word would not be sufficient if it were not also clear to human understanding. The clarity of the scriptures is a function of their divine origin as well as of the activity of the Holy Spirit, revealing the Truth of the spoken and written Word and inspiring sermons, prayers, and poems in response. The "brightnesse, and perfection of the *Gospell*" and "the cleerenesse of the text" (*Of Prelat*, CPW 1:652, 651) in coop-eration with "that eternall Spirit who can enrich with all utterance and knowledge"(*CG*, CPW 1:820–21), make sacramental union available while the "overgrowne Covert of antiquity" and the "poysonous waters" of tradition (*Of Prelat*, CPW 1:648, 649) reinforce the darkness of human understanding. It is a testament of God's goodness and wis-dom that he "could so plainly reveale so great a measure of it [his wisdom] to the grosse distorted apprehension of decay'd mankinde" (*CG*, CPW 1: 750). Since "the darknes and crookednesse is our own" (*Ref*, CPW 1:566), the Spirit, as well as our own effort, are needed to reveal the clarity of the gospel's message independently of our additions to the text. We need only to purge "that intellectual ray which *God* hath planted in us" (*Ref*, CPW 1:566) and the truth and clarity of the Word will eventually reveal itself. Milton does not give specific rules of interpretation other than to urge "obedience to the Spirit of God, rather then to the faire seeming pretences of men" (*Apology*, CPW 1:937), but instead emphasizes the sacramental nature of this clear, objective under-standing of transcendent Truth, by referring to the manna, the Old Testament type of the Lord's Supper: ". . . we doe injuriously in think-ing to tast better the pure Euangelick Manna by seasoning our mouths with the tainted scraps, and fragments of an unknown table . . ." (*Of Prelat*, CPW 1:639). He goes on to say that the Truth, another synonym for the Word,[17] although begotten in heaven, continues to dwell on

---

[17] John 14.6.

earth "in Christian hearts, between two grave & holy nurses the Doctrine, and Discipline of the Gospel" (*Of Prelat,* CPW 1:639). Once our
minds are regenerated and illuminated by the Holy Spirit, the Word is
a divine foundation for both faith and worship, doctrine and discipline.

Milton's doctrine of "scriptura sola" applies even more to the sermon because, according to St. Paul, "faith comes from hearing."[18] The
verbal sacrament is available to each member of the congregation
through the minister who is, as the Smectymnuans called him, "the
mouth of God":[19]

> ... for certainely there is no imployment more honourable,
> more worthy to take up a great spirit, more requiring a gener-
> ous and free nurture, then to be the messenger, and Herald of
> heavenly truth from God to man, and by the faithfull worke of
> holy doctrine, to procreate a number of faithfull men, making
> a kind of creation like to Gods, by infusing his spirit and like-
> nesse into them, to their salvation, as God did into him....
> (*Animadversions,* CPW 1:721)

Because the preacher must channel the Spirit into the hearts of his congregation by the force of his own words, the liturgy of the Book of
Common Prayer, especially when the Book of Homilies is used, is de-
nounced as formal, external, a violation of the Spirit. The liturgy is a
"rote lesson," and a "heathenish Battologie of multiplying words"
(*Animadversions,* CPW 1:682, 687). True discipline and worship, on the
other hand, rest in the discipline of the Word and the gifts of the Spirit:
"Certainly Readers, the worship of God singly in it selfe, the very act of
Prayer and thanksgiving with those free and unimpos'd expressions
which from a sincere heart unbidden come into the outward gesture is
the greatest decency that can be imagin'd" (*Apology,* CPW 1:941–42).

A priesthood of believers and a liturgy of the Word alone are just
two examples of reforms of worship which result from the discipline of
the Word. All offices of church government, including preaching, are
open to the congregation provided the person is "call'd by the high
calling of God to be holy and pure" and has the requisite "spirituall
gifts" (*CG,* CPW 1:843). In addition, the order, office and jurisdiction
of ministers and bishops are also reformed: there is no order of bishops

[18] Rom. 10.17.
[19] Smectymnuus, *An answer,* 12.

above elected presbyters; the minister's office consists of preaching and caring for the flock only; and his jurisdiction includes censuring wayward members of the congregation and excommunicating them as a last resort, but accepting fees from the state, imposing ecclesiastical canons, or supporting ecclesiastical courts with civil law are eliminated.

The separation of religious and civil jurisdictions is also the basis of Milton's toleration of unorthodox interpretations of church discipline, "for if there were no opposition where were the triall of an unfained goodnesse and magnanimity?" (CG, CPW 1:795). In the open encounter between truth and falsehood, many errors that God has sent will cause some uncertainty but "when truth has the upper hand, and the reformation shall be perfeted, [the errors] will easily be rid out of the way, or kept so low, as that they shall be only the exercise of our knowledge, not the disturbance, or interruption of our faith" (CG, CPW 1:796). In a passage that must have jolted his Presbyterian brethren, Milton suggests that if we look beyond the scandalous misnaming of sects, "the Primitive Christians in their times were accounted such as are now call'd Familists and Adamites, or worse" (CG, CPW 1:788). This reformation of religious life through "the struggl of contrarieties" in the pursuit of truth and the gospel takes the notion of discipline beyond the walls of any particular church and into the everyday lives of believers.

In his defense of the sects and the freedom of conscience found in the Word, Milton shifted the focus of discipline from the particular, visible church to the universal one—the temple of the heart. Because the inner temple is where the Spirit resides,[20] the individual believer cannot be forced to follow the discipline of a national church. At the same time, as Michael Fixler points out, Milton still imagines a national church, but it is one that is voluntarily joined as a result of the national regeneration which would reform church and state in fulfilment of England's covenant with God.[21] Thus, while Milton speaks of a national church built on self-discipline arising from the authority of the Word established by the Spirit, the Smectymnuans imagine a national church built on uniform worship arising from the authority of the Word enforced by the church. Even though Milton approves of presbyterial discipline and the "*union* of the reformed *Catholick Church*" (*Ref*, CPW 1:613), it is only desirable if self-discipline originating in Christian

[20] 1 Cor. 3.16.
[21] Michael Fixler, *Milton and the Kingdoms of God* (London: Faber and Faber, 1964), 101.

freedom conferred by the Word is first honored.[22]

Despite Milton's agreement with the Smectymnuans and other Presbyterians on the sufficiency of the Word in church discipline, the forms
of discipline which they found were radically different and Milton went
to great lengths to emphasize this. Milton denounces Constantine because of his confusion of temporal and spiritual power (Ref, CPW
1:553–60), while the Smectymnuans refer to him as "blessed" and
"pious";[23] he argues that the sects resemble primitive Christians, while
Thomas Edwards insists that Independents should go to Holland or New
England;[24] he approves of the equality of all and the use of forms other
than the sermon (Ref, CPW 1:819–20), while the Smectymnuans speak
only of the equality of ministers and their right to preach; he refers to
more than one discipline found in scripture, while the Smectymnuans
outline only their own; he writes of the liberty of each Christian in the
Word and Spirit, they write of the authority of the Word established by
the church. When "presbyter" is used, it denotes only the order of
church government specified in scripture and manifested in the universal, "holy reformed Church" (CG, CPW 1:861) rather than in a particular, visible church, or party, in England. He argues that "Presbytery, if
it must be so call'd" (Ref, CPW 1:610), is not such a "desperate hazard"
or an "incurable mischiefe" (Ref, CPW 1:613) as episcopacy so we
would do well to accept it—a rather lukewarm recommendation! A specific government of the church is mentioned once, and here only briefly: he includes the parish council, the "parochiall Consistory" and the
"generall assembly," but omits the presbytery completely (CG, CPW
1:789).[25] It is clear, then, that Milton grudgingly accepts presbyterial
government, but views it almost as irrelevant since discipline depends on
individual piety. Once it is recognized that every person, as God's temple, is responsible for realizing discipline in his or her own life, the form
of discipline practiced in the church can be freely chosen as long as it
responds to God's Word.

Milton goes directly to this point in The Reason of Church Government, the most closely argued anti-episcopal tract: the first reason of
church discipline is that it is written in the scriptures. Since everything

---

[22] 2 Cor. 3.17

[23] Smectymnuus, An answer, 9, 16.

[24] Thomas Edwards, Reasons Against the Independent Government of Particular Congrega-
tions. . . (London, 1641), 46.

[25] See also note 72 of CPW 1:789.

in human life turns on "the axle of discipline" (CPW 1:751), God
would never leave such an important matter to people who refuse to
govern themselves (CPW 1:754); rather, discipline is prescribed in scripture, heard in the divine voice and imitated in virtuous action:

> And certainly discipline is not only the removall of disorder,
> but if any visible shape can be given to divine things, the very
> visible shape and image of vertue, whereby she is not only
> seene in the regular gestures and motions of her heavenly paces
> as she walkes, but also makes the harmony of her voice audible
> to mortall eares. (CPW 1:751–52)

The use of music imagery emphasizes the convergence of the divine and
human in virtue—the highest expression of divine discipline available in
human life—and seems to echo a similar use of imagery by Richard
Hooker: "In harmonie the verie image and character even of virtue and
vice is perceived."[26] Adam and Eve were not without the "golden sur-
vaying reed" of discipline either: before the Fall they lived its limits perfectly, just as the angels were ordered "as God himselfe hath writ his im-
periall decrees through the great provinces of heav'n" (CPW 1:752).
The ideal of discipline as the measure and proportion inherent in individuals is also linked to the order of creation itself through the imagery
of planetary orbits. As a result of true discipline, "our happinesse may
orbe it selfe into a thousand vagancies of glory and delight, and with a
kinde of eccentricall equation be as it were an invariable Planet of joy
and felicity . . ." (CPW 1:752). Far from encouraging the "repetition of
that which is prescribed," the order of discipline allows the planets to
have a variety of orbits and still participate in a more inclusive order,
just as each Christian is free to live out his own discipline and still participate in the church. The specific directives of discipline are written in
a "typicall and shadowie" manner in the temples of Solomon and
Ezekiel, but under the gospel they are clearly inscribed in the soul of
each Christian:

> Should not he rather now by his owne prescribed discipline
> have cast his line and levell upon the soule of man which is his

---

[26] Richard Hooker, *Of the Laws of Eccesiastical Polity: Book V,* ed. W. Speed Hill, The
Folger Library Edition of the Works of Richard Hooker, 5 vols. (Cambridge: Belknap Press
of Harvard Univ. Press, 1977–90), 2 (1977): 151; bk. 5, chap.16, pt.8. See also Hooker, ed.
Edelen, 1:142; bk.1, chap.16, pt.8.

rationall temple, and by the divine square and compasse thereof forme and regenerate in us the lovely shapes of vertues and graces, the sooner to edifie and accomplish that immortall stature of Christs body which is his Church, in all her glorious lineaments and proportions[?] (CPW 1:757–5)

In his analysis of Paul's first epistle to Timothy, Milton finds that the "heavenly structure of evangelick discipline" consists in exhorting and teaching "the doctrine which is according to godliness."[27] The metaphor of discipline as measure and proportion is appropriate because St. Paul's message is one of self-discipline and its verbal equivalent—"faithful saying." The self-portraits in *The Reason of Church Government* and *An Apology Against a Pamphlet* also take on new significance: they are examples of self-discipline in response to God's extraordinary calling of a poet who "ought him selfe to bee a true Poem, that is, a composition, and patterne of the best and honourablest things" (*Apology*, CPW 1:890).

Finally, self-discipline and godliness are the grounds for legal and political reformations as well. The purpose of the gospel, as manifested in the lives of those in whom the Spirit dwells, is liberty "after which all honest and legal freedom of civil life cannot be long absent" (*CG*, CPW 1:853). The process begins with regeneration, which is expressed in godliness, and ends in "the true florishing of a Land" (*Ref*, CPW 1:571). As Milton later summarized in *The Second Defense of the English People*, discipline derived from the Word was the basis of both personal and civil reformation: "if discipline originating in religion continued its course to the morals and institutions of the commonwealth, they [the English people] were proceeding in a direct line from such beginnings, from such steps, to the deliverance of the whole life of mortal man from slavery."[28]

When treated as a whole, then, Milton's anti-episcopal tracts present a rigorous and consistent view of reformation and discipline grounded in the religious equality of each believer before God as he is revealed in his Word. Although for the purposes of controversy a presbyterial form of church government is opposed to episcopacy, a more radical discipline is advocated at the same time. In this form of discipline, a ritual of ver-

---

[27] 1 Tim. 6.3.

[28] Quoted from *The Works of John Milton*, ed. Frank Allen Patterson, et al., 18 vols. (New York: Columbia Univ. Press, 1931–38), 8:128. Cf. CPW 4:622.

bal and moral action rather than ceremonial observance is enacted when the individual, with the guidance of the Spirit in the search of the Word, chooses to act in accordance with the principles of order and measure which God has given to govern human nature. This view of discipline was expressed by Milton earlier in his career in *Comus* and would, later in his career, lead to his independency. For Milton, nothing could be further from "things indifferent" than discipline since, as the application of doctrine, it is the fulfillment of religious, ethical, and national reformation, and since only after this had occurred could he feel justified in offering his "elaborate Song" to God: "Then amidst the *Hymns,* and *Halleluiahs* of *Saints* some one may bee heard offering at high *strains* in new and lofty *Measures* to sing and celebrate thy *divine Mercies,* and *marvelous Judgements* in this Land throughout all AGES ..."(*Ref,* CPW 1:616).

UNIVERSITY OF BRITISH COLUMBIA

INDEX

Of Poetry and Politics: New Essays on Milton and His World is an edited selection of papers from the Fourth International Milton Symposium. These essays illustrate some of the best and most characteristic critical discussion on Milton today. All written specially for this volume, the essays focus on issues of context, with key studies on prophecy, poetic interpretation, gender, and politics.

Louis Martz illumines Milton's prophetic voice, Mary Ann Radzinowicz focuses on the tragic women of Genesis, and Dayton Haskin discusses Milton on Mary and Ruth. John Hale examines Milton's Latin verse, Stella Revard considers *Lycidas* and Pindar, and T.H. Howard-Hill writes of "The Rounded Theatre's Pomp." Deriving their arguments from consideration mainly of the prose are Wyman Herendeen (*Accedence Commenc't Grammar* and "grammatical tyranny"), Ken Simpson (the anti-episcopal tracts), and Achsah Guibbory (Charles, idolatrous images, and creation in *Eikonoklastes*). Balachandra Rajan, examining banyan trees and fig leaves, discusses Milton's India. Peter Lindenbaum addresses the poet in the marketplace, while Janel Mueller contextualizes Milton's nascent republicanism.

David Robertson ranges over the major poems, studying soliloquy and self; Gary Hamilton centers on *Paradise Regained* and Michael Spiller on audience in *Samson Agonistes*. Lee Johnson ponders language and innocence in *Paradise Lost*, Douglas Chambers considers "art's synopticon" in book 12 of *Paradise Lost*, John Leonard reconsiders the evidence on Milton's "vow of celibacy," Donald Friedman discusses 'sex' and J. Martin Evans empire in *Paradise Lost*, and Michael Wilding, calling attention to seeming, argues for equality between Eve and Adam.

■

P. G. Stanwood is Professor of English at the University of British Columbia. He is the author of *The Sempiternal Season: Studies in Seventeenth Century Devotional Writing* and *John Donne and the Theology of Language* (co-authored with Heather Ross Asals), and has edited texts by John Cosin, William Law, Richard Hooker, and Jeremy Taylor.

MRTS

MEDIEVAL & RENAISSANCE TEXTS & STUDIES
is the publishing program of the
Center for Medieval and Early Renaissance Studies
at the State University of New York at Binghamton.

MRTS emphasizes books that are needed —
texts, translations, and major research tools.

MRTS aims to publish the highest quality scholarship
in attractive and durable format at modest cost.

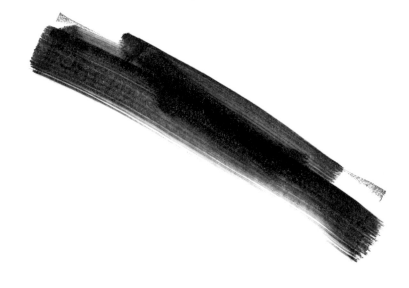